A POCKET GUIDE TO IRISH CASTLES

THE STORY OF IRELAND'S AMAZING HERITAGE

Gill Books
Hume Avenue, Park West, Dublin 12

www.gillbooks.ie

Gill Books is an imprint of M.H. Gill & Co.

Copyright © Teapot Press Ltd 2019

ISBN: 978-0-7171-7940-4

This book was created and produced by Teapot Press Ltd

Written by Fiona Biggs
Designed by Tony Potter & Becca Wildman
Picture research by Joe Potter & Tony Potter

Printed in Europe

This book is typeset in Garamond and Dax

A CIP catalogue record for this book is available
from the British Library.

5 4 3 2 1

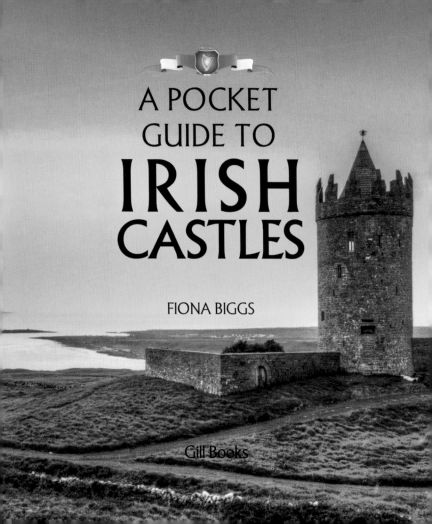

A POCKET GUIDE TO IRISH CASTLES

FIONA BIGGS

Gill Books

Contents

Introduction

Romantic, mysterious and powerful, the survivors of Ireland's several thousand castles rise out of the landscape, reminders of a time when simple stone and mortar was an effective protection against almost any enemy. The castles of Ireland chart the turbulent history of the island as it unfolded over 500 years from the 12th century. Each one has a unique story to tell, its legends and superstitions embedded in local lore. Even those castles that are in a ruinous state draw the visitor in – it's easy to imagine them as vibrant and bustling homes, garrisons and defensive outposts in more dangerous times. Usually located in strategic positions on high ground or beside large bodies of water, these powerful buildings map a story of invasion, colonisation and inter-clan warfare.

Although the Vikings were early invaders of Ireland (their first incursions dated from the end of the eighth century), they quickly settled into peaceful co-existence with the indigenous population, ultimately leaving a legacy of trading towns and fortified harbours, which became, over time, Ireland's major urban centres and ports.

After the death of Brian Boru, one of the most powerful and unifying high kings of Ireland, at the Battle of Clontarf in 1014, he was succeeded by a line of high kings who were weak and lacked the ability to control the regional rulers. The centralised royal administration in the country was gradually undermined by a series of power struggles between the minor kings. In 1167 Diarmaid McMurrough, deposed King of Leinster, asked King Henry II of England to assist him in retaking his kingdom. The king responded by giving the Earl of Pembroke, Richard de Clare (later known as Strongbow), permission to travel to Ireland with an army recruited from his nobles. It was a move that would have permanent ramifications for the country's social and political landscape. De Clare's mission was both successful and enriching – he married Diarmaid's daughter Aoife – and when Diarmaid died in 1171, his Norman son-in-law succeeded in taking over his kingdom, in breach of the laws of succession, which prohibited inheritance through the female line.

King Henry II came to Ireland later that year to claim some of its rich territories for himself and to curb de Clare's ambitions. Many of the Irish lords and chieftains swore allegiance to him, but when Henry's son, Prince John, on whom he had bestowed the title 'Lord of Ireland', came to the country in 1185 he redistributed the land of the loyal Irish among his friends in order to consolidate his rule in the country. Those Norman knights who were gifted large tracts of land by Prince John usually built fortifications on their landholdings from which to exercise their power and authority. Most of these structures were simple wooden buildings of the type known as motte and bailey.

By the turn of the 13th century the newcomers were replacing many of their quickly constructed motte and bailey fortifications with larger structures. Designed to demonstrate their power and wealth, these stone strongholds often boasted battlements, crenellations, turrets, moats, drawbridges and high curtain walls, and were capable of repelling even the largest armies. Dublin, Trim, Limerick and Kilkenny Castles were among the first major ones to be built. The large castle at Carrickfergus was built in 1180 by John de Courcy, a nobleman who was made 'Lord of Ulster' by King John. This effectively made him a petty king, and his strategic stronghold on the Antrim coast played an important role in the history of Ireland for centuries.

Successive English kings after John concentrated almost exclusively on maintaining their territories in England, and their lack of attention to Ireland facilitated the native population in their many efforts to overthrow the Anglo-Norman administration. When central authority finally collapsed in Ireland in the late 14th century, thousands of smaller castles, in reality fortified tower houses, were built by the Anglo-Norman settlers who had followed the first wave of Norman knights, in an attempt to protect themselves from the Irish clans in increasingly lawless times.

The tower houses were also favoured by Irish chieftains, who began to replace their traditional ring forts and cashels with them – one of the most famous of the clan tower houses is Rockfleet in County Mayo, home to Grace O'Malley, or Granuaile, the so-called Pirate Queen. The tower house is the most common type of castle in Ireland. These square stone edifices built over several storeys, with few windows, dot the countryside of the island, particularly along the coastline and the country's many waterways. (The county of Limerick, which straddles the Shannon Estuary, has a higher density of Anglo-Norman castles than any other Irish county.) Most of the tower houses have fallen into ruin, but others, including Dysert O'Dea Castle in County Clare, Ross Castle in County Kerry and Rockfleet are in good condition.

Leading families such as the Desmonds, Ormondes, Kildares, O'Neills and O'Donnells built stone towers and forts wherever they needed them for protection. The ruins of over 2,000 still remain.

The Tudor monarchs who seized power in England in 1485 were determined to subdue the population, both Irish and Anglo-Norman, and bring it back under English control. The second Tudor king, Henry VIII, declared himself King of

Ireland, and his daughter Elizabeth I's reign brought a flood of settlers to Ireland from the late 16th century onwards – having quashed the two Desmond Rebellions, effectively exiling the heads of the Irish nobility in what is referred to as the Flight of the Earls, Elizabeth realised that a landed population that was sympathetic to her would help keep the Irish under the control of the crown. She gifted huge tracts of land, particularly in Munster, to her favourites at court, on the understanding that they would encourage an influx of English settlers.

Over the centuries, as the Irish persisted in their efforts to regain control of their country, the great castles were called into frequent service, both as defensive structures and as a means of protecting the English population. For several hundred years the only reliable way of bringing about the surrender of a castle garrison was to lay siege to it – since most castles were well provisioned, and many had a source of fresh water within their walls, sieges were lengthy and costly. The demise of the castle as a defensive building came about as a result of developments in artillery. The first cannon were introduced to Ireland at the end of the 15th century, changing the nature of warfare on the island for ever. The heavy artillery employed during the Cromwellian campaigns of the 17th century (also known as the Confederate War), was used to devastating effect. These powerful cannon were capable of 'slighting' the walls of even the strongest castles – the 'slights' tore open the walls, and even one serious breach could render a castle's defences useless. Cromwell's armies cut a swathe across the island, destroying many of the great castles as they went.

In the years following the Williamite War (the decisive encounter of which was the Battle of the Boyne in 1690, when William of Orange defeated King James II) at the end of the 17th century Ireland's castles became redundant as defensive structures, although some were turned into English garrisons. Many of the larger castles in private ownership were renovated or extended as manor houses. Some of these were subsequently extensively remodelled to become the great houses of the 18th and 19th centuries, and have made an enormous contribution to Ireland's architectural heritage. Land was tamed and landscaped to create fashionable gardens for the enjoyment and amusement of the leisured classes.

During the Irish Civil War some of these great houses and castles were damaged in arson attacks, and a number were handed over to the new Irish state after independence. Many have been made safe or restored, and are open to the public.

Although a modern perspective gives medieval castles a romantic aura, they were conceived as completely practical edifices, designed to keep invaders out and to provide a measure of protection for those within their walls. As residences they were draughty, chilly and

Winding stone stairway inside Trim Castle.

dark, with few windows to let in natural light. The members of the castle household, usually comprising the lord's family, servants and fighting men, were all accommodated within the walls. Most of the living was communal, and the sanitary facilities were basic. The garderobes, or toilets, also had a secondary purpose – the clothing of the castle inhabitants, which was never washed, was hung above them so that the ammonia fumes would kill any lice or other small vermin living in the seams.

Castles were tailor-made for their owners, all of whom would have had a list of demands depending on their needs and circumstances – some have murder holes, sally ports and moats, while others relied on machicolations and batters to provide an extra layer of defence. The narrow spiral staircases that are common to almost all castles in Ireland were always built in a clockwise direction so that the widest part of the step was on the right as the defender descended – this allowed maximum freedom for his sword arm, always assumed to be his right arm. Right-handed swordsmen would have been seriously hampered while ascending the stairs, giving the defenders the advantage. While the larger castles were surrounded by an impenetrable outer layer or layers of curtain walls, even the smaller tower houses were usually built within a protective bawn wall.

Two characteristics of the medieval castle, which have all but disappeared today, strike the modern visitor as surprising: Castles generally had thatched roofs, which, once the castles became uninhabited, naturally decayed into nothingness with the passage of time; and the porous stone walls were coated with an underlayer of render and then with 'harling', a mixture of limewash and crushed pebbles or shells – this protected the stonework against the elements, and most castles were white, rather than grey. Their high visibility in the largely unforested landscape of medieval Ireland would have sent a stark message to would-be attackers. A great castle such as Trim must have been a magnificent sight in its heyday, its gleaming walls shining in the sunlight, colourful pennants flying from its towers.

Most of the castles detailed in this book have been chosen because they are open, or at least accessible, to the public. Opening times often vary throughout the year, so intending visitors should always check the latest information online.

Parts of a tower house

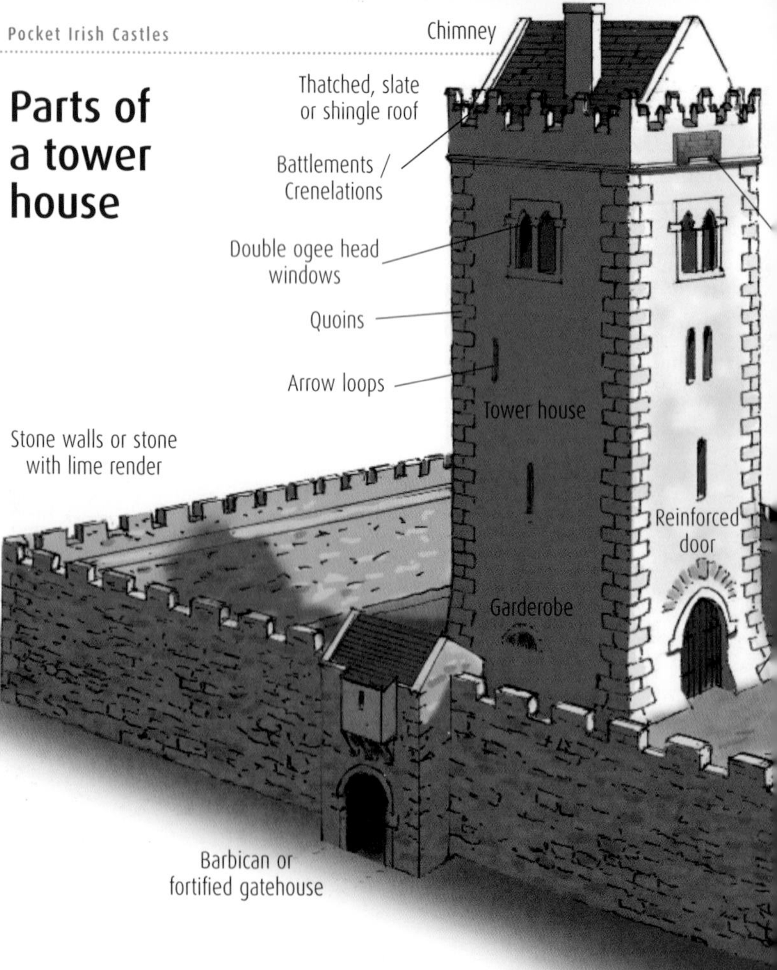

Chimney

Thatched, slate or shingle roof

Battlements / Crenelations

Double ogee head windows

Quoins

Arrow loops

Stone walls or stone with lime render

Tower house

Reinforced door

Garderobe

Barbican or fortified gatehouse

Irish tower houses were built for defensive and residential use, often with protective walls known as bawns. Most of the 2,000 or so buildings still remaining share similar architectural features. This drawing shows some of the typical features.

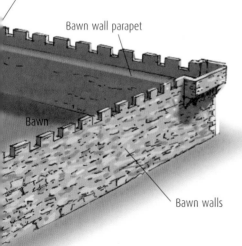

Machicolation

Base batter

Bawn wall parapet

Bawn

Bawn walls

Ruins of Clononey Castle in County Offaly.

Ross Castle in Killarney National Park, County Kerry

Provinces & counties

Ireland has historically been divided into
four provinces: Leinster, Ulster, Munster and
Connacht. The provinces of Ireland serve
no administrative or political purpose,
but function as historical and cultural entities.
Each province is divided into counties.

DONEGAL • DERRY • ANTRIM

ULSTER

TYRONE

NORTHERN IRELAND

FERMANAGH • DOWN

ARMAGH

MONAGHAN

SLIGO • LEITRIM • CAVAN • LOUTH

MAYO

ROSCOMMON • LONGFORD

CONNACHT

MEATH

WESTMEATH

GALWAY • OFFALY

**REPUBLIC
OF IRELAND**

LEINSTER

LAOIS • WICKLOW

CLARE

CARLOW

LIMERICK • TIPPERARY • KILKENNY

WEXFORD

KERRY

MUNSTER

WATERFORD

CORK

The Irish word for this territorial division, cúige,
literally meaning 'fifth part', indicates that there
were once five provinces; the fifth, Meath, was
incorporated into Leinster and Ulster.

Chapter 1
Leinster

Ruins of Carbury Castle,
County Kildare

Enniscorthy Castle

The first stone castle on this site in the middle of Enniscorthy
town was built in the late 12th century by the Norman knight
Philip de Prendergast on land that belonged to the McMurrough
Kavanaghs.

Vintage postcard of
Enniscorthy Castle.

The de Prendergasts lived in the castle until the 1370s, when it was successfully attacked and possession regained by Art MacMurrough Kavanagh, whose family retained it for the next century and a half. In 1536 it was surrendered to the crown and was burned down in 1569 when it was attacked by the Earl of Kildare.

Queen Elizabeth granted the ruined castle to a favourite, the poet Edmund Spenser, in 1581. He never lived there and the castle later came into the possession of Sir Henry Wallop, together with its surrounding lands. The castle was still ruined when Sir Henry took possession, and he refurbished and extended it. His main interest, however, was not the building, but the commercial exploitation of the surrounding forests, and the castle's strategic position at the head of the tidal River Slaney made it easy for him to export his timber.

Oil painting of Edmund Spenser.

The Irish Rebellion of 1798, also known as the United Irishmen Rebellion, was an uprising against British rule in Ireland lasting from May to September 1798. *Defeat of the Rebels at Vinegar Hill*, by George Cruikshank.

The original 13th-century castle would have been a simple tower house, but Sir Henry rebuilt it as a four-storey rectangular keep with five-storey three-quarter drum towers at each corner.

In 1649 the castle was besieged and occupied by Cromwellian forces and was used as a prison during the failed 1798 Rebellion. It was bought and restored by the Roche family, who lived in it until 1951. It now houses the Wexford County Museum.

Castle view with the River Slaney.

Johnstown Castle

The Johnstown estate was the ancestral home of two prominent Wexford families, the Esmondes and the Grogans.

The Esmondes were a Norman family from Lincolnshire who came to Wexford in 1169 with Richard de Clare. They settled in County Wexford and built defensive tower houses at Rathlannan and Johnstown at some time during the 15th and 16th centuries. Their estate was confiscated during the Cromwellian invasion of Ireland, and the Esmondes, who were Catholics, were expelled from their lands and the county of Wexford. It is said that Cromwell spent the night before his attack on Wexford town on the Johnstown estate, reviewing his troops before the next day's battle.

Oliver Cromwell, after a painting by Samuel Cooper (1609–1672).

In the early and mid-19th century John Grogan and his son Hamilton Knox Grogan built the castle in the Scottish baronial style that was then popular, and created the wonderful gardens of the demesne. They were designed by Daniel Robertson, who was responsible for the gardens at the Powerscourt estate in County Wicklow. Covering 1,000 acres, the Johnstown estate includes two lakes, a folly tower, a farm and a deer park.

The original Johnstown tower house is still standing. In 1945 Maurice Victor Lakin, a descendant of John Grogan, presented the estate to the Irish nation. Nothing was done with it for several years, but it was eventually taken over by the Department of Agriculture, which established an agricultural institute in the grounds. Today the castle houses an agricultural museum.

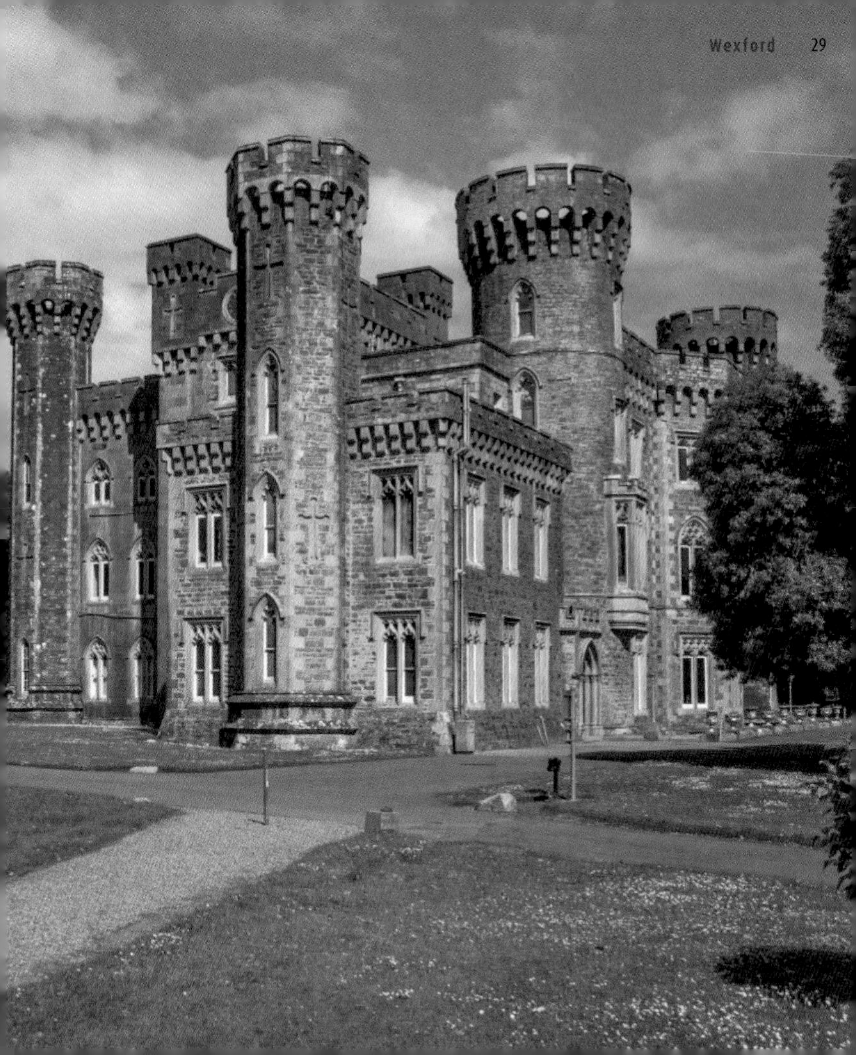

Athlone Castle

The first castle at Athlone was built by Turlough Mór O'Connor in 1129. It was a wooden structure, and no trace of it survives – it may or may not have been built on the same site as the stone castle built for King John in 1210 to defend the crossing over the River Shannon at Athlone.

The castle that dates from 1210 is the central keep of the present castle. It is a three-storey polygonal tower built on a motte, and was probably surrounded by a moat. The upper storey is furnished with machicolations and arrow loops.

In the late 13th century the castle was heavily fortified. The motte was contained within a curtain wall with drum towers at the corners. There is a sally port in the wall overlooking the river.

The castle was rebuilt once again by the Lord Justice of Ireland, Sir William Brabazon, in 1547. The curtain wall and drum towers survived the Sieges of Athlone in 1690 and 1691, said to have been the heaviest bombardments in Irish history, but they were destroyed by lightning in 1697. The entire castle was rebuilt between 1793 and 1815, when a two-storey barracks was built overlooking Main Street. Keeping up with

Defence of the bridge during the Siege of Athlone, 1691.

Drum tower at Athlone Castle.

modern military developments, gun embrasures and pistol loops were built into the walls that protected the entrance ramp. The drawbridge survived until the 1940s.

Athlone Castle, which has been of pivotal importance in the history of the town for 800 years, has been extensively refurbished by Athlone Urban District Council, who installed a modern visitor centre in 1991.

The Assault on Athlone, 20 June 1691, 1691 Siege of Athlone during the Williamite War, 1689–91.

Tullynally Castle

Tullynally Castle, to the west of Castlepollard, was built in the mid-1650s and has been home to the Pakenham family, now the Earls of Longford, for more than 350 years. It was known as Pakenham Hall for most of its existence.

The land on which the house is built was owned by the Anglo-Norman FitzSimons family and was bought by Henry Pakenham after the Cromwellian wars. He built a semi-fortified square 'plantation' house of two storeys, probably within a defensive outer wall. The house, which was much smaller than the present structure, was incorporated into later revisions and enlargements.

In 1740 Thomas Pakenham, grandson of Henry, married Elizabeth Cuffe, a grand-niece of the last Earl of Longford, and Thomas became first Earl of Longford when the title was recreated for him. The house his grandfather had built was restyled as a sumptuous three-storey Georgian mansion, and extensive formal gardens were laid out in the grounds. These were replaced several years later by a fashionable 'wilderness' garden.

In 1803, the second earl, another Thomas Pakenham, decided to turn the house into a castle and had a Gothic Revival superstructure built, with all the features that were needed to turn a mansion into a facsimile of a castle, including battlements, turrets, a moat and several round four-storey flankers. The earl installed what may have been one of the first central heating systems in the country, turning the castle into a luxurious home, far removed from its draughty antecedents.

The second earl continued to add to the castle and his English wife Georgiana redesigned the gardens. When Thomas Pakenham died in 1835, Georgiana went back to England and their son Edward, the third earl, executed his father's latest plans, doubling the size of the castle with the addition of two large wings to accommodate the large numbers of servants required to run a great house. The Pakenham family in London sent their linen back to the excellent laundry facility at Packenham Hall until the outbreak of the First World War.

The hill on which Tullynally is built overlooks Lough Derravaragh, the lake where the legendary children of Lir were turned into swans, and in 1961 the name Tullynally (meaning 'hill of swans') was restored by the Longfords.

The gardens at Tullynally are open to the public.

Birr Castle

The town of Birr is built on the ancestral lands of the O'Carroll clan of Offaly. The first castle on this site was an Anglo-Norman tower house, believed to have been built around 1170 on a motte. The original gate tower is now the centre of the present gothic-style castle building, where it is located in the lower floor.

In the 14th century the O'Carrolls seized the castle and it remained in their hands until the 1580s, when they sold it to the Butlers of Ormonde. It fell into ruin and in 1620 James I granted the castle and 1,277 acres of land to Sir Laurence Parsons, whose family had moved to Ireland from Norfolk during the Tudor plantations. Birr became known as Parsonstown, and one of Parsons's descendants was created first Earl of Rosse in 1806.

Laurence Parsons decided not to live in the tower house, but extended the gate house and used that as the family residence until his death in 1628. By the end of the 17th century, the castle had survived two sieges. The family lost much of their money and did little to improve the house during the 18th century. At the beginning of the 19th century, a gothic-style facade was built on to the house, which now faced the parklands, rather than the town. The old castle walls and the tower house were demolished and the Gothic Saloon was added.

Exterior of Birr Castle.

The Yellow Drawing
Room at Birr Castle.

The central block of the castle was badly damaged by fire in 1836. A major rebuilding project added a third storey. Famine relief work during the 1840s was responsible for the replacement of the old moat and Norman motte with a new, star-shaped moat. One of the most extraordinary innovations at this time was the building of a great telescope, the brainchild of the third Earl of Rosse, in 1842. In the 1860s a square tower was added at the back of the castle. The family still lives in the castle.

The beautiful gardens are open to the public, and the telescope, after a complete restoration in the 1990s (its structure was melted down and used for armaments during the First World War) has pride of place.

William Parsons, third Earl of Rosse.

Charles Parsons – inventor of the steam turbine in 1884.

Distant view of the castle

The great telescope,
constructed at Birr
Castle in 1842.

Charleville Castle

This Gothic Revival castle, said to be the finest example of its type in Ireland, is situated beside an ancient oak forest with druidical associations near the River Clodiagh, on the outskirts of Tullamore. In 1577 the forest and lands at Charleville were gifted by Elizabeth I to Thomas Moore, who built a manor house on his estate. The estate was later expanded to cover more than 24,000 acres. A direct descendant of Moore, Charles William Bury (made first Earl of Charleville in a second creation of the title), inherited the estate in the late 18th century and decided to build a new house. It was commissioned in 1798, work began in 1800 and the castle was completed in 1812. It was designed by one of Ireland's leading architects, Sir Francis Johnston, and is thought to be his masterpiece.

Despite the money that was poured into the building of the castle, not all of its owners could afford to live in it and it remained unoccupied for years at a time. Whenever it was re-opened by the family, they commissioned more work to be carried out on it. A particular feature of the castle is its ceilings, including a greatly admired stencilled one by William Morris in the late 1860s in the castle's dining-room, which is now open to the public. The last Bury left the castle in

1912 – by 1968 the roof had been removed, resulting in a lot of damage to fabric of the castle. A charitable trust, the Charleville Castle Heritage Trust, was set up to fund the castle's restoration, which has been ongoing since 1971. The trust hosts many events at the castle, and it has been used as a filming location on several occasions.

Facade of the castle.

Charleville is believed to be one of the most haunted buildings in Europe and has been investigated on several occasions by paranormal experts and psychics. Its most famous ghost is a child called Harriet, the third earl's youngest daughter, who died after falling down the stairs. People have reported seeing a small girl in a blue and white dress, with blue ribbons in her golden hair.

In 2013 the King Oak tree in the grounds of Charleville Castle was nominated for European Tree of the Year. Legend has it that each time a limb falls from the ancient oak, a member of the Bury family will die soon afterwards.

William Morris, by Frederick Hollyer, 1888.

Aerial view of Charleville Castle.

Slane Castle

Slane Castle was built in a very picturesque location, perched on a rock overlooking the River Boyne, close to the site of the Battle of the Boyne.

The Anglo-Norman Lords of Slane, the Flemings, had had a fortress on the site since the 12th century. As staunch Catholics they were among the leaders of the 1641 Rebellion – in its aftermath their property was confiscated by the crown. Their estates were restored by James II, but after the Jacobites were defeated at the Battles of the Boyne and Aughrim in the Williamite War the Flemings lost Slane and its lands for ever.

By 1703 Slane was owned by the Conynghams, a Scottish Protestant planter family who had settled in Donegal. They built a house on the foundations of the old Fleming castle soon after taking possession. It looked nothing like the castle does today, with many towers of different sizes and shapes. The power and influence of the Conynghams increased as the century progressed, and by the 1780s they had decided to turn Slane into a castle befitting their position in society. In 1785 the exterior of the castle was refashioned to incorporate the towers, and battlements were added to the roof. The gardens were landscaped by Capability Brown.

The next owner of Slane was made a marquess in 1816. His wife, Elizabeth, was the mistress of King George IV and there is a tale that the king was in such a hurry to get to Slane when he visited Dublin in 1821 that he had a straight road built along the route from the city to the castle!

In 1991 disaster struck when the eastern portion of the castle was badly damaged by fire. It has been restored and is once again open to the public, together with the whiskey distillery operated on the estate. Slane is probably most famous today as a venue for open-air summer rock concerts.

Capability Brown, who landscaped the gardens of Slane Castle in the 18th century, painted by Nathaniel Dance, (later Sir Nathaniel Dance-Holland).

Side view of the castle showing the
17th-century battlements added to the roof.

Trim Castle

In 1172 Henry II gave the Liberty of Meath (a much larger area than the present-day county of Meath, extending as far west as the River Shannon) to the Norman knight Hugh de Lacy. It was an attempt to push back against Richard de Clare – the king was worried that it would become a power grab, with de Clare declaring himself King of Ireland. De Lacy built a wooden fort on a piece of raised ground, protected by a ditch and a stockade. In 1176, he began to build a stone castle there.

Construction took more than 30 years, and de Lacy didn't live to see it completed. After his death the castle was finished by his son, Walter. Trim was the largest Norman castle in the country, with defensive walls enclosing more than three acres of land.

The huge three-storey castle, built on a crossing of the River Boyne on the very edge of the Pale, is still a looming presence in the town of Trim. The keep is a 20-sided cruciform tower, buttressed by four square towers, of which three are still standing. It was surrounded by a moat, and the whole structure was protected by a polygonal curtain wall and a barbican. Defensive square and drum towers were built into the wall at intervals, and additional protection was provided on one side by the swift waters of the Boyne. The windows were glassed and the roof was tiled.

In its heyday, the castle was self-sufficient, with a chapel, stables and even a mint. It is a indication of its importance that no fewer than seven parliaments were held there in the 15th century. It began to decline in the 16th century, but was refortified in the mid-17th century. It was taken by Cromwellian forces in 1649.

In the 19th century the castle was bought by the Dunsany Plunketts. They sold it to the state in 1993 and a programme of conservation was carried out by the Office of Public Works. The castle is now open to the public. It was used as a location for the film *Braveheart* in 1995.

Trim Castle

Clomantagh Castle

Clomantagh Castle, near Freshford, is a medieval tower house within a bawn dating from the 1430s. It belonged to the Butlers of Ormond until it was confiscated during the Cromwellian campaign and granted to Arthur St George. The castle changed hands again soon afterwards. In the early 19th century a farmhouse was built that connects with the first two floors of the tower. It stands on the site of the medieval banqueting hall. Originally thatched, the roof of the farmhouse was later tiled.

The Clomantagh síle-na-gig. The earless figure has small breasts hanging to the sides, prominent ribs, the left hand reaching in front of the leg to spread the vulva, and the right hand waving. No toes are depicted on the feet. What may be braided hair or a pony tail extends from the back of the head to the left arm. This síle is hard to see once the leaves are out on a nearby tree.

A meticulous restoration carried out in the 1990s returned the tower to its medieval state while maintaining the condition of the farmhouse as it would have been in the 1800s.

Clomantagh is now owned by the Irish Landmark Trust, which manages it as holiday rental accommodation. It is said to be haunted by a victim of the Great Irish Famine of the mid-19th century.

Kilkenny Castle

Dramatically situated on high ground above the River Nore, the castle at Kilkenny dominates the city and is one of the best-known castles in Ireland. It has been important since its construction in the 13th century on the site of an earlier structure.

Kilkenny came within the lordship of Leinster, which was granted to Richard de Clare. When he came to Kilkenny in 1172 he chose a section of high ground above the River Nore as a strategic site for a wooden tower house, a traditional motte and bailey. The site had been the base of the Irish kings of Osraighe. De Clare's son-in-law, William the Earl Marshall, built a square limestone castle with four towers, three of which are still standing. The castle was very strong, with a moat, double curtain wall and steep batter. An inner and outer courtyard gave an extra layer of protection, and a sally port provided an opportunity to leave the castle to make surprise attacks on the enemy.

Kilkenny has a long association with the Butlers of Ormond, who bought the castle from the crown after it was seized from its rightful owner, Joan de Bohun, heir to the seneschal of Kilkenny, who died in 1381. The family's wavering loyalty to the crown may have been the reason for the seizure – Gilbert de Bohun had been outlawed for several years at the beginning of the 14th century. The Butlers (originally FitzWalters) had come to Ireland with the Norman forces and were politically astute and steadfastly loyal to the crown. Their loyalty was well rewarded – they became wealthy and were created Earls of Ormond in 1328. The third Earl, James Butler, bought the castle in 1391 and it became the base from which the Butlers, further ennobled as marquesses and dukes, ruled the area for several centuries. It was their residence for more than 500 years.

During the Confederate Wars in the 1640s the owner of the castle was James Butler, the 12th Earl of Ormond, a Protestant. However, as Lord Lieutenant, Butler lived in Dublin, and his castle became the base of the Catholic rebel movement known as Confederate Ireland. When Cromwell besieged Kilkenny in 1650, the castle was targeted, and one of the towers and a section of the wall were damaged.

The castle was remodelled and refurbished in the modern style in 1661, and a new gate was built in the south wall. In the 18th century some much-needed maintenance was carried out after the 17th earl

married a wealthy heiress, Anne Wandesford. In
the 19th century work was undertaken to restore
the castle's original medieval appearance. The north
wing of the castle and the southern part of the
curtain wall were also restored.

The dining room in
Kilkenny Castle.

In 1922, during the Civil War, the castle came under attack by the Irish Free State forces when it was occupied by the Republican Army. The Ormonds barricaded themselves in their bedroom over the great gate of the castle with their dog, and a machine gun was stationed outside the door. The castle was badly damaged during the assault.

The Ormonds continued to live in the castle until 1935, when, their fortune depleted, they moved to London, abandoning the family seat. The castle was given (or, rather, sold for a token £50) to the Irish nation in 1967. At the handover ceremony the 24th earl, Arthur Butler, said that the family was 'determined that it should not be allowed to fall into

Sir Henry Sidney, brother-in-law of Robert Dudley. Unknown artist, late 16th century.

ruin. There are already too many ruins in Ireland.'

Kilkenny Castle and grounds are now in the care of the Office of Public Works and the castle has been the subject of an extensive programme of restoration. The castle today is faithful to the 19th-century renovations. Many areas are open to visitors, including the grand reception areas on the ground floor, the state rooms on the first floor, and some of the bedchambers on the top floor.

Fountain at Kilkenny Castle.

Leinster ruins

Now a ruin standing on the eastern bank of the River Barrow, Carlow Castle is thought to have been built by William de Marshal (Earl of Pembroke and Lord of Leinster).

Ormond Castle

Ormond Castle, built on the River Suir to the east of Carrick-on-Suir, is a 15th-century tower house with two battlemented flankers within a bawn. A grand Elizabethan manor house was added in the 16th century.

The original castle on the site was built in the early 14th century by the Butler family, who, in 1309, were granted the land on which the castle was built and were given the Earldom of Ormond in 1328. The 10th Earl, Thomas 'Black Tom' Butler, had been raised at the English court during the reign of Henry VIII and was a favourite of Elizabeth I (to whom he was related through her mother, Anne Boleyn). He developed a liking for the fashionable manor houses that were being built in England, and when he returned to Ireland he built the first manor house in the Plantagenet-Tudor style in the country, moving away from the old defensive style of architecture to a more graceful, comfortable, many-windowed structure with steep gables. The house was built in 1565 and was a favourite home of the Butlers until 1688, after which it was abandoned and fell into a state of ruin.

The house was owned by the Butler family until 1947 when it was transferred to the state. It has undergone an extensive programme of restoration and has been opened to the public. The long gallery, with its richly stuccoed ceiling, is of particular note, as are the Tudor devices and images of Elizabeth I that proliferate in the house. It is said that Black Tom harboured an ambition to marry the queen and, at the very least, hoped that she would visit him at Ormond Castle.

The Elizabethan manor house with the castle behind.

Kilkea Castle

Kilkea Castle was the medieval stronghold of the Earls of Kildare, the FitzGeralds. The land had been given to Sir Walter de Riddlesford, an Anglo-Norman knight, by Strongbow (Richard de Clare) after the Norman invasion of Ireland.

Sir Walter built the original motte and bailey in 1180. It later became a FitzGerald possession through marriage. The castle was extensively rebuilt in 1426 over four storeys with towers and crenellations. Restoration work was carried out in 1849 and there are now two two-storey wings. The castle is entered through an arch in the bawn – the arch is protected by a defensive drum tower built into the corner of the castle to the left of it. Kilkea was the family home of the FitzGeralds until the 19th earl moved to Carton House in the early 18th century, making it the family seat, and the castle was then leased to a succession of tenants. The Jesuit order leased it for 12 years, from 1634 to 1646. In their last year as tenants they entertained the Papal Nuncio, Archbishop Rinuccini. When Carton House was sold in 1949, the 8th Duke of Leinster, Gerald FitzGerald, moved back to Kilkea Castle.

The FitzGeralds sold Kilkea in the early 1960s and it was run as a hotel until 2009, when it went out of business as a result of the financial crisis and was put up for sale. It was bought by an American,

Jay Cashman, and is now being run as a leisure resort.

One of the castle's most colourful owners was the 11th earl, the so-called 'Wizard Earl', Gerald FitzGerald, who inherited the title in 1537 at the age of 12, when his half-brother, Silken Thomas, was executed at Tyburn. Gerald was educated on the Continent, where he developed an interest in alchemy, and is said to have possessed magical powers. He died in 1585 and there is a legend that he appears at the castle every seven years, mounted on a white charger with silver shoes.

Silken Thomas and five of his uncles were beheaded at the Tower of London in 1537.

Stone carving at the castle.

Maynooth Castle

Maynooth Castle, a 13th-century three-storey tower house now stands at the entrance to the south campus of Maynooth University. It is one of the largest tower houses in Ireland.

In 1176 Richard de Clare granted the lands that now comprise the modern county of Kildare to Maurice FitzGerald. The keep was constructed at Maynooth in the early 1200s. In 1316 the FitzGeralds were granted the title of Earls of Kildare and Maynooth became their principal seat. The heyday of the FitzGeralds was during the time of the eighth earl, Garret Mór, known as the Great Earl of Kildare, who governed Ireland as the king's deputy from 1487 to 1513. Under the eighth and ninth earls Maynooth Castle became a centre of political power and social and cultural influence.

In 1534 Silken Thomas, the son of the ninth earl, rebelled against the crown and the castle was bombarded by English soldiers. It proved to be no match for an onslaught by modern siege artillery fire and fell after 10 days. The entire garrison was summarily executed, and Silken Thomas and five of his uncles were later executed for treason at Tyburn in London.

The castle was restored and expanded in 1630–35 by Richard Boyle, first Earl of Cork, whose daughter had married the 16th Earl of Kildare, George FitzGerald. This restoration relegated the keep to a secondary role and the new buildings became the focus of the castle. During the Confederacy Wars much of the new construction was destroyed, with only the gatehouse and tower still standing. The FitzGeralds left Maynooth, moving first to Kilkea Castle and then to Carton House.

The Office of Public Works began a restoration project in 2000, with works still ongoing. Limited visitor access to the castle is possible.

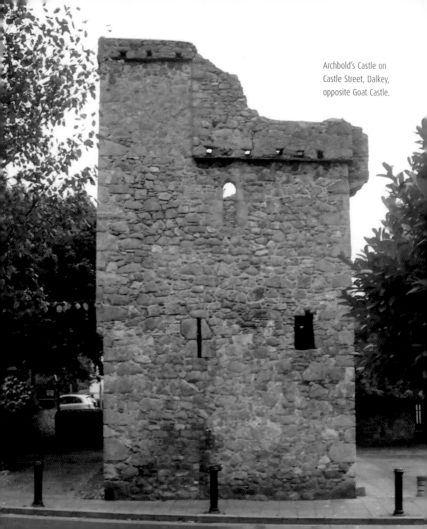

Archbold's Castle on Castle Street, Dalkey, opposite Goat Castle.

Dalkey Castle

Dalkey Castle is one of seven fortified townhouses dating from the 14th and 15th centuries – the others were Black Castle, House Castle, Archbold's Castle (situated just across the street from Dalkey Castle), Wolverton's Castle, Dungan's Castle and Yellow Castle. Dalkey Castle was built beside the 10th-century church of St Begnet on what is now Castle Street.

The existence of the seven castles evidences the commercial importance of Dalkey during the medieval period. At that time, Dublin Bay was silted up, which meant that large ships, laden with goods, found it impossible to anchor there. The deep waters of Dalkey Sound provided a solution. The merchants of Dublin, unable to land their cargoes at Dublin, successfully petitioned the crown for permission to use the harbour at Dalkey. Heavy cargoes were offloaded there and transported in smaller boats to the city of Dublin. The seven castles of Dalkey were built to provide well-defended storage for goods awaiting onward transport into Dublin.

Dalkey Castle, the largest of the seven castles, was originally known as The Castle at Dalkey. The main storeroom was on the ground floor, with further storage on a mezzanine floor. The living area was on the first floor, with sleeping quarters above. The defenders of the castle could safely keep a lookout from the castle's two turrets and the crenellated battlements. A machicolation over the heavy front door allowed stones and other heavy objects to be dropped on would-be attackers. Those who successfully breached the entrance found themselves trapped under a murder hole.

As the largest of the seven castles Dalkey Castle is believed to have been the centre of administration in the town during the medieval period. The importance of Dalkey as a harbour declined in the early 19th century when a large 'asylum' harbour was built at Dún Laoghaire, a little further north along the Dublin coastline. From the mid-19th century the castle was utilised as a meeting place for the Dalkey Town Commissioners, and when Dalkey Town Hall was built in the 1890s, the ground floor of the castle was used as its foyer.

Dalkey Castle was also known as Goat Castle. This curious name was first used in the early 17th century, when Dalkey Castle was owned by the Chevers (or Cheevers) family of nearby Monkstown (they were later exiled to Connacht by Cromwell). Their name was an Anglicisation of the French 'chèvre', meaning 'goat'.

Dalkey Castle and Heritage Centre is open to the public, providing living history tours and the opportunity to explore Dalkey's creative heritage in its purpose-built Writer's Gallery.

Part of the walls of
Dalkey Castle.

Dublin Castle

Dublin Castle was the centre of the British administration in Ireland for centuries, serving also as the residence of the sitting Lord Lieutenant. When the Anglo-Irish Treaty creating the Irish Free State was signed in 1921 the British handed the castle over to Michael Collins, the leader of the new provisional government of Ireland. It is now an Irish government complex and is used on state occasions, including presidential inaugurations, beginning with that of the first president of Ireland, Douglas Hyde, in 1938. It is the administrative centre for the Irish presidency of the European Union.

The first structure at Dublin Castle was built in 1204 by Meiler FitzHenry. He had been ordered by King John to construct a defensive castle that would protect the city, the administration of justice and the king's treasure. FitzHenry chose a strategic location at the confluence of the River Liffey and its tributary, the Poddle, which may have been the site of a much earlier ring fort. A portion of a Viking fortress can be seen in the castle's medieval undercroft.

Building work was completed in 1230. The castle was built to Norman specifications, without a central keep. It was a square surrounded by tall curtain walls with a round tower at each corner.

The moat was filled by diverting the river. The buildings within the curtain walls were wooden and the complex was badly damaged by fire in 1684. The reconstruction obliterated most of the medieval origins – the only parts to have survived above ground are the Record Tower, built around 1230, and the base of the Bermingham Tower. The battlements were added in the 19th century.

As it is today, the castle was used for many different purposes, and has had a varied and sometimes colourful history. It was the location for the Court of Castle Chamber, the highest court in the land, equivalent to England's Star Chamber; it was the crown treasury in Ireland – in 1907 the Irish crown jewels were stolen from the castle and have never been recovered; it has served as a house of parliament and a banqueting hall, and has been used as a prison for Irish rebels and insurrectionists throughout its history.

On the morning of Easter Monday 1916 a small and poorly armed contingent of the Irish Citizen Army seized the entrance and guardroom in an attempt to turn the castle into the headquarters of the rebellion. There were only 25 soldiers in the garrison at the time and a larger Irish force could probably have taken it. However, British reinforcements were sent from Royal Barracks (now Collins Barracks) and Portobello Barracks (now Cathal Brugha Barracks) and the rebels were soon in retreat. A pike (the definitive symbol of Irish revolt) dropped by one of the rebels in Upper Castle Yard, now an exhibit in the National Museum of Ireland, shows how inadequately armed some of the insurgents were.

Apart from state occasions Dublin Castle has many functions today: the offices of the Revenue Commissioners are located in a new building within the Castle Yard; the collections of the Chester Beatty Library are housed in purpose-built museum; and the museum of An Garda Síochána is also located there.

The castle is a major tourist attraction maintained by the Office of Public Works, and many of the state rooms can be visited. St Patrick's Hall, which is used for state occasions, is decorated in gold and blue (the official coat of arms of Ireland is a gold harp on a St Patrick's blue background) and has one of the best examples of a painted ceiling in the country. The castle gardens, to the south of the state apartments and the Chapel Royal, are sited on or near the spot of the original 'dubh linn' or 'black pool', a Viking harbour and trading base, after which the city is named.

St Patrick, decorating a doorway at Dublin Castle.

Howth Castle

Howth Harbour was one of the main ports of entry on Ireland's east coast and this magnificent castle on a promontory reflects the town's importance. Howth Castle has been occupied by the same family for more than 800 years. The first Lord of Howth, Almeric, came to Ireland in 1177. He is said to have won a decisive battle on the feast of St Lawrence, which gave him possession of the Howth peninsula. He took the name St Lawrence and his descendants (the Gaisford-St Lawrences) are still living in Howth castle.

Almeric's wooden castle was built overlooking the harbour,

The walls at Howth Castle.

but in 1235 another castle, also wooden, was erected on the site of the present castle. A stone structure was built in the middle of the 15th century, and some of the earlier structures were incorporated in the castle as it is today. The current appearance of the castle dates from 1738, when it was extensively renovated, rebuilt and extended. There were further renovations and additions at the beginning of the 20th century.

There are several legends associated with Howth Castle, the most famous of which involves Grace O'Malley. It is said that when she was returning from her historic visit to Queen Elizabeth in England in 1576, she landed at Howth and made her way to the castle, expecting to be invited to dine and pick up provisions for her voyage to Mayo. Instead, she found the gates closed against her. She felt that the slight against her was in breach of Irish rules of hospitality, so when the young St Lawrence heir was brought to the harbour to see Grace's ship, she abducted him and brought him to her stronghold in Clew Bay. She released him on the condition that the gates of Howth Castle would never be closed at dinner time, and that an extra place would always be laid for an unexpected guest. To this day, the extra place is always laid. There are several versions of the tale. However, as Grace in fact visited Queen Elizabeth in 1593 at a time when there was no St Lawrence heir of the same age as the abductee, the dates don't tally, but it makes a good story!

The castle is a family home and, until recently, was not open to the public, but there are now guided tours in June, July and August, for which booking is essential.

Howth Castle
viewed from a rocky
outcrop on Howth Hill.

Malahide Castle

Home to the Talbot family for more than 800 years, Malahide Castle dates back to the 12th century. It was built by Richard Talbot, Earl of Shrewsbury. In 1185 Henry II gifted him the lands and harbour of Malahide for his services to the Norman invasion of Ireland.

Talbot built a motte and bailey castle to the south-east of Malahide, and the remains of the motte can still be seen there. Around 1250 a stone castle was built on the site of the present castle – little is known of its construction or appearance. By 1486, according to a contemporary sketch, the castle had a three-storey keep and the original east wing (extended around 1475) had been retained. The west wing was added between 1550 and 1640.

The 17th century was a troubled time for the castle and its residents. In 1639 Lord Stafford tried to take control of the castle and the port of Malahide, with its valuable customs rights. The Earl of Ormonde billeted a garrison of 200 soldiers in the castle during the Irish rebellion of 1641. In 1649 the castle and lands were seized by Cromwell's troops

and the castle was occupied until 1660 by the Lord Chief Baron of Ireland, Myles Corbet. It was then reoccupied by the Talbots, and although 13 members of the Talbot family died fighting on the losing Jacobite side at the Battle of the Boyne in 1690, their landholdings were not confiscated.

After a fire in the west wing the drawing rooms were rebuilt in the late 18th century and two round corner towers with turrets were constructed, giving the castle its Gothic Revival appearance. This was enhanced by the addition in the early 19th century of the square turreted entrance block. In 1831 the title of Baron Talbot of Malahide was created for the family. The seventh Lord Talbot inherited the title and the castle in 1948 and carried out some improvements and modernisation.

Swords Castle

Located in the centre of Swords, beside the River Ward, the castle was built in 1200 as the manorial residence of the first Anglo-Norman archbishop of Dublin, John Comyn, who reigned from 1181 to 1212 and built a new town of Swords, relocating it from the opposite side of the river. Although the castle was not designed as a defensive structure, it had to be capable of withstanding an attack, and it was enclosed within a high pentagonal perimeter wall.

The accommodation included a gatehouse, a chapel, a banqueting hall, farm buildings and living quarters for the entire episcopal entourage, including knights, squires and monks.

Throughout the four centuries after the first stone was laid, the castle was regularly extended and revised. By the 14th century it was twice the size of an average Dublin manor house. The castle was built using the local limestone, with imported red sandstone dressings. In 1324 a new archbishop's palace was built in Tallaght, and Swords was turned into a church court, with the castle being managed by a constable. The Constable's Tower was built in the mid-15th century during a period of fortification. Swords Castle by this time had sustained damage, most probably during the military campaign by Edward Bruce (brother of Robert) in 1317. By 1583 it had fallen into ruin, being described as 'the quite spoiled castle'.

Panoramic view of the castle battlements.

The castle was sold to the Cobbe family of Donabate after the Church of Ireland was disestablished in 1871. The castle was crumbling, appearing on contemporary ordinance survey maps as a ruin, and the area enclosed within its walls had been made into an orchard. A Bramley apple tree from the 1890s is its oldest survivor. Some areas of the castle have disappeared completely.

In the 1930s the castle was placed under the guardianship of the Office of Public Works and was bought by Fingal County Council in 1985. Restoration work began in 1996. The Constable's Tower and the chapel have been restored, as has the three-storey accommodation block known as the Chamber Block. Swords Castle was used as a location for the television series *The Tudors*.

Vintage print of Swords Castle.

Dublin

Carlow Castle

Built on a rocky mound at the confluence of the Rivers Burren and Barrow, Carlow Castle is believed to be one of Ireland's earliest keeps. It was built by William Marshall in the early 13th century, on the site of an earlier motte and bailey wooden fortification constructed by Hugh de Lacy at the end of the 12th century.

The castle was rectangular in form and had drum towers at each corner, with defensive crenellated battlements and a batter. Although the middle floor had mullioned windows, the towers and upper floors were furnished with arrow loops.

By the 14th century the castle was the property of the crown, and Edward III's son, the Duke of Clarence, lived there. He strengthened the fortifications so that he could move the royal treasury from Dublin to Carlow, but it was soon moved back to the safety of Dublin Castle. The next owners were the Earls of Norfolk, but the castle was confiscated in 1537. In 1616 it was bought by Donogh O'Brien. It was captured in 1642 during the Confederate Wars, but was liberated by General Ireton of the Commonwealth army and given back to O'Brien.

In 1813 Dr Philip Middleton leased the castle with the intention of turning it into a mental asylum. While his improvements to the castle were under way the east wall and towers collapsed, and today only one elevation remains, the western wall flanked by two round towers.

In 1996 Carlow Castle was given into the care of the Office of Public Works and has been declared a national monument.

Huntington Castle

Huntington Castle in Clonegal was built on the ruins of a 13th-century Franciscan monastery, itself built on a site of druidic worship. After the dissolution of the monasteries in the mid-16th century the monastery was abandoned, and the land was later given to Laurence Esmonde, a member of an English family who had been elevated to the peerage in 1622 for his military services to Elizabeth I and James I.

Huntington looks every inch the baronial castle, but its structure evolved over several centuries, with each extension designed according to the fashion of the times. In 1625 the first Sir Laurence Esmonde built a three-storey fortified tower house which served as a garrison and was taken by Cromwell's troops as they advanced on Kilkenny in 1650. The tower house now forms part of the present structure. Additions and alterations began in the 1680s, carried out in the first instance by Esmonde's grandson, another Sir Laurence. In the 1720s yet another Sir

Laurence built an entire new wing.

A further extension was built in the mid-19th century, at which time the crenellated battlements were added. Direct descendants of the Esmondes, the Durdin-Robertsons, still own the castle.

The monastic history of the site continues in the beautiful gardens, which include an excellent example of a yew walk, planted over six centuries ago. An artificial lake powered one of Ireland's first water turbines, which provided Huntington's electricity from the late 19th century.

The detailed guided tour of the castle includes a visit to the Temple of Isis in the dungeons of the old castle.

Chapter 2
Munster

Minard Castle ruins in County Kerry.
The castle was built by the Knight of
Kerry and destroyed by the forces of
Oliver Cromwell.

Dungarvan Castle

Strategically located at the mouth of the River Colligan, Dungarvan Castle, a royal castle in the English style, was built in 1185. Ships could anchor next to it and the castle's occupants could keep watch over the small strip of land linking East and West Waterford.

The original castle comprised a rare shell keep enclosed by a polygonal curtain wall. It was built in the water, so that the castle had a natural protective moat. The keep was connected to land by a wooden bridge leading to a small enclosed yard on the mainland. The keep contained the great hall and living apartments. In 1262 a round tower was built in the north-western corner and the height and thickness of the curtain wall were augmented. The corner gatehouse, with its D-shaped flankers, was built in the north-eastern angle of the wall, complete with a murder hole and space for a portcullis. It is believed that the moat on the land side of the castle was filled in during the 14th century.

No further changes were made to the castle until the 16th century, when advances in the techniques of warfare called for the construction of gun loops and a wider entrance to accommodate gun carriages. A cannon platform was added to the top of the gatehouse. In the 18th century a two-storey barracks was built inside the castle walls. During the Civil War the castle barracks was taken over by the Republican Army, who fired it as they departed. An Garda Síochána was set up in 1922 and the restored barracks was used as the local Garda station for the next 65 years.

After the Garda left the castle in 1987 it fell into a state of disrepair, but was later restored by Dúchas, who have opened it to the public.

Gateway at Dungarvan Castle.

Members of An Garda Síochána.

Lismore Castle

Built in a beautiful position with panoramic views over the Blackwater Valley to the Knockmealdown Mountains, Lismore Castle dates from the 12th century and has a rich royal and ecclesiastical history.

Until the end of the 12th century, Lismore Abbey had been one of Ireland's most important monastic settlements. When Henry II visited in 1171 he chose the site of the abbey for a castle and, following the Norman sacking of Lismore town in 1173, his younger son, the future King John, began building a castellum in the abbey grounds in 1185. When John was crowned king in 1199 he gave the castle to the Church and it was used as the palace of the Bishop of Lismore until Sir Walter Raleigh leased it in 1589. Raleigh later bought the castle, but when he was imprisoned for high treason in 1602 he sold it to Richard Boyle, later the first Earl of Cork, who landscaped the estate in the style of an English country manor.

In 1753 the castle was acquired by the Cavendish family when the fourth Duke of Devonshire married the heiress to the earldom of Cork. Their son, born in 1748, made many improvements to the castle, including the building of a bridge across the river in 1775. The sixth Duke of Devonshire, William Cavendish, succeeded his father in 1811 and immediately began to turn the castle into a grand Gothic-style building, with towers, crenellations and a gatehouse. The architect of the Palace of Westminster, Augustus Pugin, transformed the chapel of the bishop's palace into a medieval-style banqueting hall, complete with choir stalls and stained-glass windows. A new bridge was built in 1858, replacing the older one built by the fifth earl, and it was at this time that the beautiful lower garden was created.

Lismore is still owned by the Devonshires, who live there for several weeks each year, and although the castle is private the gardens are open to the public.

Views of the gardens at Lismore Castle.

Reginald's Tower

This important landmark was built in the 12th century on the site of an earlier Viking fort. It was part of Waterford's Anglo-Norman defensive chain of walls and towers, one of three towers that form a triangle known as the Viking Triangle – the others were Turgesius Tower and St Martin's Castle – and one of 17 towers that encircled Waterford city. Only six of these towers remain today, of which Reginald's is the largest (the other survivors are the Watch Tower, Double Tower, French Tower, Semi-lunar Tower and Beach Tower).

Plaque on
the wall of
Reginald's Tower.

Reginald's Tower is a squat circular structure, tapering slightly towards the top, with a conical tiled roof. It has four storeys, connected by a spiral staircase. It is Ireland's oldest civic building and the only one that has a Viking name (Reginald is an Anglicisation of Raghnall, which is, in turn, a Gaelicised version of the Norse Røgnvaldr). When it was built, its location on the site of its Viking predecessor, a piece of high ground between the River Suir and a tributary of St John's River (since drained), was a strategic one. The capture of the original Viking fort by the Normans in 1170 led to the fall of the city of Waterford.

Reginald's Tower has had a colourful history. One of the most notorious events to take place in the tower was the marriage of Strongbow (Richard de Clare) to Aoife, daughter of Diarmaid

McMurrough, King of Leinster, giving the Normans their first foothold in Ireland.

During the first centuries of its existence the tower served as a mint, a prison and an arsenal. King John visited in 1210, and Richard II came to the castle twice, in 1394 and 1399. In 1649 Waterford was fruitlessly besieged by Cromwell's army, but in 1650 they were more successful – a cannonball from that second siege is still lodged in the wall of the tower. It is said that James II surveyed his lost kingdom for a final time from the top of the tower after his defeat at the Battle of the Boyne.

The tower came into the hands of Waterford Corporation in 1861 and became the official residence of the Chief Constable. In 1954 the last resident moved out and the tower was turned into a museum. During the Second World War it was a designated air raid shelter. It is now the home of the Waterford Viking Museum.

Entrance to Reginald's Tower.

Reginald's Tower.

The Marriage of Strongbow and Aoife, by Daniel Maclise, painted in 1854. It is on permanent display in the National Gallery of Ireland, Dublin.

Cahir Castle

Cahir Castle, situated on an islet in the River Suir, is one of the largest castles of its date in Ireland. In 1142 Conor O'Brien, Prince of Thomond, started building a castle near the site of an earlier stone fort, a cathair, which gave the place its name. Construction of the castle continued into the 13th century.

In 1375 Edward III granted the castle to James Butler, first Earl of Ormond, in recognition of his loyalty to the crown. The castle was improved and enlarged in the 15th and 16th centuries, and by 1599 the castle had achieved its present appearance. The keep, tower and most of the defensive walls are still in good order.

Cahir Castle is one of the best defended castles in the country. It was built as a series of walled courts, with an additional perimeter wall on the riverbank. The large rectangular keep in the innermost courtyard was the original gatehouse. The entrance to the main courtyard, possibly with the original gate arch and an unusual double machicolation (reconstructed in the 19th century), was moved alongside the keep in the 15th century.

In 1542 the first Baron Cahir was created and Cahir Castle, previously the principal seat of the Earls of Ormonde, became his baronial seat. The castle was besieged by the Earl of Essex during

the Tyrone Rebellion in 1599 and was captured after three days of artillery bombardment. Until then, the castle had been considered impregnable, but its walls were no match for heavy cannon fire. Lord Cahir formed an alliance with the Earl of Tyrone and was arrested for treason in 1601. However, he succeeded in obtaining a full pardon and Cahir Castle was returned to him.

Robert Devereux, 2nd Earl of Essex, by Marcus Gheeraerts the Younger, c.1597.

Castle gate with cannon.

During the Confederate Wars the castle was besieged twice, in 1647 and 1650, and was surrendered on both occasions without a drop of blood being spilt.

The castle fell into ruin in the late 18th century when the Butlers moved into their town house in Cahir. It was partially restored in the mid-19th century. Cahir is an Irish Heritage Town and Cahir Castle is now managed by Dúchas, the Irish Heritage Society.

Nenagh Castle

Nenagh Castle was built in 1220 by Theobald FitzWalter, an ancestor of the Earls of Ormond. It was the main seat of the Butlers of Ormond until 1391, when they moved to Kilkenny Castle.

The cylindrical castle keep, which is all that remains intact of the castle, is said to be one of the finest examples of a round tower house in the country. The whimsical touches, which have given it iconic status, were added in the 19th century.

The four-storey keep was incorporated in the curtain wall, which enclosed a large pentagonal courtyard. It has arrow loops and a large machicolation (now closed off) over the entrance. Only a few fragments of the walls, gatehouse and east tower remain, but the keep has been restored.

During the 15th century the keep was occupied by the O'Briens, but by 1533 it was once again in Butler hands, and had several changes of ownership in the period leading up to the Cromwellian invasion. In 1703 the Duke of Ormond sold the castle to pay off some creditors.

The keep gets its unique appearance from the clerestory-style windows around the top of the tower, added in 1860, together with the decorative crenellations, by the Bishop of Killaloe. It increased the height of the tower by 30 per cent and was done with a view to turning the keep into the bell tower of a cathedral that was never built.

Roscrea Castle

Built on high ground near the River Bunnow, Roscrea stands apart from many Irish castles in that there was no pre-Norman fortification on its site. A wooden motte castle was built in 1213 by King John and was replaced by a moated stone castle in 1280 when it was discovered that there were silver deposits nearby.

The castle is also unusual in that there is no keep – it consists of two D-shaped corner towers built into the curtain walls that enclose a courtyard. The larger tower is three storeys high.

In 1315 the castle was granted to the Butlers of Ormond, who retained possession of it until

1703. In the 15th century the fourth Earl of Ormond, James Butler, built a huge gate house with a drawbridge and portcullis. This became the castle's main living area.

In 1646 the castle was invaded by Eoin Roe O'Neill with a large army of 1,200 men. Almost all the occupants of the castle were killed. O'Neill invaded the castle again in 1649 and looted it of almost its entire contents, including kitchen utensils and women's clothing. The castle's occupants surrendered to Cromwell in 1650 and it was occupied by General Ireton for a month.

During the Williamite War William of Orange ordered the demolition of the castle to prevent it falling into enemy hands, but it was saved when it was made clear to him that it provided a haven for English settlers.

In 1703 the Duke of Ormond sold the castle to King's Hospital in Kilmainham and it was sold on to John Damer in 1722. He built a house in the castle grounds and the family lived in it until 1798, when it was turned into a military barracks. It was later used as a TB sanatorium, a library and a school.

Damer House was slated for demolition in the 1970s but was taken over by the Irish Georgian Society and has been meticulously restored. The house and the gate house of the castle are open to the public.

Eoin Roe O'Neill

The Rock of Cashel

Legend has it that the Rock of Cashel, rising high above the surrounding Tipperary plain, was formed when St Patrick routed the Devil from a mountain cave some distance away. The Devil bit off a piece of the mountain but spat it out when he realised he had broken a tooth. The piece of rock landed in the plains of Tipperary. St Patrick's dates don't tally with this story, but it provides a fanciful explanation as to why an enormous limestone rock dominates the surrounding plain.

Legends aside, the Rock has been fortified since the fourth century, when King Cormac of Munster built a ring fort here. It was the seat of the kings of Munster until the Normans arrived in Ireland at the end of the 12th century. St Patrick is said to have to come to the rock in 446, when he converted King Aengus to Christianity, and the Rock, otherwise known as St Patrick's Rock, became an important Christian site. It is thought that Brian Boru, was crowned high king at the Rock of Cashel in 964.

At the beginning of the 12th century King Murrough O'Brien (a great-grandson of Brian Boru) gave his fortress on the Rock of Cashel to the Church and it quickly became a religious centre. A 28-metre round tower, built using the dry-stone method, is still standing, although conservationists have mortared the stones in the interests of safety. In 1127 Cormac's Chapel was built on the orders of the King-Bishop of Cashel, Cormac McCarthy, and construction of a large cathedral began in 1169. It took 65 years to complete and was consecrated in 1234.

In 1647 Cromwell's troops invaded the city and the stronghold. The church treasures were plundered, the Irish troops were massacred, the priests were murdered and 3,000 of the townsfolk who had taken refuge behind the castle walls were burned alive. The Rock of Cashel was never returned to its former glory and, in 1749, in what has been criticised as an act of vandalism on what was considered a jewel among Irish ecclesiastical buildings, the Anglican archbishop of Cashel, Arthur Price, ordered the roof of the cathedral to be removed.

Restoration on the site, which is open to visitors, is ongoing.

Glin Castle

Glin Castle has been owned by the FitzGerald family for more than 700 years. In the 1170s Thomas FitzGerald was given land in western Limerick and built a small castle at Shanid, several miles from Glin. In the 13th century the title of Knight of Glin was created – the holder of the title is head of one of the three branches of the Geraldines of Desmond.

The original castle is a now a ruin, devastated by crown attacks in the 16th century. The family moved to the site of the present castle and built a thatched longhouse. In the 18th century they became Protestants and were able to participate in the social and political life of the country. Their elevated status required a grander house

and a many-windowed three-storey extension was attached to the longhouse. Although the exterior was quite plain, the interior was, and is magnificent – the house, which boasts the only flying staircase in Ireland, was lavishly decorated and furnished.

In the early 19th century, the 24th knight refurbished the exterior of the house with crenellations, mullioned windows and other Gothic details, and it was afterwards known as Glin Castle. The top floor of the castle was unfinished until the late 20th century, when the rooms were finally plastered. The family moved into the wing and the main house was let. The 29th knight died in 2011 – as he had no male heir the romantic title died with him and the castle was inherited by his daughters. It was put up for sale in 2015, but was later withdrawn and remains in the family.

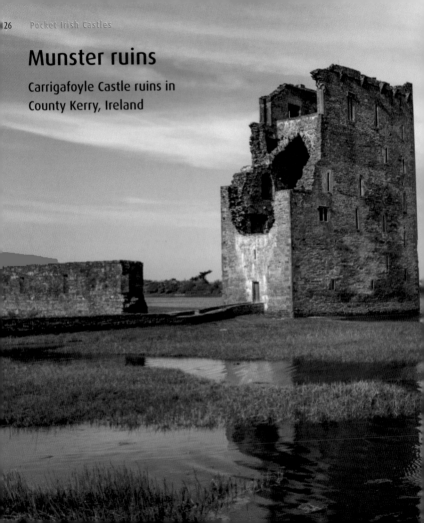

Munster ruins

Carrigafoyle Castle ruins in
County Kerry, Ireland

King John's Castle

Located in a prominent situation on an island in the River Shannon in Limerick, the magnificent King John's Castle was built in the 13th century on an older Viking site. The remains of the Viking settlement were uncovered during excavations in 1900. St John's is one of the best-preserved Norman castles in Europe.

Limerick Cathedral, the site of the burial of Domhnall Mór Ó Briain.

The Normans arrived in the area of the Shannon in 1172 and Domhnall Mór Ó Briain burned the city of Limerick to the ground in order to prevent it falling into the hands of the invaders. He died in 1194 and the Normans captured the area in 1195. At that time the King of England and Lord of Ireland was John, the youngest son of Henry II. He gave the city of Limerick its royal charter in 1197. In 1200 he gave orders for a castle to be built on the Shannon boundary in order to protect the city from raids by the Irish clans. The huge castle was built to a plan that was unique at the time, a move away from the square Anglo-Norman tower houses that dot the Irish countryside. Instead of having a square tower

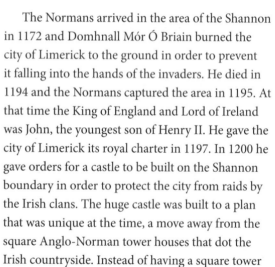

or keep within a courtyard that was bounded by a wall, King John's Castle is a series of large drum towers, with a bulwark and a huge gate house, all connected by a high curtain wall. Accommodation within the castle walls would have been built out of wood. A natural moat was created by the strategic siting of the tower on an island and the castle was connected to the other side of the river by a bridge, which was later replaced by Thomond Bridge.

The completion of the castle in 1210 ushered in an era of great peace and prosperity for the city. It was an important port and trading centre, but King John, who died six years after the completion of the castle, never visited it. He had a mint set up in the north-western corner of the castle, an indication of the importance of the structure.

Despite its impressive size, strong construction and easily defended situation, the castle came under frequent attack from the O'Briens and the MacNamaras, who even managed to take possession of it for a while in the 14th century. It was badly damaged in the first of several sieges that took place in the 17th century. In 1642 the castle was besieged by an Irish army under the leadership of Garret Barry. He had none of the siege artillery that would have made it possible to breach the walls, so he undermined them instead, digging away the foundations. The Protestants who had taken refuge in the castle after the Irish rebellion of 1641 surrendered just before the castle walls collapsed on top of them. The foundations were so badly damaged that some of the walls had to

Tapestry of King John hunting.

be knocked down. The walls were further damaged during the Siege of Limerick by siege engines and mines.

In 1651 Cromwellian troops under the command of General Ireton blockaded the city of Limerick. Despite being offered generous terms the defenders refused to surrender. The siege lasted for almost five months, and as many as 5,000 people died of illness and starvation before the terms of surrender were agreed. The English troops took over the castle and this occupation marked the end of the long period of prosperity and social power enjoyed by the Catholic population of the city.

There was a brief Catholic resurgence in 1690 and a Williamite army was repulsed by Jacobite forces inside the castle. The women in the castle are said to have thrown stones and broken bottles at the enemy during the fighting. In 1691 one of William's generals, Ginkel, took a number of important Irish towns, including Galway, Cork and Kinsale. Limerick held out until Ginkel starved the population into signing a truce, known as the Treaty of Limerick, said to have been signed on the Treaty Stone (on the far side of the river) which can be seen from the castle.

King John's Castle had a complete renovation between 2011 and 2013 and the castle, its visitor centre and interactive exhibits are open to the public.

Listowel Castle

Listowel Castle is sited on a steep bank overlooking a ford on the River Feale, a site that was very easily defended. The castle was built in the 15th century by the Anglo-Norman FitzMaurice family, the Earls of Desmond, but it is believed to have been constructed on the site of an earlier castle, probably dating from the 13th century.

The town of Listowel, north of Tralee, developed around the castle, which is now in the centre of the town. The ground plan of the castle was square, with a large square tower at each corner. It was equipped with gun loops and has a shallow batter at its base.

Vintage postcard of Listowel Castle.

The FitzMaurice family seats were at Ardfert and Lixnaw, but Listowel was extremely important to them as a defence in their constant battles with the O'Neill clan and the forces of the English crown. The ford effectively made a stronghold of the castle. It was captured in 1600 by Sir Charles Wilmot after a 28-day siege during the first Desmond Rebellion, and was the last Desmond bastion to fall. It became the property of the Hare family, later ennobled as the Earls of Listowel. It was abandoned and became uninhabitable at the beginning of the 19th century, when many of the stones used in its construction were removed to build some of the houses in the town square.

Today, all that remains of what must have been a very imposing structure is the front of the castle – two tall four-storey towers (the living quarters of the soldiers and the castle servants) connected by an unusual closed arch. The original crenellations have gone. The Office of Public Works began a programme of restoration in 2005, cleaning the stonework and building an external staircase to the rear of the facade.

Maurice FitzGerald, Lord of Lanstephan, as shown in a manuscript of the *Expugnatio Hibernica*, written in 1189 by his nephew, Gerald of Wales.

Ross Castle

Situated on the edge of Lough Leane, Ross Castle was built in the late 15th century on an ancient copper mining site. The five-storey square tower house was the home of the O'Donoghue Mór, chief of the O'Donoghue Ross clan, and was well defended with a square bawn, drum towers on each corner of the bawn, machicolations on two opposite corners of the tower house, crenellations, a murder hole and a batter. Given the extent of its defences it is not surprising that Ross was one of the last castles in Ireland to surrender to Cromwell's forces.

After the second Desmond Rebellion in 1580 the castle was occupied by the MacCarthy Mór, and it was a MacCarthy who defended the castle against Cromwell's army of 4,000 troops under General Ludlow, surrendering only when it came under sustained artillery fire from a boat on the lake. The castle was confiscated and given to the Earls of Kenmare, who added a long fortified house to the tower house.

During the Williamite War the castle was converted for use as a military barracks and the bawn was removed in the 18th century to allow a more permanent barracks to be built. Ross housed a garrison until 1825, after which the roof of the barracks was taken off and the castle was fitted with some larger windows.

The great hall, with its two large windows, minstrels gallery and magnificent oak roof, has been restored, together with the vaulted ceilings of the bedchambers. There is a legend that the O'Donoghue Mór watches over his castle from his resting place at the bottom of Lough Leane, where he landed after being sucked out of one of the castle windows together with his horse.

Cannon situated in the castle walls.

Vintage view of the castle.

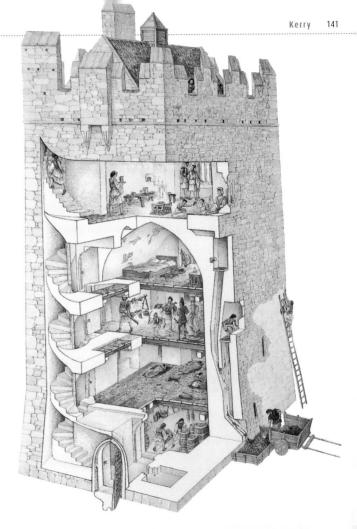

Castle interior. Drawing commissioned by the Irish government and donated to the museum.

Baltimore Castle

Baltimore Castle, which stands on a sandstone ridge overlooking Baltimore Harbour, is known as Dún na Séad, which translates as 'the jewel fort', its poetic name cloaking a more mundane reality – the occupiers of the castle were the collectors of taxes on ships entering Baltimore Harbour.

The castle was built in 1215 by Lord Sleynie, a descendant of Robert FitzStephen, who was granted half the kingdom of Cork by Henry II. It is a two-storey rectangular keep within a bawn, probably built on the site of an earlier ring fort. The castle had several arrow loops, battlements and a machicolation, but it would have depended largely on the bawn to keep the inhabitants safe from attack.

An Irish clan revolt in 1261 ousted many Anglo-Normans from their strongholds and it is thought that the O'Driscolls took possession of Dún na Séad at that time. It was their seat for more than 300 years and the family prospered during their time there, enjoying a lavish lifestyle. All that changed after the Battle of Kinsale when the castle was forfeited to the crown. In 1631 Baltimore was attacked by Algerian pirates who took 107 local people as slaves, but they didn't succeed in breaching the castle's defences.

In 1649 Cromwellian troops were garrisoned at the castle, and after they left it gradually fell into ruin. The current owners, Patrick and Bernie McCarthy, began a meticulous restoration in 1997, faithfully following the plan of the castle and renovating its original features.

Baltimore harbour in West Cork.

Blarney Castle

Blarney may be the most famous castle in Ireland because of the stone set in its battlements that is said to impart eloquence, or the 'gift of the gab', to anyone flexible enough to bend over backwards to kiss it.

Blarney Castle, located near the River Martin in Cork, is an imposing five-storey tower house that is believed to date from 1210, replacing an earlier wooden structure on the site. The stone fortification was destroyed in 1446 but was rebuilt by Cormac MacCarthy, Lord of Muskerry. The castle came under siege during the Irish Confederate Wars (1641–53) and was captured by Cromwellian forces in 1646. Within 20 years it had been returned to the ownership of the MacCarthys by Charles II, who created Donough MacCarthy first Earl of Clancarty.

The fortunes of the MacCarthys took a downturn after the Battle of the Boyne in 1690 – the fourth Earl of Clancarty, also Donough MacCarthy, was captured and his lands became forfeit to the crown. The castle was sold to Sir James St John Jefferyes, governor of the city of Cork, in the early 1700s.

Subsequent generations of the Jefferyes family built a manor house near the keep, and a cylindrical tower, with an arched top portion, was added in the mid-18th century. The tower is still standing, but the house was destroyed by fire, and in 1874 a Scottish baronial-style mansion was built near the lake to replace it. Around this time a Jefferyes married a Colthurst, and the Blarney demesne is still occupied by the Colthurst family.

The castle itself is now partially in ruins, although some of the rooms and battlements are accessible. The Blarney Stone, or the Stone of Eloquence, is at the top of the castle, set into the wall below the battlements. Legend has it that it is the stone on which the kings of Ireland were crowned.

The castle is set in acres of parkland planted with rare trees and shrubs, and in the enclosed area known as the Rock Close there are ancient stones believed to date from the pre-Christian era in Ireland, when the druids were a power in the land.

Beautiful view of
hanging flowers in
the castle gardens.

Waterfalls
at Blarney
Castle.

Desmond Castle

A three-storey square tower house with a storehouse to the rear, Desmond Castle was built around 1500 by Maurice FitzGerald, ninth Earl of Desmond, as the customs house for Kinsale port when Henry VII granted the customs of the town of Kinsale to the FitzGeralds. There was a flourishing wine trade between Ireland and the Continent and Kinsale had been designated a wine port in 1412. One of the perks of the grant of customs was the right to claim a barrel of wine from every cargo that was landed in Kinsale. In 1579 the 15th Earl of Desmond launched an unsuccessful rebellion against Elizabeth I, and the customs of Kinsale was one of the many rights the FitzGeralds lost when their lands were forfeited and the castle became the property of the crown.

The tower was turned into a naval prison in 1641, when a new customs house was built. It became known as the French Prison, because

many of the prisoners were French. They were kept in overcrowded conditions and were half starved. As a consequence, disease was rife. A fire in 1747 killed 54 of the prisoners and damaged the tower.

American prisoners captured at sea during the American War of Independence were also held in the castle. They were helped by the local people who provided food and assistance in escaping.

During the Great Irish Famine in the mid-19th century the need for assistance was so great that the local workhouse was overwhelmed, and Desmond Castle was pressed into service as an overflow facility, with some 200 inmates living in much the same conditions as the prisoners had endured. The castle was abandoned after the famine, eventually

Exhibit in the International Wine Museum.

being given into the care of the state in 1938. It was declared a national monument, but languished until the 1990s, when it was restored and opened to the public.

Today the castle houses the International Wine Museum, honouring Kinsale's early involvement in the wine trade. Many of those who escaped persecution in Ireland from the 17th to the 19th centuries, the Wild Geese, lived out their years in France, and hundreds of them established vineyards there. Their names have been immortalised by their wine labels and the museum tells their story.

Drishane Castle

Drishane Castle, a four-storey crenellated square stone tower house, was built near the confluence of the Finnow and Blackwater rivers in the middle of the 15th century by the Lord of Munster, Dermot McCarthy. A small round tower was built beside it. The castle was surrendered to Elizabeth I in 1592 and was recovered by the family in a regrant.

Between 1641 and 1653 the castle was used as a Catholic garrison in the Confederate Wars and became forfeit to the crown. In 1660 Charles II was restored to the English monarchy and Drishane was restored to Donough MacCarty, first Earl of Clancarty. The Williamite War of 1689–91 resulted in the loss of the castle once again. In the aftermath of the wars it was bought by the Hollow Sword Blades Company and was sold to Henry Wallis in 1709. He built a large house near the castle in 1728, which was the Wallis family residence until the late 19th century.

Drishane was a British garrison during the 1867 rebellion and became a convent in 1909 when it was bought by the Sisters of the Infant Jesus. They ran it as a girls' boarding school until 1992.

Kanturk Castle

Construction of Kanturk Castle was undertaken by Dermot McCarthy in 1609. It was built as a four-storey rectangle with five-storey square towers on each corner. The date of the castle is reflected in some of the Tudor-style architecture – an Italian Renaissance-inspired door and mullioned windows sit alongside the more traditional tower house architecture that was the norm in Ireland. It was built beside the Dalua, a tributary of the Blackwater. Building work was stopped in 1618, when English settlers in the area objected to the size and fortifications of the castle. It is not clear whether construction was ever finished. Today the castle is an imposing shell. It has no roof, and the floors, if they were installed, have gone.

The castle was built of limestone and is said to have been constructed by seven stonemasons, all of whom were called John, or Seán – it was known as Carraig na Shane Saor (the Rock of John the Mason). The main entrance door is set very high, on

One of the castle's towers.

the first floor, and it is thought that this may have been for defensive reasons – or that it was intended to build a flight of steps up to the doorway.

In 1641 the castle was mortgaged to Sir Philip Perceval, who removed many of the castle's fine fireplaces and had them installed in another of his properties.

The National Trust was founded in 1895. In 1899 the owner of Kanturk Castle, the Countess of Egmont, donated it to the National Trust (it became the ninth property held by the Trust, and the only one in the Republic of Ireland), on the condition that it be maintained as a ruin. In 1951 the trust gifted the castle to An Taisce, finally transferring the title deeds in 2000. Kanturk Castle is now a national monument.

Kilbrittain Castle

The oldest inhabited castle in Ireland, Kilbrittain is said to have been built by Cian, son of the high king of Ireland, Brian Boru. The castle, originally a tower house built within a bawn, dates from 1035 and probably replaced an older fortress built by the O'Mahony clan.

The siting of the castle was strategic, and it overlooks the surrounding countryside. It has been owned by many of the ruling families of Ireland, including the McCarthys and the Anglo-Norman de Courcys, who extended the castle. They lost it to the McCarthys in the early 15th century. A keystone from the castle dated 1556 records the tower as having been built by Donal McCarthy and his wife Margaret FitzGerald. Following a sustained attack in 1642 during the Confederate War, the McCarthys surrendered the castle to the Cromwellian forces.

The castle then came into the hands of the Stawell family, who built the three-storey house that incorporates the original tower house. The house was partially burned down in 1920 and was restored in 1969 as a residence for the inventor Russell Winn.

Kilbrittain has more well-preserved features than many castles, including machicolations, gun and arrow loops, crenellations and a good example of a bartizan on the south-west corner. A four-storey tower was built around 1830. The remains of the original tower house and bawn are still standing.

Kilcoe Castle

Kilcoe Castle sits in a superbly defensive position on the edge of Roaringwater Bay in West Cork. It is a many-storied, two-level tower house (the corner tower is taller than the main building) built within a protective bawn, and it dominates the coastal landscape. It was built in or around 1450 by the Dermod MacCarthy clan on a two-acre islet in the bay, with the bawn built right on the edge of the water. The surrounding waters are shallow, and attacking warships were unable get close enough to aim their cannon accurately at the castle.

The actor Jeremy Irons, who has carried out a restoration of the castle.

In the first years of the 17th century, when many Irish castles in West Cork fell to the English after the Battle of Kinsale, Kilcoe held out longer than most had been able to, and it was the last to fall. Conor O'Driscoll, who had the castle at that time, finally surrendered to the invaders in 1603. The castle, uninhabited, fell into a state of disrepair. In 1972 it was sold to Edward Samuel, who built a causeway connecting the island to the mainland, but didn't undertake any repairs to the castle buildings.

In 1998 the British actor Jeremy Irons bought Kilcoe with his wife, actor Sinéad Cusack, and they have undertaken a painstaking restoration of the castle, down to an ochre limewash of the exterior of the castle itself.

Kilcoe Castle is a private residence and is not open to the public.

Macroom Castle

Macroom Castle is believed to have been built in the 12th century during the primacy of the Uí Fhloinn clan in the kingdom of Muskerry. It was probably built on the site of an earlier fortification, strategically located at an important river crossing. The owners of the castle are thought to have been the Carew family. They were ousted by the McCarthys, who held the castle until the mid-17th century, restoring and extending it in the 16th century.

In 1602 the castle was besieged and the owner, Cormac McCarthy, was arrested. The castle was damaged by fire for the first time in its history. The Papal Nuncio, Cardinal Rinuccini, stayed at Muskerry for four days during the 1641 rebellion.

Bishop MacEgan of Ross oversaw the installation of a Confederation garrison at the castle in 1650. When the castle was besieged by Cromwellian soldiers, the garrison set fire to it and escaped to rejoin the rebel army. The castle was burned again by General Ireton, Cromwell's son-in-law, later in

the war. The castle was given to Admiral Sir William Penn, whose son, also William, founded the American state of Pennsylvania. The castle was returned to the McCarthys after the restoration of the monarchy in 1660, and was renovated and enlarged for the second time in its history. The fourth Earl of Clancarty, Donough MacCarty, was loyal to the Catholic cause of James II in the Williamite War and his estate became forfeit to the crown after the Battle of the Boyne.

In 1703 the castle was sold at auction to the Hollow Sword Blade Company and it was sold on to a lawyer and politician, Francis Bernard. It was leased to the Hedges Eyre family, who bought the castle in the 19th century. Olivia Hedges-White, who inherited the castle at the end of that century, was married to Arthur Guinness, heir to the brewing family, later Lord Ardilaun. In 1922 Macroom Castle was burnt, for the fourth and final time, by anti-Treaty forces during the War of Independence. Lady Ardilaun sold the demesne to a local consortium of businessmen, to be held in trust for the townspeople.

In the 1960s the castle was in such a dangerous condition that it had to be demolished. All that is left of it is the handsome gateway, some walls and one square tower.

James II

Bunratty Castle

Dominating the landscape around it, Bunratty Castle was built on the site of a 10th-century Viking trading post on the Ralty River, a small tributary of the Shannon. The present castle is the last of four castles built on the site – the first, erected in 1250, was a defensive wooden tower built on an earth mound by the Norman Robert de Muscegros.

In 1276 Edward I granted de Muscegros's lands in Thomond to his friend and adviser, Thomas de Clare, who replaced the wooden tower with a stone castle. This was the focal point of the town of Bunratty, which had a population of around 1,000 at that time. In 1318 the town and castle were completely destroyed after a battle between the Irish and the Normans. The Normans were routed and de Clare's son, Richard, was killed.

Bunratty Castle was restored by the Edward II, but was again destroyed by the Irish in 1332, this time by the O'Brien and MacNamara (Mac Conmara) clans of Thomond. The castle was granted to Sir Thomas Rokeby, who rebuilt it in 1353. It was destroyed again during an Irish assault, and it fell out of Norman English hands for ever.

The MacNamaras built the present castle in 1425. Although structurally it is a simple tower house, its very large scale was intended to demonstrate the power of the family. In 1475, the largest clan in north Munster, the O'Briens, direct descendants of Brian Boru, took possession of the castle after a battle. It became the stronghold from which they ruled the surrounding territory for almost two centuries. They swore allegiance to Henry VIII in 1543, surrendering their Irish royalty, and were granted the title of Earls

Bedroom at Bunratty Castle.

of Thomond. The fourth Earl, Donogh O'Brien, made Bunratty his main seat. The castle as it is today is how it would have been in his time. In 1646 the Papal Nuncio to Ireland, Cardinal Giovanni Battista Rinuccini, visited Bunratty, and was effusive in his praise of the castle and its grounds:

> *I have no hesitation in asserting that Bunratty Castle is the most beautiful spot I have ever seen. In Italy there is nothing like the palace and grounds of Lord Thomond. Nothing like its ponds and parks and its three thousand head of deer.*

Oliver Cromwell invaded Ireland in 1649, and Bunratty was one of many Irish strongholds that surrendered in the face of complete annihilation.

The O'Briens left the castle, never to return. Bunratty and its lands were granted to several English families in succession, the last of whom were the Studderts. In 1804 they left the castle to live in Bunratty House (in the castle grounds), and the unoccupied castle fell into disrepair over the next one and a half centuries. The roof of the great hall collapsed at the end of the 19th century, adding Bunratty to a long list of ruined Irish castles.

In 1954 Bunratty was given a new lease of life when it was bought by Lord Gort, who restored it to its former glory, with the assistance of the Office of Public Works, the Irish Tourist Board and Shannon Development. The restoration is the most complete of any castle in Ireland. It has been furnished with original medieval furniture and artefacts. It was opened to the public in 1962 and was bequeathed to the Irish nation in 1975.

Bunratty Castle hall.

Doonagore Castle

Doonagore Castle is a 16th-century tower house built by Tadgh Mac Turlough Mac Con on the site of a much older ring fort.

The castle is unusual in that it is built of sandstone, rather than the limestone that is abundant in the surrounding area (although some of the castle's decorative features were carved in limestone), and it is one of only three round tower houses in the Burren region. It had four floors over a cellar, and there was a vault between the first and second floors. It was well defended with arrow slits, a machicolation jutting out from the battlements over the doorway, and a bawn. It is strategically located on a high hill overlooking Doolin and is now used as a navigation point by boats coming into the pier at Doolin.

In 1582 the castle was granted to Sir Turlough O'Brien of Ennistymon. The 170 captured survivors of a Spanish shipwreck were hanged at the

castle in 1588. After the 1641 rebellion the castle was granted to John Sarsfield and later that century it came into the possession of the Gore family – it is known locally as 'Gore's Castle'. By then it had become very dilapidated and the Gores carried out a programme of repairs in the early 19th century. Half a century later it was owned by the Nagle family and had fallen into a bad state once again. It was bought and renovated in the 1970s by an Irish-American, John Gorman, whose family still owns it.

While Doonagore Castle is not open to the public, it's worth a visit for its spectacular setting, with its uninterrupted views over the Atlantic.

Dromoland Castle

Dromoland Castle, near Newmarket-on-Fergus, was the ancestral home of the O'Briens, the Barons Inchiquin, who are descended directly from Brian Boru. The present building, completed in 1835, is probably the third construction on the site. The dark-blue limestone, baronial-style mansion was described in 1855 as 'one of the most beautiful and desirable residences in Ireland'.

In the 11th century a defensive tower house was built on the elevated site above the lake by Donough O'Brien, son of Brian Boru. It is said to have been similar in structure to Bunratty Castle, another O'Brien stronghold. By 1551 it was in the hands of Murrough O'Brien, first Earl of Thomond and Baron Inchiquin, who swore allegiance to Henry VIII in 1543 and resigned his own royal title of King of Thomond. He rebuilt the castle at Dromoland.

Murrough's son and heir, Donough O'Brien, was executed for treason, and his property was forfeited

to the crown. Dromoland was granted to Sir George Cusack, who was murdered by Turlough O'Brien. There followed several years of wrangling over which branch of the O'Brien clan owned Dromoland. The dispute went to arbitration in 1613 and was decided in favour of the Earl of Thomond, although the property did eventually revert to a direct descendant of Murrough O'Brien, Sir Donough O'Brien, in 1684.

In the meantime, the tower house had been leased to the Starkey family who had extended it. Sir Donough continued to build on and improve until the house was described as 'a handsome Grecian building'. When he died in 1717 his grandson, Edward, inherited his title and the Dromoland estate. The castle was completely redesigned and was turned into a 10-bay, two-storey house in the Queen Anne style that was then popular. The fourth Baron, another Sir Edward O'Brien, inherited the castle in 1794 and decided to rebuild it. Work started in 1822, and by 1837 it was 'a superb edifice in the castellated style', with four linked castellated turrets. Sir Edward was the father of

William Smith O'Brien, leader of the Young Ireland rebellion of 1848.

William Smith O'Brien, leader of the Young Ireland rebellion of 1848, who was born at Dromoland.

The fortunes of the Barons Inchiquin took a downturn when the land acts of the late 19th and early 20th centuries compelled them to sell their farmland to their tenants. In 1921, Dromoland, like many of the great houses of Ireland, was earmarked for destruction by the IRA, but was reprieved when the local people insisted that the Inchiquins had been fair landlords.

Without the income from the farmland, Dromoland became increasingly difficult to maintain. In 1962, the 16th Baron Inchiquin sold the castle and 330 acres of land to an American industrialist, Bernard McDonough, who restored Dromoland as a luxury hotel.

Lord Inchiquin built a new residence, Thomond House, on a hill overlooking Dromoland and lived there until his death in 1968. Thomond House is now owned and occupied by the 18th Baron Inchiquin, Conor O'Brien.

Dysert O'Dea Castle

In 1318, when Richard de Clare attacked the Lord of Cineal Fearmaic, Conor O'Dea, he was defeated at the Battle of Dysert O'Dea and the Normans were driven out of the Corofin area for over two centuries. A six-storey tower house was built on the site of the battle by Diarmuid O'Dea, a direct descendant of Conor O'Dea, between 1470 and 1490. After the fall of Limerick to Cromwellian forces in 1642, the castle was used to house a small garrison of Roundhead soldiers. When they were leaving, they demolished the battlements of the castle, the upper floors and the staircase.

Cromwell granted the castle to the Neylon family, but it was returned to the O'Deas after the restoration of the monarchy in 1660. The O'Deas lost the castle once again after the Williamite War, in which they supported the cause of James II. The lands were given to the Synge family, but the castle was unoccupied after the O'Deas left and gradually fell into ruin. In 1970 it was bought by John O'Day of Wisconsin, who restored it and leased it to the Dysert Development Association. It now houses the Dysert O'Dea Archaeology Centre and has won an award for being one of the most authentically restored castles in Ireland.

Knappogue Castle

This late medieval tower house in Quin was built in 1467 by Seán Mac Conmara (later MacNamara), and in 1571 it became the principal seat of the MacNamaras. It is a relatively squat, square, three-storey tower house, furnished with arrow slits and machicolations for defence.

Knappogue Castle whiskey.

The castle remained in the possession of the family until the Cromwellian invasion of Ireland, after which it was confiscated and gifted to Arthur Smith. Smith lived in the castle from 1659 to 1661, when the castle was returned to the MacNamaras after the restoration of the monarchy in Britain.

Francis MacNamara, High Sheriff of Clare, sold the castle to the Scott family in 1800. Major renovations and extensions were undertaken and extensive gardens were laid out. In 1885 the Scotts sold the castle to Theobald FitzWalter Butler, 14th Baron Dunboyne, and it became the Dunboyne family seat.

Reunion of the East Clare Brigade of the Old IRA at Knappogue Castle on 8 May 1968. During the War of Independence Clare County Council held its meetings at Knappogue Castle, guarded by the East Clare Flying Column. Michael Brennan, General of the East Clare Brigade, used the castle as his headquarters at that time.

The Butlers added a west wing to the castle, along with a clock tower and gateway. The work was carried out by the Pain brothers, who were responsible for much of the work on great Irish country houses. The appearance of the castle has changed little since then.

During the War of Independence the castle was used as the headquarters of the commander of the East Clare Brigade of the IRA.

In 1927 Knappogue demesne was sold to the Irish Land Commission, but ownership of the castle was transferred to a local farming family and it fell into disrepair. In 1966 it was bought by an American, Mark Edwin Andrews, who carried out an extensive restoration with Bord Fáilte and the precursor to Shannon Heritage, the Shannon Free Airport Development Company. The tower house was returned to its original state and the later additions and extensions were sympathetically restored. Andrews leased part of the castle to the state and then sold it to Shannon Development in 1996.

Castle gardens.

Newtown Castle

Now part of the Burren College of Art, Newtown Castle in Ballyvaughan is a meticulously restored, rare, cylindrical fortified tower house, one of just 30 in Ireland. Its square pyramid-shaped base is unique and would have served as a substantial batter. The conical roof gives it a fairytale appearance.

It was believed that Newtown was built around 1550 by the O'Brien clan leaders, although recent excavations point to late 16th- or even early 17th-century origins, but it was soon taken over by the Ó Lochlainn (or O'Loghlen) clan, the most powerful in the area – Charles O'Loghlen was known in the locality as 'the King of the Burren'. The O'Loghlens were still in residence in 1839, and the castle was noted to have been in a good state of repair. The occupant at the end of the 19th century was Peter O'Loghlen – he was known as 'the Prince of the Burren'.

The castle fell into ruin at the beginning of the 20th century but was restored in the 1990s as an exhibition centre for the Burren College of Art, which opened in 1994. The castle has many defensive features – arrow and gun loops, a murder hole and machicolations. The battlements and roof were an important part of the reconstruction, which reinstated the allure wall behind the crenellations.

O'Brien's Tower

O'Brien's Tower, perched dramatically on a headland of the Cliffs of Moher, looks like a good example of a defensive medieval castle, but was in fact built in 1835 by a local landlord, Cornelius O'Brien MP (a descendant of King Brian Boru). He intended it to be an observation point (and tea room) for 'strangers visiting the magnificent scenery of this neighbourhood', although there are those who say that he built it to impress the woman he was courting at the time.

In the Victorian era, tourism was becoming increasingly popular with the growing population of middle-class people with good disposable incomes. O'Brien realised that the local economy would benefit from the development of an area of such majestic natural beauty into a tourist destination, providing employment locally.

As well as the tower, O'Brien built a wall along the cliff so that visitors could enjoy the views in safety – he had boasted to his fellow MPs that he could build a fence a mile long, a yard high and an inch thick. He achieved this at Moher using slabs of the local Liscannor slate. This beautiful stone was subsequently adapted as a domestic building material, and was used extensively on the floors of farmhouses. It was said that O'Brien built everything around Moher except the cliffs.

The three-storey stone drum tower, with an adjoining two-storey drum tower and arched gateway, has a castellated viewing platform with sweeping views (on a clear day) out over the bay towards the Twelve Pins in Connemara, the Aran Islands, Loop Head in County Clare and the Kerry mountains.

Chapter 3
Connacht

An aerial view of Annaghkeen Castle, situated beside Lough Corrib in County Galway.

Ashford Castle

The original Ashford Castle was built in 1228 on the banks of Lough Corrib beside the site of an Augustinian monastery that dates from 1128. The castle was constructed by the Anglo-Norman de Burgos, who acquired the site when they defeated the O'Connor clan of Connacht.

The de Burgos built several castles in the province, with Ashford as their main stronghold. More than three and a half centuries later, in 1589, after a fierce battle between the de Burgos and Sir Richard Bingham, the English governor of Connacht, a truce between the factions granted Ashford to Bingham, who added a fortified enclave to the castle. The impressive building we see today was built in stages, added to and extended by the various owners over the centuries.

Dominick Browne, Baron Oranmore, was given the Ashford estate by royal grant in the late 17th century, and by 1715 the Browne family had established the Ashford estate and built a French-style chateau, which still displays the Browne coat of arms. The castle was occupied by the Brownes up to the early 19th century. In 1852, Sir Benjamin Guinness, the wealthy owner of the Guinness brewery in Dublin, bought the property, expanded the estate to 26,000 acres and added two large extensions to the castle. Following the fashion of the time, he planted thousands of trees and landscaped large areas of the estate. His son, Arthur Guinness, given the title Lord Ardilaun in 1880 (Ardilaun is a small island on Lough Corrib), inherited the castle in 1868. He added a castle to the chateau, rebuilt the entire west wing and constructed a six-arch bridge over the river with two impressive battlemented towers at the entrance.

Lord Ardilaun and his wife had no children and the title died with him in 1915. The Ashford estate passed to the Iveagh Trust (which represented the Guinness family) and it was sold in 1939 to Noel Huggard, who converted the castle into a luxury hotel. Since then it has had several owners, all of whom have run it as a hotel, and it has had many famous visitors, including John Lennon, Ronald Reagan, Brad Pitt and Pierce Brosnan.

Kildavnet Castle

Situated in the strategic south-eastern corner of Achill Island, overlooking Achill Sound, Kildavnet Tower is an excellent example of a 15th-century square tower house. The four-storey tower was built by the O'Malley clan in 1429, but its more famous association is Grace O'Malley, born a century after the tower was constructed. Known as Grace O'Malley's Castle, Kildavnet is one of several Connacht strongholds associated with the so-called Pirate Queen (see also Rockfleet Castle, page 196).

The castle is 12 metres high and is vaulted above the first floor – the only access to the higher levels is a hole in the corner of the vault. There is no longer a stairway, so the upper storeys of the tower are not accessible. Kildavnet was built for defensive reasons – it protected the waters of Achill Sound, which links Clew Bay and Blacksod Bay. There are few windows, and some arrow slits and machicolations provided the defensive features. The castle was further protected by a bawn, the remains of which can still be seen.

The name Kildavnet is a reference to the Achill church built by St Dympna – Cill Damhnait – in the 7th century.

Rockfleet Castle

Rockfleet Castle is a four-storey, 16th-century tower house built on a good vantage point in a narrow and easily defended channel on the north shore of Clew Bay. It was relatively easy to defend, with arrow loops, a batter, two machicolations on opposite corners and a naturally strategic position with water on two sides (it is almost completely surrounded by water at high tide when the ground on the land side becomes waterlogged). It has a large chimney, which facilitated a fireplace in the top floor chamber, accessible via a spiral staircase. Access to the middle floor was by wooden ladder, which could be removed in the event of an attack.

The castle, one of five medieval tower houses built on the shores of Clew Bay, is most famous for being home to Grace O'Malley, also known as Granuaile, or the Pirate Queen. She lived there with her husband, Richard Burke, from 1566. Grace O'Malley was the chief of the O'Malley clan and controlled most of the west coast in the late 16th century. She had a fleet of 20 cargo ships which she kept moored at Rockfleet and used to carry out raids on merchant ships.

Richard Burke died in 1583 and Grace became the owner of Rockfleet. Ten years later the English captured some of her fleet of ships, taking Grace's brother hostage. When Grace appealed in person to Elizabeth I for the return of her brother, the queen released him, and the captured ships, on the condition that Grace would use them to defend the English cause.

After the Irish Civil War a descendant of Grace O'Malley restored the castle and the Office of Public Works has carried out additional works to make it safe for visitors.

Statue of Grace O'Malley at Westport House.

The meeting between Granuaile and Elizabeth I.

Rockfleet Castle stands
guard at Clew Bay.

Athenry Castle

One of the few surviving examples of a medieval walled town in Ireland, Athenry has an imposing castle on the Clareen River, built between 1235 and 1241 by Meiler de Bermingham. He was granted a charter by William de Burgo, who had conquered much of the province of Connacht. Athenry town was built around the castle and was walled in 1316 so that it could be defended against attack. Large portions of the walls are still standing.

The castle is built on a rectangular plan. The ground floor was used for storage. A large hall, the main reception area, is accessed from the entrance to the castle on the first floor. The importance of this space is evident from the detailed carving used to decorate the door and window surrounds. There is no fireplace in the hall – the fire was built in the centre of the room and the smoke escaped through an opening in the roof.

Built primarily for defence, the castle has few windows, and the battlements are equipped with tall arrow slits. The base of the castle fans out in a batter. In the 15th century a second roof was added to the castle, and it is still there today, rising above the parapet.

Athenry Castle was repeatedly attacked by the kings of Connacht, the O'Connors, but they were finally repulsed in 1316. The castle and town diminished in importance after that date and never really recovered from the damage inflicted by Red Hugh O'Donnell in 1596 during the Nine Years' War.

The castle has been restored by the Office of Public Works and is open to the public.

Statue of Red Hugh O'Donnell.

Aughnanure Castle

Built around 1500 by the O'Flaherty clan, Aughnanure has a lovely setting near Oughterard on a rocky islet close to Lough Corrib. It is a six-storey tower house, one of more than 200 similar structures in County Galway. It was strategically built over a small river so that supplies could be delivered by boat, and the flowing water has carved out caverns underneath the castle over the years. Aughnanure is an anglicisation of 'achadh na nlubhar', which means 'field of yews'. Today there is just one remaining yew tree.

There was an earlier castle on the site of Aughnanure, said to have been built by the first Earl of Ulster, Walter de Burgo, or de Burgh, who had expelled the O'Flahertys from their ancestral lands in Connemara in 1256. However, by the end of that century, the O'Flaherty clan controlled all of western Connacht (Iar Connacht), extending from the western banks of Lough Corrib to the Atlantic ocean. Aughnanure became their stronghold. They were regarded as a 'mountainous and wild people' by the citizens of Galway, who put up a plaque on the western entrance to the town: 'This Gate was erected to protect us from the ferocious O'Flahertys.' The clan remained at odds with the people of Galway until well into the 16th century, even after they had submitted to Henry VIII in 1537.

Even within the O'Flaherty clan there was infighting, with a member of a junior branch, Morogh an dTuadh, betraying a plot hatched by his kinsmen against the English. Elizabeth I's army marched against Aughnanure in 1572 and the castle fell. It was given to Morogh as a reward and he refurbished and fortified it. It fell in and out of O'Flaherty hands for the next three centuries, and was bought by the Commissioners of Public Works in 1952. It was declared a national monument in 1963 and restoration work was undertaken. Aughnanure is managed by Dúchas, and has been described as 'the finest fortified dwelling upon any of the shores of the Corrib'.

Although the castle fell to an English army in 1572, it was strongly and defensively built, with a small circular watch tower at the south-eastern corner. The tower house was in the middle of the courtyard, surrounded by two walls, overlooked by a gallery patrolled by sentries. There was a protective projection for archers and bartizans with musket loops jutted out from the third floor. Just inside the entrance there is a 'murder hole', which allowed stones and other objects to be dropped onto the heads of unwelcome visitors. The living quarters were on the third floor of the tower, and the clan leaders held court on the top floor. A banqueting hall built over the river is said to have had a trapdoor in the floor that was used for disposing of unwanted guests. The thatched banqueting hall has fallen into ruin, with only its eastern wall left standing.

The castle is open to the public, opening times dependent on the time of year.

Stamp of Aughnanure Castle, issued by An Post in 1982.

A medieval arch over a window at Aughnanure Castle. The arch features some ancient stone carving and decorative detail.

Connacht ruins

Easkey Castle, County Sligo

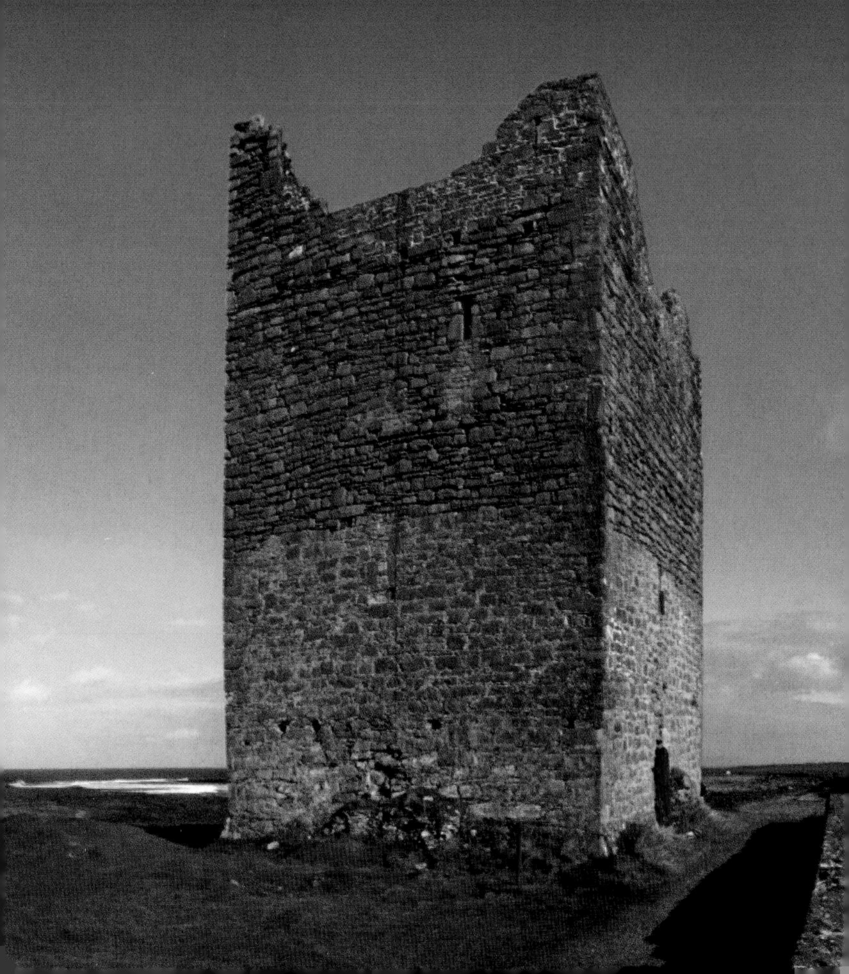

Dunguaire Castle

Dunguaire (meaning the fort of Guaire, an early king of Connacht) is a 16th-century tower house built by the O'Hynes clan of south Galway in 1522 on a rocky promontory on the south-eastern shore of Galway Bay. The clan had been a prominent one in Galway since the 6th century, and it is thought that they had previously lived at the ring fort whose remains can be seen near the castle. The location is very strategic – surrounded by water on three sides, Dunguaire would have been easily defended.

The four-storey tower was well built for defensive purposes. It is surrounded by a bawn and the keep has four machicolations and a strong batter at its base. The O'Hynes clan were big cattle farmers and would have traded their produce in Galway city, easily and most safely accessible from Dunguaire by sea.

In the 17th century the castle came into the hands of the Martyn clan of Galway. Galway's mayor, Richard Martyn, bought the tower in 1642, intending to turn it into his residence. He modernised it with the most up-to-date comforts, including window glass and chimneys. The Martyn family retained ownership of the castle until 1924, although when they moved to Tulira Castle near Gort in the 19th century, Dunguaire, unoccupied, fell into a state of disrepair.

The castle was bought in 1924 by the writer and surgeon Oliver St John Gogarty, who undertook its restoration. It became a centre for Celtic Revival poets and other literary luminaries, including W. B. Yeats, George Bernard Shaw and J. M. Synge.

Lady Christabel Ampthill bought the castle after the Second World War and completed the restoration begun by St John Gogarty. It was later acquired by Shannon Development and has become a major tourist attraction, reputedly the most photogenic castle in Ireland!

Portumna Castle

Portumna Castle, overlooking the River Shannon where it enters Lough Derg, is a semi-fortified house built in 1618 by Richard de Burgo (Burke), fourth Earl of Clanricarde. It served as the main seat of the de Burgos for more than 200 years. Architecturally it is a perfect example of the bridge from defensive medieval tower house to Renaissance manor house and was unrivalled for style and sophistication in Ireland at the time. It is regarded as one of Ireland's first great houses.

Portumna Castle is a large rectangular structure, built over three stories, with large, symmetrically placed windows replacing the more usual arrow and gun loops. There were some defensive features, including a protective bawn, part of which still survives, and flanker towers that housed gun ports.

The building was groundbreaking in that it was laid out in the Renaissance style that had been a feature of French and Italian architecture for more than a century, but which had not been imported to England or Ireland. Apart from its layout, the Renaissance features are few, limited to the Tuscan-style gateway and the curved gables that interrupt the crenellations at the top of the castle. The Earl of Clanricarde was extremely wealthy and no expense was spared in the construction or finishing of the castle, which was lavishly decorated in the French style.

The castle was abandoned when it was gutted by fire in 1826. In 1968 the Office of Public Works reroofed it and rebuilt the great chimney stacks. Work on the restoration and repair of the castle is ongoing and the ground floor and the formal gardens are now open to the public.

Richard de Burgo, 1250, Abbey of Athassel, Cashel, Tipperary.

Thoor Ballylee

Thoor Ballylee, situated on the Cloon River in Gort, was described as 'Ireland's most important building' by the poet Seamus Heaney because it was home to William Butler Yeats and his family from 1919 to 1929.

William Butler Yeats.

Built in the 14th century by the powerful de Burgo family, the tower is a typical square Anglo-Norman stone keep on four floors, with one room on each floor. The larger windows on the lower floors, untypical of a defensive tower house, were added by Yeats so that more light was admitted to the interior of the building. The poet worked in a room on the ground floor, and the main bedroom was on the top floor. There is plaque on the wall inscribed with a poem:

> *I, the poet William Yeats,*
> *With old mill boards and sea green slates,*
> *And smithy work from the Gort forge,*
> *Restored this tower for my wife George;*

And may these characters remain
When all is ruin once again.

The romance and poetry of living and working in a tower house were probably diluted by the inconvenience and discomfort of damp walls and a lack of electricity.

When Yeats bought the tower in 1916 it was called Islandmore Castle, but he changed the name to Túr Ballylee (Ballylee Tower), anglicised to Thoor Ballylee. Even thought he didn't live there after 1929, the tower and the two adjoining cottages remained in the possession of the Yeats family. The tower fell into disrepair, but was bought by the Kiltartan Society in the 1960s and was restored and opened as a Yeats museum on 20 June 1965, the centenary of the poet's birth. Its proximity to the river means that it is flooded from time to time (the damp is always visible on the lower part of the outside of the tower) and in 2009 was so badly inundated it had to close. The Irish government was in financial crisis at that time, and, despite the tower's literary significance, no funds were made available for repair work until 2102. Thoor Ballylee reopened to the public in 2015.

Interior of Thoor Ballylee, Gort, County Galway.

Classiebawn Castle

Perched on a small promontory on the Mullaghmore peninsula, Classiebawn Castle rises impressively out of the landscape. The castle was built in the late 19th century as a country house for the heir of Lord Palmerston, a British prime minister. The land on which it is built had come into the possession of the Temple family, later created the Viscounts Palmerston, in 1694. The first building work carried out was on the harbour at Mullaghmore in the first half of the 19th century.

The castle was built in 1874 in the baronial style, with a tall cone-roofed turret gracing the top.

For a relatively recent construction, the castle's history is quite turbulent. It was commandeered by the Irish Free State Army in 1916. In 1920 the IRA plotted to destroy it but a strong show of local opposition to the measure caused them to abort their plans. There were reports of destruction to the castle in 1921, after the owner, Lieutenant Col. Wilfrid Ashley, asked the British prime minister for protection. In 1922 the IRA held three hostages at Classiebawn in order to procure the release of three IRA prisoners under sentence of death. In 1923 local

Republican volunteers were detained in the castle by the Free State Army until they could be transferred to Finner Camp in Donegal.

In 1925, Ashley closed up Classiebawn for good. When he died in 1939 his daughter, Edwina Mountbatten, inherited the estate. She began a renovation programme in 1943 which finished in 1949. She died in 1960 and Classiebawn was inherited by her husband, Lord Louis Mountbatten, a member of the British royal family. He spent summers at the estate and had a boat, *Shadow V*, built from timber from the Classiebawn woods.

Lord Mountbatten, by
Philip de László, 1925.

When internment was introduced in Northern Ireland in 1971, Lord Mountbatten and his family were given a full-time security detail, which increased in number over the next three years. In 1979 Mountbatten offered Classiebawn to the Irish state, rent-free, but Taoiseach Liam Cosgrave refused to accept it.

Later that year Mountbatten and four others were blown up by an IRA bomb on the second incarnation of *Shadow V*. In 1991 Classiebawn and 3,000 acres of its estate were bought by Hugh Tunney, a businessman from County Tyrone. He died in 2011 and the property is now owned by his estate.

Sunset over Classiebawn Castle.

Parke's Castle

Situated on the banks of Lough Gill, Parke's
(or Newtown) Castle was completed in 1610
by English settler Captain Robert Parke. It is a
fortified three-storey manor house built on the
site of a 15th-century O'Rourke tower house
set within a large pentagonal bawn. An officer
from a shipwreck of the Armada, Francisco
de Cuéllar, once enjoyed the hospitality of Sir
Brian O'Rourke. He wrote that 'Although this
chief is a savage, he is a good Christian and an
enemy of the heretics and is always at war with
them.' O'Rourke was arrested for his treason
in harbouring an enemy and was executed
in London in 1591. Parke bought O'Rourke's
forfeited castle during the Elizabethan
plantation, and the family lived in the manor
house until the end of the 17th century, since
when it has been unoccupied.

Sir Brian O'Rourke was
convicted of treason and
sentenced to death at
Tyburn, London.

All that is left of the tower house is the base,
which has been excavated and can be seen beside the

manor house. Although Parke retained the bawn he demolished the tower house, using the stones to construct the manor house, which is built into the bawn wall. The castle was well defended, with one wall of the bawn built at the edge of the lake, and two round flanker towers guarding the northern end. The gate house is in the southern wall, and there are also a postern gate and a sally port. The castle had a moat, probably filled by water diverted from the lake.

The Office of Public Works has carried out an extensive restoration of the castle, which is open to the public.

Chapter 4
ULSTER

Dunseverick Castle,
County Antrim

Killyleagh Castle

Some parts of Killyleagh Castle beside Strangford Lough, near Ballynahinch, date from the 12th century, but, having been redesigned in the mid-19th century, the castle now looks like a typical château in the Loire Valley in France, with round turrets on the corners, a steeply sloping roof and a gate lodge.

John de Courcy built Norman fortifications on the site in 1180. By 1602 Con O'Neill of Clandeboye owned a sizeable part of north Down, but when an attack on English soldiers in the area led to O'Neill's imprisonment, his wife offered half his lands to a local Scots landowner, Hugh Montgomery, in return for his negotiation of a royal pardon for her husband. O'Neill was pardoned, but his lands were divided in three by James I, with the area that included Killyleagh going to James Hamilton. A 1625 map shows a single tower on the site of today's castle. Hamilton built a bawn and gate house. His son, the first Earl of Clanbrassil, built the second tower. The castle was besieged by Cromwellian troops in 1649 and they blew up the gate house from the lough. The earl fled, leaving his family behind, but the castle was eventually returned to him on payment of a fine. The second earl built the third tower and reinforced the bawn, and the castle remained unchanged for centuries.

In 1697 there was a dispute over the inheritance of the castle and the probate court divided it in two. One of the parties to the dispute received the main house and towers, and the other was given the bawn and gate house, effectively blocking the entrance to the main house, and a new doorway had to be made. The branch of the Hamilton family that had been allocated the main house was gifted the gate house in 1860. The Hamiltons have lived at the castle continuously since they first came into possession in the 17th century. One of its owners, Archibald Hamilton Rowan, was a founder of the Dublin Society of United Irishmen. The castle was assaulted by the IRA during the War of Independence, but it was not seriously damaged.

Narrow Water Castle

The first castle on this strategic site on the banks of the Clanrye River near Warrenpoint was a simple keep built in 1212 by Hugh de Lacy, first Earl of Ulster, as a defence against river-borne attacks on Newry. It was one of several Anglo-Norman fortifications in this part of Down.

The original castle was destroyed in the 16th century and in the 1560s a three-storey rectangular tower house was built as a garrison for the English soldiers detailed to guard the narrow point of the river where it meets Carlingford Lough. It was built within a bawn, bounded on two sides by the river, which provided a natural defence. The tower is fairly typical of the tower houses built in Ireland from the 14th to the 17th centuries, with arrow and gun loops, machicolations and cleverly contrived internal garderobes. Some thought must have gone into the construction of the castle as it is unusual in not having a spiral staircase – the straight staircase was built into the castle walls.

The castle was captured in 1580 by Hugh Magennis, Chief of the Mournes, but was retaken by the English in 1596. Sir Conn Magennis recaptured it during the 1641 rebellion and it was successfully defended against Cromwell's troops in 1644. In 1670 it was sold to Francis Hall, and the Hall family owned it until 1956, operating a salt works from inside the bawn between 1744 and 1819. It is now a national monument.

In 1836 the Halls built an Elizabethan Revival-style castle, also called Narrow Water Castle, near the tower house.

Scrabo Tower

Scrabo Tower soars above Newtownards to the west, a well-known landmark that is visible from most of north County Down. From a distance, with its conical turrets and roof, it looks like a medieval Scottish tower house, but it was built by in 1857 as a memorial to Charles William Vane, third Marquess of Londonderry, in recognition of his efforts to alleviate the suffering of his tenantry during the Great Famine in the mid-19th century. When he died in 1854 there was a lot of discussion, not about whether a monument should be erected, but about where it should be built. It was decided that the location of the monument would be Scrabo, and that it should take the form of a tower house.

A strict budget of £2,000 was set, but the original plans for the tower house were extravagant and had to be modified – the amended design shortened the tower, reduced the size of the round flankers and

dispensed with the buttress walls. Despite these concessions, and even though the interior was left unfinished, the project still went 50 per cent over budget.

Scrabo was never intended to be an empty monument and it was leased to a quarry foreman, William McKay, whose descendants were tenants for more than a century. They finally handed back the keys in 1966, at which time it was discovered that water penetration (caused by the omission of the buttress walls from the plans) and lightning strikes had caused a good deal of damage to the fabric of the tower. The Department of the Environment carried out a programme of remedial works, repointing the stonework, replacing windows and doors and inserting structural ties. They also installed lightning conductors,

essential on a tall building in such an exposed location.

The tower opened to the public in 1983 and visitors who climb to the battlements can enjoy excellent views of Strangford Lough, the Isle of Man, the Scottish coastline, Ailsa Craig and the Mountains of Mourne.

Charles William Vane, third Marquess of Londonderry, by Sir Thomas Lawrence (1769–1830).

Doe Castle

Built at Sheephaven Bay near Creeslough, this four-storey tower house was a stronghold of the mercenary Scottish MacSweeney clan intermittently for two centuries and was known in Irish as Caisleáin na dTuath, the Castle of the Territories. This was later Anglicised as Doe Castle. The castle's origins are unclear – it may have been built in 1425 by Nachtan O'Donnell, but there is no official mention of it until 1544, and it has the appearance of a contemporary Scottish tower house.

Doe Castle was built in a highly strategic position. It is bounded on three sides by water, and the landward side was protected by a deep fosse carved out of the rock, which may have been filled by water diverted from the bay. The keep was surrounded by a bawn. The castle was later extended on the south and east sides and there are two drum towers – one inside the bawn and one at a corner of the bawn wall serving as a flanker. The tower house has been coated with the lime render that would have been usual when it was first built, providing a stark contrast with the stone bawn that surrounds it.

Stories about the castle abound. Some say it was used to shelter shipwrecked sailors from the Spanish Armada and that Red Hugh O'Donnell was fostered there.

The castle changed hands several times and was owned by George Vaughan, MP for Donegal, at the end of the 18th century. He did some restoration work and built a new entrance to the tower house on the east side. The estate was later bought by Alexander Stewart of Ards, who leased it to a succession of tenants. It was abandoned in 1890 and fell into ruin. In 1932 it was bought by the Irish Land Commission and has been vested in the Office of Public Works since 1934.

Ulster ruins

Grianán of Aileach, a 6th-
century Irish ring fort in
Donegal, covered in snow.

Donegal Castle

Donegal Castle was built in 1474 by Hugh O'Donnell, chieftain of the O'Donnell clan of Tyrconnell. Some historians believe that the castle, built in a strategic defensive position beside the River Eske, stands on the site of an earlier Viking settlement. Its main building is a fortified tower house or keep, and a turreted manor house and gate house were added in the Jacobean era. The castle is surrounded by a partially restored curtain wall.

The castle was damaged by fire in 1589 and was partially destroyed during the bitterly fought Nine Years' War, which lasted from 1593 to 1603. In 1607 the leaders of the O'Donnell clan, together with about 90 Irish earls, left Ireland for the European continent in what has become known as the Flight of the Earls. Although they had intended to muster support on the continent, they spent the rest of their lives in exile, and Irish rule in Ireland came to an end.

In 1611 Donegal Castle and its lands were granted to an English army captain, Basil Brooke. The O'Donnells had damaged the castle before they left, but Brooke undertook extensive renovations – he built the manor house and gate house, embellished with windows, turrets and gables that were out of keeping with the castle's original defensive purpose.

The Battle of the Boyne, by Jan Wyck. It was one of the key battles of the Williamite War (1688–1691).

During the Williamite War, the Brookes aligned themselves with William of Orange and defended the castle against James II's Catholic army. The castle remained in the hands of the Brooke family until 1898, when ownership was transferred to the state. By then it was a ruin, although the Brooke coat of arms was (and is) still in situ in the banqueting hall. The castle was completely neglected until 1988, when a restoration of the keep was undertaken.

The castle is open to the public, who are free to explore the rooms that have been restored.

Interior of Donegal Castle.

Glenveagh Castle

Although at first glance Glenveagh looks every bit the medieval castle that has evolved into a Scottish-style baronial manor, with a round tower, turrets, a square four-storey keep, battlements and windows so narrow that they could, conceivably, be arrow loops, it was in fact built in the late 19th century.

Glenveagh was constructed between 1870 and 1873 by Laois-born John 'Black Jack' Adair, whose cousin, John Townsend Trench, designed it to resemble Queen Victoria's castle at Balmoral in the Scottish Highlands. Adair's family belonged to the minor landed gentry of County Laois (known under the British administration as Queen's County) and John Adair went to America to seek his fortune. Once he had amassed one, through land speculation, he returned to Ireland, where, while on a tour of Donegal, he was smitten by the incredible beauty of Glenveagh. In 1859 he bought 28,000 acres of land there and began building the castle soon after his marriage in 1867. As a landlord he was renowned for his cruelty, evicting 244 tenants from his lands in 1861 to improve the aesthetics of the estate.

Adair died in 1885 and his American wife took over the running of the castle and the estate, improving and extending the castle. When she died in 1921 the castle was sold to a Harvard professor,

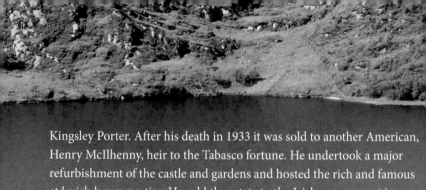

Kingsley Porter. After his death in 1933 it was sold to another American, Henry McIlhenny, heir to the Tabasco fortune. He undertook a major refurbishment of the castle and gardens and hosted the rich and famous at lavish house parties. He sold the estate to the Irish government in 1975, and Glenveagh National Park was created. McIlhenny presented

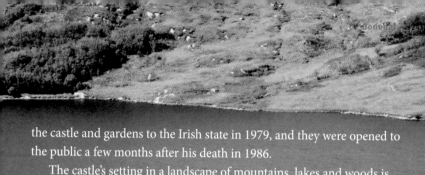

the castle and gardens to the Irish state in 1979, and they were opened to the public a few months after his death in 1986.

The castle's setting in a landscape of mountains, lakes and woods is stunning. The visitor centre has information about the estate and visual guides to the national park. The castle can be visited only with a guided tour group.

Carrickfergus Castle

In 1180, 11 years after the Norman settlement of Ireland began in 1169, John de Courcy invaded Ulster and began to build a castle at Carrickfergus, on a rocky basalt promontory jutting into Belfast Lough. He constructed a simple keep and inner ward.

When King John visited Carrickfergus in 1210 he realised how strategically placed the castle was. Carrickfergus, one of only a few walled towns in Ulster, became a royal garrison town and was the main centre of the English crown's administration in Ulster during the Middle Ages. In 1226 Hugh de Lacy, Earl of Ulster, added drum towers, a gate house with a portcullis and an outer ward. Carrickfergus was the backdrop to many of the important events of Irish history over several hundred years and is the best-preserved example of an Anglo-Norman military building on the island of Ireland.

As one of the most strategic military structures in Ireland Carrickfergus Castle was the target of many military operations over the six centuries after its enlargement. It was attacked and besieged by the Irish, Scots, rival English kings and the French.

In 1597 the governor of Carrickfergus, John Chichester, was killed in an ambush carried out by the MacDonnells. Two years later his brother, Arthur Chichester, took over John's role as governor and

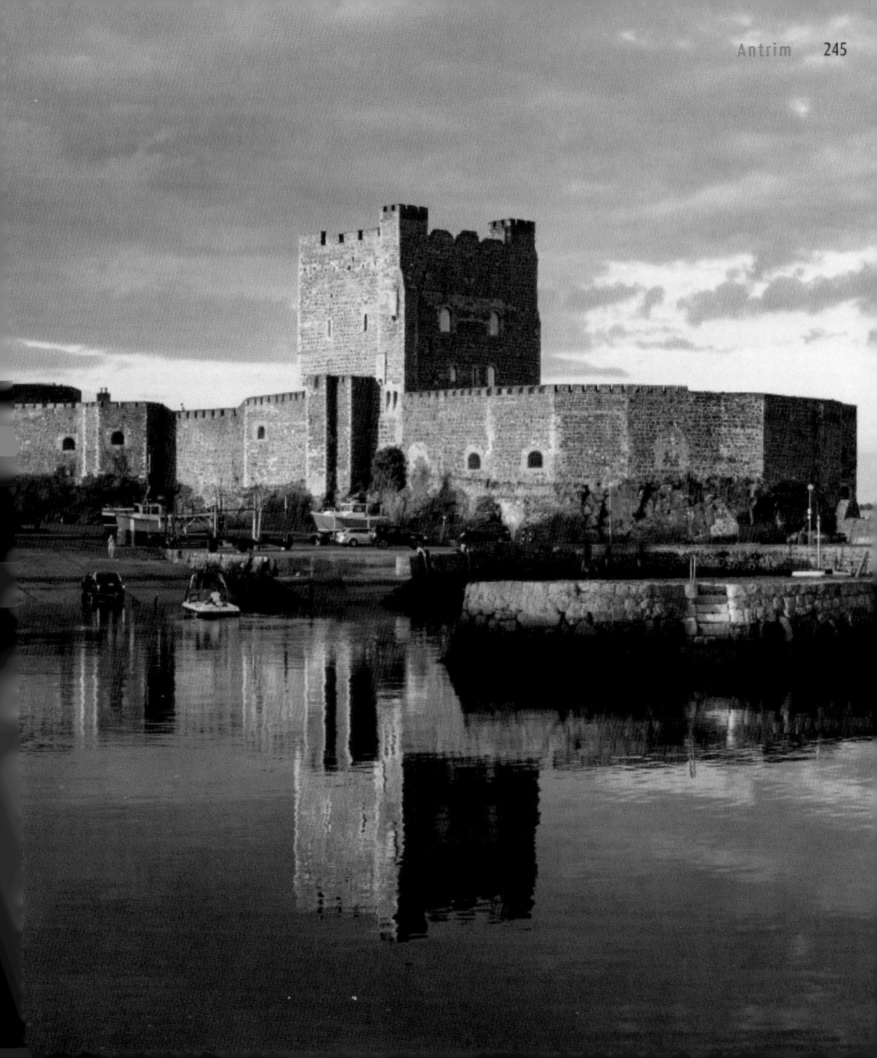

succeeded in bringing lasting peace to the town, planting the area with English and lowland Scots.

In 1641, Protestants fleeing from a rebel attack took refuge in the castle, using it as a base for a counter-attack on the Catholic rebels. In 1649 the Parliamentarian army occupied the castle until Charles II was restored to the throne. In 1688, during the Williamite War, the castle garrison was loyal to James II and the town and castle were besieged in 1689. The garrison surrendered after a week. Almost a year later, in June 1690, William of Orange disembarked at Carrickfergus en route to the Boyne and his decisive victory against James.

Re-enactment of fighting from the castle walls.

French forces attacked the town in 1760 – the castle garrison surrendered but the French were caught after a pursuit by the British Navy. In 1797 the castle was used as a prison for captured United Irishmen.

Carrickfergus Castle was occupied by a military garrison for more than 750 years, the longest tenure of a castle garrison in Ireland. It also served as a 19th-century military prison and armoury. In 1928 the castle was handed over to the Ministry of Finance so that it could be preserved as a national monument. It was used as an air raid shelter during the Second World War.

King William III (1650–1702), by Godfrey Kneller (1646–1723).

Dunluce Castle

Dunluce Castle is the most spectacularly located castle in the entire country, described by St Oliver Plunkett as 'a place washed on all sides by the sea'. Built on a rocky promontory in the wild North Sea, this dramatic fortress has given rise to legend and superstition and has been used as a film location on several occasions (it was Pyke, seat of House Greyjoy, in the television series *Game of Thrones*). Although the first castle was built here in the 13th century by the second Earl of Ulster, Richard de Burgo, the site, which is now connected to the mainland by a precariously narrow bridge, had been used defensively since the days of the Viking invasions.

The large drum towers on the eastern side of the castle are thought to date from the 14th century, but none of the other remains (it has never been restored) can be dated any further back than the 16th century, and little is known of the history of the

castle prior to then. It was owned by the Lords of the
Route, the McQuillans, from 1513, but was seized by
the MacDonnells after the Battle of Orra in 1583 and
became the home of the chief of the MacDonnell
clan of Antrim. In 1584, Sorley Boy (Buí, meaning
blond) MacDonnell took possession of the castle.
When a ship from the Spanish Armada, the *Girona*,
was wrecked on the Giant's Causeway in 1588,
Sorley Boy installed four of its cannon in the castle
and used the proceeds from its booty to modernise
the castle. He swore allegiance to Elizabeth I and
his son Randal was made first Earl of Antrim by
Elizabeth's successor, James I.

Dunluce ruins.

After Sorley Boy MacDonnell's death in 1590,
Dunluce became a grand castle. Randal MacDonnell
built a fine manor house within the castle walls, and
his son (also Randal), the second Earl of Antrim,
and his wife Katherine, one of the wealthiest women
in England, refurbished the house in a very lavish
style and added more buildings outside the castle
walls. It was their main residence in the late 1630s.
MacDonnell was arrested during the Irish rebellion

of 1642 and the contents of the castle were dispersed by Cromwell's government. In 1666 the second earl reoccupied the castle and lived there until his death in 1683.

After the Battle of the Boyne in 1690, the fortunes of the Jacobite MacDonnells went into decline and they abandoned Dunluce for nearby Ballymagarry House. The castle has not been inhabited since then and has fallen into disrepair and ruin over the centuries. It is, however, open to the public, and has an informative visitor centre.

Legends associated with the castle include a resident ghost (said to be Maeve, daughter of one of the Lords McQuillan, who was smashed on the rocks below the castle as she tried to escape with her lover), and the collapse of the kitchen into the sea, killing seven cooks.

Enniskillen Castle

Enniskillen Castle, constructed beside the River Erne in the early 15th century by Hugh Maguire, has been important throughout its history. It was built in the north-western part of the Maguire clan's territory and it guarded one of the few passes into Ulster.

The original castle was a small tower house protected by a bawn. It was frequently attacked and was burned to the ground in 1508 during an assault by Hugh O'Donnell. It was rebuilt as a much larger rectangular keep, and was besieged on no fewer than six occasions by the O'Donnells, the O'Neills and the English between its reconstruction and 1602, when it was once again destroyed, this time by Niall O'Donnell.

The castle was completely rebuilt in 1607 by Captain William Cole and was remodelled the following century into a barracks. There is a central two-storey keep surrounded by a curtain wall, strengthened with several bartizans. The

base of the keep incorporates the original Maguire tower house. The Watergate, built around 1616, was one of two flanker towers, and the only one still standing. It incorporates two circular turreted towers, known as tourelles, which gives the castle its characteristically Scottish appearance.

The castle was the Cole family residence until 1710, when it was destroyed by fire, having withstood a Jacobite siege in 1690. It was

rebuilt as a barracks in the last decade of the 18th century and it was in military use until the 1950s.

Enniskillen is now a national monument owned by the Crown. It has had a major renovation and now houses the regimental museum of the Royal Inniskilling Fusiliers, a regiment with its origins in 1688, when the people of Enniskillen took up arms to defend their town against the forces of James II.

Picture credits

The publisher gratefully acknowledges the following image copyright holders. All images are copyright © individual rights holders unless stated otherwise. Every effort has been made to trace copyright holders, or copyright holders not mentioned here. If there have been any errors or omissions, the publisher would be happy to rectify this in any reprint.

p1   Shutterstock
p3   Shutterstock /P Kosmider
p9   Teapot Press
p14   Teapot Press / Bob Moulder
p15   Wikipedia
p16   Shutterstock / Lyd Photo
p18   Teapot Press
p19   Teapot Press
p21   Alamy
p22   Teapot Press
p23   Wikipedia
p24   Flickr / Maxwell
p25   Shutterstock / Panaspics
p26   NPG / London
p27   Shutterstock / Johnstone / Osher Avzirov
p29   Shutterstock / Johnstone / Monicami
p30   Wikipedia
p31   Wikipedia
p32   Alamy
p33   Wikipedia
p33   Shutterstock / R Semik
p34   Shutterstock / R Semik
p37   Birr Castle Gardens & Science Centre
p39   Birr Castle Gardens & Science Centre
p40   Birr Castle Gardens & Science Centre
p41   Birr Castle Gardens & Science Centre
p41   Shutterstock
p43   Shutterstock / Dontsu
p44   Wikipedia / J Gillet
p45   Wikipedia
p45   YouTube / Unknown
p46   Alamy / Christopher Hill
p48   NPG London
p50   Wikipedia / Sitoman
p51   Shutterstock / Gigashots
p52   Shutterstock / J Ross
p54   geograph.org.uk
p55   Flickr / Marc Evans

p56   Flickr / Psyberartist
p59   Flickr / Eric Verleene
p60   Flickr / Lis
p61   Flickr / Chris Brooks
p62   Shutterstock / Walshphotos
p65   Alamy / Manfred Dietsch
p67   Alamy
p68   Alamy
p69   Teapot Press
p71   Shutterstock / Words
p72   Wikipedia / D Doghaus
p75   Shutterstock / Fabianodp
p79   Shutterstock / Lauren Orr
p79   Shutterstock / L Rigg
p81   Shutterstock / Plekhanova
p83   Wikipedia / O'Dea
p84   Shutterstock / Spectrumblue
p86   Shutterstock / Trabantos
p87   Shutterstock / A de Raadt
p89   Flickr / Eamon Murtagh
p90   Wikipedia
p91   Shutterstock / Keith Ewing
p93   Shutterstock / Walsh Photos
p94   Shutterstock / A Bartyzel
p96   Shutterstock / Paul Brady
p98   Wikipedia / Sea
p100 Wikipedia
p101 Shutterstock / Ewing
p102 Shutterstock / Walsh Photos
p105 Shutterstock / Paul Vowles
p106 Shutterstock / C Dorney
p107 Shutterstock / C Dorney
p108 Wikipedia
p109 Shutterstock / C Dorney
p109 Shutterstock / C Dorney
p109 Shutterstock / C Dorney
p111 Shutterstock / D Ortega Baglietto
p112 NPG / London
p112 Shutterstock / Krechet

p113 Shutterstock / HakBak
p115 Alamy / Warren Kovach
p117 Shutterstock / Nikki Gensert
p118 Teapot Press
p119 Shutterstock / N Gensert
p121 Shutterstock / Thomas Bresenhuber
p121 Shutterstock / Rudi Ernst
p124 Alamy
p126 Shutterstock / Gabriel
p128 Shutterstock / John Armagh
p128 Shutterstock / Piotr Machowczyk
p131 Wikipedia
p132 Shutterstock / P Kosmider
p132 Shutterstock / Pierre Leclerc
p134 Teapot Press
p135 Shutterstock / Morrison
p136 Wikipedia
p137 Wikipedia
p138 Shutterstock
p140 Wikipedia
p140 Shutterstock
p141 Wikimedia
p143 Shutterstock / A Bartyzel
p143 Shutterstock / Timaldo
p145 Flickr / NLI Commons
p146 Shutterstock / Padden
p147 Shutterstock / FreedomFix
p147 Shutterstock / F Migawki
p149 Shutterstock / F Migawki
p150 Customs and Excise, Wine Museum
p151 Shutterstock / Rrrainbow
p153 Shutterstock / D Leeming
p155 Shutterstock
p156 Shutterstock / P Kosmider
p158 Shutterstock / LaCameraChiara
p159 Shutterstock / P Kosmider
p160 Shutterstock

p162 Shutterstock / Sharkshock
p165 Shutterstock / P Kosmider
p166 Shutterstock / Anton Ivanov
p167 Shutterstock
p168 Shutterstock
p172 Shutterstock / Shutterupeire
p174 Wikimedia
p175 Shutterstock / P Kosmider
p177 Shutterstock / Shutterupeire
p179 Shutterstock / P Kosmider
p180 Shutterstock / Enricobaringuarise
p181 Shutterstock / Lukasz Pajor
p181 East Clare County Library
p182 Shutterstock
p185 Shutterstock / P Kosmider
p187 Shutterstock / A Safuanova
p187 Shutterstock / Freeskyline
p188 Shutterstock / David Steele
p191 Shutterstock / Lyd
p193 Shutterstock / B Rybacki
p194 Shutterstock / Joanna K-V
p196 Shutterstock
p197 Wikipedia
p197 Wikipedia
p198 Shutterstock / Colin Majury
p200 Shutterstock / Rihardzz
p201 Shutterstock / Rolf G Wackenberg
p203 Shutterstock / Kwiatek
p205 Shutterstock / Kiev Victor
p205 Shutterstock / Fotoaray
p206 Shutterstock / Sean O' Dwyer
p209 Shutterstock /P Kosmider
p210 Shutterstock / Gabriela Insuratelu
p211 Wikipedia

p212 Flickr / James Stringer
p213 Shutterstock /Everett
p215 Alamy
p216 Shutterstock /P Kosmider
p217 Shutterstock / M Maslanka
p218 Shutterstock /P Kosmider
p219 Wikipedia
p220 Wikipedia
p221 Wikipedia
p222 Shutterstock
p225 Shutterstock / Nahlik
p227 Shutterstock / Jason Ruddy
p228 Shutterstock / C Majurly
p230 Shutterstock / C Majury
p231 NPG / London
p233 Shutterstock / M Maslanka
p234 Shutterstock / Ian Mitchinson
p236 Shutterstock /Rob Crandall
p238 National Gallery of Ireland
p239 Shutterstock
p241 Shutterstock / Benjamin
p242 Shutterstock / Alexilena
p245 Shutterstock / Nahlik
p246 Shutterstock / Riccar
p247 Scottish National Gallery
p248 Shutterstock / Daz Stock
p250 Shutterstock / Keith Robinson
p251 Shutterstock / Michal Durinik
p252 Shutterstock / Helioscribe
p254 Alamy

COVER
Shutterstock / Teapot Press

Madrigal

A Closely Guarded Secret

Le Douse

Christophe Medler

Published by le Douse Publishing
Copyright Christopher Robert Medler
All rights reserved

This book is a work of fiction. It includes many historical figures and events that actually happened, some of those events have been adapted to fit the storyline. All other names, characters, places, and events are products of the Author's imagination or are used fictitiously. Any resemblance to actual persons living or dead, events or localities are entirely coincidental.

ISBN 9798505741214

Printed in Great Britain by Amazon

Cover Design by Carrie Webster

Madrigal

Dedicated to

my Grandsons

Jack, Matthew, Theo and Adam

Our greatest goal in life
is not in never failing,
but rising
every time we fall.

Confucius

Acknowledgements

This Novel would never have been written
without the love, support, and dedication of
my Editor and Fiancée

Lyn McCracken.

With thanks also to
Margaret Scrase and Gill Smith.

Author's Note

I first got the idea for writing this Novel from watching a TV docudrama about Highwaymen in the 17th century, and how many were ex-Cavaliers from the English Civil War of 1642 – 1649. They were adept horsemen and had all the skills to suit the role. Some of them chose only to rob Parliamentarian sympathisers and gave a large part of their bounty to impoverished ex Civil War soldiers of both sides.

Research led me to find out that a few leading Historians believed there was a plan drawn up that could have either prevented or ended the War. That plan, termed Madrigal to reflect the number of its protagonists, is the cornerstone of the novel, and became The Closely Guarded Secret.

The story is fictional, set against the backcloth of the Civil War and its aftermath. It includes many historical figures, and events that actually occurred during that period of history.

Christophe Medler

Part I

England, Summer of 1642

A Country Divided

1

It was the Summer of 1642 whilst in Newark that the young Edward Sackville and Sir Robert Douse learned of the existence of a closely guarded secret plan, named "Madrigal".
Sir Robert's experience and intuition caused him to suspect that the plan might prevent the looming Civil War.

The 4th Earl of Dorset, Edward Sackville, the father of young Edward and a member of the King's Privy Council, was

KING CHARLES 1

a confidant of the King. He, together with Sir Robert Douse, Head of the King's Secret Service, had been summoned to report to King Charles at the Great Hall of the King's Manor in York. It was in respect of failed negotiations on the "Nineteen Propositions" that they had participated in at Newark. The Propositions had been presented by Sir Thomas Fairfax, and other Parliamentary representatives who still advocated a Monarchy but with limited powers. Fairfax wanted a Parliament representing the people and with the power to raise taxes, as well as being in control of the militia.

'Damn Fairfax and his nineteen proposals', The King was heard to bellow, 'he has had his head turned by Hampden and the rest of those traitors'.

England was on the brink of Civil War and the country was divided between Royalists and Parliamentarians. Most of the aristocracy, landed gentry, and rural England, particularly in the North and West of the country had sided with the King. Most of the cities and towns supported Parliament.

York had been declared the Capital of England by the King, much to the displeasure of Parliament who were already in discourse with him over his rejection of their nineteen-point Petition of Rights, the Reformation of Parliament and accepting that the role of the Monarch was not absolute.

London was a staunch Parliamentarian supporter, and the City was a source of great income to them. Of the other cities only Oxford, which was to become a Royalist stronghold, was wholeheartedly for the Crown, and its University colleges donated their gold and silver plate to the Royalist coffers.

Earl Sackville went to York accompanied by his son The Honourable Edward Sackville, from their seat at Knole House in Sevenoaks, Kent. It was an archiepiscopal palace built for The Archbishop of Canterbury in 1456 and it reflected the family's status and wealth as one of the most influential in the Court of the King. It was reputed to be the largest private 'calendar' house in England, with 365 rooms, 52 staircases and 12 courtyards, and had nearly 1000 acres of deer park.

Also participating in the negotiations at Newark was John Hampden, one of the "five" traitors Charles had previously attempted to arrest. On 4th January, Charles, accompanied by his armed Kings men, had stormed into the House of Commons, and attempted to arrest Hampden and four other members of Parliament for treason, but having been tipped off, they had already flown the nest. Charles issued a Proclamation ordering the citizens of London to give up the fugitives, but the City members of the Guildhall sided with Parliament as did the Regiments of The Inns of Court. His attempt to coerce Parliament by force had failed, many had turned against him, and it was one of the key events leading directly to the outbreak of the Civil War.

In the grounds of the King's Manor, taking a stroll in the cool summer's breeze with the sweet smell of jasmine permeating the air, was Sir Robert's son, Christophe. He looked magnificent in his Cavalier's fancy tunic in the colours of his father's ancestral coat of arms with coruscating blues and shades of green, as resplendent as the peacocks strutting their way across the lawns of whose feathers adorned his wide brimmed hat.

Robert was descended from landed gentry, Willian Le Douse, whose family were recorded in Norman-French charters in 1287. Christophe had inherited his father's tall, lean, and muscular frame, but with flowing locks of fair hair and sparkling blue eyes, his good looks were from his French mother Marguerite's genes. Unlike his father, he was famed for his martial spirit, sometimes reckless, almost foolhardy courage, but with a capacity for being dashing and romantic. Characteristics which were to come to the fore in battle, and unknown to him at the time, in his future adventures as a Highwayman.

Christophe was joined by the young Edward, looking equally splendiferous in full Cavalier regalia. Born into aristocracy to rule, Edward had been educated as a gentleman and scholar, polite and courteous, somewhat reserved with an upright gait. Much shorter than Christophe, he had dark hair with brown eyes and though not handsome, was considered to be one of the most eligible bachelors in the country. He was destined for a military career serving the Crown as befitted his forebears.

They were close friends and of kindred spirits having known each other from their alma–mater days at Christ Church College Oxford. Unbeknown to them, from that day on, their lives would never be the same again.

'Madrigal, that's an unaccompanied medieval chanson comprising of three to six players, isn't it?' enquired Edward.

'I much prefer a romantic ballad' replied Christophe, the less learned of the two, 'history was never my strong point, I was always far too interested in them young maidens in The Bear. Why do you ask?'

'Sir Robert and I overheard the name at those last negotiations at Newark, something about a closely guarded secret' responded Edward. 'Father said there's still time for a negotiated settlement.'

'I wouldn't wager my Bay on that, them Roundheads are spoiling for a fight' exclaimed Christophe, 'time enough for secrets, it looks like we are heading for war, my brother in arms.'

At that point, The Earl and Sir Robert appeared from the Manor looking rather forlorn.

'It's war', sighed the Earl, 'God help this country and spare the righteous.'

'The King has lost his patience with Fairfax and rejected all of Parliament's claims' said Sir Robert rather dejectedly.

Robert turned to Christophe, and with some trepidation hugged and kissed his son saying 'Godspeed Christophe, wear the colours of the Dorset Royals with pride. We may never see each other again, but let no man put our love for each other asunder.'

Christophe said nothing, having not taken in quite what this meant, and how much it would affect their lives.

'You too Edward' said the Earl addressing his son more formally, 'your forebears will be proud of you.'

Edward too was silent.

Christophe looked across to Edward. Both young men, still only in their early 20's would be on the front line as Officers of the King's Cavalry. The lives of dozens, if not hundreds of foot-soldiers would depend on their decisions, on their bravery, skill, and compassion. They exchanged glances, saying nothing, their hearts beating fast with the adrenaline now pumping. The excitement of youth and belief that they were indestructible winning over their fear of death on the battlefield.

'What will you do now, Robert enquired of The Earl?'

'I shall ride with The King; I have committed a troop of sixty fine horsemen from my estate at Knole to join the Kentish Royal Cavalry under the command of young Edward.'

'Christophe has been given the command of the Dorset Royal Cavalry, and I too have committed men from Chaffeymoor to fight as foot soldiers in the infantry.'

'It is far from me to ask the same of you Robert, for I know only too well the nature of your appointment as his Head of Secret Service by the King. I abhor the thought of war, let us hope that the conflict will be short. Should that not be so I implore you Robert to seek out allies and find a way to a declaration of truce and a negotiated settlement.'

And so, the country descended into a Civil War that was to divide the nation. It lasted almost a decade, and it was a further decade before the Restoration of The Monarchy in 1661, described by some as "Constitutionally as if the last nineteen years had never happened".

The war transpired to be a messy and muddled affair characterised by numerous minor skirmishes, assaults and sieges of county towns, castles, and fortified houses, often changing hands from one side to the other and in some cases back again.

Divisions and disputes would often split families apart, from the aristocratic society down to peasants and the poor. Allegiances were fluid and the changing of sides common.

The King was a devious and complex character, who tended to say one thing in public and do something quite different when in the company of close personal advisors in private. This together with his inclination to frequently follow contradictory policies simultaneously, often caused confusion amongst his supporters.

This cauldron of contention and confusion across the nation created an environment ripe for Agents, Spies and

Conspirators. The opportunities and incentives to engage such persons were almost limitless.

Unbeknown to young Edward and Sir Robert, John Marchal, a Parliamentary spy, was also present at Newark. On becoming aware of their knowledge of the existence of Madrigal, he had vowed to eliminate them both before they could find out its true nature, and its protagonists.

Sir Robert left York determined to find a way of making a negotiated settlement between the King and Parliament possible, and to avoid all the bloodshed. He needed to discover the nature of 'Madrigal' and with the help of his network of Royalist Agents and Spies this shouldn't be too difficult. Little did he know that his quest was to tear both his family and the country apart.

He was also unaware that in every step of his journey, Marchal was not far behind.

2

Charles gathered his army over the following few weeks and left York in July. He set off to recruit more troops in Staffordshire and Shropshire, known to be areas of strong support for his cause. They all headed for Nottingham where Charles raised his standard on 22nd August making an effective declaration of War against Parliament, then marched his army onwards towards London.

On the 22nd of October just outside Banbury, near Oxford, in the village of Edgecote, they rested in overnight billets. The Royalist Army now numbered over 15,000, although much of the infantry were armed with only clubs or scythes, while the better equipped Parliamentary force, also numbering around 15,000 were half trained and poorly disciplined.

That night, after dark, a Royalist spy on reconnaissance sighted and captured a Parliamentary trooper who revealed the local whereabouts of a large Parliamentarian army. It was led by The Earl of Essex and billeted at Kineton on other side of the Warwick to Oxford road below Edgehill.

After goading the Parliamentary army, on the afternoon of Sunday the 23rd the Royalist army started to descend Edge Hill where, upon his arrival, the King declared to his army to 'Uphold the Protestant Religion, the Laws of England and the History of Parliament', a somewhat ironic speech to some of the lowly Musketeers and Pike men, as many had been poorly treated under the current regime and by their local landowners.

The Parliamentary army, led by Essex, with Sir William Balfour leading their Horse on the left flank and Lord Fielding on the right, fought a fierce battle, with both sides letting off a volley of ineffectual cannon fire.

The Royalist Cavalry was commanded by Prince Rupert, the Duke of Cumberland, who had been appointed by the King as "General of the Horse". It consisted of two Companies each of five Divisions. Edward, and Christophe both distinguished themselves in battle leading their Divisions as Captains of the Kent, and Dorset Royals, respectively.

Christophe, the more experienced cavalryman having previously fought alongside the King in the Scottish campaigns was heard to cry 'Dieu et Mon Droit and Long Live the King' charging almost recklessly forward on the right flank under Prince Rupert. Edward was deployed on the left flank under Sir Henry Wilmot and by comparison to Christophe was more controlled, more disciplined.

The Royalist Cavalry on each flank drove the Parliamentarian Horsemen opposing them off the field and into flight. The Parliamentarian infantry however, pushed their counterparts back, but the Royalists held firm. Darkness was approaching and the battle petered out, both sides exhausted, both sides claiming victory.

Both Charles and Essex, as respective Commanders in Chief of each army, and as was customary after battle in an act of chivalry, allowed the opposition to recover their dead and wounded from the battlefield.

Mutilated bodies were everywhere, some still alive with horrific wounds, some with heads, arms and legs missing, some with gaping open wounds all torn apart, from cannon fire, lead shot, and slashing blades, some even with pikes still embedded in their bodies.

One young infantry soldier, hardly distinguishable which side he had fought on, and barely alive with his intestines spilling out of his lower body like a bed of eels from the nearby

River Dene, was heard to cry out for his Mother. He died shortly thereafter.

A local clergyman took it upon himself to be responsible for the burial of some three thousand combined casualties, gathered from the battlefield and scattered in the lanes and villages nearby.

Three thousand souls slaughtered because of a King's intransigence and refusal to relinquish any of his powers, and Parliament's determination to bring about change. This was only one battle of many to come.

The clergyman offered prayers for their departed souls, every one of them someone's father, son, brother, husband, lover. Some with families who never knew what had happened to their loved one other than that they never returned from the war. In the case of those of higher rank or mentioned in despatches, their families would have heard of their sacrifice in their glorious cause.

Edward and Christophe eventually met up after the battle, fatigued but none too worse for wear save the tear from the right shoulder to left mid-drift of Christophe's tunic as a result of a slashing sword blade from a Parliamentarian.

'Look what the bastard did to my tunic' said Christophe with his customary grin. 'He's ruined it. I will have to order another one, at least it will be clean and lacking in blood-stains.'

They shared a flagon of wine and having first examined it to see how much mould was growing on it, ate some hunks of stale bread with cheese under the shade of a tall oak tree that was resplendent in its autumn colours, Edward stretching out on the ground and staring at the overcast sky. His father had been in the fighting and he had not seen or heard from him, and he wondered if he had survived or was lying in amongst the many bodies still rotting on the battlefield.

It bothered him a little to find that he merely wondered whether his father had survived, but that he was not overly concerned and rushing to find out, which, he mused, was telling of his upbringing. Brought up by Nanny in the nursery, boarding school from age 7, then straight to Oxford, he hardly knew his father.

The two Bays, exhausted from the demands of battle, drank from a babbling brook, and chewed on the lush pasture.

'Did you see Ramsey's lot take flight?' asked Christophe, smelling the cheese which was more than ripe and turning his nose up 'I must have downed at least six, we chased them all the way into Kineton where they scattered.'

He offered the remains of the pungent food to a more conciliatory and thoughtful Edward, still lying flat out, who propping himself up on one elbow to examine the offering replied in his more formal, plum in mouth elitist manner,

'It was all I could do to hang on to Black Bess', his faithful Bay horse, 'let alone despatch Parliamentarian cavalrymen. I just hung on and charged in the hope they'd get out of my way.'

They sought out a comfortable warm billet in a local farmhouse, the occupant being loyal to the Royalist cause. Having slept well, they rose at dawn and breakfasted on oat cakes and eggs cooked by the farmer's wife on her kitchen range, washed down with a tankard of ale.

While they slept, the farmer's wife had made some temporary repairs to Christophe's tunic, at least rendering it wearable. 'Marvellous' said Christophe with a grin. 'Perhaps not quite as good as new, but it will keep out the chill and make me look like a very brave Cavalier, don't you think? Fresh from battle, the ladies will love it' he said laughing and parading around the room showing off his newly mended 'battle scars' with a huge smile on his face.

Edward looked to the heavens shaking his head. He was used to Christophe showing off, but it always made him smile. There was never a dull moment in his company.

They thanked the famer and his wife and offered to recompense them for their hospitality which was refused with both gusto and well wishes for their future engagements with those 'braggarts and traitors'.

Saddling up their respective horses, Edward and Christophe re-joined the King's army not long after dawn. Charles had refused to leave his troops and spent the night at the base of the hill. It was cold and miserable and many of both Royalist and Parliamentarian troops had also left the battlefield to seek warmer billets in neighbouring villages.

That morning the King led the remains of his army back to the Edgehill escarpment. They were tired, weary, dirty, hungry, but were ordered to head off in the direction of Banbury and Oxford, a 9-hour march south for the foot soldiers. Edward sought out his father. He was so pleased to find he had not only survived, but was unscathed, and they embraced, something they did not normally do, with the Earl thanking the Lord for their safe deliverance from battle.

Meanwhile, Essex left with what was left of his Parliamentary army to march to Warwick, just 15 miles and 5 hours north. The wounded were left in makeshift field hospitals and were often tended by the local village women, but even with their best efforts and that of skilled surgeons, many did not survive.

The cries of men in agony from their wounds and on the edge of death was constant. The cold October night had allowed some of the wounds to congeal however, saving many from either bleeding to death or succumbing to infection with the subsequent amputation of limbs. Officers fared a little better, usually being taken to nearby hospitals where they had proper beds, food and nurses that had had at least a basic training, and their next of kin were usually informed that they had survived.

Before departing, The King sent a messenger to Essex offering a pardon to any man who laid down his arms and swore their allegiance back to the Crown.

Essex refused to even consult his troops.

3

Meanwhile Sir Robert had decided that his first course of action would be to go back to Newark to find the trail of Fairfax and Hampden and any clues as to their associates.

He took after his Norse forefathers who had settled in Northern France in the 12th Century, tall, handsome, and muscular with reddish brown hair and brown eyes, an unbridled sense of eloquence, crafty and cunning, and this had stood him in good stead as a Royalist spy in the past.

His great, great, grand-father Gilles le Douse had fought in the 'hundred-year war' on the side of Henry V1 against King Charles V11 of France, as did many French landowners in Normandy, eager to protect their lands and lifestyle afforded them under English rule.

After the defeat of the English in Bordeaux in October 1452, Giles fled with his wife Evette and baby son Jean to England and was rewarded by King Henry with the ceding of 50 acres of land in the parish of Bourton, in Dorsetshire. The land included a derelict farmhouse on the lower fields, ideal for raising cattle and sheep.

A hilltop provided magnificent views across the woodland, fields, and the village of Bourton, and on a clear day to Mere, a larger village some 3 miles away.

Jean adopted the English version of his name, John, and, on growing up at 18 years of age, married the adjacent land-owner's daughter Mary. The family and descendants became

prosperous as farmers and import merchants of fine French Silk and Tapestries destined for the London fashion houses.

Their grandson, Robert's father, William le Douse, and his wife Evette, had by then accumulated enough wealth to build Chaffeymoor Grange on the top of the hill in 1630, moving in with Robert their only child, by then 10 years old.

Upon growing up, and at the age of 18, Robert embarked on a journey to Normandy to seek out where his forebears lived near the port of Honfleur on the Normandy coast. He returned six months later with his bride to be, Marguerite Elizabet de Harcourt, daughter of Le Duc de Harcourt. They had first met in Rouen when Robert, having looked round the magnificent cathedral, gallantly picked up a silk kerchief that Marguerite had dropped when perusing fine silk scarves and the like in the marketplace. It was love at first sight.

But that was a long time ago. After bidding farewell to Christophe in York the previous evening, Robert left just after dawn to ride the seventy miles from York to Newark on the Great North Road. His Chestnut thoroughbred mare, Keagan, bred for speed and stamina with part Arabian blood lines, could make the journey, without any hold ups in ten to twelve hours at a good pace, and he would arrive the following day as time was of the essence.

Newark-on-Trent was a Royalist stronghold with a well-fortified and vital garrison that posed a threat to Parliamentarian forces in the East of England. It dominated the River Trent which surrounded the town only to merge downstream thus creating an island. It was also at the crossroads of the Great North Road and The Fosse way, a vital communications hub linking the Royalist headquarters in Oxford to the Royalist strongholds in the North east of the country.

It was late evening by the time Robert entered the town by the North Gate. The weather had been fair, and he had made good progress despite the road being well worn and rutted in places through constant wear and tear from all manner of humanity from peasants and drovers, cattle, and geese, to soldiers, gentlemen, aristocracy, and clerics. He had managed to avoid a small troop of Parliamentary forces around the Sheffield area by diverting onto bye-ways before re-joining the main road further south near Doncaster.

Travelling incognito, he then sought out the lodgings used by Fairfax and Hampden in Newark during the negotiations that had been held in nearby Kelham Hall. It was owned by William Sutton, a distant relative of The Earl of Rutland and former moderate Member of Parliament. The Hall had been considered by both parties to be neutral grounds.

Robert knew that they had stayed at The Queen's Head in the marketplace, an Inn representative of 16th century architecture, timber framed with close studded walls and with good stables on the opposite side of the road.

The Inn was heaving with much merriment amongst its patrons. It had been market day, a popular event amongst the local townsfolk. Many farmers, drovers and stallholders were selling their cattle, geese and wares to townsfolk and gentlemen, whilst cooks and manservants of local landed gentry were sometimes accompanied by their mistress if the householder had gone off to war. Many were celebrating their day, some spending their takings on ale, wine, women and song or gambling at "All Fours" a popular English Tavern and Inn card game. In one corner were two gentlemen playing Baccarat, a new form of the ancient Roman game of Tabula, with two Charles 1st silver pounds on the side, being the wager between them on the winner of the game. Some of the onlookers were waging bets of their own with each other in smaller monetary denominations.

Having obtained lodging for the night and stabling his horse, Robert ate a most welcome hearty meal consisting of Pottage, a type of soup usually of unknown ingredients, as just about anything left over or available was put into the Pottage pot, from cabbage to squirrel and pigeon. This was served with a hunk of freshly baked bread followed by Game Pie and local vegetables. Relaxing over a goblet of wine Robert sat back in his chair and looked around the room.

His stomach was full, and he smiled in satisfaction. He suddenly belched, an indication that he had enjoyed a good meal and a compliment to the cook. It erupted rather loudly, far more so than Robert had expected, and he laughed to himself at its exuberance. He was a good-looking man in his early 40's, well dressed and attractive, and he knew it. A trait he had passed on to his son Christophe.

He used all his charm to engage in conversation with the serving wenches and observed that one of the servers seemed to be in charge of the rest. Having assumed her to be the daughter of the proprietor, he called her over to his table.

The young girl, Primrose, looked as pretty as a peach, with a fair complexion and short blonde wavy hair. She was buxom, wearing an untrimmed woven striped cotton gown over a plain dark underskirt and white linen apron. She had looped her skirt to both keep it off the floor and clean, but also to mimic the elaborate skirts of the more fashionable gowns of merchant's wives and landed gentry. Her cap of white ruffle cotton was trimmed with red ribbon, and she wore white thread stockings and buckled shoes. In her waistband was a large linen kerchief to wipe off any debris left on the tables.

Foregoing wearing stays, which restricted her movement, Primrose had pinned her gown close in front thereby emphasising her ample bosoms. She looked harassed by how busy she was and by her demanding customers who were getting more boisterous, no doubt influenced by the amount of ale and wine consumed over the course of the day and evening.

'I was here back in April my fair maiden, and two gentlemen from London were on the next table. Do you recall?' Robert casually enquired. 'They would have been well turned out with an air of authority and with southern accents.'

'Why do you ask good sir?' replied Primrose, who actually remembered very well as she had thought at the time that Robert was rather attractive.

'I have some unfinished business with them', proffered Robert, looking into her eyes and smiling whilst trying hard not to look at her breasts which were at eye level and almost popping out of her chemise.

'You mean those Parliamentarians? They didn't fool me; you can spot them a mile away' said Primrose rather scornfully. 'What did you want with them anyway? I would have thought that they were not your sort of company' she said, making sure her breasts stayed within inches of Roberts face. 'I just wondered whether you might have overheard their conversation, that's all' said Robert in a more friendly way.

Primrose wanted to sit on his lap, wanted to feel him against her. Yes, he was quite old, but he was charming, had a lovely smile and looked as though he knew how to treat a lady. That is what she wanted to be, a lady, or at least be treated like one by a true gent, not the riff raff she normally had to deal with.

I'm not one for eves-dropping, my father would chastise me if he thought that.' She said rather coyly.

'I'll make it worth your while if you can remember anything, anything at all' said Robert very quietly, still looking into her eyes, and realising that this young lass was rather struck by him. 'Did you hear any mention of a secret or names of other people not present?'

'Now you mention it I did hear the words "secret plan" and some name sounding like "magical", or something like that, that's why I remembered it.'

'That is wonderful', said Robert trying to put on his sexiest voice. 'What about other names?' he asked nonchalantly, picking up his wine glass.

'No, no names, but later one of them talked about escaping with four others and a "sixth" member that the King knew nothing about' she whispered. 'He also mentioned to the other gentleman that the unknown sixth member was vehemently against "magical".

Robert had heard enough. Realising that was all that Primrose knew, he took her hand and gently kissed the back of it.

'You have been more helpful than you can imagine' he said, holding her gaze.

He took out his money pouch and then gave her a silver half crown, minted in Oxford, and worth five times her weekly wage of six pence per week, and half of that of a conscripted soldier.

'Sshhhhh' he said as he placed it in her hand. 'It's our secret.'

Unknown to Robert, ensconced on a nearby table and eavesdropping on their conversation, had been none other than Marchal, himself disguised as a local tradesman dressed in plain clothes as if he had come straight from the market so as not to draw any attention to himself. He had followed Robert at a safe distance all the way from York and had discovered from the Innkeeper that he was only staying the one night on his way south to London.

Marchal had heard enough, he decided that Robert had to be eliminated as soon as possible on the open road in the morning, making out that he had been accosted by Highwaymen and had been shot as he tried to defend himself.

Robert retired for the night, throwing his clothes on the armchair, and sat almost naked next to the fire on a low wooden stool. *Bbrrrrr it's chilly tonight* he said to himself as he sat looking into the flames, his mind whirring.

He thought rather pensively of what he had learned from Primrose.

What could the connection of the "five" have to do with Madrigal, other than the unidentified sixth member who had plotted against the King, who was vehemently against Madrigal and had so far avoided discovery and arrest by his network of Agents and Spies.

Was this the chink in the armour which could lead to the discovery of the true nature of Madrigal, which if revealed, could have avoided Civil War, and who was the sixth member of the traitors?

Climbing into the high iron bedstead he decided to set off for London early in the morning. He pulled the blankets tight around himself and lay there wishing Marguerite his wife, the love of his life, was lying next to him. He wanted to feel the warmth of her body, caress her, and run his hands over her curves.

It would be a three-day ride, staying overnight in Huntingdon and Hatfield, so giving his horse Keagan, named after the English for "Born of Fire", a less taxing ride to preserve her energy. Upon reaching London he would seek out his associates.

Marchal, meanwhile, didn't bother to undress in his room as he intended to leave at the crack of dawn, before Robert had risen, to find a suitable place on the road to Huntingdon to ambush him.

Ten miles south of Newark, near the village of Aslockton, on the edge of The Vale of Belvoir, the road meandered through a thicket, an ideal hiding place for Marchal with brush and tree cover and a good view of the road coming round a bend.

It was a fine late summer's morning with sun beginning to burn off the early morning mist, and dew still on the ground. Marchal, knowing that Robert would not be far behind, found his perfect spot, settled his horse, and waited patiently for him to come into view fifty yards away.

Robert, feeling calm and relaxed after a good night's sleep, was going at a leisurely pace, and humming to himself, as he came round the bend. Keagan's ears pricked up, a sign that something was afoot. Robert pulled on the reigns slowing from a canter to a walk and drew his ready primed Dog-Lock Cavalry pistol, with its external safety catch known as "The Dog" half cocked.

At that moment Marchal appeared out of cover, face covered with a bandana, wearing a Tricorn hat, and looking every bit like a Highwayman, his charged pistol drawn and levelled at Robert. Robert knew that his pistol, modified with a rifled barrel, was more accurate and had a longer effective range than a standard issue flintlock. Marchal fired first, misjudging the speed and distance of Robert, his lead shot, having little penetrating force at twenty-five yards nicked the collar of Robert's cloak. Not knowing who his assailant was, Robert fired at 20 yards mortally wounding Marchal who toppled from his horse. Robert dismounted quickly and checked the prostrated body on the ground. Upon turning him over and removing the bandana he exclaimed 'Marchal', who was in his death throes with the lead shot having ripped through his garments and torn open his chest just below his heart.

Giving him a sip of water, Robert knelt close and whispered in Marchal's ear, 'Who is the sixth?'

Marchal, lungs filling with his own blood, murmured 'It's too late, the war has begun.'

'For God's sake go in peace and tell me who he is!' pleaded Robert, kneeling beside him and holding his head in his hands.

'You will find him at the Inns of Court in Holborn' sighed Marchal, coughing up dark red blood, almost black with lack of oxygenation.

'His name man, his name for God's sake!'

'The Lawyer............' he gasped in his dying breath.

Robert sat on the ground next to the body for quite a few minutes, his head in his hands. Life was cheap, murder and killing common place, but he had just killed a man.

'It was self-defence' he uttered to himself.

He buried Marchal in a shallow grave, it was the least he felt he should do. No words were said, only his own thoughts.

For there go I, same vocation, born into different heritage and beliefs, but a soldier in God's eyes.

4

Robert continued his journey, more determined than ever, dropping Marchal's horse off at the next village with the local Farrier. 'A gift from the King. His previous owner, a Parliamentary Spy, no longer has need of him.'

The Farrier could not believe his luck and smiled. Thanking Robert and taking the horse's head in his hands, he said 'I shall call him Charlie.'

Having topped up his leather costrel with water, Robert bade the farrier farewell.

'Long live the King' the farrier cried, as Robert and Keagan trotted off re-joining the main road.

It was still mid-morning and another fifty miles to ride. He continued his journey to Huntingdon untroubled and stayed overnight at The Manor House in Hemingford Grey, three or four miles east of the main road. The Manor was one of his "safe houses" situated the length and breadth of the country and used by Robert and his network of Agents and Spies loyal to the King. It was maintained by Denzel Briggs, a hardened ex-professional soldier and life-long friend who had fought alongside Robert in the Scottish Campaigns of 1639 and 1640.

The manor was built of local stone, surrounded by a moat, with a long sweeping lawn to the front, abutting the River Ouse at the rear. It had many internal passages, hiding places and escape routes and was an ideal stop-over for Robert and his associates.

Denzel's maidservant, Kimberley, dressed more befitting as his mistress than as a servant, lived on the premises, and had prepared a simple meal of cold meats and cheese with freshly baked bread, fruits from the orchard and the walled kitchen garden and served it with a large flagon of fine French Burgundy wine, which the English called "Claret".

The wine had been imported to London in barrels from Bordeaux, produced from grapes in the Gascony region of France. One of Denzel's passions, some might say vice, was to keep a cellar of fine French wines which continued to mature in the cool damp atmosphere.

Kimberley was younger than the fifty-year-old Denzel, but not as young as one might associate with a maidservant. She was mature, but had retained her youthful looks, not pretty but beguiling in her own way with long flowing dark tresses tumbling over her neck and shoulders. She wore a simple but elegant lightweight dress, inspired by the French fashion of the day.

Robert thought that she must have Spanish or Portuguese blood in her, but her English was impeccable, and he had no doubt that she must be Denzel's mistress.

He also had a manservant, Richard, the son of his late brother who had been killed in the Scottish campaign. Richard had been taken in by Denzel when he was wounded in the fighting in the North. He tended the garden, gathered logs for the huge inglenook fireplace in the Great Hall and the bed chambers, and generally looked after the Manor.

After the meal in the Great Hall, Robert and Denzel retired to the withdrawing room for another goblet of the fine claret and to smoke tobacco in a clay pipe, a relatively new pastime amongst gentlemen since its introduction from the Americas in the late 1500's.

The room, although as high as The Great Hall, was much smaller and cosier. In here was a small inglenook with large church candles on wrought iron candlesticks dwindling in the fireplace. It was furnished with sofas and huge tasselled cushions, with mullion windows overlooking the moat and the lawns beyond. It was a fine September evening with a pair of peacocks strutting across the lawn.

Robert confided in his host that his mission was to go to London to find out more about the protagonists of the Petition of Rights and those members of Parliament still loyal to the King.

He did not elaborate on the name Madrigal or the clues that he had deduced regarding the "sixth" member of the so called "five" traitors. He could not take the risk of Denzel being arrested as a Royalist Agent and interrogated by Parliamentarian inquisitors, a fate leading to ultimate death.

'What do you know about the "five" traitors and their relationship with the Barristers and Clerks of the Inns of Court?' asked Robert indulging in another glass of claret.

'Very little. The only thing I know is that it is a hotbed of support for the Parliamentarian cause. Your best way forward is to seek out Agent Elliot, he can usually be found at The Angel Tavern, in Angel, Islington, or the safe house in nearby Tolpuddle Street. I believe that he has a spy employed as a clerk in Greys Inn Court who may be able to find out what you are looking for.'

'How well do you know Elliot, is he to be trusted?' asked Robert.

'I've known him all my life, I would trust him with my life, we grew up together in Kent' replied Denzel, somewhat hurt by the inference that he could be anything otherwise.

'Then that's good enough for me my old friend, let us toast The King.'

'The King', they cried in unison, raising their goblets, and downing the contents. 'Let us have another flagon of that fine wine, I may not pass this way again for some time.'

Denzel returned from his cellar with a refill of the flagon drawn from a recently tapped barrel. 'How long is this war going to last Robert?'

'I fear that it is going to last some few years yet, time enough for me to find out what I need to know and report back to the King.'

'Stay for a while then. You're safe here, and you and Keagan could do with some respite. We can play bowls during the day, weather permitting, and cards in the evening together with nephew Richard. It will give you time for your thoughts, who knows when we might see one another again.'

Bowls was a well-established game, first played in Elizabethan days on outside lawns with hardwood "Bowls" shaped to give a curved bias when "bowled" forwards. The aim was to get your own bowl nearest to a brightly coloured smaller ball at the far end of the lawn.

Robert retired after sharing several flagons of the fine wine.

Denzel had retired not long after Robert to find Kimberley waiting in his bedroom dressed only in an alluring bodice and petticoat. She knew how much Den, as she called him in the boudoir, enjoyed foreplay before the final act of intercourse.

He quickly tore off his own garments and after disrobing her, full of desire for her taut smooth body, started kissing her passionately and fondled her rounded breasts, moving down causing Kimberley to moan and quiver in ecstasy. When sated by each other's foreplay, and with great tenderness, and love for each other they made love.

It was not long before Robert's suspicions were confirmed. Lying in his large oak framed bed, he could hear the soft rhythmic sounds of love making and the occasional groan of pleasure from above.

He suddenly had an overwhelming longing to see his beautiful French wife Marguerite, who he had left back at their Manor House, Chaffeymoor Grange, at the beginning of Summer.

He closed his eyes and thought of the glorious few days that they had spent together before his departure for York to meet up with the King.

He pictured them together in his mind, strolling hand in hand in the large meadow beyond the Grange. There was a light warm breeze. Buttercups glistening in the sun, wild grasses and tall white daisies stood against the clear blue sky, and soft fragrant smells drifted in the breeze. Birds were chirping, insects flying, bees buzzing around the heads of the daisies, and lying with Marguerite, making love for that last time before he departed, left him with a peacefulness never to be forgotten.

Robert had a love for the Renaissance poetry of the great bards, Marlowe and Shakespeare.

Their poems typically consisted of lyrics depicting love, tragedy, or pastoral forms. Their goal was to capture the very essence of beauty and truth.

At that moment he was particularly minded of Shakespeare's Sonnet 18 'Shall I compare thee to a Summers day? He knew it off by heart:

Shall I compare thee to a summer's day?
Thou art more lovely and more temperate:
Rough winds do shake the darling buds of May
And Summer's lease hath all too short a date...

WILLIAM SHAKESPEARE

He finally slept well in the knowledge that he was on the right path in tracking down the sixth member of the conspirators against the King. He now felt that he was getting nearer to discovering what was the "closely guarded secret".

The late summer's weather was kind for several days, warm, with blue skies and soft white clouds billowing like the canvas sails of a three-mast merchant ship. It was nigh on a week before Robert decided to move onwards. He left early on a slightly overcast morning, there had been a change in the weather, and it was threatening to rain.

Richard had already saddled up Keagan and so, bidding farewell to Denzel, Richard and Kimberley, Robert set off to re-join the Great North Road and head south to his next stop-over at The Swan Inn, Welwyn, near Hatfield, a market town, twenty miles north of London.

5

The journey to Hatfield was uneventful with the odd shower of rain and a drop in the temperature signalling the end of Summer and the commencement of Autumn. There was still warmth in the sun when it broke through the dismal rain clouds and Robert enjoyed the ride through the undulating hills and vales of Cambridgeshire and Hertfordshire, covered here and there by beech woods.

He planned to stay at The Swan Inn, an old coaching Inn with origins as far back as the 14th Century, located on the High Street of Welwyn just six miles north of Hatfield.

Before leaving York, The King had asked Robert to call on William Cecil, 2nd Earl of Salisbury, who resided in Hatfield House, eight miles south of Welwyn. He was a member of the King's Privy Council and as a Member of The House of Lords' Moderate Party, had refused to throw in his lot with any of the political factions. This made him vulnerable when the civil war broke out. His lands at his other estate, Cranborne Manor, in Cranborne, Dorset, suffered vast depredation at the hands of Parliamentarians.

Despite two of his sons siding with Parliament in the Civil War, Cecil remained neutral, content at Hatfield where he had spent much of the 1630's redeveloping the house. He created a sanctuary, giving patronage to budding musicians and artists including John Tradescant, a landscape architect and gardener, who designed and laid out the forty- two acres of gardens.

Having arranged his lodging and stabled Keagan, Robert sought out an errand boy through the hospitality of The Swan Inn's Innkeeper. The boy was asked to ride to Hatfield House and deliver a sealed letter addressed to the Earl and await a reply.

Later in the evening, whilst Robert was dining, the boy re-appeared with a reply from the Earl agreeing to receive him at ten o'clock the following morning for a sherry, a sweet drink imported from Spain. Robert gave the boy sixpence for his troubles.

He retired early to give some thoughts as to why the King had asked him to specifically call on the Earl, and what might be gained from such a meeting, pleasant no doubt that it would be. He also thought of what he might glean from such an audience knowing of Cecil's almost unique position of maintaining his neutrality, no doubt influenced by both family and close friends siding with Parliament, whilst at the same time the King had no doubt as to where his true loyalties lay.

Cecil knew many of The King's Court and fellow members of the Lords together with many prominent House of Commons members of Parliament. He was close friends with his son-in-law Algernon Percy, 10th Earl of Northumberland and Phillip Herbert, 4th Earl of Pembrokeshire who had sided with Parliament and the King respectively, much to his dismay and heartache.

After a hearty breakfast and settling his bill, Robert saddled up Keagan and rode over to the palatial Hatfield House.

Galloping across the Deer Park and arriving promptly as requested, he was met by the Footman dressed in splendid livery consisting of a fine coat and waistcoat embroidered in the Earl's colours, stockings and buckled shoes, no doubt as a statement of the wealth of the occupier.

He was escorted to the morning room overlooking the magnificent, landscaped garden at the rear of the house.

The Earl was waiting for him and immediately beckoned Robert to join him and sit in the other one of a pair of heavily carved English Oak Wainscot chairs. They had padded leather seat cushions and a carved armorial of the Earl's coat of arms on the back. Robert smiled to himself as he sat down as, although beautiful to look at, Wainscots were very upright with flat wooden seats, and even with the leather cushion must have been the most uncomfortable seats in Christendom, apart from the church pews. The chairs were angled towards one another in the bay window overlooking the garden, with a small wine table between them on which stood a decanter of fine Montilla sherry from the Cadiz area of Spain and two hand blown twisted stem glasses.

The Earl poured them each a glass of sherry and enquired, 'what brings you here fine Sir?'

'Your grace, The King before heading off to war, beseeched me to call upon you on my way to London,' replied Robert.

'Please call me William' said the Earl, handing the glass to Robert and holding tightly onto the wooden arms of his chair as he cautiously lowered himself into it.

'How was Charles when you left him?'

'Somewhat subdued I'm afraid William, on hearing of my failed negotiations with Fairfax on The Petition of Rights, but full of determination to maintain his divine right to rule and sure that God was on his side.'

'That may well be so Robert, but I'm afraid that his effort to govern by 'Personal Rule' has proved deeply unpopular, because the Assembly is seen as 'the representative of the people' and the best guarantee of the public welfare.'

'Now, how can I help you?'

'He asked me to deliver this sealed letter addressed you, my Lord.'

The letter was on vellum and sealed with the King's own seal, decorated with the Royal insignia. It was then folded and tied with red silk and sealed again.

William opened the letter from Charles:

King's Manor
York
25th May 1642

2nd Earl of Salisbury
Hatfield House

Dear William,

You are one of the few Lords and other members of Court and The Privy Council that I can still trust in these troubled times. Please offer Sir Robert Douse assistance in anything that he may require of you and treat anything he may ask of you as if it were I that was asking. He has my upmost support as my Head of Secret Service and has pledged his loyalty to me unto death.

Robert seems to think that there may have been a plot to reach an agreement in my favour, a secret if you like, drawn up by a few members of Court but also involving Fairfax and others, to concede certain privileges to the Crown and prevent war breaking out.

At the negotiations that Robert attended, he heard the name "Madrigal", a reference to a closely guarded secret, mentioned by that traitor Hampden. If you have any knowledge of such a plot, or any party involved, now is the time to reveal it my dear friend.

I acknowledge the difficult position that this puts you in with two sons siding with Parliament and fighting against me, however, I command you for the sake of England and the Crown, if you know anything, anything at all about this matter, to reveal this knowledge to Sir Robert.

Charles R

William looked up at Robert and offered him his unbridled attention.

'Have you heard the name Madrigal before?' enquired Robert.

'Only too many years ago to remember, it's an unaccompanied medieval chanson performed by three to six players is it not? Oh, I see where you are coming from. I presume your quest is to establish what the secret, named Madrigal was, if it still exists, and who its three to six participants are.'

'You are very perceptive William, have you ever heard of the term Madrigal in the hallowed halls of the Lords, or as an aside at meetings of the Privy Council? Or elsewhere perhaps, when entertaining at the lavish parties you like to hold at Hatfield?'

'No, not the name, but there were, and still are, many of us who opposed war and felt that a negotiated settlement with Charles was and still is possible.'

'Yes, whoever they are, they are certainly learned, intelligent, highly astute and skilful in the art of deception,' said Robert. 'It has just occurred to me, could Madrigal have a double meaning, a clue if you like.'

William wandered thoughtfully across to the fireplace and turned to Robert before replying:

'I presume that you mean that the consortium of Royalists and Parliamentarians seeking to reach a secret agreement, are three to six members, and that there is also another meaning. The other meaning being, there are at least three people who would do anything to prevent such an agreement?'

'Exactly' said Robert. 'One of those is now known to have been Marchal, who tried to assassinate me on my way down to see you, but I turned out to be the better shot. Another is almost certainly his employer, Sir Oliver Cromwell. A third is possibly the undisclosed Member of Parliament who was part of the plot to remove the King back in January.'

'I see what you mean' replied William.

'I know this is difficult for you' said Robert, 'and I respect your loyalty and trust of your close colleagues, friends, and family, but I must ask you to name any fellow sympathisers to the King's cause, openly or in secret, that you think may feel strongly enough to be part of such a plan. I must also remind you of the contents of Charles' personal letter to you to assist me in any way you can.'

William stood up, went over to his Davenport desk, withdrew some parchment paper and quill pen, and proceeded to write down several names. Without signing the paper, he folded it and handed it to Robert.

'I am sorry that I can't be of more help Robert, I don't envy this perilous task you have taken on and may God be with you.'

'Your Grace, thank you, you have been more than helpful, you have enabled me to figure out more clearly what I have to do. I seek to repay the confidence you have shown in me and restore Charles to his rightful place as our divine King.'

It was now close to noon and Robert, politely refusing William's offer of further refreshments, decided to travel onwards to London. William summoned his Footman to have Robert's horse prepared ready for him to leave.

Mounting Keagan, Robert bade William farewell and set off once more to re-join the Great North Road to head further south through Hertfordshire to the safe house in Angel Islington, North London.

The ride was uneventful, the weather much cooler than of late with late Summer on the wane and Autumn fast approaching.

Robert rode through villages grown up and spilling out from the urban sprawl of London and he was glad to see the smallholdings and market gardens with fields of vegetable and fruit being grown for the London markets. The air permeated with the smell of human and animal excrement, brought by the cartload from London mixed with straw to improve the soil and yield of the crops.

Upon reaching Chipping Barnet, ten miles North of London and again at Highgate on the outskirts of London, there were a considerable number of Parliamentarian troops stationed ready to thwart any advance of a Royalist army and send word to the Capital.

Robert, as usual, was travelling incognito as Robert Asprey, a London Merchant who had been to Huntingdon, Nottingham and Newark taking orders from wealthy patrons for his business's fine leather goods. He was holding a forged passport, endorsed by Parliament's Office of Trade and Goods, which 'authorised free passage to and from London and Nottingham and all towns between' and could traffic freely through areas controlled by the Parliamentarian army.

He made his way down through Highgate village, pausing at the top of North Hill to take in the spectacular views across London to Angel Islington, some two to three miles from the city centre. There he knew his way to the safe house in Tolpuddle Street arriving in late afternoon.

The safe house was rented and looked after by husband-and-wife team John and Jenny Kingsman, lifelong Royalist supporters, sworn to secrecy by Robert and paid handsomely the sum of £15 per annum to cover the cost of rent, upkeep and safe shelter for Robert and any one of his Agents and Spies who had a secret password to identify themselves.

The House was typical of most commercial and dwelling houses in the suburbs of London outside of the main city walls. It was in a row of distinctive Tudor vernacular houses, timber framed filled with wattle and daub, black and white and checkerboard in appearance. It was five stories high with jetties projecting the upper floors encroaching over the street below.

On the lower two floors Robert had created a leather tooling workshop to support the subterfuge of his fine leather goods business, using the best local tanneries and also importing fine leathers, often already tooled with exotic design, from Italy and Spain.

At the rear of the property was an access lane and at the bottom of the house's small courtyard were stables and an outhouse. The outhouse contained straw bales for horses bedding, fodder, and a bucket toilet which was emptied daily, or more frequently if necessary, by John. He tipped it onto a composting heap in the lane behind, awaiting collection by 'Nightmen' who transported it by the cartload to the small holdings and market gardens in the surrounding villages.

Having settled into his new surroundings for the foreseeable future, Robert set about contacting his network of Spies across the city.

He had William Cecil's list of names to go on, one or two of which surprised Robert to the point of almost disbelief that they could be involved. He decided that he would have to personally follow up the list in order to maintain and protect both William's integrity and the identity of those named on it.

Who were the Royalist protagonists who had secretly negotiated Madrigal with Fairfax, and what are its contents that was so devastating that they could have undermined the Parliamentary cause and stopped the advent of war?

6

The King and his closest supporters hastily withdrew from London to York in January 1642, six months prior to the outbreak of war. Within months, most northern cities previously loyal to the Crown, including York were lost to the Parliamentarians and the King and his entourage moved to Oxford, where he declared it the Royalist Capital of England.

This left a body of politically displaced and bitter citizens in London. Many were hostile to the programme of the more radical puritan Parliamentarians. This void was exploited by the Royalist high command in Oxford. The leadership of London's Royalists, traditionally vested in the 'Grandees of the Metropolis', was no longer confined to the elite but extended down through a diverse range of social groups.

It was from within these groups that a network of Agents and Spies were recruited by Robert, including Elliot who resided in the safe house in Angel Islington.

Clandestine communications between Oxford and London were handled in a variety of ways. Royalist Agents, many of them women, were frequently able to outwit the not very vigilant surveillance by Parliamentarian Officers. Messengers, scouts, and spies, often disguised as hawkers or beggars, constantly travelled between the two cities.

All of Roberts Agents knew only of two others to receive or pass messages to, that way if anyone were to be arrested and tortured by Parliament's Inquisitors, they could only give up two names, apart from Robert's.

This was a well-known subterfuge so as not put the whole network at risk. Robert, who was known to the Parliamentarian hierarchy as The King's Head of Secret Service, was the only one who knew most of them either by name or in person.

On that first evening at the safe house, Robert dined with John and Jenny catching up on life in the city and any news or gossip they may have picked up that they felt he might be interested in.

Agent Elliot also resided in the house. He came home late after a drinking session at the local Tavern, The Angel, with Matthew Makepiece, a Clerk at a legal practice in Gray's Inn Court, and one of his trusted spies.

John and Jenny cleared the dining table and left Robert and Elliot to have a private conversation over a late-night glass of wine. Robert had not met Elliot before and was initially guarded in their conversation.

'Denzel tells me you are lifetime friend of his and grew up together Elliot, tell me where was that?' enquired Robert seeking to establish Elliot's credentials.

'Den and I grew up together in a village near Sevenoaks in Kent, my father tended the lands of the Earl of Dorset and Den's father was the local blacksmith.'

'You knew the young Edward then, the Earl's second son?'

'No, not personally, he was part of the local landed gentry, and us mere working folk. We often saw him out riding of course, from a young age, and now we hear he is a Cavalier, Captain of The Kentish Royals.'

Satisfied as to the bona fide credentials of Elliot, Robert continued, 'Denzel told me that you have cultivated someone loyal to the King as a spy within the Inns of Court?'

'Yes' Elliot replied, 'Matthew Makepiece, I have known him some six months now and I am satisfied that his loyal intentions can be trusted.'

'I understand that the Inns of Court are rife with supporters of the Parliamentary cause. I am particularly interested in finding out the name of a lawyer reputed to have been part of a conspiracy against the King before the war for which Hampden and four others were sought for treason.'

'Next time I see Makepiece, I shall instruct him to make careful observations and enquiries of such matters' Elliot replied. 'He goes drinking with many of the other Clerks of all three Inns of Court who are also loyal to the King. If there is anything to be found out I'm sure that Matthew will uncover it.'

'Just a name Elliot, just a name, we don't want to be playing our hand too soon.'

They enjoyed a few more glasses of wine together, with Robert appraising Elliot as to how the war was proceeding and Elliot giving his views as to the situation in London. He made the first move saying,

'That is enough drinking for me in one night if you please Robert, I shall retire and set about your request in the morning.'

Robert was only too happy to agree and, not long after, retired to his own room at the top of the house. The room had been fitted out to his needs, with a comfortable bed with chamber pot, a washstand with a bowl of fresh water, towelling to dry himself and Flagons of both water and wine with drinking glasses. It also had a writing desk equipped with parchment, quill pen and ink together with chair in one corner.

Perhaps more importantly, it allowed an escape by way of direct access on to the rooftops should the premises be raided by Parliamentary troops, in which case they could be held at bay by John and Elliot whilst he made good his escape.

Over the course of that Autumn and Winter, Robert and Elliot set about their separate enquiries. Robert to trace and establish who amongst Royalist supporters in London could have been party to "Madrigal" and Elliot to find out who was the "Lawyer" in Gray's Inn Court that could be the sixth member of Hampden's parliamentarian plot before the war.

The Autumn was suddenly a stark contrast to the glorious Summer past, with misty mornings, sharp, crisp, days, often following an overnight frost, falling leaves sparkling of wild colours just before dying on the ground, earthy smells of fields cut and harvests gathered, birds gathering for migration, smoke billowing from early evening fires lit in dwellings large and small, and the most wonderful images of the sun going down in blood red colours.

Robert eliminated a few of the names from Cecil's list known to have been killed in the war so far, and he was left with two. The first name on the list was Kathryn Stuart, Lady d'Aubigny, a high-spirited widow of George, Lord d'Aubigny, a cousin of King Charles, who was killed in action at Edgehill.

Kathryn, a prominent member of Court in Oxford, was allowed free passage by Parliament to travel to London to settle her husband's affairs. She remained in London before returning to Oxford next Spring when the weather was more clement for such a journey.

Robert left his calling card, "Robert Asprey, Leather Merchant, and Holder of the King's Royal Warrant", at her London address in a fashionable square north of St James's Palace and called back the following morning. He carried with him an open letter, signed by King Charles, addressed to "Whom it might Concern", vouching for Robert and commanding all good citizens and supporters in service of The Crown to "receive and give knowledge and cognizance of any matter's requested".

He was received by Lady d'Aubigny's footman and escorted to the morning room. She entered shortly thereafter and greeted Robert, 'No introductions necessary, Robert, Charles has spoken highly of you in the past, how may I be of assistance?'

It did not go unnoticed by Robert that the King was not aware of any of his aliases that he used in the course of his duty. *Had Cecil told her to expect him to call upon her? If so, why?*

'My Lady, William Cecil, The Earl of Salisbury, thought that you may be of help with a matter vital to the outcome of the war and the return of Charles as de-facto Head of Parliament'.

Kathryn, although middle aged, was still an extremely attractive woman, and was very aware of it. She indicated for Robert to take a seat near the window, and sat opposite him on a chaise longue, arranging her beautiful silk skirt and ringlets to ensure she looked at her best.

'Please call me Kathryn. Of course, I know William well from Court in London, but I've heard he has withdrawn from society and lives almost as a recluse in Hatfield. What are such matters you refer to?'

'I am attempting to uncover a secret plan, named "Madrigal", the name of which I overheard at the last official negotiations with Lord Fairfax and others on The Petition of Rights.'

'I have not heard of the name; what can such a plan be about?' asked Kathryn.

'I cannot go into too much detail for reasons of security but suffice to know that I don't know much about it myself. I believe that Madrigal could still undermine the Parliamentary cause and force a truce in the war and negotiations favourable to Charles. Do you know of anyone who would risk life and limb to participate in such a plan?' asked Robert.

Kathryn paused, and looking out of the window replied. 'I have heard rumours of such, from within Court and also from my own Agents. I can give you three names but cannot guarantee that they would ever be involved. Edmund Waller, the famous poet, Austyn Lamborghini and Alexander Hampden a younger cousin of John Hampden.'

The name Alexander Hampden took Robert by complete surprise, causing him to sit up straight. It only reinforced his belief how many families had been torn apart in the side they had taken in this conflict.

He wondered; *if Alexander Hampden was involved, how many other prominent past or present Parliamentarian supporters were also involved?*

'Would you take some tea Robert, or do you prefer coffee?'

'Tea would be most welcome Kathryn; I believe you may have unlocked one of the many secrets of Madrigal.'

7

Over a light lunch of Game Pie and pickles at The Angel Tavern, washed down with a tankard of ale, Robert pondered on the names that Kathryn, Lady d' Aubigny, had given to him. The revelation that one of them was Alexander Hampden, a younger cousin of the traitor John Hampden, had taken him aback.

He always thought that some leading Parliamentary supporters, such as Lord Fairfax were against the war and thought that an accommodation could be reached with the King, but never envisaged that the likes of Alexander Hampden could be involved in Madrigal.

Whilst he thought that the young Hampden was possibly the best lead to follow, he decided to find out more about the other two names, Edmund Waller, and Austyn Lamborghini.

Waller, he had heard of, and was even fond of some of the Poems that he had written. Waller's mother was a cousin by marriage to Oliver Cromwell, and he himself was well educated at Eton and Kings College Cambridge. He entered Parliament at the age of sixteen back in 1624 and was considered to be an eloquent orator seeking to appease both sides of Parliament, but despite family ties to Cromwell, was more latterly outspoken in favour of the King's cause.

Robert thought that Waller could well be party to such a daring plan such as Madrigal. As with the young Hampden he decided to hold fire and reflect before pursuing the two of them. He then turned his mind and attention to Austyn Lamborghini.

He knew nothing of Lamborghini other than he was the Grandson of an Italian Count, so he would need to discover just who he was through Elliot's network of Spies in London and ask them to find out more about this mysterious man. He left the Angel Tavern feeling a little more positive. He had some leads to follow that could be useful.

Meanwhile he had other matters of State demanding his attention, and Madrigal, although of utmost importance, had to be dealt with amongst his many other duties.

Lamborghini turned out to be a young firebrand, handsome, well-educated thanks to a legacy from his Grandfather which allowed him to live like a gentleman of private means. He was outspoken in his political views in support of the Monarchy. What was more interesting to Robert, was that young Lamborghini was a protégé of Waller, he wrote love poems, led a mysterious life but was popular with young middle-class men and ladies.

It seemed to Robert inconceivable that Lamborghini could be involved in a clandestine plot such as Madrigal, but nothing surprised him any more in the 'game of espionage'. Nevertheless, the link to Waller kept coming back in his mind.

That evening he caught up with Elliot over supper at the house. Jenny had cooked a pottage, made with mutton cutlets and a knuckle of veal, slowly simmered in wine and water for several hours on her kitchen range, with oats and barley, a variety of herbs, thyme, marjoram and parsley, marigolds and beets, borage and sorrel with a little salt. This was served with sippets of small pieces of toasted bread.

It was delicious, made with so much meat, more of a stew than a soup and they tucked into it with gusto. They were privileged as a result of Robert's generosity to be able to afford meat.

'Anything to report Elliot?' enquired Robert, investigating his bowl and searching with his spoon for more pieces of meat.

'Not yet Robert, I have briefed Makepiece, who will discreetly put out feelers amongst his fellow trusted clerks at the Inns of Court.'

'Good man. Just remember we don't want to scare off this Lawyer we are seeking. When you think you have identified him, I want to deal with him myself.'

'Aye, I understand, but it may be some weeks' said Elliot, sitting back and wiping his mouth with his linen napkin, 'perhaps even months before we get close to him.'

'This war will be raging for some time yet, I fear, a few weeks more in our quest is not going to make much difference, better to proceed with caution than to expose ourselves to the traitor.'

The next day Robert decided to put Waller and Lamborghini under observation for a few weeks to follow their movements, note who they met, where, and if possible, eavesdrop on any conversations they were having.

After telling Elliot what his intentions were, Robert decided to meet Bob Thatcher, one of Elliot's Spies already known to him. They met that day for lunch at the Boars Head Inn in Eastcheap, near the main meat market for London, where butchers' shops and stalls lined both sides of the street selling all sorts of comestibles, foodstuffs, home-made pickles, jams, and such like.

The market was busy with cooks and domestic servants going from shop to shop, stall to stall to see what was fresh to market and the lowest prices. Those employed by gentry were looking for the best cuts of meat, those of the lower classes often for offcuts or offal.

The channels in the middle of the cobbled street were being sluiced to clear the blood and guts of animals being butchered and some smaller ones, like piglets, ducks, and chicken being slaughtered at the market itself.

As Robert approached the Inn at 12.00 noon, he could hear the bells of St Clements Church pealing in the adjacent Clements Lane.

Robert, a known admirer of Shakespeare's plays and sonnets, recalled that The Boars Head Tavern, as Shakespeare called it, was supposedly the favourite resort of Falstaff and his friends in the 15th Century play Henry 1V Part 1.

He arrived first and positioned himself in a corner booth where he could see the entrance. It was relatively private, and almost unobserved by other patrons, none of them being within close hearing distance. Thatcher arrived shortly thereafter and immediately recognised Robert but made his way to the bar, purchased a tankard of their finest ale, and then ever watchful, casually made himself over to Robert's booth.

'Good day Bob how goes thee?' greeted Robert.

'I'm well, thank you Sir, busy as ever keeping my nose to the ground, passing despatches on, the usual demands of your hierarchy. What brings you to London, Sir Robert?'

After ordering more ale and lunch Robert proceeded to brief Thatcher on the task ahead.

'I have a task for you and your closest associates only. I am instructed by King Charles on this matter, and it is to remain the utmost secret. There has never been a more important assignment than this, compared to those that you have performed in the past, or that may be asked of you in the future. Suffice for you to know that your efforts could help to bring about the end of this needless war and restore Charles to his rightful place as our country's Monarch and Defender of the Faith.'

Thatcher had indeed performed most admirably for the Royalist cause risking his life on more than one occasion. Robert had no doubts to his loyalty to both himself and to King Charles.

'Good God Robert, pray what is it?'

The two men moved closer together so that they could speak quietly.

'I need you to observe two persons, Edmund Waller and Austin Lamborghini, who may be acting in concert with others in a plan favourable to the King, but I must know who is involved and what it means before I present it to the appropriate parties. It has a code name of "Madrigal" and may also have some leading Parliamentarians involved.' Robert shifted in his seat and looked around the room to check that they were not being spied on.

Satisfied that no-one could overhear them, he continued,

'I want them followed, I want to know who they meet, where and when, and if possible, without putting yourself and others at risk, eavesdrop on their conversations. I shall be staying at the safe house for at least the Autumn and Winter, and you can let John know when you have something to report.'

Robert now had both Elliot and Thatcher briefed and could concentrate his own efforts on Alexander Hampden.

8

Several more weeks passed by without any more news from Elliot and nothing startling from Bob Thatcher about Waller and Lamborghini. Robert was beginning to realise that his quest to solve the mystery of Madrigal and also find out who the "sixth" traitor was proving to be more daunting than he first thought on leaving York over six months ago, full of optimism.

He had to remind himself that he had come such a long way and was still convinced in his own mind that at least one or more of Hampden, Waller or Lamborghini held the key to opening Madrigal's "box" and revealing the secrets within. He had risen to Charles' Head of the Secret Service because he was perceptive, intuitive with an enquiring mind, and as he thought back, he was convinced that Kathryn was holding something back.

She had given him the names but something in the way she acted told him that she was not telling him everything. How did she know who he was when she greeted him that morning back in the resplendent Autumn? He had left his calling card the day before with the name of Robert Asprey, so had no reason to produce Charles' letter of authentication, and yet she knew it was him. Was she more involved than she was letting on, and why had she so easily and quickly revealed the names to him?

It was now late November with shorter days and longer nights, damp mornings and evenings, blustery overcast days with the occasional burst of the late Autumn sun. Robert was mindful that winter would soon be upon them and the naysayers and astrologers were predicting another harsh winter.

He continued to look into the background of Hampden and who were his closest friends and associates.

Hampden turned out to be somewhat of a mercurial character, much younger than his older cousin John, and considered to be the "black sheep" of the family. His political views were diametrically opposite that of John's. He was a staunch Royalist supporter and often engaged in protesting against Parliament. He was even involved in riots on the streets of London, but always managed to slip away before the inevitable beatings and sometimes arrests by Parliamentary soldiers.

The surprise to Robert was that he was sometimes engaged in clandestine meetings with Waller. Waller, the poet, was known for his Royalist support and was prominent among the moderate so-called constitutional royalists, but unlike most of his parliamentary allies chose not to join them in Oxford and continued to occupy his seat in Parliament.

Bob Thatcher had reported back to Robert that Hampden was never to be seen in public with Waller, which Robert deemed to be suspicious. *Could they both be involved in Madrigal?* Lamborghini however, was publicly deemed a protégé of Waller's, often seen in his company, particularly at music and poetry soirees. His actions, some would say his worship of Waller, even created rumours as to whether he was more of a muse to him than just a poetic protégé.

Robert thought, *could the three of them be involved together?*

It seemed unlikely, Austyn Lamborghini appeared to be the odd one out, an effeminate, weak person of Italian breeding. He had no political ties to the other two. Other than his time spent with Waller, which was not inconsiderable, and often in private, he was a mysterious person, rarely seen in the company of others and appeared to have no other close friends or associates.

He was however trying to get some of his poems published and did now and again visit a printing shop in Clerkenwell. Printing presses had proliferated in the 1640's and were now a key resource to both Parliament and Royalist alike in the publication of propaganda to win over the hearts and minds of the public. Most were now written in plain English, some were distributed free, others on sale on the streets for a few pence. This particular printing shop, Blackwells, was known by a few Royalist activists as a supporter of their cause, and where one could get unofficial propaganda leaflets produced in secret. This news was encouraging to Robert and the first real lead discovered for some time.

17ᵀᴴ CENTURY
PRINTING SHOP

He decided to visit the printing shop under the guise of Robert Asprey, seeking to have some advertising leaflets printed for his leather business. It was a short walk south from the house in Angel Islington towards the city centre, to the printing shop in North Clerkenwell which was situated in a run-down area still suffering from its past notoriety.

As it was a suburb beyond the confines of the London Wall, North Clerkenwell was historically outside of the jurisdiction of the puritanical City Fathers. Consequently, there were basic tenements in various states of disrepair housing all manner of people of the lower classes. Poor people, several crammed into single rooms, beggars, pickpockets, people without any trade, plus stables, ale houses, gambling dens in taverns and numerous brothels. One or two "black market" trades and businesses had sprung up in recent years including the Blackwell's printing shop.

Having visited the printing shop and engaged in conversation with the owner and master printer Bembo Scrase about having one hundred leaflets printed, Robert sensed that there was something not quite right, something not quite bona fide about the business.

He decided to return that night with Elliot.

They returned well into the night. It was in darkness when they stepped off the main street into Caxton Lane where the printing house was located. A full moon with little cloud cover enabled them to find their way without carrying lanterns which may have given them away.

Finding their way to the rear of the premises, it proved easy to force the lock on the rear door to gain entry. Elliot lit two shielded lanterns providing enough light for them to find their way around.

As Robert suspected this was no ordinary printing shop.

Upon searching the basement Robert quietly cried out 'Look here Elliot'.

There was all manner of anti-Parliamentarian propaganda and even instructions on how to make crude incendiary grenades, as well as a concealed small arsenal of weapons.

The evidence against Lamborghini continued to grow.

'There is more than the eye can see in young Lamborghini' Robert said to Elliot. 'He is clearly a staunch Royalist supporter and like many heroes in history would appear to be willing to lay down his life to restore the Monarchy'.

'It just goes to show Robert, the most unlikely of suspects are often the masterminds behind any caper' whispered Elliot as he looked around the room at the large Gutenberg Style printing press, with the type set in place for the next propaganda leaflet.

'Oh I don't think he is the mastermind, but he could well be one of our three to six conspirators, some might say heroes, behind Madrigal. However, he could lead us to that mastermind and expose the leading Parliamentary supporters who also risked their lives in supporting it'.

They returned to the house and had a swift brandy to warm themselves up before retiring for what was left of the night.

Robert was restless and found sleep hard to come by. His mind wrestled with the nights events but moreover he was longing to see Marguerite and Christophe again. He had promised them that he would be home for Christmas which was now only a few weeks away.

An exchange of despatches to and from Oxford confirmed that he would ride over there on the 21st of December to meet up with Christophe, stay overnight, then the two of them would ride south west to Dorset and to Chaffeymoor Grange, arriving on Christmas Eve.

9

On the morning of the Wednesday 21st, it was a crisp, cold, bright misty morning with an overnight frost, so typical of late December with the air permeating with the smell of smoke from the overnight fires in dwelling houses right across London and the suburbs. Some, no doubt, were down to just glowing embers awaiting to be stoked up again, but thankfully it had not snowed, and the ground was firm. The worst of the forecast bad winter's weather was yet to come. It was to be a long, one-day journey to Oxford and Robert prayed that the weather stayed calm.

He mounted Keegan his faithful horse, bade John, Jenny and Elliot 'Farewell and Merry Christmas, one and all, spend it with your families and make merriment. I shall return in the New Year'.

'Godspeed Robert', cried Elliot, as Keagan trotted out of the yard and into the lane to make his way, incognito as Robert Asprey. He would head north west out of the suburbs towards Gerard's Cross and onwards to Oxford, passing through High Wycombe.

Robert was pleased to get out of London to the countryside. The weak sun soon burned off the last of the morning mist and he was glad to be able to breath in the fresh country air once he had cleared the suburbs and on the road to High Wycombe, a stop-over point for the London to Oxford Mail Coach. It was located on the banks of the River Wye, a clear chalk stream ideal for bleaching paper pulp and subsequently linen and lace.

The journey was pleasant and uneventful through the Chiltern Hills until he reached the outskirts of the town which was currently held by Parliamentarians. He was stopped at a check point and rather than attempt to go on a lengthy detour he decided to rely on his subterfuge and the forged papers he held giving him free passage to Oxford. The Parliamentary Officer on duty took a cursory look at Robert's papers and waived him through.

He stopped for lunch at The George and Dragon Inn.

Having observed the strength of the troops occupying the town he then continued his journey unhindered until he reached Shotover on the Cheyney road on the outskirts of Oxford where there was a Tollgate.

The Tollgate had been there for centuries and now served as a Royalist check point before allowing anyone to continue and descend Headington Hill into the City. In the 10th century, Oxford became an important military frontier town between the Kingdoms of Mercia and Wessex, so was well used to being on the frontline of any skirmishes. Its population were mostly Royalist supporters, and the Universities were staunch supporters of the Royalist cause.

Robert went through the same checks by a Royalist Officer as he had done at High Wycombe with the Parliamentarian Officer. The Royalist Officer, Captain Neal Artfellow, was equally nonchalant in checking his papers, a point Robert would make to the duty officer upon his arrival at the garrison in the city centre. It seemed no wonder to Robert that Agents and Spies on both sides of the war found it relatively easy to move across the country unhindered.

After reporting to the Duty Officer at the garrison, Robert rode over to the Bear Inn on Blue Boar Street, opposite Bear Lane, and just north of Christ Church College which were to be his lodgings for the night and provide stabling for Keagan. He had sent word for Christophe to join him there for supper and to catch up on each other's lives since they last met over six months ago.

Robert made sure that Keagan was stabled and settled for the night before making himself comfortable in his room. After splashing and soaping his face with water, washing away the grime and dust from his days ride, he changed out of his riding clothes into something more comfortable and presentable for a respectable visiting Merchant.

He descended the oak staircase to find Christophe, looking resplendent standing at the bar supping a tankard of the Innkeepers finest Oxford ale.

Christophe, upon seeing his father, had to fight back the tears in his eyes, such was his emotions and delight at seeing Robert again.

'Father, I am lost for words' he cried, finding it difficult to speak, as he wrapped his arms around Robert giving him a huge bear hug.

'Christophe my boy, I am so glad to see you, you have made both your mother and I very proud. We both love you like no other and cannot wait to celebrate Christmas together like old times.'

They enjoyed each other's company for a few hours, talking and laughing about everything and anything, from old times when Christophe was growing up at Chaffeymoor Grange to the horrors of the Civil War. Christophe recounted how much he was looking forward to Christmas and to seeing his Mother and Sarah, mother's Scottish cousin from the Isle of Islay, and her husband Paul who was of Welsh ancestry. They acted as Housekeeper and Handyman and lived at the Grange.

They shared a sumptuous supper and drank a bit too much wine considering the journey ahead which would take them two days. The time flew by before Christophe finally returned to his unit and Robert to his bed for the night.

'Good night son, we leave at eight o'clock sharp, the road should not be too slippery for the horses at that hour.'

'Good night father, sleep well, it is wonderful seeing you again, I can't wait to see Mother.'

Christophe duly arrived in the morning at eight a.m. sharp to find Robert already saddled up and ready to go. The sun had barely risen but they both considered it safe to trot the horses and made their way to the South West Gate of the city.

Christophe was no longer dressed in his fine Cavaliers tunic which now showed the scars of battle, having been repaired more than once by seamstresses. He was wearing a simple outfit more befitting as one of his father's employees in the leather business and carried forged papers to that effect provided by Robert.

The journey would take them south west to Marlborough where they would stay overnight, then south through Pewsey to join up with the Great South West Coach route from London to Exeter. Then westward to Mere the nearest village to home at Chaffeymoor.

They both relished the thought of their ride across The Downs to Marlborough. Then it was south through the Vale of Pewsey and the Savernake Forest before the landscape petered out to the great Salisbury Plain north of the Great South West Road.

As they set off, they felt safe in the knowledge that much of country south west of Oxford was in Royalist hands. The ride across the downs was glorious and gave both Robert and Christophe the chance of a fine gallop over lush grassland.

'This is wonderful' cried Christophe, 'to be able to adopt a full charge, wind in our hair, without facing Parliamentary Horse in full charge towards you.'

When they had slowed down from a canter to a trot alongside each other, Robert could not help but think of how brave were the likes of Christophe and those fine young Cavaliers, charging the enemy staring possible death or mutilation in the face, though they did not think of themselves as brave.

'You are a fine horseman young man, it seems such a long time ago when you mounted your first pony, do you remember?'

'How can I forget father, you taught me well. Honeysuckle was a beautiful New Forest pony; I remember you taking me to the horse fair at Salisbury to pick her out. I was so excited'.

'I remember it well, and it's wonderful that we have her foal Blaze with us at Chaffeymoor now. He is now a fine stallion and Paul exercises them every day in your absence.'

They continued on down to Marlborough which was traditionally neutral in the Civil War. They arrived just one month after a minor skirmish between a small band of local Parliamentarian supporters and a Troop of Royalist soldiers which resulted in some looting and burning of dwellings. Robert and Christophe were appalled by the behaviour of The Royalist Troops who had since left the town. Fortunately, The Marlborough Inn in the marketplace was left untouched and provided fine lodgings for their overnight stay.

The next morning it was the 24th, Christmas Eve, the weather was still fair and calm, but Robert suspected that snow might fall later in the day. After a hearty breakfast, Robert and Christophe set off in high spirits with thoughts of home. Robert longing to see his beloved Marguerite again and Christophe his mother, so dear to him, not forgetting Sarah and Paul.

Once again, the early part of the ride was through magnificent countryside, down through the Vale of Pewsey and onwards across the Salisbury Plain. They made good time, unhindered, and joined the Great South West Road by early afternoon. After going west for a few miles, they stopped briefly to take in the wonder of Stonehenge, a prehistoric Neolithic ring of standing stones, some over twelve feet in high and six feet in diameter.

Although still some twenty miles from home, Robert felt he was back in his homeland with the rich soil supporting a variety of agriculture. They passed a number of farmhouses

and it did not seem long before they were entering Mere where they paused at The George Inn and downed of tankard of ale to quench their thirsts before continuing their journey.

They were soon turning off into a narrow lane leading to the hamlet of Bourton just over the border from Wiltshire into Dorset. Chaffeymoor Grange, a magnificent 17th century stone manor house set in glorious grounds, was up on the hillside overlooking Bourton.

As they turned into the grounds it was dark and the temperature was falling fast. Robert exclaimed exuberantly 'Home at last'!

They were first heard by Paul who had been bedding down the horses and collecting more logs for the fires in the bedrooms. He couldn't see them yet, but heard the horses coming up the long winding drive, so rushed inside crying out 'They're here, they're here'.

Marguerite and Sarah came rushing out, Marguerite overcome by tears as Robert and Christophe dismounted. Before Robert could say anything, she managed to get out the words

'Joyeux Noel mon amour' before the tears streamed down her face.

Robert threw off his riding hat and embraced her, holding her head gently in his hands he kissed her sweet lips and replied 'Joyeux Noel ma femme belle, son merveilleux d'etre a la Maison.'

Christophe too was also full of emotion at seeing his beloved mother again. He swept his hat before him like a true cavalier and said to her

'Joyeuse mere de Noel, je pense a vous tous les jours.'

After reciprocal Christmas greetings between Robert, Christophe Sarah, and Paul, they all entered the warmth of the Grange, the smell of roast beef wafting from the kitchen.

It's so good to be home, thought Robert.

10

Christmas was one of the highlights of the medieval calendar, it was the longest holiday of the year, typically the full twelve days of Christmas from the 25th of December, Christmas Day, right through to the 6th ^{of} January, the Twelfth day of Epiphany.

As they entered the hall of the Grange Robert and Christophe were immediately struck in awe and wonder at the lengths Marguerite, Sarah and Paul had gone to decorate the house.

Garlands and wreaths of holly, with glossy green leaves and bright red berries, ivy with its smooth shiny leaves with small yellowish flowers and black berries, bay with lustrous dark green leaves, often used in cooking stews and pottage, and other winter foliage gathered in the grounds adorned the house throughout. Doors, windows, walls, and sideboards nowhere was left without embellishment.

In the Grand Hall, the double planked oak table, big enough to sit up to twenty people, had a magnificent centre-piece with all manner of foliage woven through and around a large eight-piece silver candelabra. Two smaller ones were at either end of the table and all three were decorated with gold and silver trinkets which sparkled in the candlelight.

A double ring of mistletoe hung from the ceiling of the Withdrawing Room under which couples might kiss, removing the jewel like berries with each peck. They would all withdraw to this room after dinner each night for dinks, games, dancing, and much merriment.

It was now early evening and Sarah had laid on a welcome table, set up in the Morning Room, of mince pies and other pastries, thick fruit custards, oranges, figs and dates. Decanters of sherry and brandy with ornate small glasses were set out ready to toast the welcoming home of father and son.

Sometime later, after they had all eaten and refreshed themselves with glasses of sherry or brandy, Marguerite and Sarah bade their leave. They and went off to fill the copper bathtubs in Robert and Christophe's bedrooms with hot water which had been heated in large copper cauldrons on well-tended fires in each, the water having been carried upstairs earlier by Paul, a heavy time-consuming task.

The copper bathtubs were freestanding and could easily be moved when empty. They were the height of home-bathing fashion, only affordable by aristocrats, landed gentry and gentlemen with private incomes. They were boat shaped rising in a curvature at each end and could sit two people toe to toe. The more adventurous amorous couples took full advantage of this.

Downstairs Robert just had time before his bath to chat with Paul for a while about managing the estate:

'Tell me, how you have been coping?' enquired Robert.

'Quite well really' he replied, reaching for the last mince pie across the table. 'The lower fields are let to the farmer Peter Quince who tends and raises sheep on them, and we have organised shoots in the copse for pheasant, woodcock and lark for which local gentlemen pay us a handsome fee. Sarah looks after our own gaggle of geese and ducks, as well

as the house with the help of young Olivia, the Blacksmith's daughter from the village.'

'What about maintaining the house? The Grange does not look after itself, especially in these harsh winters we have been having.'

Paul got up from his chair and wandered over to the inglenook, placing a large beech log in the centre of the fire. He kept the beech in a separate corner of the log store for use at Christmas as it burned so brightly if stored for a year.

That will cheer the room up, he thought to himself and turning to Robert said,

'I do most minor maintenance and repairs myself. Anything I can't handle on my own I usually call upon Parker the blacksmith and his brother-in-law Hugo.'

'Well, you seem to have everything well under control Paul. Any sign of any Parliamentarian intruders?'

'We are well off the beaten track here, but I did hear of some Parliamentarian Troops passing though Mere some time back.'

At that point Marguerite entered the room to say that the bathtubs were ready for Robert and Christophe. Sarah reminded everyone that supper would be served at eight o'clock in the Great Hall.

To have a hot bath was a luxury to behold for both Robert and Christophe. For Christophe, most days on the road as the life of a Cavalier it would only be a wash of the hands and face with hard soap, made of olive oil, soda, lime, herbs and water. An all over dousing would take place per chance upon a river or lake deep enough to submerge.

Robert was more fortunate; he was either staying at a safe house or lodging in Inns that would have bathtubs but partaking in a hot bath no more than once a week.

At Chaffeymoor they were able to enjoy bathing, not only in hot water, but also with home-made soft soap, made by

Sarah with mutton fat, wood ash, soda, flowers from the estate and herbs from the kitchen garden to create a sweet smell.

Robert, accompanied by Marguerite, ascended the Great Oak Staircase to the master bedroom which had been tastefully furnished by her with a combination of English and French furniture. A huge English oak four poster bed dominated the room softened by an exquisite French Armoire and Dressing table. Oak floors were adorned by baroque silk floor coverings from France, the height of French fashion in Paris.

In one corner was an elm washstand with marble top and matching china wash basin, and chamber pots. Alongside was a magnificent copper bathtub matching the one in Christophe's room.

Marguerite helped Robert disrobe and get into the bath. She made him lie back and relax whilst she lovingly, softly, soaped him all over, using the best of Sarah's soaps with a permeating lavender smell and a sponge imported from southern France.

Robert was in ecstasy, home with his beautiful wife who he had adored since first sight on a Spring day in Normandy, some twenty-five years earlier. He soaped and washed his hair, face and closely trimmed beard followed by Marguerite pouring warm water all over him from head to toe. He stepped out of the bath, still a lithe, fit man for his late forties, while Marguerite draped him in towelling to dry off.

Whilst Robert was drying himself, Marguerite pulled back the covers on the bed and then started to remove her own clothing. She had got as far as removing her outer garments when Robert, giving in to his desires came over and removed her silk underwear and stockings himself.

Overcome with emotion he still marvelled at the sight of her beautiful body, which still retained her youthful figure despite just turning forty-three years of age. Slim, nubile, so

serene, with those large green eyes, wide smile, and pert breasts. He led her by the hand to their bed and they lay in each other's arms in bliss. Passionate kisses flowed and slowly and sensually, they explored each other's body culminating in marital union, in love with each other.

They both dressed for the evening in practical but stylish clothes befitting their status in the community, but mindful that they would all be attending midnight Holy Communion at St Michael's Church in Mere.

Sarah and Paul were already downstairs in the Withdrawing Room having set out the dining table in The Great Hall. Roaring fires of birch and ash wood were in both rooms to keep the cold at bay.

Christophe finally appeared, just on time, refreshed from his bath, looking handsome as ever decked out in clothes he kept at Chaffeymoor. He wore a ruffled white shirt, scarlet waist coat and matching silver short coat and breeches all made from the finest French silk.

It was not for him to hold back on false modesty as a courageous Cavalier loyal to the King, sure in his own mind that he would turn the heads of many a fine local damsel when attending the church service.

That evening, Sarah had laid on a simple supper of cold meats, trout from the nearby River Stour, local cheeses, pickles, and home baked bread. Red and white wines were served, the ladies mixing theirs with water and honey to sweeten the taste. Desserts were thick fruit custards, figs, dates, oranges and nuts served with a jug of spiced red wine.

They all enjoyed supper together, reminiscing of better times and catching up on Christophe's adventures. The evening passed quickly, and it was soon gone eleven o'clock and time to think about riding over to St Nicholas's Church.

Making sure that all of the fires were battened down and safe, Paul prepared the Gig and hitched up Blaze to it. He would take Marguerite and Sarah, Robert and Christophe accompanying them on their own horses. They left just after eleven thirty to arrive in good time.

At the church they were greeted by the Reverend Banks and his wife Rosemary. Robert reminded him of Marguerite's previously extended invitation for them, together with their daughter Claire, to join them all at Chaffeymoor for Christmas dinner, starting at six o'clock in the evening. The vicar thanked Robert most kindly and said that he only had one morning service tomorrow, Christmas day, and they would love to come.

After the service, at which Robert made a most generous donation when the collection plate came round, there were greetings of 'Merry Christmas' and the shaking of hands among the congregation.

As they rode back to Chaffeymoor there was a full moon lighting their way, and the first flakes of snow began to fall.

CHAFFEYMOOR GRANGE,
BOURTON, DORSET

11

It was Christmas morning and when drawing back the heavy drapes of their bedroom Marguerite called out 'Look Robert, how wonderful the garden and beyond looks with its blanket of virgin white snow. You can you see the footprints made by the fox crossing the lawn. She'll no doubt be lying outside the kitchen door waiting for some scraps.'

Robert, still a bit sleepy, mustered himself and crossed the bedroom to the window. Looking blearily out, he put his arms around Marguerite and kissed her gently on the nape of her neck saying,

'I do so love you; you are a joy to behold.'

Marguerite turned round and they shared a passionate loving kiss, wishing each other 'Merry Christmas.'

Once downstairs, they all shared a hearty breakfast cooked by Sarah, and whilst eating, decided the order of the day. Sarah and Marguerite would set too and start preparing for the evening's celebratory dinner. Robert had also invited Peter Quince and his wife Lin and their two daughters Lottie and Kelli, making twelve for dinner, so there was a lot to prepare.

Robert, Christophe, and Paul would go for a morning's ride and they would all meet back at the house with a small gathering of other guests that they had invited for drinks and tasty morsels at twelve noon. Guests included young Olivia who helped around the house, her mother and father, the

blacksmith Paul Parker, his wife Kim, her brother Hugo Birch and a few other villagers who had helped around the Grange in this past year. It was Robert's opportunity to thank them all for their help and service, and to wish them all a prosperous and healthy New Year. Marguerite had made up small gifts for each of them, as a token of their gratitude.

After the last of their mid-day guests had left, Marguerite and Sarah made sure that the roast meats were on the spit and starting to cook slowly, and the vegetables and other items were ready and prepped for later. They then joined the menfolk in the Withdrawing Room for the opening of gifts and to play cards or chess.

Robert had bought Marguerite an exquisite gold necklace with a drop pearl nestled between two rubies, made by the renowned Goldsmith Richard Hoare of London. Marguerite gave Robert a fine small silver snuffbox engraved "Forever yours, Marguerite". They kissed upon exchanging gifts under the mistletoe.

Gifts were exchange by one and all, Christophe gave his mother earrings matching her gold necklace, with a single pearl droplet on each. She in turn gave him a gold signet ring bearing the le Douse family crest, which also adorned the two diamond shaped oak panels each side of the stone fireplace in Withdrawing Room.

The Grange was warm, it was comfortable, it was beautiful, it smelt of Christmas, with the foliage decorations, the wood fire on which they were burning pinecones and chestnuts, the smell of roast meat permeating through from the kitchen, and, with a brandy in his hand, Robert looked around the room, surrounded by the people most dear to him, and smiled the smile of a contented man. *What more could a man want,* he mused to himself.

As they made up an odd number for cards, Christophe, despite being the youngest, took advantage to have an afternoon snooze in one of the comfortable armchairs.

At around four o'clock Marguerite and Sarah left the men to their own devices to attend to the evening's meal. Paul made sure that all the fires were made up and safely burning, including in the bedrooms to keep out the winter's chill, and Robert shook Christophe awake and despite its light layer of snow, the two of them wrapped up well and took an afternoon stroll around the peaceful garden in their leather riding boots.

'It's hard to believe we are in the midst of a Civil War' said Robert, pausing to admire the view across the valley.

'You don't know how wonderful this is father, such peace and respite from the horrors of the war. I tell you, it's not for the faint hearted. I have witnessed young men mortally wounded on the battlefield crying out for their mothers and thought that, only by God's grace was I still alive.'

Robert put his arm around Christophe's shoulders as they walked. 'Let us just enjoy the moment Christophe, your mother is overjoyed at seeing us both back at the Grange.'

Back in the warmth of the house, everyone freshened up and dressed for dinner ready to receive their guests at around six o'clock. Robert welcomed them all, ushering them into the Withdrawing Room to meet Christophe and Paul for drinks and morsels before the main event. It was usually Paul who served drinks to the guests, but on this occasion, Christophe took over, treating Paul as one of the guests, and being extra charming to the Reverend Banks' daughter, Claire, who blushed and was enchanted by this charismatic young man.

The Withdrawing Room was furnished with a number of Baroque style French sofas with huge cushions, matching armchairs, a chaise-longue and a pair of English elm side chairs, all tastefully upholstered in the finest cloth and velvet. There were matching side tables and small wine tables alongside each sofa and amongst the armchairs. Huge tapestries depicting aristocratic life in England and France hung on panelled walls, and the oak floors were adorned with hand woven silk rugs from the Orient.

The stone fireplace with its roaring fire had a large cast iron fire basket with matching ornate andirons either side, all made by Parker the blacksmith, who had been a guest for drinks earlier, and who was very proud to see his work appreciated by such high-ranking people and in such a grand setting.

Farmer Quince and his daughters Lottie and Kelli being only fifteen and thirteen years of age were grossly animated and entertained by Christophe's watered-down stories of Royalist victories in the war, whilst Claire, being somewhat infatuated, had eyes on Christophe for quite different reasons. Christophe, knowing this, enjoyed throwing her the odd glance and smile.

Marguerite made a brief appearance, looking quite stunning in a very simple but elegant emerald green gown. She mingled with the guests, chatting away, completely at ease and contented. Shortly thereafter she made her apologies, said that dinner would be served at seven, and disappeared back to help a harassed Sarah in the kitchen.

They had asked Olivia's parents if she could come back for a couple of hours at seven to help Sarah serve up the main meal and then come back the following morning for an hour or so to help clear up the kitchen for which she would be well rewarded. She was delighted to do so, not only for the money, but she loved being in this beautiful house where it was always warm, where even the crockery was beautiful, and she was treated like a member of the family with respect and kindness.

She would have happily come in to help for free, especially as Christophe was home. He had bowed and kissed her hand once. It was some time ago, but she knew she would never forget that moment, even though she realised she could never be anything to him. His father was a 'Sir' and his mother was actually 'Lady Marguerite' even though she rarely used the title. She was just a girl from the village, but she still thought he was wonderful and was happy just to be in the same four walls as him.

Marguerite returned shortly before seven, having rushed upstairs and changed into the most elegant, flowing evening dress that she had made, importing the silk from Paris. It was in glorious gold and green matching her sparkling eyes. It took on the style of French Court dresses, with a draped skirt, tight bodice, and low neckline trimmed with lace showing off her breasts. She wore Robert's gold, ruby, and pearl necklace with the matching pearl earrings from Christophe. *Stunning, magnificent, and mine* thought Robert as she announced in her slightly French and charming accent:

'Ladies and gentlemen, dinner is served if you would like to make your way to The Great Hall.'

The table was laid out with a long lace table runner, setting off the silver candelabras and cutlery. Soup dishes for the first course and glasses for wine and fresh water from the Grange's well, sat beside bowls of scented water to be shared by each of two diners with hand cloths.

Olivia had come in to help Sarah and had permission to eat any leftovers returned to the kitchen. She was a hard-worker and very diligent, and she loved working in this beautiful house. Even washing up the precious bone china and silver cutlery was a pleasure. These were things she would never encounter at home, comfortable as it was, but most of all she loved it because she was treated with kindness and respect. The tureens often came back half-full, so, being in the kitchen alone, she had a feast, not bothering with a plate, but picking at all the wonderful things with her fingers and popping them straight into her mouth. There was still plenty left over for a large and rather wonderful parcel for her family.

Sarah had changed into an evening dress and put on a cloth smock over the top whilst she served up dinner with Olivia, sitting down with everyone for each course, usually, rather hot, and out of breath. She was a brilliant cook who obviously enjoyed her food and her own cooking, very attractive in a homely way, but not elegant like her younger cousin

Marguerite, and she spoke with a gentle soft Scottish accent. Robert poured out wine and water for everyone.

Olivia appeared with the first course of oyster soup served in two large tureens with ladles, and sippets of freshly baked bread. Trying to avoid Christophe's eye as she knew he was watching her intently, she hurriedly put the tureens on the table for someone, anyone, to serve, and scurried back to the kitchen, her heart pounding.

Before any meal was Grace: The Reverend Banks invited everyone to stand, bowed his head, clasped his hands, closed his eyes, and said in his Dorset drawl:

'Lord, for the food that today we celebrate with you
For the rest that brings us comfort, joy, and ease,
For our homes where memories linger
We give thanks to you for these.'
Heavenly father, we ask that you give guidance
And protection, to our most loyal King Charles 1
And all of God's soldiers who follow him.
We ask that our own dear Christophe does
Honour in battle in your name, and bring him
Home safely to Chaffeymoor'
'Amen'

The remaining soup and all of the dishes were cleared away and replaced by pewter plates upon which the fish and main courses would be eaten. The fish course consisting of two large platters of whole salmon, dressed to the nines, trout, herring, eels and oysters was served, and after a short interlude and a digestive of mulled wine with herbs, the central candelabra was removed to the sideboard.

Paul helped Sarah to carry in the main event on huge pewter platters. There was roast goose, suckling pig, beef and mutton joints and a roast Boar's head sat proudly at the centre of the table. Various sauces thickened with breadcrumbs accompanied the meal, having been made with the juices and fats from the meats, plus herbs and spices. Tureens of vegetables from the kitchen garden or stored in the cool kitchen scullery,

were also served. Celeriac, leeks, onions, winter greens and the newest of vegetables, potatoes. It was just a magnificent feast to behold.

'Marguerite and Sarah, you have done us all proud, not forgetting the efforts of Paul', Robert said over the humdrum of excited conversation around the table.

Marguerite just turned and smiled at Robert, so happy, so content.

At around ten o'clock Peter Quince tapped his wineglass and stood to propose a toast.

'Robert and Marguerite, we all thank you most graciously for inviting us here to the Grange to share this magnificent feast with us on this Christmas day. Thank you also Sarah and Paul.' He said looking towards them and acknowledging the work they had put in to make this meal possible.

'Robert and Christophe, we shall be saddened when you have to leave us, and we wish you God-speed when you do. We cannot ask Robert too much of his work in the King's name, but we all pray for both you, and Christophe. May God give you both the strength and fortitude to see through this conflict. I therefore propose a toast to 'The Douse family.'

They all cried 'The Douse Family' in unison downing the contents of their glasses.

As was a tradition at the Grange, they all retired to the Withdrawing Room for games and dancing. Olivia set out desserts in the Morning Room for later treats and served coffee in the Withdrawing Room. She then cleared the table with the help of Sarah, who helped her make up a generous parcel of food to take back to her family.

'Take care walking back to the village Olivia, come by in the morning at around ten o'clock.'

'Thank you, Miss Sarah,' she replied, as she headed off home in the dark and the snow.

After a few games of Blind Man's Bluff and The King Who Does Not Lie, the Vicar lead them all in singing their chosen favourite carols accompanied by Christophe playing the harpsicord, the learning of which was one of his "penances" of a privileged education.

Christophe then led off with tunes of the day encouraging everyone to dance. Marguerite, who was an accomplished player, took over for some of the time, much to the delight of Claire who jumped at the chance to grab hold of Christophe and waltz him round the floor.

They all laughed, danced, ate sweet deserts, figs and nuts, and drank their way well into the night, even Vicar David got tipsy. 'It's the Lords wish' he cried as he whirled Marguerite around the dance floor, and they all laughed, including his devoted wife Rosemary.

After the last guests had departed with a small present from Robert and Marguerite to be opened in the morning, "Boxing Day", the night sky was clear with a waxing moon. Paul made sure that the house was secure, and all fires bedded down and safe for the remainder of the night.

They all trooped off to bed, weary, sated, and happy. Robert, rather tipsy and feeling very happy, said,

'Good night all, you are my family and I love you all, thank you for such a wonderful celebration.'

'Good night Robert we all love you too' replied Sarah with a smile.

On New Year's Eve to see in the New Year, Christophe performed the ritual of being the "First Foot" across the threshold, as that person had to be male, swarthy, perhaps fair-haired, and best of all with flat feet. They all agreed that Christophe came closest of all to that description.

Christophe needed to go back to Oxford to be there by the end of the holidays on the 5th. Robert would accompany him until the turn off for the road to Pewsey and Marlborough. He would then continue his journey to London, staying overnight at The Three Cups Inn in Stockbridge.

As Robert and Marguerite lay with their arms round each other in bed on that last night, after making love for the final time, they pledged their love to each other.

'Come back safely to me Robert my love, you are my life and soul, I love you as brightly as the stars do shine.'

'I love you too my darling one. You are my first and last love, there has never been anyone else nor will there be.'

Tears began to flow, sweet kisses followed until they finally drifted off to sleep in each other's arms. Tomorrow was another day, and it would take care of itself.

12

Robert arrived back at the safe house around mid-afternoon on the 5th to be received and greeted by John and Jenny.

'Happy New Year Robert, I trust the holiday at Chaffeymoor was everything you wished for' said John.

'That and more my friend, how about you and Jenny?'

'We had a grand time thank you Robert' said Jenny, 'it is good to see you again.'

'It's good to be back. Any news from Elliot?'

'He is out at the moment, but he said he would be back later to catch up with you.'

Upon his return, Elliot had little to report with London practically shutting down for the holidays.

They all dined together that evening on a light supper made by Jenny, a welcome relief for Robert after all the rich food over the holiday period.

Over the next few weeks Robert needed to gather his thoughts and go over his progress to date: Who were the protagonists of Madrigal and its true meaning? He also needed a breakthrough in his quest to find out who "The Lawyer" was who was so determined that Madrigal was never to be made public.

He referred to his notes which he kept in a secret hiding place in his room, hoping that seeing them afresh, a 'eureka'

moment might make it all clear. Unfortunately, that was not the case.

The harsh winter predicted by some was now well and truly upon them. It was now mid-January, with the odd snow flurries and temperatures barely rising above freezing point at any time of day and deep, deep, frosts all night causing the River Thames to freeze over. The ice was many inches thick and well capable of holding The Frost Fair which was becoming an almost annual event now with such harsh winters.

By the end of January, a temporary street was built on the ice from Temple to Southwark with all manner of things being sold. There were rows of tents, each boasting some delight to the fairgoers, from food and drink of every sort imaginable to toys, books, and souvenirs.

Coaches plied on the River as they would do in the streets, sliding on skeets, to and from Westminster to Temple, 2 miles east, and many other landing stages on route.

A great deal of activities and entertainment took place, ice skating and sledding, nine pin skittles, horse and coach races, puppet plays, jesters leaping and telling jokes, poets and lyricists orating their prose. It created a carnival atmosphere to be enjoyed by all from landed gentry to tenement dwellers getting some relief from their dismal existence and struggles of winter.

Food and drink were both plentiful. One of the main culinary draws was the roasting of an entire ox. Though this would have taken about 24 hours to cook, when it was done one animal would have fed as many as 800 people. There was also sliced mutton and mince pies, gingerbread, hot apples, and oysters, as well as hot chocolate, tea and coffee among the delicacies.

Spit roast Ox was a particular favourite of King Charles who was known to have attended the Fair on many a previous occasion.

The tents selling alcohol were among the most popular. Called "fuddling" tents, selling a variety of particularly potent

gin-based drinks including Old Tom, a sweet, light, but undeniably potent drink. Purl was a waterman's favourite; served hot it was a combination of gin, spices and wormwood wine. 'Mum' was another popular beverage in the fuddling tents, being a spiced ale concoction.

Robert and Elliot had decided to go to the Fair together to get some light relief from their day-to-day quest, to have fun, compete against one another at skittles, and down many a tankard of Mum.

It was the hunting ground for pickpockets and thieves who could expect no mercy if caught by either the public or the authorities. It was commonplace for dead bodies to be found in the early hours after dawn, victims, and perpetrators.

The Fair only lasted a matter of a few days and when cracks started to appear in the ice, the town of tents and stalls disappeared as quickly as they had been erected. The next morning a dead body was found at the bottom of the steps at Temple.

Robert was still taking a leisurely breakfast, nursing a hangover from drinking too much Mum the night before at the Fair. Suddenly Elliot, who had returned to the house soon after departing, came bursting into the room in an agitated state.

'Whatever is the matter?' asked Robert.

'He's murdered; Matthew Makepeace has been murdered' Elliot cried out.

Makepiece, his spy at the Inns of Court, was found that morning with his throat slit from ear to ear at the bottom of the steps at Temple. They could only surmise between them that he had been discovered by "The Lawyer" who had then had him murdered before he had time to reveal anything about him, let alone his name.

'Come and sit-down man, have some coffee or would you like something stronger?'

'It is a bit early for me Robert, but the death of young Matthew has really hit me hard. You know what it is like when

you take on a new recruit, train them in the art of espionage and send them out to do your bidding. You form a strong bond with one another. He was to me like the son I never had.'

Robert called out for Jenny and asked her to bring a decanter of Napoleon Brandy and two glasses. She returned and set them down.

'Good God Robert, is he all right?'

'He is OK, he has just had a bit of a shock, that's all.'

Robert and Elliot were always careful not to divulge too much about their activities to John and Jenny, although they were well aware of their roles in life.

Jenny, knowing not to ask too many questions, then retired to the kitchen to plan that evening's supper.

Robert poured them both a generous measure of brandy and waited for Elliot to calm down. After he had regained his composure and appeared to be more rational, Robert asked him to go through, slowly, and concisely from the beginning, what Matthew had reported back, however seemingly unimportant. He knew that sometimes it was the little things that are easily dismissed as not being relevant at the time, that turn out to be a hidden clue crucial to their quest.

Elliot proceeded to report on Matthew's enquiries and observations including those of Jack, Adam, and Theo, three of his Spies. They worked as Clerks in the Inns of Court, at Lincoln's Inn, the Inner Temple, and Middle Temple.

Robert had heard most of this before but there was one item that made him stop Elliot in his tracks and repeat what he had just told him.

Just a week ago, Jack, who worked at Lincoln's Inn, had told Matthew what he had overheard one day in Chambers when William Lenthall, Speaker of the House of Commons, and a learned Member, was visiting Chambers for lunch with other prominent members of The Inn.

Jack had to deliver an urgent message from a wealthy client to Sir Hugo Boseman, Head of Chambers, who was in conversation with Lenthall during the lunch.

He overheard Lenthall refer to a former member of Chambers, a lawyer named Edward Floyd, who had been impeached by the House of Commons back in 1621 for insulting the Prince Palatine, the son in law of the then King James 1, and also his wife Elizabeth of Bohemia, the King's daughter.

Floyd had been sentenced to life imprisonment and degraded from the title of a Gentleman. Following a petition to the King by none other than the then Prince Charles, James 1 exercised his prerogative of mercy in the case of political prisoners.

Lenthall was heard to mention that Floyd had struggled to continue in his legal practice, and the poor fellow had recently been disbarred. He had been accused of blatant favouritism towards a known Parliamentarian criminal, and abuse of Privilege in Court. He accused the Judge of being biased and in the pockets of Oxford, deemed to mean the King.

Nothing further had been heard of Floyd who had apparently disappeared into obscurity with his illegitimate daughter, Lysette. She had been the outcome of a liaison with a noble high-born Lady of Court, rumoured to be the wife of a Peer of the Realm, who was off fighting the war alongside the King. Clearly, there was no love lost between Floyd and the Royalist cause, despite the then Prince Charles's intervention on his imprisonment.

Both Lenthall and Floyd were of interest to Robert. Lenthall had risen to the heights of being appointed Speaker of the House, and had famously defied King Charles on his attempt to arrest the "five" traitors, saying to Charles,

'I have neither eyes to see nor tongue to speak in this place but as this House is pleased to direct me whose servant I am.'

However, in his last speech to the House in the King's presence, he talked of reconciliation and invited Charles to rid himself of false counsellors.

Robert allowed Elliot to finish his recollection of all of Matthew's reports before thanking him for his memory and briefing him on where to go next.

He rose from his chair and crossed the room to Elliot who was downing the last few dregs of the brandy. Patting him on the shoulder he said:

'Well done Elliot, you are a fine Agent, worthy of the trust that both The King and I place in you. You may well have inadvertently, but concisely, put me on the path of this anonymous Lawyer who we suspect to be the "sixth" member of the conspiracy against the King, and who would go to any lengths to see that Madrigal is never made public.'

'What do you want of me now Robert?' asked Elliot, holding out his glass for a re-fill.

'Just go about your normal business, keep your eyes and ears open to anything that may be either to the advantage or a threat to the Royalist cause. You should also interview Jack, Adam and Theo and form your own view as to who would be best placed to replace Matthew as your principal spy in the Inns of Court.'

'I will do that; he will be hard to replace but I have one of them in mind. I'll reserve judgement at this time.'

Refilling Elliot's glass, Robert continued

'That's fine. I have every confidence in you to make the right decision, in the meantime I have other matters of State I must attend to.'

13

Meanwhile, the Civil War continued unabated with skirmishes across the land until the end of March 1643 with The Battle of Seacroft Moor, which was a resounding defeat of Parliamentary forces in the North of England, led by Sir Thomas Fairfax.

Another decisive victory followed for the Royalists at Stratton in Cornwall on the 16th of May with Christophe leading the Dorset Royals with distinction. Following Stratton, the mood and confidence of Charles and his officers and troops were running high.

In London, unknown to Robert, a plot by Sir Nicholas Crisp, a wealthy merchant and militant Royalist, had been uncovered by Parliamentary spies towards the end of May. It was to seize the City by organising an uprising of all known militants. Merchants, shopkeepers, and tradesmen down to the poor would be brought together into a cohesive fighting force organised along army lines.

It seemed to Robert that Madrigal, a peaceful plan, organised by more moderate Royalist and Parliamentary supporters was not the only "closely guarded secret", with Crisp's plot setting another example of Charles's tendency to run several secret campaigns together, sometimes overlapping or conflicting with each other.

Robert was aghast that Charles had not made him aware of Crisp's plot, which could have a major bearing on his quest to uncover and reveal the secrets of Madrigal.

His intuition about Katherine, Lady d'Aubigny was right. He discovered that she was, by association, caught up in the plot and she had sometimes acted as Crisp's courier taking secret messages to associates in London.

Edmund Waller, Henry Heron and Alexander Hampden, the three names given to him by her, were part of Crisp's plot, and were arrested on the instructions of Cromwell.

Crisp had fled back to Oxford. Kathrine was arrested and imprisoned in the Tower but later released upon the intervention of the French Ambassador, with no charges brought against her as she herself was not involved in the plot.

Waller was arrested and confessed to being part of it and gave evidence against two others involved, Richard Challoner and Nathaniel Tompkins, Waller's brother-in-law. All were found guilty of Treason; Waller received a heavy fine and a short term in prison and upon release went into exile. Challoner and Tompkins were hung.

Alexander Hampden died in prison before trial and Henry Heron was released without charge and retired into obscurity.

This immediately ruled out Edmund Waller, Henry Heron and Alexander Hampden as suspects. Katherine's involvement in Madrigal, however, was still questionable.

Meanwhile, Christophe, having been called to arms to fight in his native West Country at the Battle of Stratton, led the remnants of The Dorset Royals to join up with Prince Rupert's army at Chinnor in Oxfordshire on their way to reinforce Oxford, now the Royalist Capital of England.

He was overjoyed to see his good friend Edward, still holding his upright gait, riding his faithful Bay as if he were out for a Sunday jaunt. It was clear to Christophe that Edward had lost all his fears and reticence that he displayed at Edgehill and was now a seasoned Cavalier.

It was early summer, on a cool but not cold evening with a bright moon-lit sky, and nearly a year after they had left York. After setting up camp at Chinnor, near Oxford, Christophe found Edward, sprawled, laughing, and relaxed enjoying a flagon of wine with his troops.

'How goes thee Edward' cried out Christophe as he advanced towards him.

Edward leapt up almost overcome with joy and embraced his old friend.

'Better for seeing you. Your heroic deeds are well known throughout the realms of Charles's army and supporters across the breadth of the land', he said with pride.

Christophe replied modestly 'No more so than you my dear friend, and all those that have fought for the King's cause. We have all lost many a fine man along the way, friends, and family alike, and many a fine young Cavalier of the Kentish and Dorset Royals. Let us toast absent friends and may they rest in peace.'

Edward's troops all stood to attention as they cried in unison 'Absent friends.'

'Now Edward, let you and I catch up on times old and new.'

After a long night listening to each other's news, reminiscing of their families and their days at Oxford together, and drinking too much wine, they manged to sleep for a few hours before the call to arms in the morning.

Prince Rupert's army set off for the short ride to Oxford entering the city to widespread cheering from Royalist troops, the aristocracy, city folk and peasants alike.

In London, the high command of the Parliamentarian Army, Fairfax, Essex, and the rising star both politically and in the field of battle, Colonel Oliver Cromwell, met secretly and concurred that the taking of Oxford would be huge blow to Charles and his supporters, and would give rise to a quick ending of the war. It was agreed that Essex, Chief

Commander of the Parliamentary Army, should have the honour of taking Oxford.

Royalist Cavalry under the command of Prince Rupert, having ridden out of Oxford under the cover of darkness on the night of 17th to 18th of June, raided Parliamentary positions around Chinnor. As they were returning to Oxford they were pursued as far as Chalgrave by Parliamentarian Cavalry under the command of John Hampden. Rupert halted his troops, turned, and ordered a counterattack which scattered Hampden's forces before reinforcements could arrive.

Both sides regrouped and a battle commenced along a bridleway, bounded by a double line of thick shoulder high hedgerows, marking the parish boundary. The skirmish was all but over by the time that Essex arrived with reinforcements. A decisive victory for the Royalists. It once again proved the effectiveness of Rupert's Cavalry.

In the fighting Hampden was shot twice in the shoulder and in the aftermath was taken to The Greyhound Inn in Thame.

On hearing about Hampden, Charles, somewhat surprisingly considering he had attempted to arrest him for treason prior to the war, offered the services of his surgeon. This demonstrated how chivalry prevailed in those days. Hampden's wound, however, became infected and he died six days later.

Robert heard in despatches that Christophe had once again distinguished himself in battle and had come through unscathed. He was also made aware of the death of John Hampden. Death was a consequence of war, but Hampden's death meant one less source of finding out who were the Parliamentarians who supported Madrigal.

It was now nearly the end of July 1643 when Robert heard in despatches of further Royalist victories in the West Country at Lansdown Hill on the 5th of July, and Roundway Down on the 13th followed by a costly victory by Prince Rupert in the storming of Bristol on the 26th.

The tide seemed to be turning in favour of King Charles, but Robert knew only too well that one decisive victory for Parliament could change things overnight.

Christophe and Edward had fought gallantly in all three battles coming through virtually unscathed bar a minor injury to Edward having succumbed to a glancing blow just below the shoulder blade. He was checked out by The Surgeon General who sewed him up with three gut stitches and passed him fit for Battle.

Robert sat at his desk one morning in his room at the safe house in Angel Islington. Springtime had come and gone, and it was now the height of Summer. It was warm, long forgotten the harsh Winter and mild Spring. He had thrown open the window to let in the breeze along with the sound of people and trade below; the sky was clear blue, dazzling like a clear diamond, with the occasional white cotton fluffy cloud drifting by.

He decided that he really needed to take stock of where he was in his investigations, to set down on parchment all of the protagonists involved, the arguments and evidence for and against each one, and with the hope of cross referencing and linking associations and friendships, find a way forward in his quest.

There had to be a way, he was still missing something.

14

After drinking several cups of strong coffee to help him to focus his mind on the task ahead, Robert set forth to summarise where he was in his quest. He would write a short precis of any person he had ever considered might be involved in Madrigal, their background, known associates, actions and rationale for suspecting them or otherwise. Most of all he would put down in writing his own instincts and his reading of body language, this being an art he had developed over his years of spying and intelligence gathering.

He sat at his desk overlooking the street below, it was early afternoon, and the street was still busy with street peddlers and shops open to sell their wares. The crowds queuing earlier for their daily bread at the bakers and such meat as they could afford at the butchers had waned. Islington was transforming itself into a more desirable area and run-down premises were being restored into more fashionable residences. Shoemakers, Drapers, Milliners and Haberdashery shops were opening up to sell to the newer middle classes.

Robert pulled out several sheets of parchment and sharpened his quills. His inkpot already stood on the desk full of black ink made from bark of hawthorn cut in the Spring, dried, and then boiled in water and wine until it evaporated into a thick black substance to which iron sulphate was added to form the ink.

Sitting back in his chair, quill in hand, he referred to several notes he had made in code, lest they be discovered by a Parliamentary spy. He started with who he believed to be the main instigator of Madrigal, Thomas Fairfax, and wrote:

Sir Thomas Fairfax, *Parliamentarian, 3rd Lord Fairfax of Cameron, English nobleman, peer, politician, and Lieutenant General of the Parliamentary Army in the English Civil War. He headed the Parliamentary Commission at the final negotiations on "The Nineteen Proposals". He had previously served under Charles and was always known to have wanted a negotiated settlement. In his opinion, Charles's stubbornness to yield on any one of the proposals, prevented this and led to war. Was Fairfax the main protagonist?*

John Marchal, *Parliamentarian. He was present at the negotiations but not one of the Parliamentary Commission. He attempted to prevent the discovery of Madrigal by any means and was shot and killed when he attempted to kill me. Gave me the reference to "The Lawyer".*

William Cecil, 2nd Earl of Salisbury. *Neutral but with Royalist sympathies, member of The Privy Council, friend of King Charles, two sons fighting on behalf of Parliament. He gave up the list of four names to follow up on, two had died in the war, one was Lady d'Aubigny, and the other was Geoffrey Chambertin a moderate Parliamentarian who had inherited considerable wealth from his Royalist grandmother. Was Cecil conflicted by his sons fighting the Parliamentary cause? There was more than the eye could see with old William, perhaps time had caught up with him and he no longer had the fight in him to see it through. Is it possible that he conspired with Fairfax?*

Katherine, Lady d'Aubigny, *A Royalist and an English lady, married into French aristocracy, arrested as part of Sir*

Robert Crisp's plot to encourage an uprising in London, but freed through the intervention of the Ambassador of France. She gave up the names of Waller, Heron and Hampden too easily, there was more to her than she revealed. Why would she "give them up". Did she know of the Crisp plot and needed a diversion to Madrigal?

Geoffrey Chambertin, a moderate Parliamentarian, who had inherited wealth from his Grandmother, The Dowager Myra Chambertin and was rumoured to have friends amongst the Parliamentarian elite.

He was yet to be investigated; it was unlikely Chambertin was involved directly but he could lead me to a high-ranking Parliamentarian who was.

Edmund Waller and Alexander Hampden, Royalists, both part of Sir Robert Crisp's plot. Waller was currently in prison and would be exiled upon release the following year, Hampden died in prison.

Henry Heron, a Royalist and one of Crisp's low-level Agents, arrested as part of Crisp's plot but released without trial. Little was known of him; he certainly was not part of the Royal Court.

Austyn Lamborghini, Waller's protégé, a young militant Royalist engaged in violent demonstrations and sabotage. It was unlikely that he was one of the protagonists of Madrigal but he might be involved playing a minor role running messages between those that were.

Agents Denzel and Elliot, Royalists. He reminded himself what he had said to William Cecil 'Whoever they are, they are learned, intelligent, highly astute and skilful in the art of deception.' If he did not know better, he would wager that one of his Agents was involved. Could either Denzel or Elliot, his two most senior Agents, be involved? Highly Unlikely

The Lawyer Parliamentarian. He believed that almost by chance, Elliot had probably discovered who he was. It seemed highly probable that the lawyer was Edward Floyd, until

recently a former member of Lincoln's Inn. He had been dis-
barred from practising as he had accused a High Court Judge
of being in the pockets of Oxford, deemed to mean The King.

He then tried to summarise his current thinking to enable him to find a way forward and decide his next steps.

He was convinced that Fairfax was involved, and he would confront him when he had identified all of the others. He was equally convinced that there had to be at least one other leading Parliamentarian involved, as yet unidentified. It was unlikely to be another high-ranking officer fighting at the forefront of the conflict. Robert considered this hypothesis, it had to be someone in Court circles, with Parliamentary sympathies or a politician.

William Cecil had all the hallmarks of being one of the major protagonists alongside Fairfax. A nobleman, skilled in politics and as a diplomat. Robert thought, why, despite the King's personal appeal to him in his letter, William did not reveal more to him. A conflict of interest, a change of mind, a fear of being discovered and Parliamentary reprisals putting at risk his son's inheritance, perhaps. Something was causing him to hold back. He decided to visit William again in due course and rely on William's friendship with Charles to help him put the pieces of the jigsaw together.

He needed to find out a lot more of Geoffrey Chambertin and try to connect him with Katherine Lady d'Aubigny and others. Although the uncovering of the Crisp plot appeared to be a major setback, it had in fact done him a favour. He no longer had to worry about Waller, Heron and Hampden and it had strengthened his doubts about Katherine.

Lamborghini was a strange one, high born with a silver spoon in his mouth. He mixed with the Avant-guard set of London; artists, poets, writers, and musicians who could never have envisaged that beneath that effeminate exterior there was a hardened member of the Royalist resistance. Robert decided that he needed more evidence, and he must try and find a link between him and the other suspects. He would put Elliot onto this one.

He found it hard to think that Elliot could have anything to do with Madrigal based on his experience of living with him at the safe house in Angel Islington for some time, and the diligence shown by Elliot in their investigations. However, he could not at this stage rule out Denzel, his Agent for South Midlands, and East Anglia, despite the convivial stay at The Manor at Hemingford Grey near Huntingdon. He trusted Elliot and would question him about Denzel's background. Is there anything there or had he heard anything on the grapevine that might suggest that Denzel was involved.

The afternoon had passed without a sign of Elliot and it was now early evening. Robert bound his notes, now several pages of parchment, and put them in his secret hiding place in the eaves of the roof. God help us that we never have a fire, he thought. He knew where he might find Elliot at this hour, so he told Jane to expect them for supper at around eight o'clock.

He wandered off towards The Angel Inn, in fine fettle, with a sense of achievement that despite its ups and downs he was still confident of unlocking the "closely guarded secret" of Madrigal.

15

Robert, having briefed Elliot the night before over supper as to his task to investigate Austyn Lamborghini further, set out to find out more about Geoffrey Chambertin. It was not a name known to him; he could not be expected to know everyone in high society in London. Geoffrey Chambertin turned out to be the grandson of the late Dowager Myra Chambertin an heiress to part of the fortunes of the Gevry Chambertin family of wine growers in the Burgundy region of France. His father Francois Chambertin was also a wealthy merchant, importing fine wines from France including those from the family's estate and others in the Burgundy region.

Geoffrey, a young man in his early twenties, had been educated privately and at King's College, Cambridge, where he mixed with a number of sons of leading Parliamentarians. Upon graduating, he refused to go into the family business setting himself up as an importer of fine French furniture which was all the fashion of London socialites.

He was known for being flamboyant, dressed in fine clothes, a womaniser and gambler with a house in Soho, one of the most fashionable parts of London. Soho was also the centre for Gentlemen's Clubs and gambling dens. His gambling losses caused the downfall of his business and the timing of his inheritance was a blessing as he continued to lead the life of a gentleman, despite his dwindling fortune.

Robert deduced two things from this intelligence, firstly Chambertin would know a number of leading Parliamentarians through being friends with their sons at Cambridge. Secondly his gambling debts might leave him open to blackmail by those he owed money too.

He needed to find out who his closest friends were at King's College, so decided to go up to Cambridge and see the Master of King's and enquire of Chambertin, who would have graduated some six years ago.

He advised John and Jenny that, all being well, he would be back within the week and set off the following morning with some trepidation, as East Anglia and Cambridge in particular, were Parliamentary strongholds with control of the town being given to Oliver Cromwell.

Cambridge Castle had been re-fortified and was occupied by over one thousand Parliamentary troops and would remain so for the remainder of the War. Although there was such a large Parliamentary presence, the University Colleges were, on the whole, still loyal Royalist supporters.

Robert travelled incognito, as he had done many times before, as Robert Asprey, Merchant of Fine Leather Goods, with a forged travel passport authorised by Parliament giving him unhindered travel between London and Cambridge.

Despite the assurance of the forged travel papers Robert was unusually nervous, but remained controlled, disciplined, and determined.

He travelled with his faithful Dog-Lock Cavalry Pistol, which was ideal if attacked on the open road, but concealed in his clothing and his baggage were his dagger and one of the newly invented Pocket Pistols, which he been asked to trial by the Royalist Army high command.

The journey took him back out of London the way that he had come in from Hatfield, and he would retrace his steps staying overnight once more at The Swan Inn in Welwyn.

It was another glorious Summer's day and Robert was glad to be out in the countryside again, away from the oppressive nature of the London streets, and breathing in fresh air. The trees and hedges were now in full bloom and the fields either lush with pasture and wildflowers or bursting with signs of the burgeoning Autumn crops. It had every sign of being a good Harvest. He felt safe on this part of the journey recognising the landscape and villages he passed through. His heartbeat only raced once as he passed a small troop of Parliamentary Horse Soldiers as he neared Hatfield. They hardly acknowledged him as they continued on their way.

The Swan Inn was as welcoming as ever and Robert spent a relaxing evening dining under magnificent thick sturdy oak beams dating back to the 14ᵗʰ century.

In the morning he partook of their renowned hearty breakfast and set off for Cambridge, fortified and in good heart, but well aware of the possible dangers ahead. It was a risk he had to take. He had more than a feeling; his "sixth sense" was telling him that Chambertin might well be the link to other leading Parliamentarians involved in Madrigal, alongside Fairfax.

The Great North Road took him north from Hatfield to Letchworth, from where he travelled north eastwards through Royston and Great Shelford to Cambridge. The closer he got to Cambridge the more aware he was of an increasing number of Parliamentary Troops, either out on Patrol or garrisoned at strategic points along the way.

Was Cromwell gathering a large East Anglian Army to join Essex for a major confrontation with the Royalist Army which was under the command of King Charles and Prince Rupert, he thought. When he was back in London, he would send a courier to advise Rupert of his observations.

He entered Cambridge in the afternoon having ridden through Grantchester and over Grantchester Meadows alongside the River Cam, making his way along Silver Street, past Queens' College to the city centre and The Blackmoor's

Head in Market Square where he would stay the night. After handing over Keagan, his horse, to the stable yard hands he registered with The Innkeeper and settled into his room, throwing his doublet and hat onto a chair, and removing his long boots.

To be wearing no boots in the summer's heat felt so good, especially after a long ride, and he also undid the buckles on his breeches below his knee, letting them bag as loosely as his shirt. Padding around the room in his stockinged feet, he sat down at the small table by the open window. A welcome breeze was blowing the linen curtains and he could see and hear the market traders in the square, their goods protected from the sun under colourful awnings.

The table in his room was set with a quill, ink and hand-made paper, and Robert sat for a while and composed an introductory letter seeking an audience with the Master at King's the following morning.

KING'S COLLEGE, CAMBRIDGE

It was a short walk to King's, and as the letter was written under his real name, but saying he would be arriving under his alias, Asprey, Robert decided to deliver the letter personally to the College Gatekeeper, asking that it be delivered to the Master as soon as possible.

The inner city was surprisingly absent of Parliamentary Troops, just a few officers finishing a long leisurely lunch before returning to the Castle or their billets outside of the city.

He felt reasonably safe walking the streets, but safer back at The Blackmoor.

Robert was aware that King's in particular, was still loyal to The King and it was not long before he received a reply requesting that he come by at ten o'clock in the morning. He dined and retired to his room early, not wishing to be drawn into conversation with other patrons. The following morning he rose late, so just had a meagre breakfast, together with strong coffee, enough to fortify himself to face the day.

He informed the Innkeeper that he would collect Keagan later that morning then he set off for King's College on foot, arriving promptly at ten o'clock. The Gatekeeper had been informed of his pending arrival and he was escorted to the Master's House where he was met by his housekeeper and shown into the Library.

Samuel Collins: the eighteenth Provost Master of Kings since its foundation in 1441, welcomed him warmly. The Housekeeper brought them coffee and left them to conduct a private conversation, making sure that they were not to be disturbed. Collins signalled to Robert to take a seat and enquired as to his request for an audience. Robert, unlike his normal reticence, decided that if he was to make progress in his quest, he had to take a huge gamble.

'Master, I am here at the request of the King' he said, offering Collins the letter signed by Charles vouching for him and requesting all persons to offer him assistance.

Collins returned the letter to Robert and said, 'please call me Samuel, Robert, I am the King's obedient servant as are most of my Fellows at King's College, and many of the other Colleges within Cambridge.'

Robert breathed a sigh of relief and proceeded to inform Samuel of his need for information about Geoffrey Chambertin.

'When do you think he graduated at Kings?'

'It must be six or seven years ago judging by his age.'

Samuel went over to his library shelves stacked high with academic works and College Year Books. He pulled out those for 1636 and 1637.

'Yes, here he is, he graduated in 1637.'

'Is there any way we can tell who his contemporaries were whilst he was here?' enquired Robert.

'Of course, The Yearbook shows all those that graduated that year and who their sponsors were, predominantly their fathers. Take a look' he said, handing the large leather-bound, hand-written book over to Robert.

Robert could not believe his good fortune, in amongst those listed there was one name of a leading Parliamentarian which immediately caught his eye and gave Robert cause to think. Could he have finally found one more leading Parliamentarian involved in Madrigal as well as Fairfax?

William Lenthall? Robert had come across Lenthall in Elliot's investigations at Lincolns Inn which led him to Edward Floyd, the probable "Lawyer" seeking to stop Madrigal coming to fruition. He never thought at the time that Lenthall himself could be involved, nor was he on his list of suspects.

William Lenthall, the Speaker of the House of Commons, whilst outwardly a staunch supporter of Parliamentary ideals, had no sympathy for the diehard protesters seeking radical ecclesiastical reform. In 1642 he had argued forcibly for The Commons to send a peace proposal to the King which Robert knew only too well came to no avail.

Robert did not explain to Samuel as to why he wanted to know of leading Parliamentarians who had sent their son's up to King's, nor did Samuel ask. After exchanging a few more pleasantries, Samuel talked of the difficulties of continuing education at King's with a Civil War raging across the country.

The fact that Cambridge itself was at relative peace, being a strong fortification held by Parliament and under the control of Cromwell, strangely helped. There were still some sons of leading Royalists at King's completing their degrees, but within the confines of the College it was part of the College's mantra that freedom of opinion and speech still prevailed.

Robert bade Samuel farewell 'I can't thank you enough Samuel, you can be sure I shall tell the King of your most valuable assistance.'

'Godspeed Robert, whatever your quest is I wish you well in your endeavours. If there is anything more I can do for you just let me know by secret courier. I will respond by letter or I could come down to London, which I often have to do on College business or in seeking new benefactors.'

Robert walked back towards The Blackmoor's Head to collect Keagan and head off on his return journey to London. On leaving King's he hurried across King's Parade then proceeded up Bridge Street. Just before Market Square he turned down a narrow alleyway that lead to Blackmore Yard.

He was about halfway down the dark alleyway, which was no more than a short cut, no businesses, no shopfronts, no people, when out of the shadows stepped a man, pistol in hand who called out 'Asprey, if that is your real name which I doubt, you are a traitor to Parliament.' Robert had no time to think, only react; he pulled the Pocket Pistol from his tunic and shot the man dead with a bullet between his eyes. Thankfully, the retort from the pistol was not very loud and Robert decided to risk searching the body.

His assailant was short, stocky, and muscular. He was swarthy with facial hair but not a full beard. In Robert' opinion, he was fit, a fighter but not a soldier. His tunic was simple and contained a hidden stiletto dagger. He had all the hallmarks of an assassin.

Robert searched his tunic and boots and found no other items to identify him other than he was wearing a gold signet ring with an engraved coat of arms. He took the ring off his finger and managed to drag the man's body and push him into a cellar entrance before hastily exiting the alleyway into Blackmore Yard.

He had no idea how, if at all, his subterfuge had been discovered, but suspected that the Gatekeeper at King's may have been a Parliamentarian informant, reporting on any suspicious visitors to the College. He was concerned for Samuel's welfare but reasoned that although he was a known Royalist sympathiser, the College continued to be neutral, educating both Royalists and Parliamentarian sons alike and therefore he was not considered to be a threat by the Parliamentarian High Command.

Robert hurried across the yard to The Blackmoor's Head but before saddling up Keagan he had a quick look at the signet ring. He could not be sure without further examination, but it looked like the arms of Oliver Cromwell.

How much did Cromwell know? Marchal reported to him, so did the assassin laying in the cellar in Blackmoor Yard. His subterfuge as Robert Asprey had been compromised and he was on Cromwell's home turf, but was that the reason he was the subject of another attempted assassination?

He vowed to himself to be extra diligent in future, two attempts on his life were no coincidence.

16

Robert rode out of Cambridge the way he came in. He set off on his journey back to London at a walking pace, so as not to draw attention to himself, until he entered Grantchester Meadows and then sped up to a canter. He stopped off again at The Swan Inn north of Hatfield where he was warmly welcomed back by the Innkeeper and his staff.

He was sorely tempted to seek another audience with William Cecil at Hatfield House to confront him. He had an intuition that, despite the King's personal letter to Cecil, for some reason he had held back information on Madrigal, crucial information, when they last met.

He dined and decided to sleep on it rather than just rush in. If William was involved, he was likely to be the main Royalist protagonist, and Robert reached the same conclusion he had done with Fairfax. He would not reveal his hand to either of them until he had identified the others involved. He reasoned to himself that he might skilfully try to bring about a meeting with the two of them in secret at the appropriate time. He wanted to confront them, reveal his evidence and findings to them, have them confirm those people involved, alive or dead, and divulge what the objectives were behind Madrigal.

He arrived safely back in London at the safe house in Angel Islington the next day, late afternoon and unsaddled Keagan in the back-lane yard and stables. John was in the yard

emptying the outside bucket toilet in the outhouse, shovelling the excrement in with the horse manure and straw, and heaping it onto the mound in the back lane for the "Nightmen" to collect.

'Welcome back Robert, I trust you were successful in your venture and nothing happened untoward?'

Robert trusted John as more than just a loyal Royalist, but he did not share with him the life and works of a Royalist Agent and Spy. He obviously knew Robert and Elliot's roles in life, but the least detail he knew the better.

'Very well thank you John, I am always amazed how I can move around the countryside unhindered with a Civil War going on all around me.' Robert left it at that and was pleased to be back.

He greeted Jenny as he entered the back kitchen. She was already preparing supper, a simple spit of game slowly turning on her cooking range, to be served with vegetables and herbs. He asked her for some coffee and her own baked biscuits to be brought up to his room, and to let him know when Elliot arrived home for supper.

He wearily climbed the four flights of stairs, changed out of his riding attire and his heavy long leather riding boots, washed his hands and face in the bowl of cold water and felt a bit more refreshed. He then dressed in much lighter day wear, not intending to leave the house again that day.

On looking at his broad oak bedstead with its soft duck down, feather and horsehair mattress, he resisted the temptation to take an afternoon nap. Perhaps later he thought, I must update my notes on my discovery and add Lenthall to the likely suspects. It was all he could do. Carefully concealing his parchments back into their secret hiding place, he finally gave into his fatigue from the journey, lay on the bed and drifted off to sleep.

At around five o'clock there was a soft knock on the door just loud enough to wake him.

'Come in' called Robert. It was Jenny to tell him that Elliot was home.

'Tell him I shall be down shortly if you will please.'

Robert rubbed the sleep out of his eyes and splashed his face with cold water again to make himself more alert. He descended the stairs to find Elliot sitting in the small snug off the dining room, relaxed, smoking tobacco in a china clay pipe.

'How goes it Elliot, any more news on Lambo?'

'Not much news I am afraid Robert. He continues to lead the life of a gay poet about town, meeting up with his avant-garde gay friends and being invited to recitals and music soirees to read poetry and entertain the young nouveaux-rich of society.'

'Where does he go, who does he meet, what does he get up to?' Robert replied somewhat tersely.

He admired Elliot, he was a good Agent, tenacious, and he employed a small group of loyal spies, but Robert thought he reached his own conclusion to an enquiry rather too quickly without reporting the full facts.

'Yes, sorry', replied Elliot somewhat sheepishly.

'He can often be seen leaving his house with a handsome young man, almost a boy, who had been in residence for some time.' They dressed as dandies, Lamborghini sometimes wearing a cerise shirt with great flapping sleeves and wide turquoise linen breeches, imitating the look of a Cavalier, with a pink feathered hat and wearing rouge make up. The boy was often dressed either as a page boy or as a sailor.'

Re-lighting his pipe, he continued,

'they always left by a carriage, usually with the drapes drawn so as not to draw too much attention to themselves.'

Robert intervened 'It seems that since King James's public love affair with Robert Carr, homosexuality has become tolerated in society, provided there is no demonstration of public indecency, even though it is a criminal offence.'

Elliot continued 'Sometimes in an afternoon they would go to the theatre to see an afternoon performance of a

Shakespeare play, but mostly in the evening they went to an

A 17ᵀᴴ CENTURY
MOLLY HOUSE

early form of "Molly House" where like-minded gentlemen, some cross-dressing as ladies, would attend.'

Molly houses were often little more than a large room, lavishly decorated in colourful silk drapes, with "loveseats" for two, chaise-lounges and room for music, dancing, and much drinking. There were private side rooms for couples to retire to, to engage in sexual activities.

'Any more signs of his subversive activity, riots, blowing up Parliamentary statues or buildings?' enquired Robert.

'None at all, in my opinion he is just a young gay radical poet, easily drawn in now and again by the excitement of subversive activists causing mayhem and making a political statement in the name of The King.'

'I think you are probably right Elliot, keep someone on his tail for a few months just in case we are missing something.'

'Aye, I will do that, might I enquire how your trip went?'

'Interesting, remarkably interesting indeed' he said with a smirk, his eyes lighting up.

'What is it Robert, what on earth have you uncovered?'

Leaning forward in his seat, he said

'You recall William Lenthall, the Leader of The House of Commons, who almost accidentally gave Jack, your spy at Lincolns Inn, the name of the "Lawyer'.

'Yes, but why in God's name is he of interest to you?'

Robert moved his chair a little closer.

'I want you to do this personally, but I recognise that you cannot make yourself available for twenty-four hours of the day, so choose only the best, most reliable spies available to you to assist you. You are about to undertake the most confidential, and perhaps the most dangerous, assignment that you have ever performed for me in the name of the King.'

Elliot also leaned forward, listening intently, and in a loud whisper said:

'Don't concern yourself Robert, I will only use Jack, who I have since promoted to the senior role as Head of my spy ring following the death of poor Matthew.'

'That gives me much reassurance. I want Lenthall investigated, followed, but quicker than the Lamborghini assignment, as speed is of the essence. I particularly want to know more of his private life outside of Parliament. You must on no account let yourself or Jack be discovered by Lenthall or his associates. There is a side to him that we know nothing about.'

Robert got up and headed for the door, indicating to Elliot to join him.

'Good, now let us be off to The Angel and down a couple of tankards of the landlord's finest before returning for Jenny's supper, which is smelling divine roasting in the range.'

17

Cannon fire roared and all hell was let loose. It was dawn on a miserable, wet, and misty morning of the 20th of September 1643 after days of heavy rain at Wash Common and Round Hill, south west of Newbury in Berkshire. Parliamentary cannons, under the command of Major-General Phillip Skippon, roared from the top of Round Hill, an ideal defensive location consisting of numerous agricultural enclosures. The Parliamentary Army was under the overall command of the Earl of Essex. Their fire was aimed at Royalist troops, led by King Charles himself, on high ground to the south.

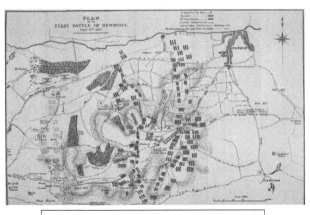

MAP OF THE BATTLE OF NEWBURY 1643

The Royalist responded by launching an all-out attack on Parliamentary troops on the western side of Wash Common. Prince Rupert, with Christophe and Edward leading the Dorset and Kent Royals, made three full charges across the common before clearing the Parliamentary Horse off the high ground, whilst Brigades of Royalist Foot led by Colonel Henry Wentworth and Colonel George Lisle attacked Round Hill.

Sir John Byron with his brigade of Royalist Horse charged Round Hill on its northern flanks but after being initially pushed back, Skippon called upon reinforcements of well-trained reservists from the London brigade, supported by several more cannons. After several assaults in an attempt to take the Hill, the Royalists were forced to abandon their headlong attack.

The fighting around Wash Common and Round Hill continued until around dusk. The men were exhausted from fighting all day on the heavy, sodden ground and the air was thick with smoke and the smell of gunpowder.

At a Royalist council of war that night the younger officers were all for continuing the battle the following day but supplies of black powder and musket-shot were low. King Charles resolved to pull back to Oxford and the battle was not renewed.

The Earl of Essex and his army were allowed to leave Newbury unhindered and to continue their march to London. It seemed to Christophe that Chivalry still prevailed despite the carnage around them.

That evening he assessed the number of casualties of his own Troop. He had led a full complement of sixty Horse into the first charge across the common. Ten lay dead by the end of the third, and another six were recovered wounded from the battlefield.

After rallying the survivors, he immediately went to inspect and give leadership and comfort to the wounded. Three more would succumb to their wounds that night, the others would recover and soon be back in active service, but 13 had now lost their lives just from his troop, and they had gained no ground.

He was about to leave the makeshift hospital tent when he recognised the colours of the Kentish Royals and an officer laying prone on a mud-spattered stretcher in one corner.

It was mayhem, with medics and surgeons hastily tending to the most seriously wounded. Christophe cautiously approached the officer who was barely conscious and bleeding profusely from an open wound on his right leg, despite a tourniquet having been tied tightly to stem the bleeding.

It was Edward. Although only semi-conscious, he was in agony, writhing on the filthy canvas, his loss of blood leaving him a deathly pale.

He had been recovered from the battlefield barely conscious, and the initial prognosis was that he would have to have his right leg amputated as it was severely cut to the bone by a slashing blow from a Parliamentary sword. As it was unlikely that he would survive surgery, and if he did, it would leave him open to infection leading to gangrene, he was not considered a priority.

Without hesitation Christophe sought an audience with Prince Rupert and pleaded the case for him to intervene on behalf of Edward, and the Prince immediately instructed the Surgeon General to act. He personally took over and worked a miracle by operating and saving both Edward's leg and his life. Having survived the surgery against all odds, Edward was taken to Oxford for months of nursing care and rehabilitation. His war in the field was over.

Robert heard in a despatch that Christophe had once again come through the Battle of Newbury with flying colours but was sadly reminded of the terrible price being paid in the war with the news of Edward. He resolved that when next in Oxford he would visit him.

For months now he had been dealing with despatches from his Agents and Spies reporting of plots and subversive actions by Parliamentarian supporters to undermine the King's war efforts. On one such occasion he was able to send word to the garrison at Oxford of a planned attempt to the blow up the huge arsenal of weapons, ammunition, and gunpowder they has stored in barns at Headington on the outskirts of the city.

A small group of Parliamentary partisan forces, operating outside of the Regular Army but under the overall control of Oliver Cromwell, were highly trained in guerrilla tactics. They attacked at dawn one morning under cover of dark rain clouds, only to be met and cut down with a volley of fire from Prince Rupert's infantry.

Not one was allowed to survive, the injured were dispatched by a single pistol shot to the back of their head. Robert's report exposing the plot together with Rupert's, which contained details of the action that night, were filed in the Royalist Army Archives in Oxford marked 'Top Secret'. Cromwell dismissed the disappointing news as just another incursion to weaken the Royalist resolve.

Autumn and Winter came and went as quickly as the scudding clouds on that bright but frosty February morning. The country had enjoyed relative peace since Newbury with news of only minor skirmishes between the opposing armies in the war. It appeared to be at a stalemate, much like Robert's quest. He was aware that each side would be regrouping, recruiting more men, re-arming and training for the next major battle that might, just might, be the turning point in the war, but if only he could solve the mystery of Madrigal, he might be able to stop this bloodshed.

This damn war he said to himself. It was constantly on his mind as he travelled around London dealing with the Matters of State pertaining to his role as the Head of His Majesty's Secret Service. *Husbands, sons, brothers, friends are being slaughtered, women and children are starving with no-one to support them. It has to stop. I have to find a way.*

He continued to miss and long for Marguerite more than ever. They had managed to send Christmas greetings to each other, together with a small gift, by way of secret couriers.

Marguerite wrote a deeply loving and personal letter to Robert, virtually repeating her wedding vows to him.

Chaffeymoor Grange
Bourton

18th December 1643

My darling Robert,

Time seems to stand still here at Chaffeymoor without you. It is Christmastide and I awake longing for you to walk into the bedroom, disrobe, and make love to me. I miss you so much. I rub my sleepy eyes and realise it is all but a dream, a glorious dream.

My thoughts go back to last Christmas, all together celebrating with family and friends from the village. Even Reverend Banks still regales what fun it was. It was wonderful and magical.

Sarah and Paul are fine and send their love. The winter gales blew the roof off the stables but Paul with the help of Hugo has made a good repair. Hugo reckons it will hold for a good few years yet. Blaze has sired a foal to Flame, Hugo's mare. He has named it Firebrand, a wonderful gesture, don't you think?

I do so love you my darling and will forever, until my dying day and beyond in the afterlife. Please God, come back safely to me and in good health. Promise me that when this ghastly war is over and you have completed your quest, that you will come back to me, to live out our days, together, at Chaffeymoor.

Your beloved wife,

Marguerite.

The letter brought tears to Robert's eyes, a thing only Marguerite and Christophe were capable of doing. He missed her gentleness, her touch, her laughter, so much.

Robert had also written to Christophe in Oxford, sending Christmas greetings, wishing him well and good fortune in forthcoming campaigns. He enquired as to Edward's health, and enclosed a finely tooled leather wristband with the simple script "Carpe Diem, Father".

Christophe's reply told him little about the Royalist's preparations for a major battle for security reasons, but it must surely come soon. He told his father that he was well and in good spirits. He had been commended to The King by Prince Rupert for his gallantry at the Battle of Newbury having single handily chased down, engaged, and killed Captain William Willet of The Earl of Essex's Lifeguards.

He also had news about Edward. He had recovered well but he now walked with a distinctive limp and had to have the use of a walking cane. Being back on his feet he had been appointed to an administrative position in Oxford, responsible for the securing and supply of munitions and armaments to the Royalist Troops in the field.

Edward was also in love and engaged to a Miss Bridget Wray, daughter of The Honourable Edward Wray of Oxford, and had asked Christophe to be his best man at his wedding the following year.

It had been a mild Winter in London, such a change not to see the Thames frozen over as it was last year. The weak Winter sun actually felt warm on Robert's back as he took a brisk walk from the safe house over to Hampstead Heath and back for some daily exercise.

Stand up straight, he would say to himself as he walked, *shoulders back chin up, stop slouching,* as Marguerite often told him.

He spent many hours ensconced in the safe house, most days sat at a desk, bent over reports and devising counter measures against perceived threats to the country, writing instructions to his Agents and Spies. That was when he wasn't having clandestine meetings and discussions with prominent loyal members of the Commons and Lords. Even then he was sitting, so a brisk upright walk was an important part of his day when he had the chance.

The Heath as it was known locally, was a sandy swampy area of heathland some three or four miles from the city centre. It ran along a sandy ridge between Highgate in the East and Hampstead in the South-West. In the South-East corner a steep hill gave one of the finest views across London. It was rumoured that Robert Gatesby, the mastermind behind the Gunpowder Plot of the 5th of November 1605, planned to watch the Houses of Parliament blow up and cause the death of King James from the top of this hill.

After returning to the house Robert retired to the Snug to muse over where he had now got to in his investigations into Madrigal. He felt frustrated and somewhat shackled in that his investigations had slowed down considerably. He had eliminated many suspects and circumstantial evidence and perhaps more importantly his own instinct led him to narrow down the probable protagonists. He needed a breakthrough.

It finally came from Elliot after months of investigation into William Lenthall. It appeared that Lenthall too had a vice, not unlike Lamborghini in many ways, but as a red-blooded heterosexual.

18

Sam, a regular companion to Edward since he had recovered from being wounded at Newbury, appeared one day to exclaim 'What's this I hear about you being engaged to be married, you're a dark horse'.

Edward had known Sam since their days at Christ College, his full title being Viscount Samuel Fitzherbert son of the 3rd Earl of Guildford, Surrey.

The town of Guildford, along with most of Surrey, was a strong supporter of the Parliamentary cause, but certain Royalist members of the aristocracy, particularly members of the Lords, were tolerated by them under their freedom of speech legislation, providing it was not considered subversive in nature.

Sam spent his time between Oxford and his father's estate on The North Downs straddling Surrey and Hampshire. Their ancestral home was a large 15th century Manor House on the Petersfield Road, the coaching route to Portsmouth. He lived the life of a gentleman, with a generous family allowance and a house in Turl Street in the centre of Oxford. At Christ Church, he was known for his exceedingly good looks, and flamboyant nature, which he used to his advantage with ladies of all ages, from his "bedder" who cleaned his rooms, to the barmaids at The Bear and even daughters and wives of the local landed gentry.

Edward and Sam's fathers met regularly in the Lords, both advocating the return of the Monarchy, with King Charles on the throne but with a more liberated Parliament. Sam supported Charles but more from the point of leading a hedonistic lifestyle, a lifestyle that would not be tolerated under the puritan Parliamentarians.

At Christ Church, Sam had been closer to Christophe who was easily led astray by him in engaging in the social life of young undergraduates, as opposed to Edward who was more inclined to academic study. Sam knew he would inherit the title of 4th Earl of Guildford by birth right whatever his academic achievements were, whereas Edward was second in line to his older brother Richard so felt under more pressure from his father to prove his worth and standing in the family.

Christophe had no such pressure, he was not of noble birth, his father was in the hierarchy of King Charles's administration and was paid well for his services, but it was his mother's inheritance from wealthy French aristocrats that paid for Chaffeymoor and his education. On more than one occasion Sam had led Christophe on a tour of Inns and Taverns of Oxford ending the night in a house of ill repute.

'I'm in love Sam, with the most wonderful English Rose as you will ever meet,' said Edward.

'Come on then who is she, and how have you managed to keep this a secret?'

'It has all happened rather quickly, a whirlwind romance you might say.'

'My God Edward, who is she, I hope she is not just a gold digger you being the son of an Earl?'

'Of course not you idiot, only you could say such a thing having had all the dalliances and assignations you have had since we have known each other. I can remember when all three of us went to Bicester for a week-end break from College and we had to make a hasty retreat after you came flying back to our lodgings being pursued by the husband of a rather voluptuous lady you had met and bedded earlier in the evening.'

Sam smiled. He remembered the occasion well, and the rather voluptuous lady who had almost suffocated him, burying his face in her very generous breasts.

'Well, I wish you well my friend, I assume Christophe will be your best man' he said as he wandered around his old friend's office, peering at the leather-bound journals that were lined up on huge shelves. He couldn't help but run his finger over a particularly old looking one, only to find it covered in dust.

'He shall indeed Sam, he has already accepted but I will be honoured if you will be my second attendant.'

'The honour is all mine Edward, I shall be delighted, when is the wedding?' he asked, wiping the dust from his finger down his breeches.

'We have set a date for Christmas Eve, 24th December, God willing Christophe comes through any future engagements with Parliamentary forces.'

'Speaking of which where is the hero?'

'He's out on patrol at the moment but he should be back by this evening. We had planned to dine together.'

Edward started packing away his reference books and walked over to the window to see the church clock. It was coming up to 6pm so time for him to leave for the day.

'Then we shall all three dine together, and it's about time we met this young lady of yours. Prey do tell me more about her.'

'Walk back home with me and I will tell you all on the way, and we can have a brandy while we wait for Christophe. Her name is Bridget Wray, she is not high- born Sam, but she is the most caring, kind, and beautiful young lady as you would ever meet. She is a nurse. She nursed me back to health upon returning to Oxford after my surgery on the battlefield of Newbury. Her father is a wealthy merchant, importing fine cloth from France and Italy, so you should have no worries that she is a "gold digger" and with her father's allowance and mine, together with my pay, we shall live quite comfortably here in Oxford.'

They reached Edward's front door and he let them both in.

'Her father, Henry, has graciously accepted my father's offer that the wedding be at Knole House, so it shall be a rather grand affair. Father has invited the principal guests to stay on over Christmas.'

'Oh, marvellous, so who is to be on the guest list then?' asked Sam looking around the front drawing room for the decanter of brandy and some glasses.

'Our respective families, obviously, yourself and Christophe, father would like your parents to attend, and I would like to invite Robert and Marguerite,' said Edward as he gently moved Sam out of the way so that he could get to the drink's cabinet.

'Ah, the beautiful and most elegant Marguerite, she will no doubt turn the heads of many an Earl, let alone their wives.'

'Sam, that is Christophe's mother you are talking about, behave, you are supposed to be a Viscount and a gentleman!'

19

Robert was feeling down hearted, and the war continued unabated with no side seeming to be gaining an advantage over the other. He thanked God that Christophe was such a fine horseman and so capable of handling the heavy long bladed sword of a Cavalier. Of Christophe's original Troop of sixty strong, only half remained alive, the fittest, most capable and some would say the luckiest. The departed had been replaced by new recruits, all fine young horsemen, some as young as seventeen years of ag

Elliot had diligently and meticulously gone about his investigations into William Lenthall over several months. Much of Lenthall's time was devoted to the House of Commons and there was no obvious political connection between him and the few leading Royalist supporters in the House of Lords. However, early on in his investigations, Elliot had reported back to Robert, that in his private life, Lenthall had a penchant for visiting the seedy brothels in Clerkenwell and South Bankside.

It never seemed to amaze Robert that despite plenty of opportunity to engage in promiscuous sexual activity with well-bred ladies of society, men such as he and many of the aristocracy, felt the need to demean themselves by frequenting brothels.

Brothels, of different kinds, had of course been around since time immemorial but had proliferated during the war to satisfy the needs of soldiers of all ranks, all backgrounds, often far away from home for long periods of time, facing death at every battle, every skirmish.

This was different thought Robert. There were two exceedingly high-class establishments that had grown up on the South Bank and were run by the infamous Elizabeth Cresswell and Demaris Page who had accumulated small fortunes at the expense of their respective clientele. In the main, these were the aristocracy and Gentlemen about town who paid highly to satisfy their desires. In such establishments Earls and Lords would greet each other as if they were attending a soiree and it were an everyday occurrence.

Elliot however, had frequently observed Lenthall, taking a carriage to Clerkenwell, dressed down from his normal attire to look more like a merchant so as not to draw attention to himself. There he would enter seedy, squalid, insalubrious establishments where any and every possible sexual practice, some might say deviant, were on offer for extraordinarily little cost to a man of his standing.

MOTHER WARD'S BROTHEL

He more often than not went to Mother Ward's establishment run by Carolanne Ward. Robert had thought that this could have led Lenthall to being open to blackmail, but Elliot could find no evidence of such.

Robert, as when in Cambridge, decided that he had to take a huge gamble and a decisive move if he was to make real progress. He was going to set a trap for Lenthall and blackmail him into revealing his true colours. He needed to brief Elliot on his plan when he saw him that evening.

Elliot arrived home early in mid-afternoon giving them plenty of time to go through all of his evidence on Lenthall before supper.

They ensconced themselves in the front room and Robert led the proceedings.

'Now, remember when we were going through your investigation into Lamborghini, the devil was in the detail, so let's start at the beginning leaving nothing out, nothing to chance, however insignificant you may have thought of it at the time.'

Elliot went meticulously through his investigation and confirmed what he had already reported.

'Did you ever go into any of these establishments yourself and observe whether Lenthall repeatedly asked for any one particular girl.'

'I'm sorry Robert, I could not bring myself to sink so low. Is it important?'

'It could be vital' proclaimed Robert.

'Well, I did ask young Jack to go in on the pretence that he was looking for some company, but I'm not sure that he would have observed whether he asked for a particular girl,' said Elliot looking rather worried as he hadn't asked Jack to find that out.

'Don't concern yourself, it wasn't specifically in your brief, but we need to see Jack with some urgency. Where can we find him at this hour?' Robert got up and headed for the door

'Well, his local tavern is The Tabard Inn in Southwark, and he can usually be found there any time after six in the evening.'

'OK, go and hail a carriage in the High Road and I shall just let Jenny know we shall be back around eight o'clock for supper.'

Southwark was only some three or four miles from the Angel Islington, and they arrived at around five o'clock.

Thankfully, Robert thought, Jack arrived earlier than normal not long after them.

Jack greeted Elliot, 'What brings you here, have I done something wrong?'

'No, of course not. This is Alexander, a friend in our same line of business, that's all you need to know, now let us find us a quiet table in the corner where we can talk in confidence.'

"Alexander" went and got three tankards of ale whilst Elliot sat Jack down and quietly started to ask him about what he observed when he frequented Mother Ward's brothel in Clerkenwell.

Robert joined them, but just observed, as Jack recalled every detail of his experience, his observations, right down to the names of the prostitutes he had come across.

'Ann is the most experienced there' he said, 'legs up to her armpits and does anything you want. Hannah specialises, you know, only does it one way, so their services and charges differ.'

Elliot had trained him well.

'Well done Jack. Now this is extremely important, did you notice if Lenthall had a particular favourite amongst the ladies?'

'Why yes of course, he usually asked Mother Ward for Janny Welcher who practises a speciality of the house as a dominatrix, involving sadomasochism. She's not your usual prostitute like the others.'

'Are you absolutely sure? This is vitally important information, and we need to be certain.'

Jack leant forward, and almost in a whisper confided:

'I heard him ask for her on more than one occasion and saw him go off with her once. She walks around half naked in leather thigh-boots and chains and things, carrying a horse whip, and she's a big lady,' he said, indicating her large bosoms and backside and moving his head in a 'you know what I mean' way.

'I'd be terrified,' he said.

'Good grief exclaimed Elliot, such depravity, and he The Speaker of The House of Commons. Thank you, Jack, you have done great service in the name of The King, we shall drink up and leave you to enjoy the rest of your evening.'

Robert and Elliot returned to the house, exuberant at their discovery about Lenthall and in good time to enjoy Jenny's supper of a steaming game pie with a golden crust. It came straight from the oven and was served with freshly dug potatoes, borage, and a thick game stock.

It looked and smelled delicious.

Robert invited John and Jenny to join them. He was in good heart with Jack's revelations and wanted to spend the evening and share his corking good mood with pleasant and easy company. Sitting back in his chair with a smile on his face, he beckoned to them:

'John, Jenny come join us, and break out the finest wine from the cellar if you please. We are celebrating tonight.'

THE SAFE HOUSE, ANGEL, ISLINGTON

20

The next morning over numerous cups of coffee in the Snug, Robert and Elliot set about plotting how to snare Lenthall into a trap involving Madam Ward and Janny Welcher. The answer was pure and simple, greed. Enough money to persuade both Ward and Welcher to enact Robert's scheme. Robert briefed Elliot as to his scheme.

'Have you any idea what it would cost to put this all together?'

'Well, I suggest that we use an intermediary from London's criminal fraternity who is well versed in such despicable practice.'

'I agree with you, it is not something I would normally condone, but if it brings us success, beggars cannot be choosers! We must avoid any trace of it back to myself or The King at all costs, even if it means eliminating those involved.'

'Leave it with me Robert but let us just be sure what evidence we are seeking.'

'What I want at the end of the day is signed statements from both Carolann Ward and Janny Welcher'.

Robert topped up Elliot's coffee cup for the umpteenth time.

'I want them to state the frequency and nature of Lenthall's visits to Madam Ward's house of ill repute, dates, services they provided, and amounts paid for them by him. The statements must be capable of standing up under scrutiny in a Court of Law but let us hope that Lenthall will not be foolish enough to deny it when we confront him.'

'Clearly understood Robert, but it's going to cost a great deal. I will report back when I have recruited such a criminal, his plan and the cost involved.'

'Very well, how long do you think that will take you?'

'Hopefully no more than a few days, a week at most.'

'OK, draw sufficient money from John that you think you will need to get him interested, with the majority of whatever fee we agree to be paid, on completion of the task.'

It proved to be easier than Elliot thought, he was introduced through a mutual acquaintance to Sean O'Halloran, one of many Irish immigrants who had settled in the Kilburn area of North London. They met at The Clover Leaf, a Tavern on the Kilburn High Road.

He was the head of one of the Irish gangs in North London. Several were involved in pickpocketing and minor theft, others in prostitution or gambling rackets. A few like O'Halloran were into more serious, dangerous crime.

He knew exactly what Elliot was proposing and had obviously set up similar "honey traps" in the past. His fee, take it or leave it, was fifty pounds; ten for Madam Ward, five for Janny, five pounds for a notary to witness their statements, five pounds for miscellaneous expenses, and the balance of twenty-five pounds for himself.

Elliot, knowing that this would be acceptable to Robert, agreed and settled on ten pounds in advance, the rest payable on Robert being completely satisfied with the signed statements.

Robert could hardly contain his delight at the news.

'Let the fox take the bait' he cried.

O'Halloran contacted Elliot a few weeks later with all the evidence on Lenthall in signed statements, duly notarised and delivered. Elliot shook his head in disbelief. *Who said crime did not pay?* he thought. He didn't enquire into his methods and hoped he would never have to engage his services again.

With O'Halloran's agreement, Elliot was allowed to take the documents back to the house for Robert's verification and approval. He had heard what happened to people that crossed the infamous Sean, so there was never any doubt that he would return and pay the man his remaining fee.

That evening Robert pondered over his next step. It had to be played right, discreetly but with purpose, and in an obtuse way, considerate of the position that Lenthall held in politics and society.

A despatch arrived later, there had been a second battle at Newbury. Robert hastily read it; he was concerned for Christophe. It was a mighty battle by all accounts. King Charles led a 9,000 strong army against a combined Parliamentary force of 19,000, including 9,000 Horse.

The Royalists were woefully short of Cavalry. Prince Rupert, with Christophe amongst the 2,000 Cavaliers alongside him, was still away in Bristol moving into Gloucestershire, whilst the Earl of Northampton's Cavalry of 800 strong had been sent to relieve Banbury.

Despite overwhelming odds against them, The King's forces were exemplary and managed to hold the Parliamentarians. News had reached Charles, however, that a reserve force of The New Model Army, commanded by none other than General Oliver Cromwell, was on its way. The King wisely decided to retreat. Robert was thankful that Christophe was not involved and that he lived to see another day. He thought that this really might be the turning point in favour of Fairfax, Essex, Cromwell, and Parliament.

He turned his attention back to Lenthall and Madrigal. His initial admiration for Fairfax, Cecil and probably Lady d'Aubigny had now turned to contempt, as none of them had the courage to come forward with details of Madrigal and put a stop to the war.

He was still determined to see his quest through and present his findings to the King and his closest allies. He would not sleep easy that night. *What if he did not resolve Madrigal by the time of the inevitable Parliamentarian victory? What would happen to Charles?*

He woke up early with determination and resolve. His sleep had been disturbed by a storm overnight that had blown in from the west with violent outbursts of thunder and lightning flashing across the sky and illuminating his room. The strong gales and heavy winds rattled the window shutters and caused some damage to the shops in the street below with debris strewn up and down the street.

Looking out of his window he could see the shopkeepers trying to repair the damage to hanging signs and awnings that had been left overnight and were now torn and hanging down in front of the shop windows. Water poured down the street, washing away the manure into the gutters which led down a slight incline to the local stream, which itself would have been in full flood.

It will smell much better now, thought Robert, *and the sun is poking through the clouds. It is going to be a fine day.*

John had been up during the storm calming the horses down in the stable in the back yard of the house and was still outside trying to stop the water that was flooding the yard from getting into the stable's straw bedding. As fast as he swept the water away it seemed to appear again. Jenny appeared and offered to help.

'Don't get your dress wet' he called to her 'I can manage, and it's giving the yard a good clean. How much damage is there in the rooms?' he called, madly sweeping with the huge broom he used in the stables.

At that moment, Robert also appeared in the yard to check on the damage. 'How bad is it?' he enquired.

'Not too bad at all, just lots of drips. No real damage, but it has come through quite a lot of the windows,' said Jenny, still balancing on a dry stone with her skirts lifted well off the ground.

'I'll see to it once I've got rid of this water' responded John. 'You'd better go and start breakfast, I won't be long,'

Hearing this, Robert called 'don't worry yourself about breakfast for me Jenny. I shall just take a pot of coffee up to my room as I have urgent matters to attend to.'

Robert was anxious to check that his notes and manuscripts hidden in his roof space were safe. He climbed onto a chair and reached within. All was well. There, hidden behind the rafters was what he was looking for, he had wrapped and bound them in an oilskin cloth, and fortunately there was no other water ingress to his room.

He now had to decide, how, where and when he could confront Lenthall. It had to be on a one-to-one basis, not an easy thing to achieve not being a personal friend of his, and Lenthall leading a busy life as The Speaker of the House of Commons. The Commons met on most days, even throughout the War. The Lords was more relaxed, and its atmosphere was often compared to a Gentlemen's club when it did sit. He needed to request a meeting of the utmost urgency, in secret, with a hint of some startling news. Lenthall would of course know of Robert and his relationship with the King. It should be something along the lines of 'to your advantage' and suggest that the meeting takes place on neutral territory, perhaps a private room at The Royal Exchange.

The Royal Exchange was built in the 16th century and was opened by no less than Queen Elizabeth 1. It is what is called a trapezium building, of four sides surrounding an inner quadrangle for merchants and tradesmen to conduct business. The upper colonnade which runs right round the building is where Robert would ask Lenthall to meet him in room number 13, unlucky for him.

First, he had to draft such an invitation. His mind was whirring. He went back to his room and sat at his desk to give some thought as to what he would write. Pulling out some dry parchment paper and a quill pen, he started, and after discarding several attempts, he settled on the following:

The Angel Inn,
Angel Islington

30th October 1644

To William Lenthall
Speaker of The House of Commons

Your most gracious Sir,

We have only been introduced but a few times before this unnecessary conflict between the King and Parliament. I am led to believe that we may have a common goal to end hostilities and achieve a negotiated settlement, with the King restored to his place as our sovereign Monarch but with many concessions to Parliament as to the running of the country for the good of all of its citizens.
I am here with the blessing of King Charles and bear news to your advantage, financially, politically and in recognition of your dedication and achievements on behalf of the people of this glorious country of ours.
I implore you to meet with me urgently, in secret, with only you and I present, no witnesses, no record of our most discreet conversation.
I suggest that I take a private room at The Royal Exchange in the name of Robert Asprey, Merchant in Fine Leather goods to conduct discussions with you on a trade mission to the colonies.
I would be most grateful if you would consent, and I look forward to your communique.

Sir Robert Douse KBE

Robert signed and sealed the letter and handed it to Elliot to deliver in person to The Sergeant at Arms at The House of Commons. Elliot picked up Leander's reply the following day at The Angel and brought it to Robert who immediately broke the seal and read the letter.

'My God Elliot, he has taken the bait! I did not expect an immediate reply. I would like to think that he has done so out of respect for The King, but I suspect that avarice has engulfed his mortal soul. He has agreed to meet me on any given Friday afternoon after The Commons has risen for the weekend.'

Robert was ecstatic, marching around his room waving the reply in the air, unable to believe that a man of such standing would actually rush to agree to such a meeting.

'Let us strike whilst the iron is hot Elliot, can you arrange for a private room at The Royal Exchange in the name of Robert Asprey for next Friday at three o'clock. That will allow the condemned man time for some lunch. I shall draft the invitation to Lenthall immediately. If you hurry you might just catch The Sergeant at Arms before close of business this afternoon.'

'I will do that; do you care for a little celebration at The Angel when I return?'

'There will be time enough for that, let us not count our chickens before they have hatched.'

Robert drafted a simple invitation to Lenthall, signed and sealed it in the name of Robert Asprey and handed it to Elliot who then sped off to The House of Commons.

It is all going too easily, thought Robert, his natural instinct kicking in. He would make sure that Elliot and Jack were armed and in the Exchange building when he met with Lenthall, just in case he double crossed him.

Assuming Lenthall breaks down after presenting him with the evidence of his sordid deeds, and concedes as to his involvement in Madrigal, he needed him to confirm who the other parties involved are, and that Katherine Lady d'Aubigny is indeed one of them.

He would need to confront her with his evidence next. As he sat back in his armchair his head was buzzing with thoughts of how to achieve this. He would leave the final confrontation with Fairfax and Cecil till last. It seemed strange to Robert that it felt as if he was putting together a case of criminality for a leading barrister to argue in court, rather than exposing a conspiracy in the King's favour.

Elliot duly returned and confirmed that he had delivered Robert's invitation to Lenthall and that he had indeed booked a room at The Royal Exchange for the following Friday at three o'clock in the afternoon. It was all going to plan.

His thoughts turned to Lady d'Aubigny and how he could engineer a meeting with her. They left each other previously on the friendliest of terms after taking tea together, *too friendly* thought Robert at the time. He could just ask to visit for a social call, maybe on the pretence that he would be passing her way. He thought that might arouse suspicions on her part, but he also suspected that she rather liked him, perhaps a little too much. As a gentleman he should just ignore her inviting glances, and he was a gentleman, but acting on this suspicion might get him the information he needed.

He did not have to wait long to resolve his dilemma. The answer came the following Friday at his long-awaited confrontation with Lenthall.

21

It was Friday at noon, and the wet and windy weather that was endured during the week had abated. *Time to expose Lenthall* thought Robert, his heart rate racing but he was still calm and collected as to the task ahead. He had the evidence, the testimony of Madam Ward and Janny Welcher as to Lenthall's sordid private life, so unbecoming of a man of his stature in public life and society. Surely nothing could go wrong in getting him to confess his part in Madrigal and the other protagonists involved.

He briefed Elliot, who would in turn brief Jack as to his role.

'Elliot you are to loiter outside of the room I am meeting Lenthall in and only intervene if you hear a scuffle or pistol fire. Jack is to roam the colonnade and be observant as to any suspicious persons who may be in league with Lenthall. I have obtained two more of the experimental Pocket Pistols, one for each of you. I am not expecting trouble, but it is better to be safe than sorry.'

'Now let us have some bread and cheese with pickles before we set off. It is not as if I don't have the stomach for this, but mine is growling with hunger. Best leave the wine for later.'

After they were replete, Elliot left to pick up and brief Jack. He had arranged to meet Robert at The Exchange at around two o'clock to reconnoitre the building and check out room 13.

Robert decided it would be better to confront Lenthall almost immediately after they had met and exchanged greetings. He wanted to put him on the defensive from the word go; there was no point in beating around the bush. He relied on the element of surprise to break Lenthall's spirit and force a confession from him without him even trying to deny any of it. He arranged a small table with seating for two and sat himself down so that Lenthall would have his back to the door of the room.

Lenthall duly arrived promptly at three o'clock and to all intents and purposes he was alone. He knocked and entered the room.

'Robert, this is a surprise, the last time we met all was well with the world and if I remember, we enjoyed a garden party at The Palace of White Hall.'

'Sit down William, I am here at the King's bidding so I will not waste any time with any pleasantries. I am aware, as is Charles, that despite your admonishment of him in the Commons when he tried to arrest those five traitors, you have on occasion spoken up for him and expressed a desire for a peaceful settlement to the war.'

Lenthall duly sat in the chair indicated and responded.

'One must be circumspect in stating such views now that Cromwell has risen to be the heir apparent to the Parliamentary cause Robert.'

'Yes, but I understand that just prior to the War and since, Fairfax, yourself and certain leading Royalists are party to a plan named Madrigal to engage with Charles and his advisors to obtain a peaceful settlement. Charles is to remain our Monarch and Parliament is to be granted a great deal more power to act on behalf of all its citizens.'

'Such talk now is, of course treason Robert; I am sorry you have wasted your time in requesting to see me.' William rose from his chair and turned to leave.

'Hold fast, William I have something here that may just change your mind.'

Robert proceeded to lay before Lenthall the sworn statements of Madam Ward and Janny Welcher. Still standing, Lenthall started to read the statements. There was an unearthly silence in the room as he read the statement from Madam Ward. He faltered and sat back down and upon reaching the page of Janny's account of their meetings, he started quivering, chewing his lower lip, his eyes welling up with tears. Once the first tear broke free the rest followed in an unbroken stream. He bent forward where he sat, placed his palms on the table and began to cry with the force of a person vomiting on all fours.

Robert produced a flask of brandy from inside his coat and offered it to him. He knew that he had his man but felt a small degree of sympathy for him. He never expected such a reaction. Lenthall took several swigs of the brandy and began to compose himself.

'Robert, I beg of you, please do not expose me, I am not a bad man I have just given into the temptation of the flesh. It is the pressure living a lie, a lie in Parliament and a lie at home. My true allegiance has always been with the King but circumstance, let alone my standing in society, has taken me down an altogether different way in life. I have never loved my wife Elizabeth. It was an arranged marriage, and I had no say in the matter, something I bitterly regret not least for the fact that she has denied me my conjugal rights for many years.'

'Pull yourself together man, I want to know all about Madrigal and who is involved, not your pathetic excuses.'

Lenthall proceeded to confirm what Robert suspected, that it was the brainchild of Thomas Fairfax and William Cecil.

'Where does Lady d'Aubigny fit in?' demanded Robert.

'Katherine is a long-time friend of Cecil. She used his influence as the Earl of Salisbury to her advantage in Court circles, a modern female "Don Juan", and snared me like a widow spider in her web. I have had a long passionate, fiery, and volatile affair with her on and off over many years. It was she who introduced me to bondage, a forerunner to more aggressive forms of sadomasochism.' Wiping his eyes with a huge linen handkerchief, he continued:

'She introduced me to Cecil at one of his many house parties and he persuaded me to be part of Madrigal. I suppose he wanted at least one other leading Parliamentarian to add weight to the cause. I did not need a lot of persuasion, I was smitten with Katherine and always believed that a negotiated settlement was the only way to achieve true peace in our country.'

'Come on William, there must be more people involved for it to carry weight with Charles and Parliament.'

'I'm sorry Robert, all I know is that after I put my signature to it, one other leading Parliamentarian who had changed sides from being a Royalist and a friend of Charles some years ago, has also joined forces with Fairfax and Cecil.'

'So that makes five of you?'

'No, only four signatories to Madrigal, Katherine knows about it and is a supporter of it, but she was considered to be a bit of a loose cannon with her chequered past, by Fairfax in particular.'

'Ok William, you now have a chance to redeem yourself, even become a hero if I succeed in my quest. I am going to introduce you to a colleague of mine, Elliot, who will sit down with you whilst you write down all that you have told me, for you to then sign it and for him also to sign as a witness to your statement.'

Robert rose from his chair and putting both hands on the table, leant forwards towards Lenthall, a beaten man still snivelling into his large kerchief. 'You shall not hear from me again, or from King Charles until I am successful in exposing

Madrigal and he is restored to the Monarchy. Go back to Parliament, speak in the King's favour, and seek God's forgiveness.'

'Thank you Robert, it feels as if I have made a true confession before God, which I shall do in due course'.

Robert beckoned Elliot into the room, smiled at him, and briefed him to take down Lenthall's statement. He left them to it and took a carriage back to the safe house. Smiling to himself on the way back, he now felt a real sense of urgency with adrenalin coursing through his veins and he was on a high.

The sun had just broken through, an omen he thought. He felt euphoric whenever he felt victory was in his grasp, and he wondered if maybe that was how some of his forebears felt when relaxing in the opium dens of the Far East. It was just as addictive. Reality soon kicked in, he still had to put the final pieces of Madrigal together. He now knew it had four protagonists: Thomas Fairfax, William Cecil, William Lenthall and one other. He still did not know its true meaning or why it may have prevented the war. It seemed true that it was supported by some of the most influential persons of both political persuasions, but was that enough?

He sat at his desk and proceeded to update his records of his long search for those involved, the evidence he had gathered, suspects he had investigated and eliminated and in particular the mounting case against Fairfax, Cecil, and Lenthall. He listed down what the key questions that he needed to ask William Cecil.

Confirmation of the three protagonists of Madrigal that he had discovered.

Who is the fourth member and why is he or she so relevant?

What does the Madrigal actually mean, what does it say, is there a written testimony signed by all four?

*Why were some Parliamentarian supporters so desperate,
even prepared to murder, to prevent it being revealed?*
*Why was it not revealed by the "four" protagonists prior to
The Civil War?*
Why has it not been revealed by any of them since?
If there is a signed testimony, where is it kept?

Once again, he wrapped up his parchments and put them
back in their hiding place. No one, not even Elliot his most
loyal Agent who had been at his side since residing in London, knew of their existence let alone Robert's hiding place.
Elliot of course, knew much of Robert's quest, after all he had
done his bidding many a time, sometimes in the most dangerous circumstances.

Robert was close, so close. It had seemed like a lifetime,
not just three tortuous years with twist and turns in every direction. There had been hope and despair, success and failure, murder and mayhem and exposure to all life's rich tapestry. It was time to confront Fairfax and Cecil together.

*How on earth was he to manage that with Fairfax, along-
side Essex, still leading the Parliamentarian war effort?* he
asked himself.

The answer to that question was a long time coming, the
Winter came and went. At the end of April, with the country
enjoying an early Spring after yet another harsh Winter, The
King decided to send his eldest son and heir, Prince Charles,
to the West Country where he continued to enjoy support
from loyal Royalist supporters. From there the teenage Prince
was taken onboard a small sailing ship to sail to Cherbourg in
France. The King said farewell to him with a heavy heart, as
if he had a premonition as to his own future.

"I do not do this lightly Charles; go join your mother in
France where you shall be safe' he said lamentably.

'God willing, I shall send for you both when this cursed
war is over. Hold your head up high Charles for one day you
too shall be the King of England.'

Robert's question to himself was not to be answered readily. He kept himself busy dealing with other matters of state before finally deciding that he must first go and see William Cecil again at Hatfield House. Their last meeting had been most convivial, William being an old friend of The King.

He sent a message by courier to William requesting an audience with him as soon as possible to discuss an urgent matter. William had a fairly good idea what Robert wished to discuss with him and invited him to come and stay at Hatfield over the course of the following weekend when there would be no other house guests present.

HATFIELD HOUSE

Having informed John and Jenny that he would be away for a few days, returning the following Sunday, Robert set off for Hatfield early on Friday, 14th of June. He knew the journey well, but somehow this time it felt different. There was an uncanny silence, no sign anywhere of troops of either Royalists or Parliamentarians.

The weather was fine, but it felt like the calm before the storm. There was hardly a bird to be seen in the sky. Robert felt uneasy but dismissed the idea as nothing more than the feeling a sailor must have when his ship was becalmed at sea in the doldrums.

William, on hearing Keagan trotting up the gravel drive came out of the magnificent main entrance doorway to greet him.

'Good afternoon Robert, welcome back to Hatfield.'

'Good afternoon to you too William, I trust that you are in good health.'

'I have nothing to complain about for a man of my age, the odd gout from drinking too much red wine', replied William with laughter in his voice.

Robert smiled and replied, 'We can all be accused of that from time to time.' William seemed in good spirits, relaxed, welcoming Robert as if they were life-long friends.

Robert pondered to himself, *is this the man that is about to unburden his soul, relieved perhaps that I am about to take up the mantle and reveal the nature of Madrigal to the world? Will it make both sides in this unnecessary and evil Civil War see sense and change the country's political spectrum for ever, for the better, and create a true democracy?*

They entered the Mansion and William beckoned one of the Housemen to carry his saddlebags and show Robert to his room.

'I will let you settle in. Make the house and garden your own, if you get lost just summon one of the staff', William said laughing out loud. 'Dinner at eight o'clock, drinks in the small drawing room at seven.'

It was now mid-summer in 1645. The poet John Milton had just published his latest works:

Songs on a May Morning

The flowering May who from her green lap throws
The Yellow cow parsley and the pale primrose
Hail bounteous May, that dost inspire
Mirth and youth and warm desire
Woods and groves are of thy dressing
Hill and dale does boast thy blessing
Thus we salute thee with our early song
And welcome thee, and wish thee along

22

Robert retired to his room to relax; it had been a long journey on another glorious summer's day. His beautiful and ornately decorated room overlooked the rear gardens of the house and the estate beyond. The drapes had been drawn to keep out the blazing sun and Robert drew them wide and opened all the windows to create a welcoming breeze through the room. The air was warm, and it was a cloudless azure blue sky.

After resting and the having a cold body wash to refresh himself, he decided to take a stroll in the grounds to gather his thoughts.

They were a wonderful mix of formality and wilderness. There were places deep within the lower wood that still retained the essence of an ancient woodland. Here Robert felt a sense of remoteness, a feeling that one might just be the first person ever to stand on that a particular spot. There were tall ancient oak, lime and beech trees. The bluebells were over, but the floor of the forest was covered with wildflowers of all descriptions and colour.

He thought that to linger here is to be transported back through time, the years just fell away and with them any cares and worries of present times. *If only*, he thought.

He made his way back through the more formal gardens to the house, where parterres of box hedging were of intricate designs and divided by the occasional old English dog rose climbing an archway.

Robert changed into more formal attire and met William in the small drawing room for drinks before dinner.

William, splendidly attired and dressed for dinner welcomed him 'I know why you are here Robert; you want to know all about Madrigal, don't you?'

Robert, slightly embarrassed that his more formal wear consisted only of a clean white shirt and a change of breeches replied 'I do William, there are probably more questions than you may be able to answer. I only wish that you could have taken me into your confidence when we last met.'

'I am so sorry Robert, you are aware that two of my sons, Charles and James, took up The Parliamentary cause and are fighting alongside Essex in the Civil War.'

William wandered over to the drinks cabinet and poured them both a glass of champagne.

'I am old and no longer care what retribution I might suffer upon exposing Madrigal, but then I feared for my sons' lives, their hereditary title, Hatfield House and all of its history. My estate in Cranborne, in Dorset, has already been ransacked and taken over by Parliamentarians as have many others belonging to my fellow Lords.'

'Why now William? The War is, by any other name, over, with the remnants of the King's army in flight.'

'I will tell you all I know Robert, but let us first just enjoy the moment, drink and dine well tonight and convene in my study after breakfast in the morning.'

They walked along the cloisters overlooking the courtyard and entered the Grand hall for dinner. Robert thought they looked lost sitting at one end of the enormous French elm dining table that stood on the black and white marble

chequered floor. Oak panelled walls hung with huge paintings, including one of Queen Elizabeth 1ˢᵗ who had spent her childhood and teenage years living here, looked down on them. The hearth of the enormous fireplace, unlit at this time of year, was decorated with a magnificent display of roses and flowers from the gardens, adding to the opulence of the vast room and filling it with a heady perfume.

They did indeed dine well with no expense spared by William. The centre piece of the main course was a saddle of venison butchered from a deer culled on the Estate, with vegetables and herbs from the kitchen garden and served with the finest French wines.

After dinner coffee was served at the dining table with the most exquisite small chocolates and pastries, now considered the height of dining elegance in capital cities all over Europe having first been created in Paris.

William then beckoned Robert to join him in the Billiard Room for a game of billiards together with a brandy and smoke of a pipe of tobacco.

The evening passed convivially with William and Robert regaling past times when England was at peace with itself and life seemed so much simpler. The puritans, the poor and the underclass of society would vehemently disagree with them, a driving force for civil war.

And so to bed. Robert could not help but think that perhaps William was indeed to become one of the last of the ruling classes. His loyalty was however to King Charles and he felt a divine duty to expose and reveal the hidden secrets of Madrigal.

He rose early. The sun was not long above the horizon and he was woken by the dawn chorus. He washed, dressed, and prepared himself for the morning ahead and assembled all the evidence he had accumulated, some circumstantial, but some, like Lenthall's statement, being an irrefutable fact.

He had already decided on the questions he needed to put to William and thought *please God William has the answers.*

William was already halfway through his breakfast when Robert arrived in the morning room.

'Good morning Robert, sit yourself down and enjoy the best bacon this side of Melton Mowbray. It is from pigs reared on the estate. The bacon is cured over oak chippings and we also have freshly laid Russet Brown hens eggs. There is a basket of fresh fruits, warm bread straight from the range and plenty of hot strong coffee.'

'Thank you William, I sense I may be needing that strong coffee with the task ahead. Thank you also for such a splendid dinner last night and your most genial and good-humoured company.'

They both continued to eat a hearty breakfast.

'The most important meal of the day' proffered William, 'shall we say ten o'clock in my study'?

They reconvened at ten o'clock and settled down comfortably in William's study in a pair of Renaissance style Italian walnut armchairs, upholstered in rich red velvet with the Earl's family crest on the facing back.

They were so William, so comfortable thought Robert, *what a wonderful life he had led here at Hatfield, in such opulence but willing to share it on many occasions with so many other creative talents from the arts and music society scene.*

There was a matching walnut desk with a deeply panelled freeze, geometric fruit wood inlay and three drawers. It had turned legs that were supported by shaped side stretchers and wrought iron crossovers. It was stunning. The room was adorned with heavy silk drapes and carpets in the Renaissance style with some less formal family portraits that were dear to William.

Robert, despite feeling a warmth towards William and considering him to be a lifelong loyal friend and servant of

King Charles, had a clear objective to achieve and thus commenced to question him methodically, diligently, and directly.

The first question was:

Who were the protagonists of Madrigal?

William answered without hesitation.

'It was originally conceived by Thomas Fairfax and myself. I subsequently asked William Lenthall to join us, having been introduced to him by Katherine Lady d'Aubigny, but of course I had met him on several occasions at the Houses of Parliament as he is The Speaker in The Commons, and I a member of The Lords. I considered him to have influence in The Commons and thought he would prove to be a good advocate for Madrigal.'

Robert then asked:

'Lenthall told me there is a fourth member. Who is he William and why is he so important?'

'It is Phillip Herbert, the 4th Earl of Pembroke Robert' replied William.

'The Earl of Pembroke!' exclaimed Robert, 'now that is a surprise.

'I thought he had a major falling out with Charles over a clash of religious beliefs, and Charles sacked him from his position of Lord Chamberlain, Duchy of Cornwall under pressure from Queen Henrietta, a staunch catholic.'

'That's right. Up until then he had been a great advocate of Charles, held many high positions of State and along with me, became close friends of the King. For some reason, he then took up the Puritans cause, joined the Parliamentarians and was coerced into going to war over his beliefs. As such, he was not party to the original conception of Madrigal, that was purely Fairfax and myself.'

William rose from his chair and wandered across to the open window. He leant on the stone windowsill and looked out across the parterre. Three of his gardeners were busy clipping the endless dwarf hedges of Box that formed the intricate patterns.

What a peaceful occupation he thought, then turned to Robert and said;

'Philip continued to support the Parliamentarians but was always one of the most moderate in his views and speeches in The Lords. However, he also believed that Charles was crucial to any settlement of hostilities between King and Parliament and was always present at any negotiations between them.'

Returning to his chair and lowering himself slowly into the seat, William continued.

'Fairfax started to believe more and more that Herbert could have a major influence on the success or otherwise of getting the acceptance of Madrigal by both the King and the staunch Parliamentarians. I eventually invited Phillip up to Hatfield from his estate at Wilton House near Salisbury in Wiltshire to discuss the matter. It seemed to him by then that there was never going to be lasting peace whatever side won the raging conflict.

He agreed that the answer could only ever be a negotiated settlement and to that end was easily persuaded to put his name to Madrigal.'

Robert was still reeling from the revelation that Phillip Herbert of all people, was the 4th signatory, but continued with his questions.

'What form does Madrigal take William; it must be more than just a belief?'

'It is Robert, much, much more than that. It takes the form of a sworn statement signed by all four of us. There are two copies, Fairfax has one and I have the other which I shall now give to you.'

William went over to his desk, withdrew a key from his waistcoat pocket and proceeded to open bottom drawer. He

hesitated before taking out a scroll of vellum tied with a red ribbon.

Holding it close to his chest as though it were a precious piece of glass that could shatter, he gingerly crossed the room. He then proceeded to hand his copy to Robert to read. It was written in script on the highest quality vellum so that it could be retained in posterity on behalf of the nation.

Robert could barely believe it. Here in his hands was the answer to a quest that had dogged him for the past 6 years. It had consumed him, disrupted family ties, questioned loyalties, cost lives, and haunted his very soul. He proceeded to read the scroll conscientiously, to finally discover what this closely guarded secret of Madrigal was about. It all made sense to him at last, not quite like finding the holy grail, but a similar sense of awe and wonderment.

It became immediately clear as to why some of the more radical Parliamentarians, having knowledge that there was such a plot, were prepared to do anything, even murder, to prevent Madrigal becoming public, let alone be presented to The King.

It was those very Parliamentarians that engaged John Marchal, a Parliamentarian Spy, in his failed attempt to assassinate Robert after he set forth from York on the fateful day back in June some three years since, when Charles decided that war was inevitable.

It was they who had also had poor young Makepiece murdered when he was getting close to finding out who "The Lawyer" was, something that might have led Robert to discovering Lenthall's part sooner.

The Madrigal statement read as follows:

To His Majesty King Charles 1, Honourable Members of Parliament and the Earls of The House of Lords

Madrigal
A Closely Guarded Secret

We the undersigned have always believed that the only way to achieve lasting peace, prosperity and democracy for our glorious country was through a negotiated settlement between King and Parliament.

On the 1st of June 1642, the English Houses of Lords and Commons approved a list of proposals known as The Nineteen Propositions and sent them to your Majesty for your consideration.

These demands of Parliament sought a larger share of power in the governance of the Kingdom. Amongst these powers were that Parliament shall have control over Foreign Policy and retain responsibility for the militia. It further advocated that the King's Ministers be made accountable to Parliament.

We believe that you Sir, our most sovereign leader, and King, are willing to make some concessions but are not prepared to accept all nineteen principles en masse.

We four, respected leaders of both Royalist and Parliamentary causes, have negotiated and sought God's divine help in agreeing the most important seven of the nineteen principles.

The King and his successors shall remain as our sovereign head of state as its Constitutional Monarch.

Parliament will supervise, in consultation with the King, all Home and Foreign Policy.

Parliament shall be responsible for the Defence of the realm and have the ability to raise armies.

The King's Ministers are to be answerable to Parliament; any new Peers may not to be appointed to The House of Lords without the approval of The King and The Commons.

Matters concerning the public, including the raising of taxes, must be debated, and decided upon by Parliament.

The education of the King's children shall be at his discretion as shall be their chosen hand in marriage.

The King will publicly pardon the "Five Members" he deemed as traitors and He shall also be granted a pardon by Parliament.

All other of the nineteen principles shall be set aside for further debate, most notably the Governance of The Church and that any citizen shall be able to continue to pursue their own religious beliefs without persecution.

We beseech thee to accept the above and commend them to the King and to both Houses for their approval.

Signed below and witnessed by God and each other, your most deferential servants:

Fairfax,   Lord General Sir Thomas

William Cecil,   3rd Earl of Salisbury

William Herbert,   6th Earl of Pembroke

William Leander,   Speaker of The House of Commons

Robert was almost lost for words.

'William, if this is accepted by all, it will form the basis of a whole new democracy for the country. What are its chances?'

'More difficult in present circumstances Robert, with minds entrenched in the machinations of the Civil War, but if we can overcome those irrational thoughts, and all the grief and suffering on both sides, I believe it is possible. Fairfax has had several clandestine encouraging talks with other more moderate Parliamentarians, politicians, and army officers alike. Phillip and myself have consulted with members of the Privy Council and The Lords. Lenthall, whist having to appear to be impartial as The Speaker in The Commons, has privately sounded out the moderates of the House. A major stumbling block may be some of the rising stars of the Puritans and in particular Colonel Oliver Cromwell.'

Robert sat back in his chair, trying to take it all in.

'You have pretty well answered all of my remaining questions, but prey tell me, why was Madrigal not revealed prior to the War?'

William rose from his chair again and wandered around the room, torn by guilt, the need to protect his family but with his conscience telling him he should have acted sooner. With a calming sense of solace, he continued:

'Fairfax and I alone had conceived the idea and thrashed out most of the document, but he, quite rightly, was fearful that it did not carry enough weight of support and would just be dismissed by Charles as he had done with all previous demands of Parliament.'

'And since?' questioned Robert.

'It is true that we now have a more compelling case and the additional support of Pembroke and Lenthall, but it was too late to stop the War.'

'I will guard this document with my life William and will judge the best time and circumstances as to when to submit it to the King and for Fairfax to make his copy public in a statement to The House of Commons.'

'Then let us partake in a sherry and drink to its success', replied William relieved that the mantle was being taken up by a younger man and the responsibility no longer rested on his shoulders.

The timing could not have been worse. A thundering of horses' hooves could be heard getting closer and closer to the house galloping up the long gravel drive.

'Why it's Charles, my son' cried William, with trepidation in his voice.

William and Robert rushed to greet Charles as he leapt, almost fell, off of his faithful steed, looking bedraggled, his tunic in tatters and covered in blood stains.

'It's all but over father, we completely routed the King's army at Naseby late yesterday afternoon, they are decimated, and I cannot see them able to continue the war. I've heard seven thousand souls were either slaughtered or wounded and captured father, and for what? The vast majority were Royalists. They didn't stand a chance. The King has fled along with the remnants of Prince Rupert's cavalry.'

'What about your brother James?' William cried.

'I'm so, so sorry father, James died a hero on the battlefield, they have recovered his body and he shall be brought back to Hatfield for all of us give him a private burial and to mourn him.'

Robert turned to William and put his arms around him in a consoling bear hug saying,

'I am so, so sorry William for your loss, let us hope that the War is truly over and that the King now sees sense in a negotiated truce.'

Tears were flowing down William's ruddy cheeks.

'It is over to you and Fairfax now Robert.'

At that moment Robert could only think of one thing, Christophe.

'Charles I am so sorry to ask this of you at your time of loss, but did you see anything of The Dorset Royals?'

'They were in the first charge Robert and as far as I could tell, seeing their regimental flag still flying, fought gallantly till the end but I have to say, few were still upright on their horse by the time it was all over.'

Robert was crestfallen, he had come so far. Christophe cannot be dead; he must not be dead he thought.

How on earth could I convey such a message to my darling wife Marguerite, that her only child, our son, was never to return to be in her arms again at Chaffeymoor.

He too was nearly in tears, but hoped and prayed for better news, and that somehow Christophe had survived and was in flight with Prince Rupert and the King.

23

Robert was in shock; it was all he could do to think straight. The war appeared to be over with the King in flight. God only knows what had happened to Christophe.

He now had only one thing on his mind, he must return to Chaffeymoor as fast as Keagan would carry him. He needed to be with Marguerite. *My darling Marguerite I have left you alone in my quest to solve Madrigal for far too long,* he thought.

'William, it may seem that I am leaving with undue haste given the sad news of James, but I am sure you will understand that I have to be with Marguerite in her hour of need.'

'Of course dear boy, I wish you well and will pray that Christophe returns to you both in good health. What will you do with the Madrigal agreement?'

'I shall take it with me to Chaffeymoor, to hide it in a place known only to Christophe and myself. I suspect that the country will be in relief rather than turmoil and my journey uneventful.'

'My dear friend, if we do not meet again, I thank you most graciously for pursuing your quest to find the truth about Madrigal, its existence and what it could mean for the future of our country.'

Robert hastily packed his saddlebags as the stable lad saddled up Keagan. Whilst doing so William had the kitchen staff prepare a food hamper to keep Robert and Keagan going on his journey.

'Farewell William, I cannot thank you enough for your irrepressible dedication to the King and for taking such risks alongside Thomas Fairfax. I only hope we are not too late for it to have a major bearing on the future of our country. I am so, so, sorry about James.'

'Thank you. James suffered all his life from a progressive terminal illness, and his last wish was to be able to fight for the rights of the common man, so he achieved his goal. God speed Robert, send a courier with the news when you hear about Christophe.'

Robert set off with some trepidation on the journey going the quickest way that he knew but it was still over one hundred and twenty miles long. It would take him 3 days going south through Chalfont St Giles across Windsor Great Park and then south-west through Spencers Wood and across Mortimer Down. Riding onwards to Pamber Heath he headed south to join up with The Great West Road at Basingstoke.

He would not seek overnight lodgings but find some leafy glade where he could rest Keagan for a few hours. He would take nourishment himself from the food parcel given to him by the kitchen staff at Hatfield House. By his calculations he aimed to be at Chaffeymoor by late afternoon, the day after tomorrow.

He rode at a good canter so as not to tire Keagan out too easily. Crossing Windsor Great Park under a full moon between midnight and dawn he found a discreet hidden glade with a small rivulet of water for Keagan to drink. He also gave her some carrots and beets included in his food parcel.

He was grateful for the rest but anxious to get home before Marguerite heard any news of the Battle of Naseby. He ate some bread and cheese and drank some wine with water, but he was not in the mood for food it was more a case of sustenance for the long journey ahead.

Dawn arrived after two hours rest that seemed like eternity. Robert saddled up Keagan and continued his journey south-west to join the Great West Road and then onwards to Cocksford Down for a second night under the stars.

In the morning he felt on safer ground, more like home territory. He met several stragglers on horseback, mainly Royalists, returning from Naseby in Northamptonshire, no doubt anxious to get back home to their loved ones. He enquired of one or two if they knew or had heard anything about the Dorset Royals but to no avail.

This made Robert even more determined to get home. He stepped up the pace with Keagan and, as if she knew what was afoot, she responded to his demands.

Mere came into view by late-afternoon, no time to stop at The George for a tankard of ale this time. He turned off and up the narrow lanes to Bourton and home. The village was silent as if it were in mourning. *Not a good sign* thought Robert.

Chaffeymoor Grange came in to view and he galloped through the grounds up to the house, leaping off Keagan as she came to a halt.

The heavy oak door opened and there stood Marguerite with tears streaming down both cheeks.

'Robert', she cried 'I thought you would never get here.' In an instance he knew that she had heard the news about Naseby, and he feared the worst.

He grasped Marguerite to his chest and murmured in her ear 'I am so sorry my love, I came as soon as I could, direct from Hatfield House.'

He then kissed her gently, but he too was in tears.

'Have you heard anything about Christophe?' she pleaded, just about managing to get the words out as her chest heaved in between crying.

'Let us get into the house, my darling one' replied Robert as he led Marguerite by the hand.

Sarah and Paul were in the drawing room, they had been comforting Marguerite ever since the news of The Battle of Naseby had reached the village.

'It's bad isn't it Robert, we have heard The Royalists were overrun and the casualties are exceedingly high. There is even talk that the King fled for his life from the battlefield along with Prince Rupert,' said Paul.

Marguerite, although being comforted by her cousin Sarah, was still distraught and crying her heart out, but listened intently.

'I am afraid so; we must just hope and pray that somehow Christophe has survived. It will be sometime before the official casualty list of officers is posted at the garrison in Oxford, but in the meantime, I shall send a courier there to Edward to see if he can find anything out.'

The days turned into weeks. Robert and Marguerite had to come to terms with the fact that they may never see their beautiful son again. His handsome good looks, blue eyes, and that cheeky smile of his that permeated love to everyone that he loved and befriended.

Marguerite had gone from being distraught to becoming withdrawn; it was if she was already in mourning despite Robert trying to remain positive.

They had heard back from Edward; Christophe was not on the list of fallen officers. He was last seen leading the final charge of The Dorset Royals, tunic slashed and bleeding profusely. He was never to be seen again.

Unknown to them, Edward refused to accept the demise of his best friend until he was able to find and return his body to Robert and Marguerite at Chaffeymoor. He reasoned to himself that Christophe was the best cavalry officer he had ever seen, and that he had tempered his earlier "devil may care" impetuous nature and honed his fighting skills to the highest degree. He was a champion, a hero, if anyone could survive the heat of the battle, Christophe could.

He said goodbye to his fiancée Bridget and set off for Naseby.

Upon arrival, some ten days after the battle there was still carnage strewn all over the battlefield. There were cannon

balls, muskets, bullets, pikes, lances and cavalry swords along with the flies, thousands of flies, laying their eggs on what was left of rotting limbs of soldiers and carcasses of dead horses.

Surviving casualties had been withdrawn to God knows where and the dead buried in mass graves in the adjoining fields. Dead officers on both sides had been retrieved, the Royalists ones initially taken to Oxford and then returned in coffins to their loved ones.

No such thing had happened to Christophe, neither had he turned up at Oxford or Chaffeymoor. He was listed as missing in action.

Edward's first port of call was to visit the local vicar at All Saints Church in Naseby. The Reverend David Canten informed him that all the non-commissioned casualties were being treated in makeshift field hospitals nearby, but the Royalist Officers had been taken to the County Infirmary at Northampton.

Edward thanked him profusely and headed off to Northampton with some haste. It had been a long exhaustive day, but he could not rest until he knew whether Christophe was alive or dead.

THE COUNTY INFIRMARY, NORTHAMPTON

He found the Infirmary, but it was bedlam. He was taken aback by the hive of industry amongst the nursing staff, field medical staff, infirmary doctors and surgeons. How could both armies have had so many officers at one battle, he thought to himself not thinking that the Battle of Naseby consisted of an amalgam of battalions and companies from all over the country.

The wards were full, and the injured and dying were lying on makeshift beds and stretchers in the corridors. He found a nurse, Sister Judy D'Arcy, and asked of Christophe Douse, Captain of the Dorset Royals.

'You will have to check the admissions list in the office down the corridor' she replied.

Edward ran down the corridor which had a stench of infected wounds and death. He approached the office apprehensively, not knowing even if Christophe was there. Staff Captain Richard D'Arcy was on duty.

'I am Captain Edward Sackville, retired', he said nervously, Edward retaining his rank he held when he was discharged to take up his current administrative job.

'How can I help you Captain?'

'I am looking for Captain Christophe Douse of The Dorset Royals.'

Captain D'Arcy did not need to check his records. 'Yes, we have him, but he is unlikely to survive the night.'

Edward was crestfallen, *no not Christophe* he reasoned to himself as if his dear friend were indestructible.

'What injuries?' asked Edward.

'It was a miracle he survived the battle. He arrived here with an open wound to his chest, spilling copious amounts of blood and with a kerchief embroidered "Chaffeymoor" stuffed in his tunic to stem the blood flow. We have kept the kerchief. The wound was from a slashing sword, no doubt from a Parliamentarian cavalryman. Witnesses tell us that he continued to fight on despite being badly wounded, even taking the flag off a Parliamentary horse after he downed their Captain on the final charge.'

Captain D'Arcy stood up and directed Edward back towards the wards.

'We have done what we can, he is as comfortable as he can be, but he has lost a lot of blood. The surgeon has sewn him up, he has a fever but on the plus side there is no infection. The next twelve hours are critical, and we just have to hope the fever breaks. There is nothing more we can do at this stage, so may I suggest you come back in the morning.'

Edward would never leave Christophe in his hour of need. 'Where is he, can I see him?' he enquired.

'Of course, he is in Ward 3, down this corridor on the left-hand side.'

Edward thanked him and made his way to the ward and entered. It was now dusk with night-time beckoning, and despite candles having been lit it was hard to distinguish one casualty from another. He made his way down the ward, the beds so close to each other the nurses could hardly get between them. There were all manner of wounds that man could inflict on one another and the smell was putrid. It was all he could do to not vomit. Holding his own scented kerchief to his nose he passed one-time fine fit young men with arms and legs missing, seeping wounds from gunshot, stabs, and slashings, some having had limbs amputated to stop the spread of gangrene from infected wounds.

At the far end of the ward, thankfully next to an open window to let in the cooling fresh air, he spotted what appeared to be Christophe. 'Yes, yes' Edward mumbled to himself choking back tears.

Christophe was semi-conscious. He had been given a draught of laudanum; opium prepared in an alcoholic solution as a painkiller. He had been dressed in a clean white shirt, but blood was still oozing from his sewn-up wound. He looked at peace with the world.

Edward grabbed one of the few chairs in the ward and sat by Christophe's bed. He would stay there all night and into the next if need be, until he knew that he had survived or had passed away.

He spent a fraught and anxious night, afraid to drift off to sleep despite his weariness in case Christophe woke up and needed the comfort of his closest friend.

Christophe drifted in and out of consciousness, delirious at times as the fever took its toll and a deathly pale from his extensive loss of blood. Edward dreaded the journey that now seemed inevitable that he would have to make to Chaffeymoor to tell Robert and Marguerite that their son had succumbed to his wounds.

It was on a Sunday, several weeks after Robert had got back to Chaffeymoor. They had been to church where The Reverend Banks had welcomed them and proceeded to give a service of praise for all those, on whatever side, who had given up their lives in The Battle of Naseby.

Marguerite could not help herself as she broke down in tears as Reverend Banks read out the names of the fallen from the village including Christophe as "listed missing in action". It was all Robert could do to console her, the women he loved and cherished with all his heart, the women that had born his only son.

They were taking coffee in the morning room with Sarah and Paul when they heard the rumbling of carriage wheels coming up the long drive on the estate.

Marguerite started trembling. As it got louder she collapsed, sending her coffee cup flying across the room. Robert quickly revived her with smelling salts, but she was uncontrollable, crying and wailing. 'No, no, my poor boy' she sobbed 'please, not my Christophe, finally coming home in a coffin to his birthplace'.

Sarah took over, holding and comforting her cousin whilst Robert and Paul went outside to meet the carriage. It was driven by a footman dressed splendidly in the Earl of Dorset's colours. *Edward has brought the body of Christophe home with honour and dignity* thought Robert.

The carriage door opened and out stepped Edward. Then just as Robert was about to shake Edward by the hand and thank him for bringing Christophe's body home, out stepped Christophe himself.

Robert looked in disbelief for there he was, supported by a cane with signs of blood from a chest wound seeping through his shirt, but smiling as only Christophe could smile.

'Hello Father, I'm in a bit of a pickle here' he said trying to lighten up the atmosphere.

Robert did not know whether to laugh or cry, his prayers had been answered. Fighting back the tears of relief, and with an enormous smile on his face, he said 'I knew I had taught you well my boy, but fancy letting a Parliamentarian give you scar for life.'

'A badge of honour dear father, a badge of honour' said Christophe laughing but cringing in pain as he hugged his father, at the same time producing his blood-stained kerchief with the words Chaffeymoor barely legible. 'This probably saved my life!' he said, laughing.

Marguerite appeared at the door, supported by Sarah. 'Oh Christophe, is it really you? she sobbed. 'God be praised.'

'Well, I am certainly not a ghost Mama' he said as he opened his one good arm to embrace her.

'Enough of you two', said Robert, tears of joy now running down his cheek 'let us all be getting inside. This calls for a celebration.'

Christophe was home, in the arms of the two people most dear to him in the world.

Chaffeymoor, my Chaffeymoor, he mused to himself. *How can I ever leave you all again?*

24

Edward left Chaffeymoor in the late Autumn after Christophe was well on the way to recovery. They had enjoyed a few weeks together whilst Christophe was convalescing, regaling their times at Christ Church and as young cavalrymen before their promotions to Captain of their respective Divisions, and the onset of war. Robert and Marguerite never seemed happier seeing the two of them in such good spirits. It was to be the last time that they would all see Edward.

He returned to Oxford to be with his fiancé. They were married on Christmas Eve at a quiet ceremony with Bridget's father giving her away, Edward's mother and father in attendance and Sam standing in for Christophe as Best Man. All the preparations for a lavish wedding at Knole House had to be foregone in the aftermath of Naseby. Edward also felt that it would be disloyal to hold such a grand ceremony without his dearest and best friend Christophe, who could not make such an arduous journey, beside him.

Robert remained at Chaffeymoor. He enjoyed the time immensely, he was back in the arms of his darling wife Marguerite, his son was recovering well. The seasons came and went, it was bliss. It was just as if time had stood still and they had all been transported back to the life at Chaffeymoor before the Civil War had raised its ugly head.

The house and its grounds had never looked so sublime in his eyes. At a time when all seemed lost around him, he realised more than ever what drew him to it when he had returned that Autumn day from France all those years ago with his young and beautiful bride.

They strolled together in the gardens which had been beautifully kept by Paul. They were hand in hand on this fine Autumn day, still in love with each other, just as they were in those heady passionate days of youth, still in need of each other as they were then when they made love in wanton abandon.

'I do so love you Marguerite, right from that moment I saw you in Ruen,' said Robert.

Trying not to show the tears welling up in her green eyes, Marguerite replied 'Je t'aime beacoup, il n'y a jamais eu quelqu'un d'autre, que tois.'

All seasons at Chaffeymoor were wonderous in the eyes of Robert and Marguerite but Autumn captured the magic of the place, as the colourful trees and shrubs start to prepare for their winter hibernation. It remained special to them both as it was the season that they first moved in, in awe of its grandeur, on high ground overlooking the gardens and woods as far as the eye could see down to the village below. They loved getting lost in the vastness of it, deciding in which bedroom they would make love in that night.

The days were often warm and sunny but with encroaching darkness and with the night-time temperatures falling there were chilly nights accompanied by early morning mists that brought Chaffeymoor to the golden threshold of another Autumn. As Robert and Marguerite rose that following morning, they drew the heavy drapes of their bedroom to gaze out at the mist hanging over the sheep and cattle grazing in the adjacent fields, the hot breath of the cattle adding to the vapour that drifts between old oak and beech trees in the lower wood.

The trees and shrubs had begun changing colour, slowly at first but then as the days shortened and the temperature fell, they quickened their pace and the shades intensified reaching a climax of changing patterns and colours.

Christophe slowly but surely regained his strength, and it was a blessing that Edward stayed for so long until he was sure that his dearest friend was well on his way to a full recovery.

Sara and Paul had been stalwart in their support of Marguerite right through the war, and in particular in more recent times when they all feared the worst for Christophe on hearing the news about the Battle of Naseby.

Robert. Meanwhile, had been kept in touch about the misfortunes of King Charles, his time on the run seeking out and failing to find allies wherever he went. He subsequently heard of the King's arrest and his eventual incarceration in London. It was now or never.

If he was ever going to save Charles and put the contents of Madrigal in the public eye, it was now. He had promoted Elliot as his de facto Head of Operations and charged him with continuing to run the network of Agents and Spies despite the cessation of war.

He decided to take Christophe into his confidence; if things did not go well for him, it would be down to Christophe, as his son and heir, to finish his quest. A quest that had consumed him, frustrated him, even tormented him at times for the last six years.

It was December 1648 as Robert and Christophe strolled the grounds of Chaffeymoor to have some time alone together. The glorious Autumn had turned to Winter with a smattering of snowflakes on the ground, the holly bursting with bright red berries, the ivy in full bloom and the mistletoe, yet to be harvested from high in the poplar trees, glistening in the weak winter sun.

As they walked Robert explained to Christophe the true meaning of Madrigal. Not the literal meaning from Christophe's days as a scholar at Christ Church, but the meaning of Madrigal, the secret that he had first heard the name of that day at Newark when he had attended the last negotiations with Parliament before the start of the Civil War.

He explained what Madrigal was, who was involved, why it was likely to have a profound effect on the country's constitution, and why it was The King's only hope of avoiding execution.

Christophe was in awe of his father, his determination, his skills as an inquisitor and as a master spy.

'Do you mean father that the war that I fought those six bloody years for, could have been avoided?'

'I am afraid so Christophe. A combination of Charles's intransigence and following that, the unwillingness of Fairfax and the other protagonists to reveal Madrigal after the War had started, allowed it to drag on.'

Christophe was overwhelmed and stopped in his tracks just as a pair of geese flew over.

'Fairfax? The Lord General of The New Model Army!' Christophe said with some amazement.

'You always spoke well of him in the years before the war, but I am still astounded that he is one of the main protagonists of Madrigal given his leading role on the battlefields!'

'It's true Christophe, he was always against the war and believed in a negotiated settlement between the King and Parliament. He even conceived, negotiated and drafted the Madrigal statement with Lord Cecil after the war had started.'

A Muntjac deer burst out of the copse and leapt within feet of them. It was as startled as they were and scampered off across the lower fields.

'Charles had acted in haste, however' continued Robert. 'After rejecting the 'Nineteen Proposals' presented to him by Parliament, he believed the whole country would support him and proceeded to declare war on Parliament by raising his standard at Nottingham'.

Both Christophe and Robert stood still, looking across the valley, saying nothing, deep in thought.

'Fairfax was aghast at Charles' action. He still passionately believed that an accommodation could be reached by a negotiated settlement on the core principles. You will recall only too well that Charles's armies had notable successes for the first two years, God only knows you were at the forefront of many of those battles.'

'And it is only by His good grace that I am standing here now, whilst many of my men were slaughtered' said Christophe, shaking his head and not really able to grasp the enormity of what his father was telling him.

'As you also knew first-hand,' continued Robert, 'the tide turned after the second Battle of Newbury and by then Fairfax was of the opinion that the weaker Charles' position was, the more likely that he would reach an amicable settlement with Parliament.'

They had reached the large, rectangular formal pond on the terrace, full of colourful koi carp swimming near the surface waiting to be fed, and both stood watching them as they spoke.

'So, what is to be done father?'

'I have hidden my copy of the Madrigal declaration scroll here at Chaffeymoor. I shall ride to London to meet up with Fairfax and demand that we present his copy to Charles's advocates, as Charles is sure to be put on trial for Treason.'

'Will he really do that father, after all he *is* still The Lord General of the New Model Army.'

'He is, but he has had many a falling out with Cromwell over his staunch political policies. I have had word that Fairfax will not agree to putting Charles on trial, let alone support, or put his name to any demand that Charles be executed for Treason. He has said he will in fact resign his position making way for Cromwell to be ordained as The Lord Protector of Parliament and its Citizens'.

'It is an awful risk Father; you will be putting your life in great danger and could be accused of Treason. Mama and I

could not bear the thought of life in Chaffeymoor without you'.

'If there was any other way Christophe, I would take it, but the whole future of the country for generations to come depends on getting Madrigal accepted by both Royalists and Parliamentarians alike. What it comes down to is, do you want this country to remain a Republic, and to bring your children, should you ever have any, into that world, or do you want it to remain a Monarchy, as it has been, very successfully, for hundreds of years?'

Robert moved closer to his son, putting his arm around his shoulders, and almost whispering in his ear, said 'we must not let your mother know the true extent of the dangers I will face, promise me that Christophe.'

'I do father, but prey tell me, where you have hidden your copy of Madrigal?'

'Somewhere only you and I know Christophe. Do you remember your favourite hiding place when we used to play hide and seek when you were a young boy?'

'You mean', but before Christophe could get the word out Robert hushed him up by putting his index finger to his lips.

They returned to the house, where the candles had just been lit giving a warm glow as they entered the hallway. They stamped their feet to clear the snow that had clung to their boots and to get the circulation moving again in their feet and toes. The fire in the drawing room, blazing away in the large inglenook fireplace beckoned them in to warm themselves up by sitting on the padded leather topped wrought iron fire club fender.

When their circulation had returned and they were warmed up they both reclined on one of the huge French Baroque sofas, a particular favourite style of Marguerites. The heavily draped silk curtains, tied back to let in the maximum dwindling light, complimented the rooms furnishings. They reflected on their earlier conversation over a heartening glass of sherry.

That evening they all enjoyed a family meal together and Robert told them that he had to return to London on urgent business without revealing the real reason.

'If only I had known' exclaimed Sarah 'we could have had an early Christmas feast.'

'That would have been wonderful,' said Robert his mind conjuring up the memory of all the glorious Christmases past, but he was in no mood for celebration.

'Perhaps next year Sarah, let us all just all enjoy the next few days together before I leave.'

On retiring to bed that night, Marguerite knew that there must be some overriding compelling reason for Robert to go back to London, she knew him so well. He would not leave them all over Christmas and New Year unless it was imperative. She would miss him so much though. *How could she enjoy the celebrations without him,* she thought, but she knew he had a very important job to do, and it was her duty as his wife to support him, whatever hardship or heartache that might bring.

Robert held her tightly but tenderly as she whispered in his ear, 'It's OK Robert, you don't have to explain the reasons for you going, it's the King isn't it?'

He didn't reply.

They then made slow, tender but passionate love to each other.

There was no rush, the night was theirs.

25

It was now the Spring of 1646 and Oxford was surrounded and under siege by Parliamentarians. Charles escaped in late April in disguise with his hair cut short wearing a priest's hassock and a Montero hat. He was accompanied by his Chaplain, Dr Michael Hudson, his Groom, together with Edward and his wife Bridget.

It was dark that night with the moon hidden behind rain clouds and they left unchallenged. Charles could not believe his good fortune; it was so easy. It would appear that the Puritans had given in to the evil drink following their successes on the battlefield.

Edward, fearing the inevitability of Oxford falling into Parliamentarian hands intended to take his wife to Chaffeymoor, and shortly after leaving Oxford Edward and Bridget headed south-west, whilst Charles and his Chaplain and Groom headed for Newark.

Edward and Bridget, riding by moonlight, soon encountered Parliamentarian troops at nearby Chawley. The Captain of the Troop demanded to see Edward's papers because he was suspicious as to why they should be travelling at such an hour of the night. Edward knew that the game was up and took the first initiative drawing his pistol and shooting the

Captain square between his eyes. He was dead before he reached the ground toppling from his horse.

This took the other troops by surprise and Edward then drew his sword and charged them as he would have done leading The Kentish Royals. He shouted to Bridget 'Flee my darling, go forth to Chaffeymoor and I shall follow.'

Edward fought gallantly but was outnumbered by ten to one. He had downed six of them before he succumbed to a series of blows when surrounded by the remaining troops. They spared no mercy, Bridget fled with all her might; it was all she could do to somehow muster enough strength and courage to find her way to Chaffeymoor carrying their unborn child.

Upon fleeing Oxford, Charles did not know who to turn to. A number of former Royalist allies seeing the writing on the wall were converting to the Parliamentarian cause. *Traitors one and all* thought Charles, *I shall make allies with the Scottish Covenanters and raise a new army.* He arrived at the camp of the Covenanters at Newark in Nottinghamshire on May 5th.

He made a fatal error in trusting them but had little choice. Charles tried to engage them in a Holy War against the Puritans of Parliament and despite appearing to go along with his plans, the Covenanters agreed terms with the victorious English Parliament in January 1647. They left to go back to Scotland but not before handing Charles over to Parliament as their prisoner.

He was taken to Northampton where he led a placid and healthy existence. He often mused to himself when hearing of the quarrels between Cromwell and his New Model Army, and members of Parliament. *There was still hope* he thought, *I shall come to a treaty with one or other and regain my power.*

Whilst there, Charles had a surprise visitor, General Thomas Fairfax. 'My Liege, there is still time for a negotiated settlement.'

They then engaged in civil conversation and discussed which of the Nineteen Principles that Charles might agree with.

When Fairfax rose to leave, Charles said to him 'The General is a man of honour and shall keep his word that he has pledged to me.'

'I give you my word that I shall do everything in my power to reach such a settlement' he replied, 'but I cannot desert the Parliamentary cause.'

In June, Charles' hopes of more talks were dashed. He was taken, unwillingly, from Northampton to the Parliamentary Army Headquarters at Newmarket, and in August moved again to Hampton Court in London where he was reunited with two of his children, Henry, and Elizabeth.

Hampton Court was a palace like no other. Built on the banks of the River Thames west of London between 1515 and 1525, it was the home of Cardinal Wolsey, and then Henry V111, so as prisons go, it was very luxurious indeed with servants galore and 60 acres of formal gardens in which to wander.

Things were looking up, he was allowed free movement in The Palace, a much more comfortable abode more befitting that of The King of England. Several more months passed, and Charles became restless, there was no sign of any overtures being made to him to reach an accommodation with him on the future running of the country.

In November he decided to escape intending to go to the Isle of Wight where the Parliamentary Governor Colonel Robert Hammond, who was Charles's Chaplain's brother-in-law, was thought to be a secret Royalist.

He misjudged Hammond, however, who instead of welcoming him, placed him under house arrest at Carisbrooke Castle. Charles was initially allowed a great deal of freedom to leave the castle and travel around the Island in his carriage, bringing a number of his household to join him at Carisbrooke. A few weeks after his arrival, unbeknown to Parliament, Charles entered into a military agreement with the

Scots to raise an Army who would march south into England to fight his cause.

The resulting Scottish invasion, together with further uprisings in England and Wales led briefly to a second Civil War. These uprisings were quickly and mercilessly put down by Fairfax, Cromwell, and the New Model Army. When the Scots were defeated in September 1648 all hope was lost.

Charles entered into further negotiations which failed at Newport, the capital of the Isle of Wight and he was subsequently transferred to Hurst Castle on the mainland, then on to Windsor and London.

His fate was sealed.

CARISBROOK CASTLE, ISLE OF WIGHT

26

The time had come for Robert to leave Chaffeymoor, it was mid-December. After tearful goodbyes to Marguerite and Christophe, farewells and good wishes from Sarah and Paul he set off once more for London. He had sent word in advance to Elliot to expect him on the 22nd as there was much to do to prepare to meet Fairfax and Cecil to decide how to proceed with Madrigal.

The ride to London would take three days, the first two day's ride was mostly in what was previously considered to be Royalist territory all the way up The Great West Road to beyond Basingstoke where he would stay overnight at the Winchfield Inn. It was as if there was one long funeral going on in each village he passed through, all in mourning for the King's capture and imprisonment.

Let us hope that it is not a premonition thought Robert to himself.

As he got nearer to London the mood of the people changed. There were several village fetes going on in celebration of the Parliamentarian victory. At one point, close to London there was even an effigy of King Charles hanging from a scaffold. Robert could not believe the malice of some people, but many believed that Charles had abused his power and there was an erosion of civil liberties.

That may be so thought Robert, *but the country had enjoyed relative peace in his time, none more so than those living in the South and West. It was only in the borders with Scotland and the North of England that real hardship had been suffered before the Civil War as a result of a series of engagements with the Scots over religious beliefs.*

John and Jenny had prepared the safe house for Robert's return. As he rode down Highgate Hill, he noticed little difference from his previous journeys, but it was a far change from that of Chaffeymoor.

Little had also changed at the house other than Elliot enjoying a few more home comforts in his room, none more so than he deserved in his new role as Robert's Deputy. John had procured a deeper horsehair filled mattress for Elliot's bed and a comfortable armchair. Jenny had made some new window drapes and a matching bedspread.

That first evening they all enjoyed a simple, but sumptuous supper together, prepared by Jenny with ample wine flowing to celebrate Roberts 'home' coming.

'At least you have not drunk the cellar dry in my absence Elliot,' said Robert.

Elliot grinned. 'John and I gave it a good go on occasions, but you had stocked it well and we left the best bottles until last.'

They all laughed at Elliot's response.

He was a good fellow, in his early thirties, rugged with a decent education. Not only could he read and write, but he was streetwise and courageous. He was also reliable and honest and had quickly learnt the intricacies of espionage under Robert's tutelage. He had had many lady friends, but never a wife, and as a result he was sometimes quite withdrawn, only coming forth when the ale or wine flowed, and he could really relax within company he trusted. He was the ideal right-hand man for Robert who always knew he had his back covered.

The next day dawned and as time waited for no man, Robert and Elliot convened in the snug after breakfast. Elliot had earned his spurs admirably in Robert's absence, continuing to run their network of Agents and Spies across the land and it was now time to tell him the full story of Madrigal.

'I knew it was something momentous but not that momentous!'

Elliot said, scratching his forehead. 'It seemed to be a lifetime's quest of yours, you were so relentless, so determined. I knew parts of it of course, through my investigations and some of the scrapes that we got into together, but never would I have believed such a secret plan could exist in a thousand years.'

'Well, it may have all been in vain with the King incarcerated and probably facing a public trial and possible execution.'

'Ok Robert, so where do we go from here?'

Robert got up from his chair and started pacing around the room, deep in thought. *The carpet on the oak boards was getting threadbare and needs replacing,* he thought to himself as he worked out what to say. Elliot sat quietly, waiting. He was used to Robert's ways and knew better than to interrupt a pacing Robert.

'The first thing I must do is seek a meeting with Fairfax and Cecil. It might be a risk too far to have it in London, so I will write a request to Fairfax and suggest we all meet at Hatfield House as soon as possible. Can you deliver it in person Elliot, I believe he is at his London residence in Park Lane over the Christmas period.'

'Of course, as soon as you have written it. Shall I request a reply by return?'

'Yes, providing it does not raise any suspicion from his Footman.'

Robert sat down at the desk, loaded his quill pen and taking a deep breath, wrote the invitation to meet up with Fairfax. This was the start of what could be a turning point, a complete change in the way England was ruled and managed for centuries. If Madrigal were accepted, Charles could be back on the throne, not facing impeachment and charges of Treason which, if found guilty, would mean execution.

Elliot returned with Fairfax's reply later that morning. Somewhat surprisingly it suggested that they all meet at Harlington Manor in Bedfordshire, owned by Edmund Wingate, a mathematician who had tutored Queen Henrietta. It turned out that not only was Wingate a supporter of King Charles, but he had also befriended Fairfax and was aware of his desire to seek a settlement with Charles.

Harlington was further from London than Hatfield House but still no more than a day's ride for all three. Fairfax had said that he had sent word to Wingate to expect them on the 27th. *Good*, thought Robert. That will give Keagan a well-earned rest. She had served him well for a good few year and had taken him many miles back and forth across the country.

The 27th could be a pivotal day. Madrigal was gaining momentum.

Robert was to spend Christmas with Elliot, who had no family as such to go to, and John and Jenny who had no children. In spite of the troubles that faced him Robert entered into the spirit of things and helped decorate the house with holly and ivy making sure that Jenny wanted for nothing in terms of comestibles.

On Christmas Eve morning, Elliot accompanied him to the local meat market where they purchased a goose for Christmas Day, and a large rib of beef for that night.

Robert slept well despite missing Chaffeymoor and the warmth of Marguerite snuggled up beside him. It had been a long ride, a long day, and the copious glasses of wine he drank during the evening no doubt acted as a sleeping draught, but he lay on his back in his bed singing carols as loudly as he could, in the mode of an opera singer, making all the actions, even trying to sing the descants, before closing his eyes and drifting off.

'You were singing well last night' said Elliot as they walked to the market.

'Was I? asked Robert. 'I don't remember singing – what was I singing? Was I in tune?'

'Carols, most robustly and yes, in tune most of the time, but it got a bit painful when you tried to sing the sopranos descants.'

'Never' laughed Robert. 'Did I really? No, you're pulling my leg.'

'No, you were singing your heart out, but it was not a problem. It sent me to sleep smiling,' grinned Elliot.

Jenny, with John's help plucked the goose and gutted it, saving the heart, liver, and gizzard to add to a sumptuous soup made by boiling the carcass with vegetables. This would last them all week as a stock pot. Jenny was a superb cook, and she did them all proud with resplendent dinners on both occasions.

They all laughed and sang odes of joy and generally made merry. Robert could not help but cast his mind to the glorious Christmases at Chaffeymoor, but he was determined to play his part in making sure that this was a Christmas not to be forgotten by the others.

Fairfax had deliberately made sure that he was the first to arrive at Harlington Manor. He had travelled up the day before the 27th as he wanted to brief Edmund as to who his guests were, and that they sought to persuade Parliament to reach a settlement with the King for the good of the nation. He did not reveal to him the secret of Madrigal.

Robert had also travelled via Hatfield House on 26th as he wanted to discuss his plans with William. He did not want any surprises when they met Fairfax.

He never failed to admire the sheer magnificence of Hatfield House, seeing it from afar as he galloped once again across the Estate's parkland. As he approached from the south along the long avenue lined with trees, the red brick façade around the courtyard glowed in the low winter sun, and the lead roofed towers and clocktower stood out proudly against the pale sky, bathed in sunshine.

He arrived in good spirits and William Cecil came out to greet him as though he had been a lifelong friend again. Kindred spirits one and all with a common purpose, Madrigal.

Later that afternoon, after enjoying William's company over high tea in the drawing room, Robert rose from his sumptuous armchair and crossed the room to look at the gardens beyond before turning to face William. 'It's now or never William' he said, 'are you sure you want to go through with this?'

'As sure as I ever will be Robert, I fear that I do not have much longer on this earth and God would not forgive me if I did not see this through to the end.'

'What about you Robert, you still have your life ahead of you with your lovely wife?'

'Believe me William, I have searched my soul and sought God's will, and I proceed with both his and Marguerite's blessing.'

'Then let us dine well tonight for it may be the last time we may see each other', said William, never missing an opportunity to dine well and drink the finest French wine in splendour.

The following morning, they left Hatfield together and rode side by side to Harlington Manor. It was an unremarkable building that had been added to over the years, hidden behind high brick walls in the centre of the town, but a Manor House just the same. They were met by Fairfax and introduced to Edmund Wingate.

'Welcome', said Edmund, 'whilst here, please treat my house as your own. Thomas has told me why you are here, and I wish you well in your endeavours.'

Robert exchanged glances with William, concerned as to just how much Fairfax had revealed to Edmund.

'I shall leave you to yourselves. My Morning Room has been prepared for you and you shall not be disturbed. There is a cold meat luncheon, wine, water, and coffee on hand, please just ring for my parlour maid if you need anything else.

I should be most honoured if you would join me for dinner tonight, and your rooms have been prepared for your overnight stay.'

Robert thanked Edmund on their behalf and added 'The honour is ours Edmund, we shall all look forward to your company over dinner'. And so the three men that possibly held the future of England in their hands retired to the Morning Room to commence their discussions. The room was comfortably but not ornately furnished, with English oak furniture as befitted the status of Edmund in society. It was not a patch on Hatfield House but nor were there many others in the country as grand as Hatfield, only the Royal Palaces and some stately homes of some hereditary Lords.

None of them were in the mood for eating, but after taking lunch with a glass of wine and making general conversation about the nonsensical nature of the war, they got down to the task in hand, Madrigal.

In the light of his standing in Parliament, Fairfax opened the proceedings but deferred to Robert. 'Robert, you have been fearless, resolute and determined to uncover Madrigal with little regard for your own safety. What is it you wish to do now?'

'If it pleases you Thomas, you too William, I am of the opinion that we owe a duty to the country to put Madrigal in the public eye. I believe that it should be laid before Parliament by our friend Willian Lenthall, The Speaker of The House of Commons. I also believe that at the same time it should be presented to the King for his approval.'

'You are missing one important thing Robert', replied Fairfax, 'Time. I am led to believe by my colleagues in the Commons that the Army and their hand-picked Members of Parliament, calling themselves The Rump, have opted for a high-risk strategy of demanding a public trial of The King. If they are successful in persuading the Commons that should be the case, we have no more than one week, two at most, before charges of Treason will be laid before Charles, and they proceed to Trial. It could all be over by the end of January.'

'In which case', Robert replied as he stood up in order to emphasise his point, 'we have no choice but to present Madrigal to the King and his legal advocates.'

Thomas looked worried and started walking up and down the room, head stooped, hands clenched behind his back. 'You do realise that once we so do, we are then exposing ourselves to being arrested and charged with Treason. What is your view William?'

'I support Robert, Thomas, we have already both sought God's blessing to our endeavours.' 'I suggest then that you and I, Robert, ride to London first thing in the morning and seek an audience with The Attorney General Anthony Steele together with The Solicitor General John Cook. If we cannot persuade them to delay the proceedings against Charles whilst Madrigal is debated in Parliament, then I am afraid all is lost.'

'William, you should return to Hatfield, keep your head down, and enjoy some time with your family. Should we be unsuccessful, and Cromwell comes calling, deny all knowledge of Madrigal.'

'I shall gentlemen, I wish you good fortune for tomorrow and beyond. Let us enjoy our dinner with our host Edmund. I do hope he has some pickled herring as an appetizer.'

This brought a wry smile from Robert, 'It feels like the last supper to me William' he said as he smiled. He turned to Thomas and said, 'you do have your signed copy of Madrigal with you?'

'Of course, Robert. I take it yours is either in safe keeping with someone, or in hiding.'

'Yes' Robert replied, 'let us pray that it is never needed.'

It is not in the stars to hold our destiny,
but in ourselves.
William Shakespeare

27

Robert and Fairfax rode back to London the following morning to Thomas's London home in St Martins-in-the-Field, a part of fashionable London with houses occupied by the aristocracy and high-born Parliamentary politicians and army officers.

GENERAL THOMAS FAIRFAX

Fairfax, or to give him his full title, General Lord Thomas Fairfax, was the eldest son of the 2nd Lord Fairfax of Cameron, a Scottish peerage that allowed Thomas to sit in The House of Commons.

The family seat was at Denton Hall, halfway between Ilkley and Otley in West Yorkshire where his father now resided for most of the time unless there was an important vote in The House of Lords.

Thomas, when not fighting wars, preferred to be in London, close to the centre of the fast-moving political landscape and home of The New Model Army.

Thomas's father, Lord Fairfax also fought in the early part of the Civil War as the General of Parliamentary Forces in the North of England initially, with Thomas alongside him as Lieutenant General of Horse. Robert knew only too well of Thomas's war record but knew little about his father.

He trusted Thomas only to the extent of matters involving Madrigal. He would not, for the safety and security of Elliot, John, Jenny and his network of Agents and Spies, reveal the location of his safe house to him.

As they cantered side by side through woods and villages, the Head of the King's Secret Service and the Lord General of Cromwell's Army were united in their purpose. Robert mused to himself that *others might not believe it, you just could not make it up.*

It was cold, very cold, just above freezing and they were draped in heavy woollen capes and fortified by a flask of brandy. Their faces were masked to keep out the cold and to all intents and purposes they could have been mistaken for highwaymen.

There was snow blanketing the ground from a heavy overnight fall, drifts making wonderful patterns piled against the hedgerows and the occasional blast of the easterly wind blew the snow into billowing clouds that shimmered in the low winter's sun.

As they quickened to a gallop across open moorland, Robert wondered what Lord Fairfax's true political beliefs were. He certainly fought the Parliamentary cause, but how close were father and son, how much, if anything, had Thomas told his father about Madrigal.

He was aware that he was getting nervous as he now relied on his mental strength to see Madrigal through to its bitter end.

Fairfax's London house was grand, a three-story brick-built town house that was a sight to behold. Architectural fashion of the wealthy was slowly but surely beginning to move away from the traditional timber framed houses with walls of wattle and daub of the 16th and earlier centuries.

It was however, modestly furnished but not to the level of the minimalist fashion of some of Thomas's Puritan Parliamentarian friends who believed that one should not adorn or worship possessions, only worship unto God.

Thomas made Robert welcome and they wasted no time in retiring to the library and study to discuss as to where they went from here. He called for some strong coffee to be brought to them with pastries and gave orders that they were not to be disturbed under any circumstances.

Robert could immediately see that Thomas was a scholar. The room was austere with oak panelled walls, a reading desk and just two comfortable leather armchairs with side tables. It faced south west and was double aspect with tall wide windows, allowing the maximum natural light to penetrate the room for easier reading.

One wall was completely shelved on the lower half for easy access to the myriad of books and manuscripts that they held. The collection consisted of all manner of subjects from the ancient texts of Plato, Aristotle, and Ancient Rome right up to the latest offerings by Shakespeare and Milton.

On the wall above the bookshelves, a carved plaque depicted a quotation by the French philosopher Descartes:

"I think
therefore I am
what is a man if he ceases to think".

RENE DESCARTES

Robert and Thomas argued back and forth the pros and cons for proceeding with speed, giving that time was of the essence. It was a huge risk whichever way they proceeded.

After some considerable thought and discussion, they both finally agreed to hold their fire until The Rump decided how they were going to proceed.

In the meantime, Thomas agreed to find out what Cromwell and the army's position was, and to counsel some of the more moderate members of the Commons as to how they were likely to vote should it come to impeachment of the King.

They had both changed their minds about what William Cecil could do to help. Robert sent word to William explaining the gravity of the situation and asking him to come down to London as soon as possible.

They now thought that despite the dangers to himself, William should counsel as many of the Lords that he felt still owed allegiance to Charles.

They decided that was all they could do for now and they would meet here on the 4$^{th of}$ January unless they heard of anything dramatic happening between now and then. New Year's Day was a Friday which was historically considered to be a day of celebration, and as it was followed by a weekend, they thought nothing would happen after the 30th. It was now the 29th.

Robert agreed that if he needed to be contacted, Thomas could leave a message for him at the Angel Inn. It was the best Robert could come up with in the circumstances, but still too close for comfort.

After exchanging pleasantries and a glass of brandy to wish each other luck, Robert returned to the safe house to brief Elliot.

Elliot looked his usual jovial self, reserved and unassuming. A mistake that many a foe had made in misjudging his demeaner for he was fearless when under threat.

'Well Elliot, as well as the joys of Christmas, it looks like we are going to be spending New Year's Eve and the New Year's celebrations together. Marguerite would laugh out loud at the thought, knowing of your reputation of having any excuse to down a tankard of ale or two. She would be sure that you were leading me astray.'

They both laughed, Robert more by way of relief from the pressures of the day.

As there was nothing more he could do given the time of year, he could relax for a few days. Elliot laughed by way of the thought of the long New Year's weekend in the company of Robert, who was by now his closest friend as well as his Principal.

'Come now Robert you will need something to take your mind off state affairs for a while and it will do you good to let your hair down! Now, tell me all about your meeting with Fairfax.'

Robert wished he could get back to Chaffeymoor to spend New Year there, but the journey to Dorset and back took too long bearing in mind he would have to be back by the 4th. He also needed to be in London in case of unexpected developments.

He enjoyed the next few days together with Elliot, John and Jenny and spent many an hour down at the Angel Inn supping the finest of the Landlord Jack Daniels's ale and playing baccarat.

On New Year's Eve the Angel Inn was heaving, full of local people laughing, singing, and drinking, seeing out the old and welcoming in the new. Robert and Elliot were ensconced at a small table in one corner enjoying the atmosphere, playing a game of baccarat, and laughing and joking with each other.

Approaching the hour of midnight Robert stretched himself and glanced across the room. It was as if these good people, citizens all, did not have care in the world.

Were they really concerned as to who was running the country?

He thought not. For most of them it could only mean one thing, more taxes to be paid to support the militia.

'Right Elliot that makes it three tankards of ale you now owe me but let us get back to the house to welcome in the New Year with the others.'

It had started to rain, the icy droplets stinging their faces as they walked into the wind. They pulled their hats down and their cloaks tight around them as they quickened their pace through the dark streets.

Back at the house the log fire was roaring and lighting up the room as they all toasted in the New Year and made wishes for the year to come, but there was only one wish that Robert could contemplate, the success of Madrigal.

Their celebrations continued into the next day. It was cold and there was snow in the air but that did not diminish the music and dancing in the street.

Most Londoners struggled to feed and clothe their families thinking themselves well off if they owned a good stout pair of boots and a change of clothes, but at the slightest excuse for a celebration they would go out onto the streets and laugh, dance and sing.

The women picked up their skirts and petticoats to dance, while the men showed off their strength as they tried to dance the way they had been told the Cossacks do in Russia, squatting and rising, arms folded kicking out their legs at the same time and invariably falling over, much to the amusement of the watching crowd.

Merchants had set up stalls selling colourful ribbons, garlands, and trinkets. Vendors were cooking on wood fired braziers and serving up tasty morsels of chicken legs, pigs trotters, mutton chops and a variety of offal, with broth and sippets of oat and barley cakes.

Jack Daniels at The Angel Inn had laid on barrels of ale and were also selling mugs of hot mulled wine. The celebrations however were short lived and Robert's hopes and wishes came crashing down on this New Year's Day, 1649 when he received a message from Fairfax.

Elliot had popped into The Angel Inn late that afternoon for a tankard of ale before supper and had been given a sealed message for Sir Robert. He downed his ale in one go, belched and then rushed back to the house.

Robert was in the snug feeling relaxed after the day's celebrations, thinking of home and enjoying a glass of wine when Elliot came rushing in, looking slightly worse for wear as he had been celebrating the day as only he knew how.

'A message from Fairfax' he cried having recognised the wax seal.

Robert broke Fairfax's seal. He opened the folded parchment and read the message in total despair, and slumped into his chair, mortified. *Should they have acted sooner?* he asked himself.

The Rump had formally declared that it was Treason for King Charles to wage war against Parliament and the Kingdom, and that they would seek approval of both the House of Commons and The Lords to impeach him and put him on public trial.

28

Robert showed Elliot the message and needed a few minutes to gather his senses. He did not expect The Rump's tactics to move over the holiday weekend, they demonstrated, even more so, that time waits for no man. Despite the lateness of the hour, and the generous consumption of alcohol during the course of the day, he needed to be with Fairfax, but he refrained from going immediately as no doubt he had house guests over the weekend.

He decided to send a message that he would be with him first thing in the morning. A reply came straight back,

'Join me for breakfast at eight a.m. Much to consider, we need to move fast', Thomas.

Robert slept fitfully that night, his mind racing as to what to do next. *Was it too late, had it all been in vain?*

It had taken him so long to track down the advocates of this secret plan that he had first heard of nearly 6 years ago. They were so determined to keep its subject matter secret, for their own altruistic reasons, that he had failed to solve it fast enough to stop the war and prevent thousands from being slaughtered. However, he might still be able to change the course of history and stop the country becoming a Republic.

The significance of leading members of both sides, Royalists and Parliamentarians, none more so than Lord General Sir Thomas Fairfax, conceiving and agreeing to a such plan

of action, was immense. If all sides accepted the plan, even at this late stage, it would ensure that the Kingdom still existed, and that Charles would still be King, granted with reduced powers. There would be a democratically elected Government and but there would not be a Republican State.

He woke up early, dawn had not arisen that long ago, washed and then dressed for the day ahead. He was determined to see this through come what may. *I have not spent the last six years exposing the secret of Madrigal only to fall at the last hurdle,* he thought to himself.

He said farewell to Elliot, John, and Jenny, not knowing when he would return, if ever. Elliot summoned a carriage at the top of the street which took Robert to St Martins in The Field and to Thomas Fairfax's house.

It was a cold miserable morning; the snow had given way to slush in the streets and the skies were dark. The horse's hooves clattered through the almost empty cobbled streets, now lined with litter from the festivities and merrymaking that had been taking place.

There were hardly any people about, perhaps not surprisingly given the early hour of the day and many a person still sleeping off the effects of The New Year's day's celebrations.

Fairfax was expecting him, taking his bag, and giving it to the housekeeper, he then ushered Robert into the morning room that had already been set for breakfast.

Over breakfast Thomas brought him up to date with the political manoeuvring of The Rump. They had called for a sitting of both The Commons and The Lords for that day, to vote on the impeachment of the King. It was an extremely unpopular move given that it was a Saturday. Thomas had no doubt that it was deliberate to reduce the numbers attending whilst making sure that all their own supporters in the Commons turned up to vote. He himself had sent word that he would not be attending.

He had a runner between the House and his home keeping him abreast of proceedings. Later that morning came the

news that unsurprisingly, The Commons had passed the motion, but the Lords thought that they could delay matters by adjourning for the week.

'Good old William' cried Robert on hearing the news, 'I knew you could do it.'

His elation was short lived, for not long after another runner turned up to say that when the Lords returned to their Chamber they found that the door had been padlocked by Cromwell aides and that the Lords would no longer be allowed to be part of this delicate and unprecedented procedure.

'What must be done Thomas? Is all lost? Will Madrigal now just be part of history, a closely guarded secret for future historians to mull over in the future?'

'I must immediately seek an audience with The Attorney General Anthony Steele together with our friend William Lenthall,' said Thomas. 'It is best that we keep your name out of it for as long as possible. Our only hope now appears to be that together they can find a way to prevent The Rump from tabling a motion and getting the Commons to pass an Act of Parliament for Charles to stand trial for Treason.'

Robert could see sense in the proposal but was wary about not being present at such discussions. In truth he still did not fully trust Fairfax not to see the writing on the wall and try to extricate himself from Madrigal. He decided reluctantly to agree, but if this failed, he would act alone.

Thomas arranged to meet The Attorney General and The Speaker at the Commons when the house rose on close of business later that day, 2nd January.

Robert stayed at Thomas's house and awaited his return, it seemed like an eternity. At one-point he left the house to walk round the square in which it was built, admire the architecture and stroll in the central communal gardens to try to take his mind off matters in hand.

Thomas returned after only one hour, it did not look good in Robert's eye.

'Come Robert, let us take a sherry together.'

'Never mind the sherry, tell me what happened', Robert exclaimed getting rather agitated at Thomas's calm attitude.

'It's not looking good Robert; I fear we may be too late.'

'Well did you present Madrigal or not?' said Robert losing his patience with Thomas.

'I made The Attorney General aware that I was in possession of information of a petition called Madrigal listing out the seven out of the nineteen principles that both sides had agreed, and that it was signed by prominent Royalists and Parliamentarians of the highest level. I did not name them.'

'And?'

'The Rump has already laid down an Act before the House to be debated and voted on tomorrow to commit The King to trial. I shall of course abstain.'

'But was the attorney General sympathetic to our argument that such a revelation as Madrigal should also be tabled before Parliament?'

'Not at all' replied Thomas, 'if anything I think his mind is already made up.'

Robert was angry but controlled, he thought that Fairfax may be a hero on the battlefield, but he has been found wanting at the time of need with Madrigal.

'Then give me your copy of Madrigal and I shall go it alone to make sure that it is presented at any trial of Charles.'

Thomas disappeared off to his study, and returned a few minutes later with the parchment, rolled and tied with a ribbon. He handed it to Robert and offered to be of any further help that may be desired of him.

Robert was uneasy. His experience heading the Secret Service had taught him to judge and question peoples' actions.

He handed that over far too easily, he thought as he hailed a carriage in the street. This was a document of momentous importance, one Fairfax had kept so secret, waiting for the right moment to present it. It could cause those signatories to be charged with Treason, but here he was, handing it over without any qualm.

They shook hands and Robert climbed into the carriage, but they parted on uncomfortable terms. He returned to the house and gave Elliot the disappointing news.

'Well, surprise, surprise it is all down to us now then' said Elliot taking it all in his stride.

The following day, on the 3rd, The Commons duly passed the Act laid down by The Rump committing King Charles to public trial and claiming that:

'Charles Stuart now King of England....had a wicked design totally to subvert the ancient and fundamental laws and liberties of his nation, and, in their place, to introduce an arbitrary and tyrannical government; and that, besides that all other evil ways and means to bring this design to pass, he has prosecuted it with fire and sword, levied and maintained a cruel war in the land against Parliament and Kingdom, whereby the country has been miserably wasted, the public treasure exhausted, and infinite other mischiefs committed'.

The punishment, if found guilty, would be a public execution by beheading.

29

The next morning Robert was in a dilemma as to how to proceed. Whatever he decided he knew that it would be the last throw of the dice and that he would be exposing himself to mortal danger. He had to reveal Madrigal at a public event where no one present could deny its existence.

There was only but one logical choice: The Trial of King Charles.

He decided that he must first meet up with William Cecil, he owed William that much to appraise him of the events of the past few days and to seek his counsel. William was currently residing in his London residence, a modest town house in Mayfair, compared to the grandeur of Hatfield House.

He sent word to William suggesting that he visit him in Mayfair that afternoon. William duly agreed by return inviting Robert to partake in afternoon tea at four o'clock.

Later that morning he, somewhat surprisingly, had another message from Fairfax, who being true to his word updated Robert on the latest political situation. The charge of Treason was being drafted by lawyers and would be put before King Charles on the 10th, he will then be committed to go on trial in Westminster Hall commencing the 20th.

It was now the 4th, and Robert discussed the latest news and his plan with Elliot over a light lunch at the house.

'At least we now know the timing of events and crucially where the trial is to take place,' said Robert.

'That may well be so, but how on earth are you going to infiltrate Westminster Hall and place the Madrigal agreement before the judges and advocates before the trial begins in earnest?'

'That is where you might come in Elliot, we need full drawings and floor plans of Westminster Hall and details of the security arrangements for the trial. I do not fully trust Fairfax, but William Lenthall may be able to help us out on this one. We shall discuss it further when I return from having tea with William Cecil.'

That afternoon Robert kept his invitation with William at his house in Mayfair. Mayfair was another one of the fashionable residential areas of London being developed to house the wealthy. It was at the western extremity of the city, beyond which was the open countryside. It was formally just a small village, Great Brookfield, which had held an annual May Fair since the days of Edward 1 in open fields beyond St James's. William welcomed Robert and showed him to the drawing room on the first floor overlooking the square. Before they had even sat down, Robert immediately told him his plan to present Madrigal at the trial of King Charles.

'We need Lenthall's help, do you think you could invite him over to join us for tea?'

'Of course, dear boy, but first let us decide on the tea. Darjeeling from India, which has a light delicate taste, or would you prefer Lapsang Souchong from China, which has a smoky aroma and flavour?'

He took a key from his waistcoat pocket and walked over to a sideboard where there was a silver tea caddy.

'Darjeeling please' replied Robert, as William unlocked the caddy and took out two spoonsful of tea leaves into a bowl. He rang for the maid who took the precious bowl away to the kitchen to infuse the tea with hot water in a bone china tea pot glazed with William's coat of arms. Tea had only been introduced recently and was scarce and expensive. Only the extraordinarily rich could afford such a luxury.

Robert was getting fidgety. 'What about Lenthall?'

William immediately sent word to Lenthall that Robert needed to discuss an urgent matter concerning The Kings' trial and asked him to come over and join them as soon as possible. He arrived in less than an hour and joined them for tea.

Addressing Lenthall, Robert said to him 'before William and I tell you any details of my final plan to try to stop the trial of the King going ahead, I need to get hold of a copy of the floor plans of Westminster Hall where the trial is to be held.'

'You cannot be thinking of infiltrating and interrupting the trial, Robert, it would be madness, you would be arrested on the spot before you got anywhere near the main chamber' replied Lenthall.

'That is why I need a copy of the plans of the lower and ground floors. Will you be made aware of the security arrangements for the trial?'

'I cannot help you on the security arrangements, other than to say it will be heavily manned by Cromwell's own security guards, however I can help you regarding the floor plans.'

Robert tried not to show his eagerness at that point but asked rather hurriedly 'Have you got copies?'

'I am afraid not Robert, but they will be held in the Building Maintenance Office in the north west corner on the ground floor below the Lobby, the way in is through the East River Front Gardens and into St Stephen's Cloister. The last window in the north west corner of The Cloisters gets you into the Lobby, once in, there are immediately stairs down to the lower ground floor.'

Robert thanked Lenthall, 'Thank you, this shall be last thing I ask of you in this task.'

'I wish you well Robert, I shall myself abstain from any court proceeding and, God help us all if King Charles is found guilty. I will not be party to signing any execution order. No

doubt that will require me resigning my position as Speaker of The Commons, but I shall retire gracefully to my country-side home.'

'William, let us all pray that it will not come to that and you shall be presiding in the Commons when Madrigal has been tabled for debate.'

Robert appraised them both with the latest news on his endeavours whilst enjoying the most splendid afternoon tea of the latest varieties together with the most delectable cakes and pastries, but of course Lenthall already knew much of it.

Looking directly at Lenthall across the table Robert asked, 'Tell me William, why did Fairfax not make more of Madrigal when you both met with The Attorney General, Anthony Steele?'

'Don't be too harsh on him Robert, it was abundantly clear that Sir Anthony had already been swayed by Cromwell and was siding with the extremist in pushing for a public trial of Charles.'

It was time to go, Robert needed to get back to the house to enlighten Elliot and to give him instructions on the next move. He bade his farewells to the two Williams, saying,

'This is probably the last you will hear from me before the trial. I wish that we could have all met under different circum-stances.'

Cecil replied, 'Good luck Robert, may God be with you, I shall pray for your success.'

'Me too Robert,' said William Lenthall. 'We may not al-ways have seen eye to eye you and I, but we both wish to see change and a more democratic country, with The King right-fully restored to the Monarchy and leader of The Church of England.'

And so Robert made his way back to the house, clear in his mind as what was required next. Elliot was waiting for him when he returned.

'Come now Elliot, I do not have the energy or inclination to go to The Angel Inn, but you may well choose to so do after I have briefed you. Let us have a sherry together in the snug whilst I do.'

Robert informed Elliot as to the whereabouts of the floor plans of Westminster Hall that they desperately needed before they could plan anything further.

'I know just the man' said Elliot with a smile. 'You remember that Irish braggart, Sean O'Halloran, that helped us gain the sordid evidence of Lenthall's dalliances with prostitutes?'

'Yes, of course, whatever it costs Elliot, we need those plans.'

'Leave it with me Robert, my first port of call is down at The Clover Leaf in Kilburn High Road.'

'I shall ask Jenny to keep a plateful of supper warm for you on the range in case you are hungry when you return, whatever the time of day or night.'

Robert duly had supper at around eight o'clock with John and Jenny and then retired to his room, exhausted from the day's events. He fell asleep fully clothed in his armchair only to be woken by Elliot coming home at some ungodly hour. He checked his timepiece, it was now 2 a.m.

He could not contain himself. Lighting a candle, he made his way downstairs and nearly put the fright up Elliot who was clearly slightly worse for wear from consuming too much ale and whisky no doubt, but still retaining all his mental faculties.

'Good God Robert. I thought you were a ghost for one fleeting moment, made my heart race you did.'

'Sorry, I could not contain myself, what news, good ones I hope?'

'It's all set, you do not need to know the details, but Sean O'Halloran and his boys will break into Westminster Hall and steal the plans on Friday night, the 8th, when The Commons goes into recess for the weekend. He was initially reluctant, but after sharing a bottle of Irish whisky, he agreed to a fee of £50 due to risks involved. The penalty for being caught is long term imprisonment at best, execution at worst.'

'Well done Elliot' exclaimed a tired but elated Robert.

Yawning and slurring his speech, Elliot continued 'the charges against The King are to be presented to him in the Hall on Sunday 10th, so Friday night before seems the best option as there will be the least number of security guards on duty.'

'Off to bed with you then, and we'll talk more in the morning, or nearer noon, judging by the state of you' Robert said with a smile.

Assuming O'Halloran is successful, Robert thought, *I have until the 20th when the trial is due to commence to plan my course of action, with the help of Elliot.*

But first, I must make out my Last Will and Testament and write a letter to Marguerite.

MAIN ENTRANCE TO WESTMINSTER HALL
1649

30

Elliot went to The Clover Leaf Inn at the arranged time of noon on the 9th to collect the stolen plans and pay O'Halloran his fee.

'That will be £ 60 if you please, said O'Halloran.'

'£60! we agreed a fee of £50' Elliot retorted.

'One of my boys was shot at and killed as we were leaving, the extra £10 is compensation to his widow.'

'Fair enough' said Elliot handing over the money, 'it's a dangerous world that we all live in Mr O'Halloran.'

Elliot hastily returned to the house where Robert was anxiously waiting, standing by the window looking intently down the busy street. It felt like a lifetime waiting for Elliot to appear between the shoppers. *Surely, he should be back by now,* Robert thought, *perhaps he has been ambushed, and the money stolen, after all £50 was a great deal of money and four times his annual salary. Perhaps O'Halloran failed in getting the plans.* His mind was racing when through the crowds he saw Elliot running towards the house. *Thank goodness* he thought as he rushed to open the front door.

'I've got them, I've got them' cried Elliot, breathless from running and doubling over to catch his breath as he entered the hallway, 'but I had to pay £60.'

Robert took the roll of parchment and indicated to Elliot to follow him into the snug. Lunch was ready and laid out on a side table, but it was cold meats, so it could wait. Studying the plans was Robert's priority, finding a way of infiltrating the building and hiding was all he could think about, so he hastily cleared room on the main table and unrolled the parchment.

Elliot saw the lunch laid out on the side table across the room and wandered across to see what was on offer. He was hungry after his busy morning and a chicken leg was ideal for him to pick up and join Robert who was by now engrossed in the floor plans of the beautiful and huge Westminster Hall. It sat a stone's throw from the River Thames in Westminster and was 700 years old.

O'Halloran had told Elliot how easy it was to gain entry by way of the Thames riverside gardens, along St Stephens Cloisters to the north west corner which abuts Westminster Hall. Then, by forcing the latch on a ground floor window, entering an ante room next to the main chamber, he had to simply go down the nearest stairwell to the lower ground floor where the Maintenance Office was located. The plan immediately came to Robert's mind. He put it to Elliot who was still enjoying his chicken leg.

'The simple ones are always the best Elliot; we shall both go to the Hall on the night of the 19th under cover of darkness. There you will force entry to the same window that O'Halloran used, and I shall enter with the Madrigal parchment concealed in my cloak. I shall then hide in the Maintenance Room until 10 a.m. as that's the designated start time of the King's Trial. After I have gained entry you shall close the window as if nothing had happened. The Maintenance Room is ideal, there will be all manner of equipment in there to conceal myself, and there will be no maintenance staff on duty it being a Sunday.'

And so, the die was cast, the stage was set, Robert felt a surge of mixed emotions, relieved in one way, elated in other ways, melancholy with thoughts of Marguerite and Christophe at Chaffeymoor. He now had just over a week to perfect his plan, memorise the layout of the Hall and put his personal effects in order.

That afternoon he visited his London lawyers, Messrs Paleman and Makepiece whose offices were in The Strand. They had been his family lawyer for three generations. David Paleman was now an old but wise man, and Henry Makepiece, was the uncle of poor Matthew Makepiece who, as clerk at Grey's Inn Court, was murdered whilst spying on behalf of Robert.

Apart from being bound by his hypocritic oath not to divulge client's business, an oath frequently ignored by many unscrupulous lawyers in pursuit of fame and fortune in the seventeen century, David, or Prof as he was known to his friends was a staunch Royalist supporter of King Charles.

MESSRS PALEMAN AND
MAKEPIECE WITH CLERK

'I shall not ask of you your intentions Robert, the least I know the better. Your Last Will and Testament is up to date and valid unless you wish to make changes.'

'No, no changes' said Robert as he sat back in his chair relaxing a little. 'That gives me some comfort. What about a Power of Attorney jointly in the names of Elliot and your good self?'

'That too is a relatively simple process, I shall have two copies drawn up for you to sign. I can sign on behalf of myself and Makepiece and my clerk can both sign as witnesses.'

Prof rang a bell to summon his clerk. I will have one copy and the other is deposited with the High Court.'

'Elliot also needs to sign but you can either arrange for him to come into my office or you can take both copies with you and get him to sign them. Either one of you can return them to this office. Unfortunately, they will have no legal bearing until one copy is deposited with the High Court.'

'Prof, time is of the essence, can I wait whilst the documents are drawn up?'

'Delighted, my boy, it will take no more than an hour, join me in a glass of the finest Jerez sherry whilst we wait. Just give me a moment to instruct my clerk and call Henry, who shall also join us.'

Whilst waiting, Robert looked around the room. It was austere, so typical even for one of London's foremost lawyers. A large leather topped "partners" desk dominated the room with two visitors high backed chairs. The walls were shelved, packed to the gunnels with legal acts, case law and client's documents. There was just one leather covered, buttoned sofa, imported from Italy as to the only concession to any form of fashion or grandeur. A drinks cabinet and side table, all sitting on a thread bare woven carpet completed the furnishings.

His clerk returned shortly after the hour and the beautifully handwritten Power of Attorney was read by both David and Henry, approved by them, and signed by all parties including the clerk as a witness. Robert took possession of both copies and said that he would have them returned as soon as he could get Elliot to sign them. He was anxious to get away, it was now four o'clock and he wanted to get to his Bankers, before close of business at five o'clock.

Hoare's, founded by Sir Richard Hoare and located at Cheapside, took on the trade of banking which historically had been the remit of several Goldsmiths in the city. Sir Richard Hoare was destined to be Lord Mayor of London.

Robert arrived at the bank with a quarter of an hour to spare and was welcomed by one of Sir Richard's senior clerks, a small round-shouldered man in his forties, who peered at him over wire-framed glasses and ushered him into a side office, clutching a large leather covered ledger close to his chest.

His financial affairs were simple. The bank had his holdings in gold and the King's currency, and the deeds to Chaffeymoor. Robert confirmed the bank's record of his holdings with the clerk and told him that his Last Will and Testament was lodged with his solicitors. He also informed the clerk of the drawing up of the Power of Attorney and that it was to be lodged with them.

The clerk duly updated the bank's records in the ledger, dropping ink from his quill onto the facing blank page as he did so, and quickly blotting it.

Perhaps, thought Robert, *that page will never be needed in my name.*

All seemed to be in good order, so he bade the clerk farewell and, somewhat relieved, returned to the house in Angel Islington. It had been another mentally exhausting day for Robert, but he had one last thing to do before he could relax. It was now close to six o'clock. He asked John if he would be so kind as to go down to The Angle Inn and summon Elliot to come up to the house immediately.

John grabbed his coat and left, knowing that he would not be asked to do that if it were not important, and within minutes they both returned in earnest.

'Sorry to drag you away Elliot, but I need to get an urgent message to Christophe at Chaffeymoor, do you think young Jack is up to the task?'

'I haven't any doubts Robert, I shall go and ask him to call to collect your message at first light tomorrow morning, which will be around 8 a.m. Will you be joining me at The Angel later?'

'Thank you Elliot, but no, I am exhausted. I shall have Jenny prepare me a light supper and will retire to write my message to Christophe. I'll leave the parchment folded and sealed in your room, if you do not mind seeing young Jack in the morning.'

A yawning Robert continued 'draw sufficient expense money from John for Jack to stay over in suitable accommodation each way. I'm sure that Marguerite will make him welcome to stay the night on arriving at Chaffeymoor.'

Robert had his supper alone and then retired to write the message, asking his son to ride up to meet him at The Winchfield Inn on The Great West Road on Thursday the 14th and to come prepared to stay for two or three nights for a spot of fishing or boar hunting. It was a few miles north of Basingstoke, Hampshire where he had stayed before when coming back from Chaffeymoor.

The next couple of days went slowly with no other news other than confirmation that charges of High Treason were put to the King on the 10th. The King appeared before his judges four times, charges with Tyranny and High Treason. The exchanges always took a similar form, with the King challenging the Court's authority and its right to try him.

Robert tried to remain active over the week ahead to try to take his mind off the task ahead.

One fine sunny morning he looked out of his window and thought *what a beautiful day. It's too good to be indoors and a dose of fresh air will do me far more good than just sitting around passing time in the smoky atmosphere of The Angel, supping ale with Elliot.* He decided to take Keagan for a ride across Hyde Park giving her much needed exercise and the January air felt good but sharp hitting the back his throat at full gallop. Holding onto his hat so as not to lose it, it was exhilarating, and given her head, Keagan flew like the wind.

All theatres had been closed by order of Parliament since 1642, but he enjoyed Elliot's company and they managed to go and see Shakespeare's Macbeth, performed one afternoon in the open air of Finsbury park. On reflection, Robert hoped this wasn't a bad omen as he perceived that the story was all about the King's belief in his divine right to rule and he was murdered by Macbeth for those beliefs.

It was now the evening of the 13th. He arranged for an early breakfast at first light and to have Keegan saddled up for his departure shortly thereafter.

He dined with Elliot, John, and Jenny, and he had one last thing to do before leaving early in the morning to ride to Winchfield to spend two days with Christophe. After dinner he bade the others goodnight, went to his room, and sat down at his desk with a heavy heart to write the most difficult letter he had ever written in his life.

The mission ahead was more than just dangerous, it was almost suicidal, and the chances of him returning to a normal life afterwards were tiny.

If I actually survive, I will almost certainly be put into prison, at least in the short term he thought. He knew that, but nevertheless felt compelled to try and save Charles from execution.

He thought of the King all alone in his cell in the Tower. *What was going through Charles's mind? Did he think it was all in vain? What will happen to his son, Charles II? Would he ever return and claim his heritage as God commands?*

As The Rump had acted so quickly there had been no time for him to return home to Dorset to explain to Marguerite or to say goodbye, as the round trip would have taken at least 6 days. He knew she would understand that he could not live with himself if he felt he hadn't done everything possible to stop this execution, and to stop the country becoming a Republic. He knew, if it came to that, she would forgive him for leaving her a widow, even though he also knew she loved him with every fibre of her being. *She will still have Christophe, and Sarah and Paul,* he told himself, *and they would look after her,* but how he wished he could hold her close and feel her arms around him one last time.

As he picked up his quill, the thought of never seeing his darling Marguerite again made him choke back tears and reach for his large linen kerchief. She was the love of his life, and had always been there for him, and he adored her.

He would leave this letter with Christophe only to be given to his Mama in the event of his death. His hand shook and his eyes filled with tears as he began to write:

Angel Islington
January 19ᵗʰ, 1649

My darling Marguerite,

If you are reading this, then you will know that I have departed this earth and am waiting for when the time comes for you to join me in the Kingdom of Heaven. I have loved you my sweetheart from that first day I saw you buying lace and ribbons in Rouen market, to the very last.

You moved me like no other and made me have a purpose in life. I have served the King all my adult life and it is in his name that I have now succumbed to death. I have never been good with words of love, more by way of physically demonstrating my love for you, but I have written this prose for you my darling:

If I should go tomorrow,
It would not be goodbye, just au revoir
For I have left my heart with you
And I have yours to comfort me.
The love that is deep within me
Shall reach you from the stars
You will feel it from the heavens and
It will comfort you and heal the scars.

Forever yours

Robert

31

The following morning, shortly after dawn, Robert set off on Keagan for the long ride to Winchfield, a journey he knew so well. The weather was kind for January, cold but bright with little wind. He made good time and swore that once he was clear of the suburbs of London, Keagan would have known her own way home.

The landscape and the villages he passed through now had a sense of normality about them although the deprivation suffered during the war was still clearly visible. There were thatched roofs, destroyed by fire from marauding troops, carts turned over with wheels smashed beyond repair, farmers tilling the land prior to sewing the coming year's crops, veterans of the war with limbs missing and many widows with small children trying to make ends meet.

He could not help but think much of this could have been prevented if only Madrigal had been laid before King and country sooner.

Before he knew it, he was arriving at The Winchfield Inn. It was late afternoon and Christophe had arrived before him, even though the journey from Chaffeymoor was longer. Despite the cold he was sitting on a bench in the garden, well wrapped up and supping a tankard of ale whilst waiting for his father to arrive.

When he saw Keagan trotting into the yard he cried out.

'Hello father, get Keagan stabled and I shall get you a welcoming large brandy. It's cold out here so I will see you inside, there is a roaring log fire in the inglenook to warm you through.'

Christophe made Anton, the Landlord, aware of his father's arrival and confirmed that they would both like dinner that evening.

'You are in luck', said Anton, 'we have some smoked trout from the local chalk stream, and the wife has managed to buy a brace of duck in the market at Basingstoke.'

Robert soon joined him, stamping his feet, and rubbing his hands to get his circulation moving, and they embraced.

'It is wonderful to see you looking so well Christophe, how is your Mama?'

'She is well father, but your absence from Chaffeymoor is taking its toll. I fear what you are about to tell me with some trepidation, as we are all aware that the King is to be tried for Treason.'

They found a quiet corner with two comfortable wing-back chairs still close enough to the blazing log fire to feel its warmth. Robert removed his heavy woollen cloak and threw it across a neighbouring chair, pulling his chair forward so that he could speak quietly to Christophe. Downing the brandy, he leant towards him and said:

'Christophe, my dear son, I am about to embark on a mission to try to save the King from trial and execution that will put my own life in mortal danger. There are therefore a number of things that I want you to do for me.'

'Anything father, you know that you and Mama are the most precious things in the world to me.'

'Firstly, my Last Will and Testament is lodged with David Paleman, our lawyer in London, and I have had two copies of a Power of Attorney drawn up. It gives both David and Elliot, who I trust implicitly, the authorisation to act on my behalf should I become mentally incapacitated, and in the event of my death will help you to exercise probate of my Will more easily.'

Christophe looked at him in disbelief.

'Secondly, I have a letter from me to your Mama for your safe keeping, only to be given to her should I meet my maker on this mission. Lastly, I want you to prepare for the future, without alarming your Mama. You should rent a suitable cottage in the village now, as a precaution should I fail in my endeavours and pay the ultimate price of an untimely death. Should Chaffeymoor be seized in retribution by Parliament, you can move and hide such valuables as the family silver and Mama's jewellery. Leave my hidden copy of Madrigal at Chaffeymoor. It is as safe there as anywhere for now, and you know where it is, should the need arise for you to have it in the future.'

Robert sat back in his chair.

'That's about it Christophe. I know I can count on you. If I do not succeed in my mission, your Mama is going to need all your strength and fortitude to see her through.'

Christophe was fighting to hold back the tears in his eyes. He was a hardened Cavalier Officer, used to battles, to death, but not to the thought of his beloved father dying. His father was not a soldier, he was Head of the King's Secret Service, not even a spy, so the notion of his death had never really entered Christophe's head.

'I will do as you ask father but is there no other way than what you have in mind?'

'I have searched my conscience. Fairfax tried and failed to get the Trial postponed by petitioning the Attorney General, but it seems that The Rump and other hardliners have made up their minds. They think Charles is guilty of Treason and should be publicly tried and executed. There seems to be no other way than to infiltrate Westminster Hall and lay Madrigal before the learned Judges and the King.'

Robert smiled at his son.

'Let us just enjoy these few days together. I thought that we might go wild boar hunting tomorrow and fly fishing on Wednesday. It is many a year since I have hunted, and this will be an altogether different experience for you compared to the pheasant shoots we had at Chaffeymoor. I have arranged for us to track, and hopefully kill, a wild boar on the Greywell Estate which is owned by The Earl of Malmesbury.'

Christophe smiled back, and taking a deep breath, nodded his approval.

'On Wednesday I thought that we might go fly fishing on the local River Dever which is a feeder stream to the River Test. The Landlord has a couple of fishing poles, lines and imitation flies that he can lend us on the proviso that anything caught is brought back to the Inn for smoking over oak chippings and put on the menu.'

'That would be wonderful father, I haven't been fishing for years since you taught me how to fish in the Mill stream in the village' replied Christophe, still reeling from the idea that his father might die.

'Marvellous, let us finish our drinks and go and get changed for dinner. I will meet you back down here in an hour's time.'

Robert told Anton of their plans to hunt and fish. Anton's eyes lit up. 'If you have good fortune in bagging a wild boar, we can spit roast it all day on Wednesday and enjoy a hearty dinner that night for all our guests, in which case I shall wave your lodging fees for the whole trip. Fair enough?'

'Sounds a fair bargain to me good Sir', replied Robert, feeling excited at the thought of their plans.

The cosy dining room was next to the kitchen and the smell of roast duck permeated through, making their mouths water. Christophe, never one to miss the sight of a fair damsel, eyed up the local lass who was helping in the kitchens, smiling at her as he caught her eye. She looked away hurriedly, but he was sure she was blushing, and that made him grin. Robert sat back in his chair shaking his head at his son's antics. He was so proud of him, but he could not help thinking he should have spent more time with him over the years, enjoying these pleasures of the countryside'.

Having dinner together, reminiscing of the wonderful life that they had both shared with Marguerite, most notably their time at Chaffeymoor, was a very enjoyable way to spend the evening, and they only stopped talking and laughing when the candles flickered their last breath.

The next morning after a hearty breakfast it was off to Greywell to hunt. They arrived at the Estate, a thirty-minute trot from the Inn and checked in at the Gamekeeper's lodge. 'The Earl said you were to be expected, is it wild boar you are after then?' enquired the Gamekeeper, Jack Sawyer.

'What are our chances?' enquired Robert.

'Your best bet is the North West corner of the estate near Nately Scures. They have been seen up there, and with the wind blowing from the south west you should approach them up wind so as they don't smell your body odour.'

'Robert thanked him for his advice and promptly gave him a bottle of French Brandy which was well received.'

Father and son cantered the two miles on the Estate road from The Lodge to the north west corner of the woods and entered them cautiously. The trees and undergrowth were bare on this winter's day. They knew that the only chance of success was not to hesitate on first sighting a boar, but to charge after it as if on the battlefield with their flint lock pistols drawn. It would be a fight to the death at close quarters, a skill that Christophe had perfected during the many battles he had fought in the War. Robert was much less adept, but he had managed to down and kill Marchal shortly after leaving York at the very beginning of the War, after his failed attempt on Robert's life, so he hoped his aim was still as good.

It was not long before they spotted a boar and it spotted them. 'Charge' shouted Christophe as if by second nature to him, and they sped after the boar at full gallop. They closed the gap to less than thirty yards and Robert aimed and fired his pistol, only to wound the boar and stop it in its tracks. The discharge of his pistol caused Robert to swerve slightly, and Kegan caught a hoof in a tree root and toppled. Both Rider and horse were writhing on the ground, trying to get on their feet, none too worse for wear, but the boar sensing blood, charged at Robert with its nose flared and tusks raised.

Christophe stopped and turned round to see his father's plight and feared the worse. The boar charged and leapt. Robert, still on his hands and knees, froze in fear at the site of the huge, angry boar bearing down on him, and then he heard the loud retort of Christophe's pistol and the boar dropped dead weight on top of him.

Christophe leapt off Forest and dragged the boar off Robert crying out 'Are you all right father?'

Robert rolled over, looked at Christophe and they both started laughing uncontrollably.

They sat for a while on tussocks of dead grass covered in frost, looking across the valley, the dead boar beside them. Taking it in turn to have swigs of brandy from Christophe's flask, they shared all the emotions God has given mankind. They had gone from uncontrollable laughter and relief, to elation, hugging each other almost sobbing. Father and son as one, willing to die for one another.

'Talk about one extreme to the other! Tomorrow we shall be at peace with the world, the only fighting will be between us and those wily trout', said Robert, trying to regain some sense of normality.

They hauled the beast, tied it secure across Kegan's back and Robert doubled up on Forest. They rode back via Jack Sawyer's Lodge who could hardly believe what he saw.

'That is a beauty gentleman, all of 80 kilos I would say.'

Christophe cut off the boar's ears and presented them to Sawyer as a sign of respect and gratitude, but they also made a great delicacy in a stew or pottage.

When they arrived back Anton was almost speechless.

'I do not believe it; you have surprised me. What did you say you two have been doing these past years?'

Robert and Christophe looked at each other and smiled. 'Oh, nothing much. Young Christophe here was a Captain of The Dorset Royals, a cavalier in the Civil War', Robert said with pride.

'Well, I never', said Anton. 'Everything for this visit, lodgings, food, drink is all on the house. If only you and your fellow men at arms had managed to keep King Charles on the throne all would be well with the world.'

If only you knew, thought Robert.

'We shall spit roast the boar for 12 hours tomorrow. It will be a grand sending off for the pair of you. Enjoy your dinner tonight, we have roast duck for you with all of the Missus's trimmings. Enjoy your day fishing tomorrow.'

They did indeed dine well, especially as there was a smooth French claret with a beautiful bouquet to accompany the duck. After dinner they both felt exhausted by the day's efforts, and full, from such a delectable meal, so retired early to their rooms for the night.

They slept well and had a late breakfast together; there was no rush. This was to be a day of total relaxation, walking the river and stalking rising trout and grayling. Anton's wife, Eleanor, had prepared them a packed lunch of bread cheese and cold meats, with some of her home-made pickles and a flask of brandy to warm them up now and then.

It was an overcast day, the early morning mist still hung over the Dever valley, crisp as you would expect in January, but thankfully not freezing. A perfect day for a winter's fly fishing for grayling and hopefully the odd trout.

After breakfast they grabbed their fishing gear. The poles were about 10 feet long and made out of willow to give them flexibility, together with fishing lines of stretched woven animal gut, hooks and a selection of fur and feather lures.

They proceeded to walk side by side on pathways across the meadows as directed to so do by the Anton and Eleanor's son Toby.

They breathed in the pure fresh air, felt free and at peace with the world. The meadows were a sheer delight even in Winter. Holly bushes were still laden with red berries, and the ground, covered in meadow mat and waiting to burst into bloom in the spring, was now awash with snowdrops. Last year's Knob Weed and bunches of Greater Mullein which would have had spikes of yellow flowers in the summer and beloved of bees, were now standing tall with architectural seed heads and cobwebs strung between them.

It is good to be alive, thought Robert despite facing death in the eye in his forthcoming deed.

They soon came across the River Dever, a small fast flowing chalk stream of no more than ten feet wide with little Ranunculi weed growth in the winter. The trout might be asleep in the margins, but the grayling were lining up in the main flow to take any tasty morsel that might float by.

They paused and rested on a fallen oak tree trunk, not speaking, just admiring the frosted landscape, and soaking up the sheer stillness and tranquillity. They were in no hurry. As many a fisherman refrained, being there is all, catching a fish is a bonus.

Whilst attaching the lines to their fishing poles and selecting a lure, feather for Christophe, fur for Robert to cover their chances of a fish, they both took a swig of brandy to fortify themselves and then cautiously approached the River.

After an hour or more Robert, who had exceptionally good eyesight, spotted a large brown trout idly lying in the margins off the mainstream under a willow tree on the opposite bank. A difficult fish to catch by anyone's standard. He gave the honour to Christophe.

'Now remember son, put your pole across the water at an angle up-stream of the fish by at least six to eight feet and drop your feather lure, which is dressed to float, so that it floats down across the nose of the fish without any drag on the line.'

'I will try father; this is a lot harder than I remember fishing in the local Mill Stream.'

'Just relax Christophe, there will be plenty more opportunities.'

Christophe approached the river on hands and knees and did exactly as his father had said. The fur lure floated down stream in the margin under the far bank, swirling in the undercurrent, and just as they thought that it had gone past the wily old trout, there was a tremendous cacophony and splash in the river as the trout leapt and took the lure.

'You have got him, hold the pole up and keep tension on the line. Let the trout tire itself out a bit before bring him in to our bank side.'

Christophe, with heart pounding and adrenaline rushing through his veins, a feeling he had not felt since that last bloody battle at Naseby, took his time and landed a magnificent two-pound trout, a large fish indeed for such a small river.

'Well done son, you are a natural, you should do it more often.'

Christophe could not help but notice his father had said 'you' and not 'we.'

They continued to have a wonderful sporting day together. Robert bagged a pair of Grayling, the easier fish to catch in Winter and Christophe another small trout of maybe half-a-pound, which they released back into the river.

It started to get colder, and the Winter's sun that had finally emerged late morning, waned and started to go down, so they decided to head back to the Inn.

On arrival, they handed over their catch to Eleanor. The spit roast was still going in the yard with the wild boar they had caught the day before rotating over a pit glowing with hot oak embers.

Son Toby in charge. Robert and Christophe stood for a  few minutes their bodies soaking up the warmth from the fire and it was all they could do to resist the temptation to slice off a piece of the boar's flesh to eat now, it smelt so good.

'Go on' said Toby, 'the outside should be fairly well done but it still has four hours to go.'

Robert and Christophe needed no further encouragement, tucking in, laughing, and regaling their day's fishing stories to Toby. That night, they all, Robert, Christophe, Anton the Landlord, his wife Eleanor, son Toby, a few other guests staying overnight at the Inn, the kitchen hand and serving girl, all enjoyed the wild boar served with all the trimmings, roast potatoes, winter vegetable and herbs and the wonderous gravy broth Eleanor had concocted with pork trimmings and wine.

For both father and son it was the culmination of two wonderous days spent together, memories not to be forgotten by either for the rest of their lives.

They each departed in the morning, no sad farewells, only embraces and words of love for each other and Marguerite.

32

Robert, now back in the safe house, woke on the morning of the 19th nursing a hangover from the night before from drinking too much ale in the company of Elliot. He rose, had a cold body wash to revive his senses and dressed casually for the day.

Tonight's the night, he thought, *tomorrow will decide England's destiny. Madrigal will win or fail on my skill and determination to see it through to the bitter end. Coffee, I need coffee, strong coffee with a few Goddard's Drops.* The drops were made from the skull dust of a hanged person, dried viper, and spirit of hartshorn, the landed gentry swore by it.

He joined Elliot for breakfast who looked as he always did, ruddy, smiling, chatty as if the night before had been a casual walk in the park. Jenny appeared and enquired what they would like for breakfast.

'I will have bacon and eggs, if you please Jenny, and fried bread', thinking from experience if nothing else settled his stomach a good fried breakfast will.

Elliot nodded and mumbled 'I'll have the same.'

'How you on earth do you manage to consume so much ale without either getting drunk or having a hangover?'

'Practice, Robert, practice' he replied laughing.

'On to more serious matters, in fact only one, the whole purpose of my destiny, the end game.'

'Oh that', replied Elliot, smiling nonchalantly, as if trying to soothe Robert's nerves. Relax, we are all set, we leave at 1.30 a.m., it should be quiet as a mouse at that time.'

The day went slowly, Robert getting more and more anxious and fidgety, pacing around the house, not like him at all. After lunch, and fed up with watching him pacing around, Elliot said

'Come on, let us take a walk down to Westminster Hall, a distance of three miles. We can trace the steps we shall take in the dark tonight; the air will do us good, and we can hail a carriage for the return journey.'

They got back around five o'clock, and to pass a few more hours, they called in at The Angel Inn for a drink and a game of Baccarat.

'I seem to recall that you still owe me three tankards of ale that I won off you from our last game at Christmas' said Robert smiling.

'So I do', said Elliot as if he had not forgotten. 'what's it to be then?'

'I'll settle the score for a large brandy if I may, my good friend.'

Elliot had his usual tankard of ale and they played a few more games without any side stakes. Before they knew it, it was past seven o'clock and Jenny would be waiting anxiously to serve supper.

They strolled back to the house with Robert thinking that he had a fine Deputy, a safe pair of hands to take over should the need arise, as it might.

Without elaborating why, Robert had asked that they all dine together that night, John, Jenny, Elliot, and himself. Nothing special, just Jenny's usual sumptuous cooking, this time it was a rabbit stew with dumplings and winter vegetables.

After supper Robert and Elliot retired to the snug to go through the plan once more, and in particular the layout of Westminster Hall and St Stephen's Chapel and Cloisters.

'Ok Elliot, go through it with me one more time.'

'We approach St. Stephen's Chapel Cloisters from the River Gardens. The north west corner of the Cloisters is adjacent to the Hall, this is where you get in through the window nearest the corner. Once in, there is immediately a stairway down to the lower ground level and to the Maintenance Office. There you hide out until 10 a.m. when the Trial is due to commence.'

'Remind me. How do I get into the actual Hall?'

'When you come up the stairs, it is right to go into the Lobby, left along St Stephen's corridor and you are then within thirty feet of the entrance on the right to the Hall. You will enter immediately behind the King's Seat facing the Court.'

'You make it sound so easy; my heart is pounding just at the thought of it.'

'Just relax Robert, you can do this, this your destiny.'

It was now getting on for 11 o'clock and Robert decided to retire to his room. He asked Elliot to knock for him at 1.30 a.m. and to come in and wake him up if he had fallen asleep.

He now had to retrieve Fairfax's copy of the Madrigal Agreement from its hiding place in the roof space of his room and go through the plan again and again in his mind. He also had to memorise his short statement that he would quickly read out to the Judges before he is surely arrested by the Parliamentary Guards.

Sleep was impossible. Robert was at a heightened state of mind. He thought of the wonderful two days recently spent with Christophe hunting and fishing, the twenty-five years of happy and glorious marriage with Marguerite and raising Christophe to be the fine gallant and courageous man that he now is.

The time had come. He was as ready as he ever would be when Elliot knocked at 1.30. They set off in pitch black darkness, taking a few minutes for their eyesight to adjust, relying only on the moonlight and the occasional lanterns on the main roads.

They had arranged for O'Halloran to provide an additional lookout and extra security should the need arise. They were to meet him on the way down to Westminster, outside the Lamb and Flag Tavern in Covent Garden. They approached the Tavern, but O'Halloran was nowhere to be seen, it was now gone 2.00 a.m. Robert was about to say, 'Where the hell is he?' when he emerged from the shadows giving them a fright.

'Sorry, you can't be too careful in my game' apologised O'Halloran.

The three of them continued down to The Strand and onwards to The River Thames Embankment and along to the gardens of St Stephen's Chapel. They were there, within touching distance, the twin turreted main entrance to the Hall, together with St Stephen's Chapel dominated the moonlit sky.

They stealthily made their way into the Cloisters and to the corner adjacent to the Hall. O'Halloran had, of course, been here before and knew exactly how to prise the window open to let Robert in.

Robert checked to make sure that the Madrigal Agreement was still safe and secure in the inner pocket of his cloak, that he had a small vessel of water to quench his thirst and then turned to shake hands with Elliot. There was no need for words, they both knew that the time had finally come, they had said their goodbyes earlier in private.

He thanked O'Halloran, saying 'You are part of history here Sean, but you can never admit to it for it might cost you your life.'

O'Halloran just smiled and nodded, for he had no truck with this Parliament either.

Elliot gave Robert a final embrace and then a leg up to the window and he was in.

A deathly silence greeted him. with a strange aroma of hallowed halls. He turned to face the window, waved a final farewell and was gone. It was pitch black, but he immediately found the stairwell by touch, and descended to the lower ground floor and into the Maintenance Room which smelled of all sorts of janitorial and maintenance items.

He hid in the far corner of the room behind what felt like an assortment of building materials and ladders. The bell of St Stephen's struck three times. He decided to try to get some sleep, dawn was around 8.00.a.m and the chiming of St Stephen's bell would make sure that he did not oversleep. He dozed fitfully until he finally heard the bell strike nine times; he could hear the hum drum of the assembly within the Hall awaiting the arrival of King Charles.

The King had been moved by Royal Barge along the Thames to Westminster the day before from Windsor Castle, where he was under house arrest, arriving at the very same spot that Robert, Elliot, and O'Halloran had gained entrance to the gardens of St Stephen's Chapel. From there he was taken to St James' Palace to await trial.

On the morning of the 20th he was escorted to Westminster Hall along crowded streets lined with people, mostly jeering, some who were still loyal to the King, cheering. Rather than taking him to the main North entrance, he was taken to the West Door to avoid the mass of people cramming New Palace Yard.

Assembled in the Hall were the 68 commissioners who would try The King out of the original 135 appointed by Parliament. The most notable absentee being Sir Thomas Fairfax, Lord General of the Army. The Solicitor General John Cook had been appointed prosecutor. The King was to defend himself as he believed he was only answerable to God and refused to plead.

The bell of St Stephen's struck ten times; it was time to act. Robert nervously emerged from his hiding place and started to cautiously climb the stairwell to the Lobby. He was unarmed but carrying a forged pass and identity papers bearing the Insignia of Parliament and signed by no less than Fairfax himself.

There were two Parliamentary guards on the other side of the door from the Lobby into St Stephen's corridor. Robert presented his pass and was allowed to continue.

He reached the entrance to the main Hall and could hear General Cook starting to announce the indictment. Cook had uttered but a few words when Charles attempted to stop him by tapping him on the shoulder with his cane and ordering him to "Hold". Cook ignored him and tried to continue.

Charles was so incensed by this that he poked and then struck Cook across the shoulder so forcibly that it broke the ornate silver tip off his cane. It rolled down Cook's gown and clattered on to the floor amid much commotion.

It's now or never thought Robert. The guards on the main door challenged Robert but he just burst through into the Hall with the Madrigal Agreement held high. He immediately came face to face with Lord General Oliver Cromwell, flanked by two more armed officers who wrestled him to the ground. It was over. He had been expected. Someone had betrayed him.

The Madrigal Agreement was wrenched from his hand by Cromwell and Robert was bound by his hands and feet, gagged, and manhandled out of the building and down to the nearby River Thames, where a non-descript barge had been sitting waiting for him. Dragged by the two Parliamentary officers who had seized him in the Hall, he was hauled into the barge, which was rowed by six oarsmen of Parliamentary Yeoman Warders of the Tower of London.

He was taken along the Thames and under London Bridge, the only bridge that crossed the Thames, to The Tower, a journey of some three miles and taking half-an-hour with the outgoing morning tide flowing out to sea. It offered Robert little or no chance of escape.

As the barge entered Traitor's Gate through the outer wall of the Tower, he looked up to see a conspiracy of Ravens

perched high on the ramparts of the White Tower as if they were acting as sentries to observe the events that were to follow.

THE TOWER OF LONDON SHOW-
ING TRAITORS GATE

A bad omen, thought Robert, *it's down to you now Christophe, I know that you will not fail me, God be with you my son.*

There he was to await execution by firing squad, without trial, with few witnesses. Robert was tied to a post, and blindfolded, his last thoughts were of Marguerite, Christophe and of course Chaffeymoor.

He heard the heavy footsteps of the firing party march out to the inner courtyard accompanied by Cromwell's deputy, his son-in-law Major General Charles Fleetwood.

Without any delay came the order to fire.

A volley rang out. The ravens scattered and his mind faltered. A second volley rang out and he descended into darkness.

He was buried in an unmarked grave on the perimeter of the courtyard.

The King's trial continued over the next week and he was declared guilty on the 27th and sentenced to death.

On Tuesday 30th January 1649, the day of the execution, the streets from St James Palace to The Banqueting House were lined with throngs of people, mostly jeering but a few shouting 'God Save The King'.

On a balcony overlooking the route stood the four signatories of Madrigal, Lord Thomas Fairfax the 3rd of Cameron, Lord William Cecil, 3rd Earl of Salisbury, Sir Philip Herbert, 4th Earl of Pembroke, and William Lenthall, Speaker of The House of Commons, paying their last respects to King Charles who glanced up at them and gave them a customary Royal wave.

He was beheaded in public view on a stage erected in front of The Banqueting House of The Palace of Whitehall.

It was a Kingdom no more.

'And when the drums of war
have reached a fever pitch,
And the blood boils with hate
and the mind is closed,
The leader will have no need
in seizing the rights
of the citizenry.
Rather, the citizenry infused with fear
and blinded by patriotism,
Will offer up all of their rights
unto the leader
and do it gladly so.'

Julius Caesar
by
William Shakespeare

Part II

England, January 1649

Revenge

and

Retribution

Le Douse

Vengeance is in my heart,

death in my hand,

Blood and revenge

are hammering in my head.

Titus Andronicus

by

William Shakespeare

33

It was early morning at Chaffeymoor on Tuesday 23" January 1649. Christophe woke with a feeling of disquiet for he knew that the King's Trial was due to commence the previous Saturday. He washed and dressed and went down for breakfast. Sarah was just laying up the table and was about to put some smoked bacon rashers and pork sausages on the range. He offered to help as Marguerite started to descend the oak staircase.

Christophe looked up from turning the sizzling sausages with a long-pronged fork when he heard the sound of a horse's hooves in the distance, pounding on the gravel drive getting louder and louder as it got closer to the Grange.

He crossed the hallway and opened the heavy oak front door and saw a stranger approaching which he thought was odd at such an early hour.

'Who is it'? asked Marguerite as she stepped down from the staircase, crossed the hallway and approached him.

At first glance Christophe did not recognise the stranger, but as he got closer, he realised that it was Elliot from his father's description of him. Elliot, father's faithful deputy, friend, and confidant. Christophe knew immediately why he might have journeyed since dawn on Sunday to reach Chaffeymoor. This could not be good news.

He turned to his Mama and held his arms out wide inviting her to be hugged and comforted by him.

'Noooooooo', screamed Marguerite, 'not my Robert' as she collapsed into his arms.

Sarah came running out, closely followed by Paul, who helped get Marguerite into the drawing room. They laid her down on the chaise-longue, and Paul fetched some smelling salts, wafting them under Marguerite's nose. She was shaking and weeping uncontrollably, calling out for Christophe.

Elliot upon dismounting only had time to tell Christophe that Robert had had been killed trying to prevent the start of the trial of King Charles, when they both heard Marguerite cry out.

'See to your horse Elliot, and then please come on in, you must be totally exhausted.'

'It was the very least I could do, I did not want you to hear the news from anyone else.'

Christophe then ran into the house to comfort his Mama.

'It can't be true Christophe, tell me he is not dead, not your father, he must be missing, wounded, taken in by a Royalist sympathiser, tell me it's not true', sobbed Marguerite.

'I'm so sorry Mama, Elliot was one of the last persons to see father alive, I fear that it must be true,' replied Christophe, fighting to control his own emotions.

Since those last few glorious days spent with his father, he had come to terms with the fact that his father was in effect saying goodbye to him. He had witnessed death hundreds of times on the battlefields, fighting on behalf of the King, sights that you could never comprehend one man doing to another, least forget, but never had he ever felt the gut-wrenching agony he now felt on knowing that he would not see his father again.

He said a silent prayer to himself:

Farewell dear father but not forgotten
For all my fondest thoughts of thee
Within my heart they still shall dwell
And they shall cheer and comfort me.
Rest in Peace Father

244

After the initial shock, when everyone had caught their breath, Sarah welcomed Elliot into the kitchen to rustle up a hearty breakfast for him, and he was joined by Paul. Christophe had lost any appetite he may have had for breakfast.

Despite the early hour of the day Christophe had helped himself to a glass of brandy and gave his Mama the occasional sip as he stayed and comforted her in the drawing room, holding her hands and staring at the crackling fire that had only recently been lit. It was cold. The fire had not had the chance of warming the large, oak panelled room yet. Marguerite started to shiver, and he reached for a quilted throw to wrap around her as she sobbed.

Dear Mama, it is my job to look after you now, he thought.

'Christophe, please invite Elliot to stay for a couple of days, the poor man, riding all this way without a bye nor leave to be with us in our hour of need. I would love to hear his stories of the good times he had with your father', she said through her tears.

'I will Mama, father came to regard him as one of his dearest friends, not just an employee.'

Christophe asked Paul to go down to the Rectory and inform Reverend Banks of Robert's demise, and apologise that they would not be attending communion the following Sunday, as they would still be in mourning.

Paul came back with the news that the Vicar was going to organise a dedication service to Sir Robert in place of Sunday Evensong. He hoped that they would all be able to attend but understood if it were too much or too soon for Marguerite.

Sarah wiped her eyes and blew her nose. Someone needed to clear away the breakfast dishes and tidy up the kitchen, but first she would take over from Christophe in consoling Marguerite.

Christophe joined Elliot in the Morning Room. It was much warmer and cosier in this small room and the inglenook was always lit first thing. The lack of chill felt good, and Christophe was able to take a deep breath and relax a little. He pushed the breakfast crockery to one side as he slid onto one of the long oak benches that ran down the side of the large oak breakfast table. Elliot, who looked dreadful, was sitting opposite, and Christophe extended his Mama's invitation for him to stay on for a couple of days.

'That's exceedingly kind of her. Please convey my condolences and tell her when she feels up to it, I look forward to talking together about what Robert meant to me and our time together in London.'

'I will do that. Now please tell me about father's last hours.'

Elliot proceeded to outline what little he knew about Madrigal in concise detail, as taught by Robert. Moreover, he told him of the plan of Robert's to break into and hide in Westminster Hall so that he could burst in and reveal the Madrigal Agreement to the Judges, Counsel and The King before the King's Trial got underway in earnest.

'He was betrayed Christophe. I don't know by whom, but Cromwell and his guards were waiting for him as he entered the chamber. I have a spy who was in attendance in the visitor's gallery who witnessed the arrest. My spy quickly dashed out, mounted his horse which was hitched nearby, and followed the carriage that took Robert down to a barge that was waiting for them. It was him Christophe, he was gagged and bound and dragged onto the barge. Then it was rowed down the Thames to Traitor's Gate, which is the entrance to the Tower from the water.'

Elliot took a swig of his customary morning tankard of ale, staring down at the table, and stopped to compose himself.

'Not long thereafter, my spy heard the loud retort of a volley of muskets, shortly followed by another, and feared the worse. Later that day, another spy, a member of the Tower's household, confirmed my worst fears. Robert had been executed without trial and is buried in an unmarked grave within the execution courtyard.'

Christophe rose and walked over to the window overlooking the drive and meadows tapering away down the hill towards the village and the Church spire. He was trying to avoid eye contact with Elliot, and he had been fighting to hold back the tears that were now streaming down his cheeks. He took out his kerchief turned and wiped his eyes and cheeks and said, 'Sorry Elliot.'

Elliot too was welling up. Two grown fighting men shedding tears for the hero of their lives, one a son, the other a best friend and confidant.

'Don't be sorry Christophe, Sir Robert was the finest man I ever knew, so morally upright, courageous, faithful to the King unto death. A hero in my eyes; one day people will see him for what he was.'

He indicated for Christophe to come back to the table and join him, and once he was seated opposite again, Elliot, who was old enough to be Christophe's father, leant forward and said:

'You now need to be strong and enact your father's instructions. I assume that you have rented a cottage nearby in the village; it is likely that Cromwell will waste no time in seizing Chaffeymoor in retribution of Robert's actions. You should pre-empt this by moving all valuables, family silver, Marguerite's jewellery, and the like to a safe hiding place, maybe not at the cottage initially as Cromwell's army might search there. Perhaps the Reverend Banks can help. Also move some of the smaller furnishings that might fit the cottage.'

Elliot reached for his saddlebag and withdrew a bundle of parchments and notes of Robert's and gave them to Christophe.

'These are all of Robert's notes and parchment's relating to Madrigal. Take them, hide them and read them when you are over the initial grief and your Mama is well settled into her new life.'

Christophe sat looking at the bundle in wonder and disbelief, saying nothing. He was still trying to come to terms with the news.

'Knowing you as Robert's son and heir, and your heroic exploits in the Civil War, I have no doubt that one day you will seek revenge on those that betrayed your father, and clear and restore his good name. I will keep an eye on both you and your mother from time to time and ensure that Robert's name lives on. You must ensure that Marguerite lives as comfortable a life as can be expected in these circumstances.'

'Thank you, I now know why father thought so much of you. I'm glad you were with him until the bitter end.'

That evening they all dressed sombrely, Christophe providing Elliot with a change of shirt which just about fitted him with some fine adjustments by Sarah, and then they all went together to the Service of Remembrance.

The church was packed to the isles with village folk and local landed gentry, so much so, many had to stand around the font at the back. The Reverend Banks gave a short eulogy remembering Robert's life with Marguerite and Christophe, his service to the King and his love of Chaffeymoor and the village.

His generosity and patronage in supporting the village and the Church will be sadly missed, he said. The congregation rose and sang Psalm 23 The Lord is My Shepherd.

Christophe said a few words and together with Marguerite, left with the congregation standing and clapping. Such a moving tribute to Robert, one of their own.

Over afternoon tea the following day, Elliot and Marguerite spent a couple of hours together alone. Christophe in passing the drawing room, even overheard Marguerite laughing at some of the stories he was telling her of the scrapes that Robert and he got up to, and of their times relaxing together down at The Angel Inn.

They all dined together, that night, no tears just their own celebration of Robert's life. After dinner, taking coffee and brandies in the drawing room, Christophe gave Marguerite Robert's last letter to her. Marguerite took her leave and clutching the letter to her heart, retired early to their bedroom. Robert had often been working away, so she often slept alone, but as she entered the room it suddenly felt completely empty without Robert's presence, and a shiver ran down her spine.

She sat on the bed and read Robert's letter as if he were there, holding her hand, smiling, and reading it to her. She had wept so many tears that day, and the letter gave her comfort. She never, ever doubted Robert's love for her, and she would cherish the letter and his memory forever.

Time is a wonderful thing:

Deeply hurt and saddened by the manner of his death, only that precious commodity *Time* would heal Marguerite's distress. She was distraught at not having Robert's body back so that she could say goodbye properly and give him a Christian burial, but in the days when death was commonplace, it was:

Time for Elliot to leave and head back to London to deal with the aftermath of Robert's death.

Time for Marguerite to start her new life as a widow and begin to overcome her grief.

Time for a family torn apart by the loss of Robert, but closer than ever because of it, to start a new chapter in their lives.

Time for Christophe to take over as Head of the family.

Time for him to avenge his father's betrayal, clear his name, and to reveal

The Closely Guarded Secret of Madrigal.

34

It was the afternoon of Tuesday, 30th January that Oliver Cromwell was alone in his room in Westminster Hall. He had returned from Banqueting House where he had witnessed the beheading that morning of King Charles 1. He took no delight in the spectacle as despite his public persona, he was a God-fearing man and was troubled by Charles's last public words. Moments before the axe fell, Charles turned to The Bishop of London, Bishop Juxton and said;

'I have a good cause and a gracious God on my side,
I go from a corruptible to an incorruptible Crown,
where no disturbance can be, no disturbance in the
world.'

The room at the Hall was austere, reflecting Cromwell's Puritan Christian upbringing in Huntingdon. The oak panelled walls were adorned by a sampler of The Lord's Prayer sewn on hessian in mute colours by his 8-year-old daughter Mary in 1645, and on his desk lay a leather-bound first edition copy of the Book of Common Prayer, finely tooled in gold leaf. The desk, with chair was of simple design and made of English oak. There was also a wing back armchair to relax and read in, and chaise-longue for when an overnight stay was necessary to conduct Parliamentary business. A small side table with a wash basin and jug sat in one corner.

Other similar sets of rooms were occupied by senior Parliamentarians with shared bathroom and toilet facilities and a common dining room and kitchen maintained by Civil Service staff employed by The House of Commons.

Cromwell's family home until 1648 had been a traditional wattle and daub property in Ely, Cambridgeshire, with exposed external vertical oak framing and latticed windows. The family, wife Elizabeth and children, then moved to lodgings adjacent to Whitehall Palace to be nearer to Parliament. Upon being appointed Lord Protector in 1653, they moved into Hampden Court Palace. Cromwell had declined Parliament's offer to be called King but was addressed as 'Your Highness'.

Looking out at the Cloisters of St. Stephen's and the gardens leading down to the River Thames, he re-read the Madrigal agreement that Sir Robert Douse had in his hand when he burst into Westminster Hall in his attempt to stop the trial of the King. Cromwell was unaware that a second copy existed and that for the time being it remained a "Closely Guarded Secret".

He had however been aware of the existence of Madrigal for many years, with several reports from his spies going way back to John Marchal's observations at the failed negotiations that took place in Newark in the summer of 1642, right up to the very latest report and betrayal of Robert's plan by "The Lawyer". He now knew the extent of the Madrigal proposals and who were its advocates and signatories.

Little did it matter now that England was a Republic. However, Cromwell sought advice from The Attorney General, Sir Anthony Steele, who presided as the Chief Judge at Charles's Trial, and from The Solicitor General John Cook, the Prosecutor, as to what should be done.

It was concurred by all of them that there was no case to answer by Lord William Cecil, 3rd Earl of Salisbury and Sir Philip Herbert, 4th Earl of Pembroke. Both were former members of the King Charles's Privy Council and were accepted as having acted in good faith to try to bring about a negotiated settlement between Charles and Parliament.

However, Sir Thomas Fairfax, Lord General of The Army and William Lenthall, Speaker of The House of Commons, were a different matter. Having sought counsel's advice, the decision for Cromwell was whether to arrest them for Treason on similar charges to that which Charles had been indicted. This would expose Madrigal publicly. Alternatively, he could deal with them in a more judicious manner and avoid any public wrath or reaction to the Madrigal proposals.

He decided on the latter. The easiest and most expedient option would have been to have both Fairfax and Lenthall 'disappear' in a similar vein to that which befell Sir Robert.

He knelt before his daughter's Sampler, adorned by an image of Christ, prayed for God's guidance, and was overcome in prayer hearing the Lord's words *'Forgive others as quickly as you would have God forgive you.'.*

Weary from the emotional effect of day's events he retired for the day to be with his family. The following day after searching his soul and praying to God for further guidance his mind was made up.

He returned to his room at Whitehall after breakfasting with his family and summonsed both Sir Anthony Steele and General John Cook to his room at 10.00 a.m. Upon their arrival he bade them both to sit. Steele being the larger of the two sat on the chaise-longue while Cook made himself comfortable in the armchair.

Cromwell remained standing by the window overlooking the cloisters. He looked at St Stephen's Chapel, paused, and turned round looking stern, solemn, and determined.

At this point both Steele and Cook were expecting him to say that Fairfax and Lenthall had 'disappeared' and suffered the same fate as Robert. Instead, he walked over to them, and facing them directly and leaning against his desk, said

'There has been enough bloodshed spilt in God's name determining our mighty cause. I have searched my soul and prayed to God for guidance in this matter. Sir Thomas Fairfax has until now served this country with distinction rising to the position of Lord General of The Army. It is true that he never wanted war and always believed that a negotiated settlement with King Charles was the most preferable option, but once the die was cast, he never, ever waivered in his duty to Parliament in the war effort.'

Standing up straight, he continued

'I am minded therefore that he should be allowed to resign from the Army and to retire gracefully as a hero. He shall be awarded a pension of £5,000 p.a. payable for life.'

Steele and Cook looked at each other in amazement. They had not expected this.

'Lenthall is a much more difficult case to answer. As Speaker of The House of Commons he chose to plot secretly with Royalists in an attempt to stop the trial of The King, instead of laying a motion before The House to debate and vote on such an approach as this Madrigal agreement', he said, waving the parchment in the air.

'We also now know he has an addiction to the sordid goings on and practices performed in the brothels of Clerkenwell and elsewhere. The man is a Traitor to Parliament and the most profound sinner in God's eyes. Had not God answered my prayers and reminded me of his own forgiveness when approaching crucifixion, Lenthall would now be lying on an unmarked grave at The Tower.'

Cromwell walked slowly to the front of his desk, in deep thought. Leaning back on it and looking across the room to the window he could see St. Stephen's glowing in a sudden burst of sunlight. As if inspired, he continued: 'I shall personally interrogate Lenthall. What concerns me most is not only the question of why he felt compelled to take this route rather than advocating in the House for an Agreement with the King, but also, whether there is another copy of Madrigal. If he cooperates, he shall be allowed to announce his resignation at the next sitting of the House, as its Speaker and as a Member of Parliament. In that announcement he shall ask God for forgiveness of his sins, state that he will willingly forego the customary pension awarded to retiring Speakers and ask Parliament to donate such sums to St. Stephens's funds for the poor and afflicted.'

He looked directly at the two men who were sitting, speechless. This was the man who had instigated the beheading of a King, and who was now showing mercy of brobdingnagian proportions.

'That, gentlemen is my final word. General Cook, will you please draw up the appropriate documents stating my decisions, for me to sign and for both of you to witness. Sir Anthony you will arrange for Lenthall to be arrested forthwith and brought before me for questioning.

Thank you both for your forbearance in this most difficult matter since approving the indictment of The King'.

With that Steele and Cook rose, bowed to Cromwell, and quickly left the room. They were stunned by what they had just witnessed, but there were sighs of relief from both.

Later that day Lenthall, escorted by two Sargent at Arms of the Commons was brought before Cromwell.

'William, we have known each other for many years so I will not waste any time, other than to say that what you reveal to me today will determine your fate. You Sir are a traitor and a sinner before God on high.'

Lenthall tried to speak, 'My Lord Protectorate, I ...' but was cut off by Cromwell before he could continue.

'Enough, you are guilty as charged.'

Lenthall was by then on his knees quivering, scared, and started to empty his bladder, the urine running down his leg, protruding through his britches.

'If you tell me what I want to know you shall be allowed to resign your position in The House and as a Member of Parliament and allowed to retire into obscurity without any pension benefits. These shall be donated to St, Stephen's for the poor, as they are far more deserving than you. Do you understand me you snivelling coward?' Lenthall murmured 'Anything my Lord.'

'Are there any other copies of Madrigal? Think carefully before you answer, the last owner met a fate that awaits you if you lie to me.'

Lenthall, proving indeed that he was a coward, decided that living was far better than the hero's death that awaited him if he refused to answer. 'There were only ever two copies, one belonging to General Fairfax and the other Sir Robert Douse. Fairfax gave his copy to Sir Robert and that was the one intended for the Judges at the King's Trial.'

'Sargent, take this pathetic excuse for a man away, get him out of my sight before I do something in the eyes of God I may come to regret.'

With that Cromwell was left to consider the implications of Lenthall's confession. Pacing around his office, he was angry, for once almost uncontrollably, and he picked up and smashed the only remaining trace of King Charles, a plaster bust.

'God help me, will I ever rid myself of you and your cause.'

There was only one answer; Sir Robert Douse must have either given his copy to his son Christophe or hidden it for him to find at a later date if he was unsuccessful in his mission to stop the trial of King Charles.

Cromwell decided that he would order the sequestration and search of Chaffeymoor Grange, Sir Robert's ancestral home. At the same time, he would issue an arrest warrant for Christophe Douse, and if the second copy of Madrigal was not found in the search, he would let the inquisitors draw out of him its whereabouts.

Should they find that young Douse had already fled, there was only one person Cromwell could trust to hunt him down, find the second copy of Madrigal. That person was Alexander Marchal, son of the late John Marchal, and now himself one of Cromwell's closest and most trusted Agents and Spies.

35

They came at dawn on a cold and frosty late February morning. A Troop of Parliamentary Horse led by Captain Henry Wiggins, accompanied by the unidentified Alexander Marchal. They had billeted overnight in Mere and came trotting up the long sweeping drive of Chaffeymoor Grange.

Sarah and Paul were waiting for them, having been aware of their presence in Mere the night before. There was no point in offering any resistance.

At least this way the house would be undamaged, unlike many that had been ransacked or burned to the ground in retribution against their Royalist owners. While it remained unscathed, there was always the chance, the hope, of returning to it one day.

Captain Wiggins was polite and read the eviction notice, signed by The Lord Protector Oliver Cromwell, taking possession of the Grange on behalf of Parliament. He warned his troops that there was to be no looting or desecration of the property or its contents. Sarah proceeded to hand over the keys whilst Paul looked suspiciously at the man in the long dark, almost black cloak who seemed anxious to be the first into the house.

He is no soldier, thought Paul, *what is he up to?* Whatever it was it did not bode well. He suggested to Sarah that she show Captain Wiggins around the property and then left in a hurry to get back to the village.

Marguerite and Christophe had already rented and moved into one of a pair of cottages in Bourton, called Church View Cottages. Sarah and Paul occupied the other. The Reverend Banks had kindly arranged for the Parochial Church Council to approve a long lease on the cottages in Christophe's name.

They were tiny by comparison to Chaffeymoor, but generous by comparison to those occupied by farm workers, labourers, and other associated tradesmen. They were more in keeping with those occupied by yeomen, shopkeepers, tradesmen, and merchants who were aspiring to move up in social circles. The beginnings of the 'middle classes.'

The cottages were each double fronted, thatched, and half-timber framed with wattle and daub plastering between the timbers. They were one room deep with a centrally placed door with latticed windows either side and dormer windows above.

On entering the cottage there was a small hallway with door either side. On the right led into the 'parlour' or sitting room with an inglenook fireplace, situated back-to-back with another in the kitchen diner. There was a connecting door to the adjacent cottage, and a window looking out the front to the church opposite.

The left-hand door from the hallway led to the large kitchen, the same size as the Parlour. The inglenook fireplace complete with roasting spit had an adjacent bread oven and the staircase to the upper two bedrooms was on its far side at the rear of the property. The kitchen area was towards the rear with a window overlooking the back yard and a pantry and buttery running the full depth on the cottage. There was space for a small dining table and chairs by the front window.

Upstairs were two quite spacious bedrooms, with room for a comfortable armchair and small table as well as the bed, and they had fireplaces backing on to each other.

The adjoining cottage, occupied by Sarah and Paul, was of the same size and reverse layout to the one occupied by Marguerite and Christophe. The rear yard which ran the full width

of the pair of cottages was large enough for stabling of two horses and a generous outside 'privy' with two private compost toilets and washing facilities. There was a large rainwater butt and a covered area adjacent to the stables for keeping logs for the fires and hay for the horses dry.

Christophe and Paul were surprised by how much they had managed to save of the Chaffeymoor furniture. They both had one each of the fine Baroque style French sofas and matching armchairs from the drawing room together with the smaller of the beds, tables and chairs. Sarah retrieved silk carpets and drapes to be adapted to fit the cottages together with kitchenware and crockery. They were elegantly furnished indeed, and it had immediately felt like home, just a miniature version.

The family silver and personal possessions had been removed by Christophe and were safely stored elsewhere. The copy of Madrigal was safely left where his father had hidden it, to be retrieved at a later date when either there was a more Conservative government or the return of Charles 11, who was in exile on the Continent.

When Captain Wiggins and his Troop had arrived in Mere, it was obvious why they had come, and Christophe wanted any handover of the house and estate to be as civilised as possible. No damage, no bloodshed, so he remained at Church View in order to avoid any provocation from them, most of whom had fought in the War.

Many of them would have been on the same battlefields as Christophe himself, and they were likely to know of his reputation as a Captain of Royalist Cavaliers and a hero to many citizens. Some of the Troop had no doubt lost friends and fellow Horsemen to Christophe's slashing sword.

Although giving up the house without a fight, he had vowed to his Mama that one day he would clear his father's name and they would all return to Chaffeymoor, their rightful home.

Paul came dashing in panting, out of breath for he had run all the way downhill taking the short cut through the wooded copse to the village.

'Whatever is it Paul?' asked Christophe realising that something had happened up at the Grange.

'Quick Christophe, you must hide. There is a suspicious looking gentleman accompanying a Captain Wiggins up at the Grange. I think he may be a Parliamentary spy.'

Christophe, always able to think quickly on his feet, immediately thought *whoever he was, it must relate to his father's execution.* Of course*, Madrigal* he thought.

'Do not follow me, it's best you do not know where I am going to hide.'

Fortunately, there were few people up and about at this un-earthy hour as he ran across the road to the Church. He looked to see if anyone was around and then entered. It was eerily quiet, and every step echoed as he ran up the centre isle to the Alter, but he knew that hidden under the Alter cloth there was a trap door above a narrow spiral stone staircase that led down to the Crypt. He hurried down the steep uneven stairs, two stairs at a time, his hands on each wall to help guide him as it was pitch black.

There were no windows, only sarcophaguses of past Lords of the Manor and priests, but he knew it well as it had been a favourite hiding place when he was a child whilst playing with other children in the village. In those days they would leave the trap door open to let in a glimmer of light, but today, he had shut it firmly behind him.

It was not long before Captain Wiggins and Marchal came galloping into the village square and made for the church cottages. Paul came out to meet them.

'Where is he', demanded Marchal as he quickly dismounted.

'Who?' replied Paul knowing full well it was Christophe they wanted.

'You know full well who I mean. Douse, where is he?'

'I've not seen him since yesterday evening.'

Marchal took a pace forward and viciously swiped Paul across the face with the back of his right hand in his studded Gauntlet.

'Do not lie to me Sir.'

With all the commotion, Marguerite, who had only just risen, came out of her cottage just as Sarah arrived back from the Grange.

Paul was badly shaken, cut and bleeding on the right-hand side of his face.

Captain Wiggins intervened and proceeded to waive a document in his hand. 'I have here a warrant, signed by our Lord Protector, for the arrest of Christophe Douse on the grounds of Treason.'

'Nonsense' cried Marguerite 'is it not enough that you have taken my husband away from me?' Sarah put her arm around her cousin to comfort her. This was unbelievable.

The Captain shouted, 'Anyone found to be sheltering, harbouring or enabling the said Christophe Douse to escape shall also be arrested.'

Marchal approached Paul, 'I ask you once again. Where is he?'

'I have no idea' replied Paul, spitting out blood from his mouth almost as a gesture of defiance, prompting Marchal to drive his fist into his stomach doubling him up, kicking him as he fell.

'Enough' cried Wiggins, an officer, and a gentleman, 'We are leaving' he said as he indicated to Marchal to remount.

He had left a Lieutenant John Bowler-Bundy and a small contingent of troops residing at the Grange until Cromwell appoints a new resident, and for now his task was over.

'Tell Douse that there is a price on his head. He will be hunted down and brought to justice' he said.

With that Marchal mounted his horse and they both left, trotting off out of the village to re-join the main contingent of horse soldiers.

Sarah quickly rushed to Paul's aid who was up on his feet, sore and uncomfortable but his wounds were only superficial and would soon heal.

'What happened up at the Grange?' he asked Sarah, still bent over, and clutching his stomach.

'I am afraid that they turned it upside down, throwing open cupboards, chests and wardrobes, searching every nook and cranny. What on earth can they be looking for?' she replied, 'whatever it is, they did not find it.'

Marguerite was sobbing at the thought of her only child being hunted down for ever more, and the desecration of her beloved house.

Later that evening under the cover of darkness, and when he considered it safe to do so, Christophe emerged from the Crypt and made his way home to the cottage he shared with his Mama.

She told him what Wiggins had said that he had a price on his head and was to be tried for Treason. She also told him that they had searched the house looking for something.

'What have you done Christophe to make them want to try you for Treason?' she begged.

'Nothing Mama' he replied. 'Nothing.'

He knocked on the adjoining door and beckoned Sarah and Paul to join them. He could not of course share with them the knowledge of Madrigal, or the whereabouts of the second copy of the Agreement.

Not only did he want to clear Robert's name, but he desperately needed to disappear. He also needed to find a way of supporting himself without relying on the family's savings as they must provide an essential income for Marguerite now.

With everyone's complete agreement he decided he would leave the following morning. His first port of call would be to go to London and see Elliot. He did not know the address of the London safe house but knew from his father's stories that they frequented The Angel Inn in Angel Islington.

After breakfast and an emotional farewell hugging Marguerite, he mounted Forest, his faithful bay horse who had been saddled ready with Christophe's saddlebags by Paul. He had a draw-string leather pouch containing five gold sovereigns and a couple of changes of clothes.

He was 25. From now on, without Robert, without the estate, without his salary from the army, the need to both earn his living and help support his Mama was uppermost in his mind.

He had been brought up a gentleman, educated at Oxford and was a skilled horseman and swordsman, used to giving orders. Proud, respected, confident, he had no qualms about his future.

He was also exceedingly handsome, with his blond locks and had inherited his Mama's good looks. He was aware of the glances and attractions he gained from many a fine young lady, from besotted girls like Claire, The Reverend Bank's daughter, to refined ladies of Court when presented at the Officers Mess at Oxford. He had had the odd dalliance during the course of the War, as many an officer did, but thought that at the age of 25 maybe he would find the love of his life on his travels, marry, and eventually settle down at Chaffeymoor.

'Au revoir Mama, je reviendrai et le nom de Robert Douse sera venere dans toute le pays'.

'Au revoir Christophe mon fils le plus cher, revenez en toute securite chaque fois que tu le pouvez'.

With that he was off, waving his hat Cavalier style and shouting

'I will be back!'

Life in Bourton became as pleasant as it could be given the circumstances that the three of them now found themselves in. They were made welcome by their friends, villagers, and shopkeepers alike. The Reverend Banks had called when they first moved in to welcome them, and his daughter

Claire came round often to see if there was anything she could do.

She had been infatuated with Christophe and any excuse to see him was 'heaven' to her. He had rather enjoyed her adoration in the past and had encouraged it with an occasional wink or smile, even though he had no feelings for her in any romantic way.

Spring arrived before they knew it, as the rest of the Winter had been mild. The cottages had no gardens but faced the graveyard and grounds surrounding the Church which was well maintained by the Churchwarden and volunteers from the village. They were adorned with a carpet of Spring flowers, crocus and snowdrops surrounding many of the graves earlier in the year, and now daffodils were everywhere. Tall foxgloves and Canterbury Bells would follow, set against the backcloth of the stone edifice of the Church itself. The first honeybees greeted every flower that bloomed.

The poet Keats described daffodils as '*things of beauty that are a joy forever, gay and glancing and laughing at the wind*'.

Despite being a Catholic, Marguerite attended the church services and took Holy Communion. She helped with arranging flowers and at fund raising events. She was particularly interested in helping widowed mothers and orphaned children in the village, whichever side their fathers had fought on.

Her income, however, was now drastically reduced without Robert's salary from the Government, and Christophe's from the army, so the generosity the family had always shown the village in the past had to cease.

Marguerite said to herself, *Mon Dieu, pourquoi m'as-tu abandonne?*

36

Christophe set off on the well-known route up The Great West Road towards London. He decided to stay overnight on the second night at The Winchfield Inn and say hello to Anton the Landlord, his wife Eleanor and son Toby who had made both Robert and himself so welcome on those memorable last few days they had spent together, hunting and fishing.

All along the route from Mere to beyond Basingstoke there were black cloths, many with RD embroidered on them, tied to trees and other landmarks as a mark of respect for both The King and Robert. This was Royalist country, and no one would forget it or Robert, to them he was a national hero.

As quick as they were removed by Parliamentary soldiers, they were put up again despite the risks of severe punishment and arrest should anyone be seen doing it.

He arrived at the Inn late afternoon and was greeted by Anton and Eleanor as if he was a long-lost son.

'Welcome back Christophe, we were so, so sorry to hear about your father's passing. The news of his gallantry spread like wildfire all through the South West and beyond I gather. It now makes sense to me as to why you were both so happy when you were last here spending precious time together hunting and fishing. You will always be welcome as our guest.'

'Thank you Anton, you too Eleanor, I have been deeply touched as I'm sure my Mama would have been, to see the all the black cloth memorials to my father, all the way from Mere' replied Christophe.

Toby had already stabled Forest and put Christophe's saddlebags in the best guest room in the Inn. He then joined the others downstairs in the bar.

Anton proceeded to fill four glasses with brandy and handed them around, then said 'Let us drink to the memory of Sir Robert, a national hero. No man has ever demonstrated such love and devotion to our late King Charles.'

'Sir Robert' he cried as he raised his glass.

They all, along with many of the other guests present, responded 'Sir Robert.'

Eleanor left them to go back to the kitchen to start preparing the evening meals and Toby, sensing that his father wished to be alone with Christophe, went outside to get on with some chores.

Anton led Christophe into the family's own private snug and poured them both another glass of brandy.

'Sit yourself down, make yourself at home, you must be weary from the long ride'.

Christophe was pleased to be able to sit and relax in one of the simple oak armchairs.

'Thank you Anton. I am so pleased and grateful to be back, you have all made me feel so welcome. Such friends and people I can trust are hard to come by these days.'

Anton downed his glass, looked up and replied with deference and respect, saying,

'When you were here last, I had no idea of Robert's standing as one of The King's most loyal and trusted servants, let alone the role he played in the service of the King. Nor did I realise that you Christophe, were a Captain of The Dorset Royals and it was only after you left that I found out about your own heroic deeds in many of the battles and skirmished of the War. What a family, what a legacy Robert has sadly left us all with', he said as he pulled up a chair.

Christophe thanked him again, and briefly told him about the seizure of Chaffeymoor and the life his Mama, Sarah and Paul were now being forced to live in cottages in the village.

'What about you Christophe, what will you do now'?

'Well, I shall set about seeking the person who betrayed my father and then attempt to clear father's name for a start. That will not be an easy task given that I am Robert's son and heir, so I may well have to go under cover for some time. I am also fearful now that Cromwell has issued an arrest warrant in my name, and there's a price on my head.'

'I wish you well in your quest Christophe. Feel free to come and stay here at any time under whatever alias you choose.'

'Thank you, Anton, I shall certainly bear that in mind if I ever need a bolt hole to escape to.'

Christophe looked exhausted. It had been a long ride.

'Right young man, off you go and rest yourself. Eleanor has put you in the Boar's Head room, quite appropriate don't you think. Dinner is at 7.00 p.m. but if you fancy a tankard of the finest, I shall be behind the bar as usual from 6.00 p.m. onwards.'

Christophe got up and dragged his weary body up the stairs to the Boar's Head Room and flopped onto the welcoming bed. It was now close on 5.00 p.m. so he thought he would have a nap for an hour or so, have a quick wash and change and be down in the bar by 6.30. He remembered that Anton kept the finest ale on tap this side of The George at Mere.

The family all joined Christophe for dinner. There was smoked local trout to begin with, followed by one of Eleanor's renown rabbit pies, potatoes, garden vegetables, and served with a most delicious sauce made from the rabbit's offal, redcurrants, herbs, and red wine. All washed down with a flagon of the best French claret.

Christophe enjoyed their company and they spent much of the evening reminiscing about the hunting and fishing trip, particularly the wild boar chase, a memory that would stay with him the rest of his life.

It was soon time to retire to bed for the night. It had been a long exhausting and emotional day. Christophe's last thoughts before dropping off to sleep were of happier times at Chaffeymoor. He was determined as long as he should live, to return it to its rightful place as The Douse's ancestral home, for one day he too hoped to marry and have a son to carry on the family name.

He rose early, eager to get on the road to London and hopefully find Elliot at The Angel Inn. Eleanor, knowing he wanted to be away early, was already up and was cooking him a 'full English' breakfast.

'Two eggs or three. Christophe?'

'Oh go on then, three please'. *That should keep me going,* he thought.

On leaving, Eleanor produced a lunch pack she had put together for him consisting of west country cheese, ham, a few tomatoes, and a chunk of bread with a small bottle of red wine. She also threw in some raw carrots for Forest.

Once again, as in his last stay, Anton refused any payment, a most generous gesture, and Christophe would never forget his friendship.

He bade them all goodbye, and Anton clasped him round the shoulders saying 'Godspeed Christophe, do your father's memory proud for I know you will. Come back soon.'

Christophe mounted Forest who seemed to know the way and trotted off to re-join The Great West Road towards London. They made good time on a fine May morning all the way to Hounslow Heath.

The Heath was a notorious spot for highwaymen, the numbers of which had swelled after the Civil War, many of whom were impoverished Cavaliers who had both the horse-riding skills and that of weaponry. It was vast, consisting of some 4,000 acres crossed by both The Great West Road and the Bath Road, with Hounslow more or less in the centre.

Mostly heathland with scrub and overgrown hedgerows, it had bramble bushes with few trees, but with swathes of wild Buddleia, Forsythia, Gorse, Rosemary and Lavender growing in the sandy soil.

As if by chance and bad luck, having started to cross the Heath, Christophe was accosted by a Highwayman, pistol drawn and bellowing the now familiar cry of 'Stand and Deliver.'

He had suddenly appeared from behind bushes, a tall rugged weather-beaten fellow with tousled hair, exuding confidence, and not even wearing a mask as a disguise.

Christophe, somewhat bemused by this action, pulled out and cocked the small pocket pistol that he kept in his outer garment, and looking his assailant in the eye, said,

'You should know full well by now Trooper to cock your pistol first before aiming it at a foe. Now carefully lower it before I blow your head off. By God what regiment were you in, I would not have given you horse room in The Dorset Royals.'

The Highwayman did as he was told whilst replying 'The Dorset Royals? Were you under the command of the infamous Captain Douse?'

Christophe just smiled and said, 'I think you could say that I knew him well.'

He shared his lunch with the young man and discovered that he had fought with the Oxfordshire Royals, coming from humble beginnings as the son of a saddler in Chipping Norton. He had been commissioned in the field and was none other than Captain James Hind. They talked about the War and the misfortunes of many a brave cavalier with no home to go back to, no army pay, nobody and no-where to turn to other than to go on the road as a Highwayman, some chivalrous, some ruthless.

Hind had rapidly gained a reputation for his daring escapades, chivalrous and courteous conduct, especially to the ladies who swooned at his rugged looks, and the twinkle in his eye. He only robbed Parliamentarians, left them with at least a £5 and gave sizeable donations to destitute Royalists, a modern-day Robin Hood.

Their conversation gave Christophe an idea. *What better alias could there be to pursue his quest, than to also become a 'Gentleman of the Road'. He would be anonymous and be able to ask questions of those Parliamentarians that he held up. With luck he might find out where his father's betrayer lived.*

But first he must go to The Angel Inn and see Elliot to find out what he knows, or can find out, about his father's last days and his betrayal.

With lunch finished, Forest rested, the last dregs of the red wine swilled between them it was time to get on the road.

Wishing each other well for the future, Hind said to Christophe 'If ever you need me, or if there is anything I can do for you, I can usually be reached or contacted through the landlord of The King's Arms in Malmesbury.'

'Thank you James, I shall not forget this encounter, and next time have that pistol cocked! Another armed potential victim will not necessarily recognise a fellow Cavalier.'

Hind just laughed and with that galloped off with the Cavaliers customary wave of his hat.

37

Christophe and Forest continued their journey safely across the remaining part of Hounslow Heath from the South West to the outskirts of London. They passed through Chiswick and Kensington High Roads and cantered up through Hyde Park and onwards to Islington. It was a route well known to Robert but the first time for Christophe who was in awe of the fine houses in Kensington and along the outskirts of Hyde Park.

Upon reaching Islington it was easy to spot The Angel Inn. It was the first Coaching Inn on The Great North Road heading out of London. It was early evening when he entered the stable yard and dismounted and tethered Forest before asking the stable lad to wash him down and give him some oats and barley. Christophe thanked the lad, gave him a farthing for his troubles and entered the Inn by the back entrance.

He strolled over to the bar and asked the Landlord if Elliot had been in that day.

'Not yet' replied the Landlord 'he usually comes in around 6 o'clock.'

'In that case, I shall have a tankard of your finest ale and some bread and whatever leftovers you have from luncheon', replied Christophe.

Jack Daniels the Landlord, drew the tankard of ale from the barrel behind the bar and called out through the serving hatch

'What do we have left over from luncheon?'

'I can do bread, ham and pickles, if you like kind Sir' came the reply from the kitchen.

'That would be most welcome, thank you.'

'You're not from round these parts then with an accent like that.'

'No' replied Christophe rather too hastily, 'I grew up in the Thames Valley between Henley and Maidenhead.'

'What do you want from that ragamuffin Elliot then?'

Luckily before Christophe could answer, his board of food arrived and he sat himself down at a small table in the corner of the room. He took his time over the light meal and drinking his ale. His thoughts turned to his father, wondering where he sat with Elliot enjoying a tankard of ale or two and playing backgammon.

As soon as he was finished, Jack was over, quick as a fletcher's arrow, to clear away his board. 'You fight in the War then? Your riding boots and bearing suggests that you are a fine horseman.'

Suddenly a voice boomed across the room from the front entrance 'That's enough of that, this young man is a friend of mine and has travelled a long way to see me, so show some respect if you please,' said Elliot with a grin.

Christophe rose from the table, never more pleased to see him, rushed over and gave him a bear hug whispering in his ear 'Don't mention my name.'

Elliot understood, and whispered back 'OK my friend, tell me later.'

'Right' said Elliot 'two more of your finest please Jack.'

He then proceeded to tell Christophe that they were sitting at the very table that he and Robert used to sit at on many occasions, having a tankard of ale as a relief from the war going on around them and the deeds of the day in their clandestine occupations.

A shiver went up Christophe's spine at the uncanny coincidence that he was sat at the very same table. Speaking quietly so as not to be overheard, he told Elliot of his mission to find out who betrayed his father and that he needed to adopt the alias of "Tristan Cheval" to avoid suspicion and arrest by Cromwell.

Elliot in turn pledged his loyalty to his father's name and to Christophe himself, offering his service in whatever way he could.

After downing the last of their ale they got up and went out to the yard and untethered Forest. Elliot then led them the short distance to the alley and the back yard of the safe house. Whilst they were stabling Forest, John and Jenny came out upon hearing him clip clop up the alley and into the yard.

Jenny instinctively knew who Christophe was, holding back tears she clasped hold of him and said, 'we were heartbroken to hear about your father, he was a great man, a national hero and we thought of him as part of the family.'

Elliot introduced them properly and advised them that from this day forth, outside of the house, Christophe was to be known as "Tristan Cheval".

'Welcome' said John, we have kept your father's room as it was when he left on that fateful day. From this day forth it shall be yours whenever you come to stay.'

After they had entered the house, John explained to Christophe the layout and took him up to the floor which was given over to Robert, and now to himself. He also showed him the escape route, out of the window onto the roof should it ever be required.

'It is now getting on for 6 o'clock. Jenny and I will bring up some hot water as soon as possible, as no doubt you would like a soak in a warm bath. Dinner is at 8.'

Christophe felt a strange presence in the room but reasoned that it was a combination of the smell of his father's clothes hanging in the French Armoire and the smell of his father's favourite lavender soap.

He sat at his father's desk and pictured him writing up his notes on his quest to solve the Madrigal secret. Opening one of the small top drawers he discovered a pile of his Mama's love letters to his father neatly wrapped in red ribbon and another pile of his own letters tied up in a blue ribbon, his father had kept them all. He was drawn to tears, a grown man, a Cavalier, and hero, but a father's son still in mourning.

Before he knew it there was a knock on the door and it was John and Jenny with several ewers of hot water which they poured into the ornate copper bath in the corner of the room.

They then left him in peace knowing that it must be an emotional wrench for him to be in his father's room, his home away from Chaffeymoor.

He was glad to get out of all of his travelling garments, and step into the bath, lay back and luxuriate, washing himself all over with the soft lavender soap.

He stepped out, rough towelled himself and lay down on the large bed which had a luxurious deep horsehair mattress, made by the local upholsterer, John Lewis. It was not long before he drifted off to sleep only to wake up with a start, disorientated and realising it must be late as the sun had already set across the London skyline.

Quickly splashing his face with cold water to both gather his senses and to freshen himself up, he got dressed in clean undergarments, a fresh white shirt and black breeches and descended the stairs.

Elliot, John, and Jenny were already seated at the dining table when Christophe entered. He apologised to Jenny who replied,

'No need, we have only just started, sit yourself down, there are pots of vegetables and sauce on the table, I shall just go and get your roast chicken,'

He sat down next to Elliot, thankful that it was a relatively light supper considering he had the snack back at The Angel.

Feeling relaxed in their company, he was only too pleased to tell them all about growing up at Chaffeymoor and stories about Robert and his Mama.

'How did it go when Cromwell's militia turned up?' enquired Elliot.

'It started all very civilised. Captain Wiggins was courteous to Sarah who handed over the house and keys. I had stayed behind at the Church View cottages that we are renting from the Church Diocese to avoid any confrontation with the Troops. However, Wiggins was accompanied by a Parliamentary spy, who turned out to be a vicious thug, assaulting poor Paul in seeking my whereabouts. Captain Wiggins had an arrest warrant for me, issued by Cromwell himself, on the grounds of Treason, and said there was a price on my head. I managed to hide in the Church Crypt and made my escape this morning.'

Elliot got up and took Christophe's tankard for a refill.

'We had already moved enough furniture from Chaffeymoor to fill both cottages, and the family silver and possessions are safely hidden elsewhere. The Reverend Banks, his family and villagers have all been wonderful and I now feel able to move on, with the help of Elliot, who I know father came to regard as his dearest, closest friend.'

Elliot blushed, any sign of it being hidden by his ruddy complexion, and said,

'Come now Christophe, we all regarded Robert as part of our family, and now he is a legend among all loyal Royalist's who are eagerly awaiting the return from exile of King Charles's son, our rightful King, Charles 11.'

After much convivial conversation, John and Jenny rose to clear away the table and left Elliot and Christophe in private.

'Come, let us take this bottle of brandy and our glasses into the snug where you can tell me your plans,' said Elliot.

They both got up and moved into the snug, Elliot putting the bottle of brandy on the small wine table between the two comfortable armchairs.

With a sigh from Christophe and a belch from Elliot they settled into the armchairs, Elliot, by custom, leaving 'Robert's chair' for Christophe. Having poured them both a generous glass of brandy, he asked what his plans were.

'The first thing I need to do, and this is where I welcome your assistance, is to find out who betrayed my father to Cromwell. I have read all my father's notes on Madrigal and it seems plausible to me that there are three possible suspects.'

Elliot interjected, 'I have been thinking the same, let us see if we have come up with the same names.'

Almost like a deadly parlour game, Christophe named his prime suspect,

'Sean O'Halloran', the Irish gangster from Kilburn who had participated in the breaking into Westminster Hall on the night before the Trial of King Charles.

'Spot on' said Elliot, 'that braggard would do anything for money and I guess in this instance the reward would have been substantial in the least.'

'My other possible suspect is Lenthall, probably under duress having been discovered himself to be involved in the plan.'

'I agree, and let me guess the third, Kathryn d'Aubigny, Lenthall's, and many others, lover. Robert spurned her advances, and it may well be that 'pillow talk' whist in bed with Lenthall gave her the idea of a means to restore her pride, as well as her wealth and status.'

'So where do we go from here?'

'A process of elimination Christophe! It's simply a process of elimination. Let's start with O'Halloran. Nobody would blink an eyelid if he were to be removed from the streets and society.'

And so the 'End Game' was afoot, a chance to honour his father's name and then reveal the secrets of Madrigal to the citizens of the country.

38

The next morning during breakfast, having slept on their deliberations the night before, Elliot and Christophe decided between them that it was hard to believe that Lenthall had a part in Robert's betrayal, after all, as he was a signatory to the Madrigal agreement. He may be of help though if he knowingly or unknowingly gave something away something about Robert's intentions to Kathryn d'Aubigny.

Their first and easiest course of action was to seek out O'Halloran, and either eliminate him from their quest, or permanently eliminate him if he proved to be guilty.

After breakfast and feeling replete, Elliot sent word to O'Halloran via the landlord at The Angel Inn, saying he had another job for him which was of utmost secrecy, and he would pay handsomely for his services. He arranged to meet him by the Royal Tea Pavilion at 'The Ring' in Hyde Park the following evening at mid-night, and he was to come alone.

The second action was to meet Jack, his trusted head of his London spy ring, to find out where Lenthall had retired to after resigning from The Commons.

That night, at around 11o'clock, Elliot and Christophe mounted up and rode to Hyde Park entering by the North east Corner and down to The Ring to be in good time to meet O'Halloran at mid-night.

Hyde Park had traditionally been a royal hunting park, acquired by Henry V111 from the monks of Westminster

Abbey. King Charles 1 created a circular track called The Ring, around which members of court could ride or drive their carriages. It was just north of the Serpentine, the elongated lake.

In 1637 he opened the park to the public and it soon became a fashionable place to visit, especially on May day.

Cromwell himself was known to enjoy riding in the park and crowds often formed as he galloped around The Ring. On one such occasion he was subject to an attempted assassination, the perpetrator escaping through the crowds.

On another occasion, with crowds gathered to watch illegally organised carriage races that had monetary prizes, Captain James Hind, the notorious Highwayman, rode into The Ring for a wager, and robbed a coach of a bag of money. He was hotly pursued but made his escape.

The Ring was surrounded in parts by tall elm trees that provided shade on a sunny day for spectators, but in this instance provided cover for Elliot and Christophe. O'Halloran had performed jobs for Elliot in the past and had no reason to doubt that this was another such venture. He rode over to the pavilion and dismounted upon which Elliot and Christophe appeared, pistols drawn.

'Beejeezus what's this?' exclaimed O'Halloran.

'Just do as we say Sean and no harm will come of you' said Elliot, 'now throw down your pistol and knife and lie face down on the ground.'

'Oi don't know what you are up to, but it had better be good or your life will be truly short.'

O'Halloran did as he was told, and Christophe patted him down for any further weapons. Elliot then began to interrogate him.

'What do you know about the arrest of Sir Robert?'

'No more than you. We both never saw him again after he gained entry to Westminster Hall that night.'

'Well someone betrayed him, and you seem the most likely.'

'Now why would I do that?' said O'Halloran trying to get up off the ground but finding Elliot's boot on his back.

'Money of course, you would sell your own sister for money.'

'I've got more than enough money to see me through to dem pearly gates.'

Christophe intervened. 'We are wasting our time' and promptly stabbed O'Halloran with his stiletto knife through the back of his hand, tearing through sinew and bone and sticking the knife into the ground under his hand.

'O'Halloran screamed in pain. 'You bastard! You will pay for this!'

Christophe then cocked his pocket pistol, placed it at one of O'Halloran's knees, a well-known Irish threat for punishment for betrayal, and through gritted teeth growled,

'I ask you again, what do you know?'

'Nothing! Oi swear on my mother's life, I don't know nuffink. I do know better than to cross someone like Sir Robert, he is a national 'ero.'

'Let him go Tristan, I think we have got what we came for' said Elliot to Christophe.

He helped O'Halloran on to his feet and gave him his kerchief to wrap round his damaged hand.

O'Halloran spluttered 'Where did you find this one Elliot?'

'You don't want to know; you really don't want to know. Now here is another £25 for your pain, and if you ever divulge what happened here tonight, Tristan here will come calling when you least expect it, and he won't have me to control him next time.'

With that Elliot and Christophe mounted their horses and rode into the night, back to the safe house.

They both rose late next morning after such an eventful night.

Breakfast came and went and not long after came forth further good news. Jack had reported back that Lenthall, had bought Southlands Manor in Denham, Buckinghamshire, a quiet country village on the Oxford Road some 15 miles west of London. He had retired there with his family and led a quiet life away from the hustle and bustle of London's city life and his former Parliamentary duties.

He also confirmed that Lenthall was still secretly seeing Kathryn d'Aubigny.

Christophe was amazed at the speed of Jack's response, it would have taken him weeks, possibly months to find out where Lenthall was now living. He realised more than ever the work his father was engaged in and the network of Agents and Spies he had built up over many years.

'Right' said Elliot, 'a day off to gather our thoughts as to how we approach Lenthall, and Christophe, *try* not to go round stabbing and shooting all our suspects.'

Christophe laughed. 'That braggard was never going to yield to idle threats, he got what retribution he had no doubt melted out to others on many an occasion.'

With that Elliot burst out laughing too, 'You are a chip off the old block for sure. Let's meet this afternoon in the snug for coffee and cake at around 4. We will discuss tactics for tomorrow, then off to The Angel for a couple of tankards of Jack Daniels' finest before supper.'

Christophe welcomed the opportunity to spend some time alone with his thoughts in his father's room. He sat at Robert's desk overlooking the street below which was busy with a hive of activity. Persons going to and from about their business, housewives looking for bargains, merchants and traders visiting the many artisan shops and workshops along the street.

Sitting proudly on the desk alongside his inkwell and quill pens he found the snuff box that his Mama had given his father at the last Christmas they all spent together at Chaffeymoor, engraved

Forever Yours, Marguerite

It contained his father's favourite snuff, Madame Grand-maison's Martinique, named for the Caribbean island where it was manufactured. It was sold in long necked bottles and had to be moistened before use. Made with Rapee tobacco and perfumed with the Island's yellow cassias flower, it had a slight cinnamon flavour with a hint of gardenia.

Christophe then went through Robert's clothes and found a magnificent finely tooled dark brown leather jerkin which fitted him perfectly. On the right cuff was embossed the Chaffeymoor Coat of Arms.

Having foregone lunch, he then moved from the desk across the room and sat in the armchair to give thought on how to approach Lenthall, who was not a strong man. According to Elliot he had immediately given in to Robert's previous demands on presenting him with the evidence of his sordid addiction to sexual perversion with prostitutes.

It seemed to Christophe that Lenthall would be easily forthcoming in telling them anything he knew, even information on Kathryn d'Aubigny, without any threats or resorts to violence. It was just a question of getting him alone to question him.

He went through the remaining personal items and found his father's last notes. Robert had studied philosophy through the ages, and he had written a quote by Plato, the Ancient Greek Philosopher, that rang true to himself before he left to perform that final perilous act of loyalty to the King:

There will be no end to the trouble of states,
or of humanity itself,
Till Philosophers become Kings of this world,
or till Kings and Rulers truly become Philosophers
and political power and philosophy
Thus come into the same hands.
Plato

39

The smell of freshly made coffee and cake coming out of the oven drifted up the stairs and brought Christophe back to matters in hand. Bounding down the stairs two at a time, he found Elliot in the Snug, tucking into the cakes.

'Ok Elliot, when and where do we go and see Lenthall? It seems he has much to tell us about Kathryn d'Aubigny', he said, helping himself to a large slice of cinnamon and apple cake that was still warm.

'I think you are right. Sir Robert once told me in confidence that when they met some time ago, he spurned her advances. Being the gentlemen that he was, he would. Jack has also discovered that her finances are dire and that she is in huge debt to the French Ambassador, no doubt being worked off partly in kind, if you get my inference. Two traits of a Traitor if you ask me.'

'We shall ride out west to Denham in the morning and take a chance in just turning up at Southlands Manor and confronting him. Drink up your coffee and eat some more of Jenny's delicious cakes, then we can be off to The Angel for a tankard of ale or two and a game of backgammon.'

The next morning, they set off for Denham, an easy ride taking less than 3 hours west on the Oxford Road. It was a fine May day 1649. Once on the open road the air began to smell fresh after the early morning rain, there were late blossoms on cherry trees and hawthorns and the smell of new growth of many fauna and flora was in the air.

Traffic on the road, was surprisingly busy with carriages, horse and carts and single riders, a reflection of the country returning to normality after the Civil War. There were farmers and small holders taking vegetables to market, merchants taking their wares to and from Oxford and many people just out for a carriage or horse ride to escape the confines of the city.

After some 2 hours or so they passed through Hillingdon and Uxbridge and soon found Southlands Manor on the outskirts of Denham. They stopped and paused by the River Colne giving their horses a rest and drink from the clear flowing water. Elliot produced his hip flask, they each had a swig of brandy and decided to just ride up to the Manor unannounced. If they were greeted by a Houseman, they would simply say it was Sir Robert Douse and partner to see William Lenthall.

'That should do the trick,' said Elliot.

And so it transpired. They were received by the Houseman and before you could say 'Long Live the King' were ushered into the Morning Room.

Southlands reminded Christophe of Chaffeymoor, it was of similar age and design but nowhere near the size or character of 'home' as he still regarded it to be.

They were soon joined by Lenthall looking white as a sheet in trepidation as to who the visitors could be and what they wanted. He relaxed somewhat on recognising Elliot from the previous unfortunate encounter.

Elliot, of course, knew of Lenthall's 'pardon' by Cromwell and his 'unofficial exile' from London society.

Lenthall invited them to sit and, eager to get rid of them as soon as possible, asked,

'What on earth are you doing here? I thought after our last agreement I would never see the likes of you again, and who is this, another one of your thugs I suppose.'

Christophe bristled, and Elliot replied, 'Let us just say he is an interested party to our deliberations.'

Elliot too, did not waste any time,

'It must have occurred to you that Robert was betrayed. Cromwell was waiting for him as he burst in on the Trial.'

'I know nothing of that, I was loyal to the Madrigal cause to the end and look what good it has done me.'

'I don't need to advise you of what evidence I hold of your sordid past do I William?'

'No, no you swore we were even.'

'It seems to us that you had nothing to gain by betraying Robert, but we believe a close acquaintance of yours may well have.'

'Don't be silly, who on earth do you think I know who would have had a hand in such a deed?'

'Why, yours and many others lover, Kathryn d'Aubigny. We know that you have been lovers for many years and that you are still seeing her. What may you have told her inadvertently or otherwise William?'

'Nothing, why would I?'

Christophe was starting to get impatient thinking that he may have to dish out some punishment of the kind imparted on O'Halloran. He got up from his chair and started pacing around the room in an agitated stance.

'Think William, think hard, I can see my friend here getting impatient. Apart from publicly denouncing your proclivities with Kathryn and prostitutes, we do not want to resort to violence, do we.'

'All right', said Lenthall keeping one eye on Christophe. 'I may have mentioned that Robert was going to attempt to stop the trial and present the Madrigal agreement to the court, that was all.'

Elliot jumped up out of his chair and backhanded Lenthall across his face, cutting his cheek with his signet ring.

'That was all?' he shouted.

It was all he could do to hold back Christophe from getting his hands on Lenthall.

'You might as well have signed his death warrant' Elliot seethed, controlling his own urge to kill him himself.

'I'm sorry, I am so sorry, please forgive me,' Lenthall whimpered.

'Where and how often do you see Kathryn?'

'We meet at least once a month; I still have a small pied-a-terre in London. 'We are due to meet on Tuesday next week, and I shall travel up the day before telling my wife I have to go up to London on business for a few days.'

'Right, this is what we shall do, write down on a piece of parchment the address of the pied-a-terre and we shall meet you there. When does Kathryn arrive?'

'She usually arrives between 3 and 4 p.m., we go out to dinner and then spend the night together.'

'Ok, we shall meet you there at around 2p.m. This is your last chance to redeem yourself William, take it or suffer the consequences.'

With that, Lenthall went over to the desk by the window and withdrew some parchment paper, quill pen and ink and wrote down the address, handing it over to Elliot.

Elliot and Christophe, without any customary goodbyes, strode out of the room, out of the Manor, mounted up and left Lenthall somewhat shocked and in pain, clasping his face from a cut cheek and a sore mouth.

'Well, that was easy, so far, so good, time for some lunch' said Elliot, who was always thinking of where the next meal and tankard of ale was coming from.

They had lunch at The Swan and Bottle Inn on the Ox-ford Road. It was next to the bridge over The River Colne on the outskirts of Uxbridge. Locally reared mutton stew for El-liot and pan-fried trout caught in the Colne for Christophe. A tankard of local ale each helped the lunch go down.

After lunch they spent a while on the bridge looking down at the wily trout darting in and out of the ranunculus, feeding on the shucks of male May Flies dropping into the river after procreating mid-air, their mate flying off to lay her eggs on the

low stalks of reed jutting out of the shallow gravelled beds at the edge of the River.

How Christophe would have loved to be spending time fishing at this most prolific time of the year for catching wild brown trout. Memories came flashing back to him of that last glorious day spent fishing with his father on the River Dever.

Then it was off, back up the Oxford Road all the way to London and the safe house in Angel Islington. It was second nature for Elliot's horse 'Barley' to stop off at The Angel for him to have a swift tankard of ale before she headed into the back-alley yard of the house.

John appeared and took control of the horses, taking off their tack and saddles and giving them both a good rub down with buckets of cold water before leading them into their own stable booths and giving them each a bucket of oats and barley and a well-earned rest on beds of straw.

Elliot and Christophe went in, passing Jenny who was busy preparing supper.

'Smells good Jenny' said Christophe, giving her a smile, 'what's for supper tonight?'

'Away with you, all will be revealed at 8 o'clock.'

It was now 6.30 p.m.

Before going up to wash and change for supper he led Elliot into the snug and poured them both a glass of Manzanilla sherry.

'I thought we should just re-cap on where we are to date in seeking who had betrayed Father. I think we can rule out O'Halloran, and probably Lenthall. Kathryn d'Aubigny could be involved. She had the motive of Father spurning her advances and is greatly in debt to the French Ambassador. However, I can't somehow see her revealing her hand to Cromwell, there must be someone else involved, but who?'

Elliot responded, 'She is well known in high society of course, but this smells of a much darker hand, someone who has a grudge against the old establishment of The King, and the Courts. Someone who possibly knows about Madrigal

and would do anything to prevent it becoming public knowledge.'

'Of course!' exclaimed Christophe. 'Reading Father's notes on his Madrigal quest he was attacked right at the beginning back in 1642 by a Parliamentary Spy called John Marchal. On his deathbed, having been shot by father, Marchal revealed that someone known as 'The Lawyer' was one of the main protagonists against any Treaty with the King and was vehemently against the publication of Madrigal.'

'That's right. How on earth could I have missed him, and I'm supposed to be the Master spy here!' exclaimed Elliot. 'It has been staring me in the face all this time. He was subsequently identified as Edward Floyd, a lawyer who had a criminal record for defamation of Royalty. He had been disbarred from practising law at Lincoln's Inn for inferring that a certain Judge had taken a bribe on behalf of a Royalist defender.'

Elliot refilled both their glasses and continued,

'No one knows where he is now, he appears to have disappeared completely to live out his old age with his daughter Lysette.'

'Well, we shall find out more next Tuesday when we confront Kathryn d'Aubigny', said Christophe. 'Shame about O'Halloran, but you can't win them all'!

They both laughed and swilled down the last of their sherry.

40

Tuesday soon came round. After lunch at The Angel, Elliot and Christophe headed down to Lenthall's Pied-a-terre in Kensington. It was just after 2.30pm when they arrived to be greeted nervously by William and ushered into the drawing room. The house and the room were decorated as one might expect of a small townhouse owned by the upper middle classes of the 17th century. Comfortable and ornate, fit for purpose for the occasional stay "in town" when visiting the theatre or socialising with friends but not of the style or standard of a fine country house.

'Please do sit down', said William, 'Kathryn should be with us within the hour. I hope we are going to be civilised over this matter, there is no need to utter threats, let alone resort to violence.'

'You do not need to remind us, as gentlemen, how to treat a lady', replied Christophe as he glanced around the room, his gaze landing on an oil painting of a rather well-built naked lady lounging on a sofa. He wondered if it was Kathryn.

'We all want the same outcome, William; we just need to know who committed the final act of betrayal and denounced Robert's intentions to Cromwell. Elliot and I have a fairly

good idea who that is, but we just need confirmation from Kathryn of our suspicions.'

As he sat down on a button backed winged armchair that faced the door, Christophe added 'You have my word Sir, as an officer and a gentleman, that no harm will become of Kathryn, even if she confesses to the dastardliest act known to man'.

'Then I accept your word Sir and will do everything that I can to persuade Kathryn to tell you the truth, for I am convinced that she did this out of desperation to try to pay off debts and maintain her position in society, rather than any malice towards Sir Robert.'

'Very well gentlemen, let us hope we are not kept waiting too long', said Elliot, also seating himself so that he could see the door.

Lenthall was stooped and frail, exhausted from his double life, his complexion and presence being that of an old man. He proceeded to serve glasses of sherry and oatmeal biscuits. Inconsequential and convivial conversation continued, but it was obvious that William was becoming increasingly agitated.

Kathryn duly arrived and after the customary kiss on both cheeks was escorted to the drawing room by William, but before entering the room, she looked into his eyes and said

'You seem rather nervous my dear, has anything happened?'

She was taken by surprise as William led her into the room.

'What's going on dearest? I recognise Elliot, and presumably by his bearing and looks, this young man is Sir Robert Douse's son.'

William was taken aback; he had not made the connection between 'Tristan' and Robert. Both men had stood up as Kathryn entered, Christophe giving a slight bow of his head, acknowledging her rank in society.

'I will come straight to the point Lady d'Aubigny, Kathryn if I may', said Elliot. 'We are here because we believe that you had a hand in the betrayal of Robert to Cromwell, which led to his untimely death. Please do not deny it. William here has told us that he told you of Robert's intention to stop the Trial of King Charles by presenting a secret agreement called Madrigal to the judges.'

Kathryn broke down. Putting her hands to her mouth and collapsing onto a chair she started to sob her heart out, real tears streaming down her face, full of remorse.

'I had no idea that the information I passed on would lead to Robert's death' she said between sobs. 'I thought that it might help his cause if I made others aware of his intentions. I admired him greatly, but I also desperately needed money to pay off my debts to The French Ambassador, who was forcing himself on me on many occasions. I needed to repay him without the knowledge of my recently married husband.'

'There, there, my dear' said Lenthall as he put his arm around her shoulders 'we all know you would never do anything intentionally to even harm a fly.'

Christophe looked to the ceiling in disbelief.

'Who did you tell, Kathryn?' asked Elliot, somewhat agitatedly. He was never one to fall for a lady's tears, especially a lady so used to telling lies and being deceitful.

'A Lawyer named Edward Floyd,' she sniffed, wiping her nose with her lace kerchief, and looking pitifully at Lenthall. 'William had once introduced us in the past, and I knew of his disbarment from office and his hatred of the Judiciary. I thought he could use the information about Madrigal to disrupt the trial.

Christophe and Elliot turned and smiled at each other with a nod, acknowledging confirmation of their deduction.

'How on earth did you find him?' asked Elliot, sitting back down.

'Oh come now! I still have a few agents and spies of my own from the old days of running clandestine messages to and from Oxford during the hostilities', she said with some arrogance.

'I never knew what Floyd did with the information I gave him' she said, regaining her composure, 'but after rumours spread of Robert's arrest, I realised what I had done and was devasted, truly I was.'

Kathryn looked at them all appealingly.

'After Charles had been charged with Treason, my husband and I arranged an attempt to release him from Parliament's captivity. It was to be on his journey to the Trial. It was unsuccessful as it turned out, but Robert and I were on the same side. I would never have willingly hurt him in any way.'

Despite such an abhorrent admission, Lenthall was hopelessly in love and devoted to Kathryn and went over to the side-table and poured her a glass of brandy. Handing it to her, she continued,

'I was paid £1,000 by Floyd for the information; enough to pay off my debts. No doubt he sold the information on to one of Cromwell's spies or even Cromwell himself for a great deal more money.'

'We need his address Kathryn' said Christophe, still unimpressed by her apparent remorse.

'Of course. He is living in rented accommodation in Balham, south of the river. Number 13 Balham Park Road, off the High Road.'

Christophe walked to the door and turned to look down on the woeful sight of this so-called beautiful 'Lady', now dishevelled, blotchy skinned and red-eyed.

'I can never forgive you Kathryn, only God can do that. As you are a Catholic, I suggest that you go to confession, confess your sins, and ask for forgiveness', said Christophe.

Elliot joined Christophe and putting his hand on his shoulder said 'let us be off to Balham and strike whilst the iron's hot. No time like the present.'

Turning to face the pathetic shamefaced lovers, he added 'You two can rot in hell as far as I am concerned, you both deserve one another.'

WILLIAM LENTHALL
SPEAKER OF THE HOUSE
OF COMMOMS

LADY KATHERINE
D'AUGBIGNY

They left the pitiful pair to reflect on their own conscience of the part they had played that led to Robert's death.

They rode straight to Balham, over the Thames by way of a ferry at Wandsworth. Christophe's heart was racing.

Was he about to meet face to face with the man who betrayed his father? What would he do if he did? Would he just shoot him? Question him? Demand satisfaction by way of a duel? All these questions were going through his head as they cantered through the cobbled streets, people ducking into doorways to avoid the pounding hooves of their steeds.

It was only 5 miles, and it was easy to find Balham Park Road off of the High Road. House Number 13 was in a terrace of six houses, with an alleyway to gain access to the back yards. It was occupied by the lower classes and looked empty, not a good sign.

Elliot thumped on the front door of number 13 but got no response, so knocked loudly on number 14. After a pause, he knocked even louder.

'All right I'm comin, no need to knock the bleeding house down', came a cry from within.

It was opened by a short, fat, frumpy woman wearing a stained apron that looked like it had been worn for years. She was carrying a large double handed basket of dirty washing which stank of body odour.

Elliot, holding his kerchief to his nose enquired, 'next door looks empty, but I was told that a friend of mine was living there with his daughter.'

'Oh him', she said looking Elliot up and down, 'I knew he was too posh to live 'ere. A bit below 'is status if you ask me, and his daughter looked as if she had the makings of a fine lady.'

'I haven't seen her since she was a young child' said Elliot, trying to convince the woman that he was indeed a friend of Ford. 'She must be grown up by now. I remember her as a pretty little thing.'

'She is' she replied, 'a real looker, with blonde hair and green eyes. They high-tailed it out of 'ere soon after Charlie lost is 'ead with him owing the landlord rent.'

'Do you know where they might have gone?' asked Elliot stepping back to try and avoid the stench of the dirty washing.

'I dunno,' said the washerwomen. 'I fink he said something about trying his luck down south, in the country, something about a distant relative who lived in a forest.'

Elliot thanked her kindly, rummaged in his breeches pocket and gave her two pence for her troubles.

'You are a gentleman, kind Sir, I 'ope you find 'im'.

She closed the badly fitting front door with her large backside, banging it shut and knowing that she could now put some meat on the family table that night.

Christophe was disheartened, swearing under his breath, and kicking a stone along the ground. He thought that they had their man. They mounted their horses and made their way back to the house; Christophe was in a sombre mood all the way and had hardly spoken. His father had been murdered because of this weasel of a man, and they had been so close, so very close. He could be anywhere now. It was all Elliot could do to persuade him to call in at The Angel.

Over their customary tankard of ale at their usual table at the back of the room, Elliot consoled Christophe and said to him quietly, 'Cheer up my friend, we have come a long way in the past two weeks. At least you now know who the braggard was who betrayed your father to Cromwell. It is now down to you to decide if and how you wish to proceed from here.'

Christophe downed the last dregs of his ale.

He already knew what was to be done; he would hunt Floyd down if it took him 5, 10, 20 years, and he'd do it by making a living as a 'Gentleman of The Road', in the forests of the South of England, from Kent through to Dorset. Floyd was somewhere in those forests, and that's how he would find him.

He would be a Highwayman known as Tristan Cheval, and taking a lead from Captain James Hind, would be chivalrous and act with honour.

41

That evening Christophe confided in Elliot telling him his plans, but after taking his advice, did not tell John and Jenny other than he was off 'to seek fame and fortune'. He promised Elliot that he would keep in touch and thanked him profusely.

'I could not be where I am without you, you're the best. I now know why father thought so much of you, and in many ways, I think of you as a member of the family'.

'Oh, be off with you, you handsome devil, the world is your oyster. I shall pop down to Bourton now and then and make sure your Mama, Sarah and Paul are OK, and see if there is anything that I can do for them'.

Christophe lay in bed that night thinking of his next move. It was in that very bed that his father had spent many nights planning how to try and end the bloodiest of wars, to try and expose the agreement which, if known publicly might just have brought the two sides to a negotiated peace. It was his efforts to end the bloodshed that had cost him his life, and Christophe was now determined to revenge his death and clear his name.

He cast his mind back to his time at Christ Church. How he longed for those carefree days he spent there with Edward. He missed his late friend so badly, another casualty of war, but he loved him like the brother he never had. They had studied Geography, and this led him to think that Floyd would most likely be in hiding in one of the small villages or hamlets in one of the two large forest areas in the South of England:

Ashdown Forest in Sussex and The New Forest in Hampshire.

If Floyd needed to get out of the country quietly, but quickly, Ashdown Forest was only 20 miles to Newhaven which had a navigable harbour on the South Coast, and The New Forest, whilst vast, is some 20 miles from its centre to Lymington Key on its southern perimeter.

Christophe decided in his own mind that he would first retrace his steps to Balham and then proceed due south for 30 miles to the Ashdown Forest, located west of Crowborough.

Before retiring he had told John and Jenny that he would be leaving in the morning. Jenny asked him for any clothes that needed a wash and Christophe duly obliged with two pairs of undergarments, two shirts looking very much the worse for wear, and 2 pairs of stockings which could almost have walked off on their own.

'When did you last wash these?' she cried taking them at arm's length.

'That's nothing compared to the pile a washerwoman that Elliot and I met this afternoon had in her arms. Boy did they stink!'

They both laughed.

'You just keep up your appearances young man, and remember you are a gentlemen on your travels' said Jenny in a maternal manner.

The following morning when Christophe rose, his clothes had been washed, dried by hanging above the range overnight and pressed. Jenny had folded them neatly and left them outside of his room. He decided a thorough wash all over with soap and water was in order to do justice to his clean apparel, and to the start of his new life.

Once dressed he sat on the chair by the window, looking out along the street as his father had done many times. So much had happened in the last year and his life had been turned upside down.

He was in sombre mood, facing up to the solitary existence ahead. He had no choice. Cromwell had decided his fate on the day he ordered his father's execution and issued the arrest warrant in Christophe's name.

He was used to being surrounded by the camaraderie of the army, of soldiers, living and supporting each other. No longer did he wear the flamboyant attire of a Cavalier, but a simple shirt and breeches, although he could not bear to part with his wide brimmed hat with its peacock feather.

From now on it would be a tricorn hat, the symbol of a Highwayman. He needed to buy one, he thought, and he needed to tie his hair back if he wanted to look the part.

What lay ahead, he knew not. All he knew was that he was on his own. The exuberance and carefree attitude he had enjoyed before the war had gone. The joy of youth long forgotten.

After an enormous, cooked breakfast he bade John and Jenny farewell.

'I shall keep your room as it is Christophe, for when you return,' said Jenny. 'If I find any cast-off clothes, I shall be sure to give them a wash and press along with the bed linen.'

'You are sounding just like my aunt Sarah back at Chaffeymoor' Christophe replied with a chuckle, and gave her a bear hug, lifting her off her feet.

'Put me down, put me down' she laughed.

'Thank you, for everything' he said. Looking across at John and holding out his hand to him, 'where would I be without you two.'

He had a private emotional farewell with Elliot, promising again to keep in touch and to come 'home' if he was in trouble. Elliot gave him £20 from left over Royalist funds to keep him in good stead for the time being. With saddle bags packed including wild boar pie left over from last night's meal for his lunch, and some oats and raw carrots for Forest, he was off.

It was a good time of year to 'hit the road', it was now late summer in 1649. He felt cheered, full of hope, invigorated, and determined by his new goal in life.

He still had his dog-lock flintlock pistol, a bag full of shot balls and his leather powder flask from his army days, together with his father's stiletto knife that he found in his room. He was confident that his skills learned as a Cavalier would serve him well in his new 'occupation'. He vowed to himself and his late father to uphold his principals as a Royalist officer and gentleman.

His route would take him across the Thames and south to Balham and then on through Oxted and Edenbridge.

Whilst trotting Forest across Thornton Heath, he remembered that he had asked Captain James Hind how on earth could he tell a potential victim was a Parliamentarian supporter.

It comes with experience Christophe, he had said. We all make mistakes at first, but you learn from their demeaner, character and response to your cry of 'stand and deliver'. Parliamentarians usually are arrogant but soon start snivelling, pleading for their lives, threatening retribution and are generally vulgar in speech.

A true Royalist, however, will often recognise you as an ex-Cavalier, sometimes even address you by name, but usually as 'Good Sir', and they are generally polite and courteous. Most of them when you refuse to rob them, will offer a generous donation to the poor and destitute ex-soldiers who I support.

Christophe stopped for lunch at the pond on the Heath to gather his thoughts and give his horse Forest a rest and a drink. Still feeling that he would be nervous on the first occasion he held up a carriage, he felt relieved that he had the £20 Elliot had given him, and his own £5. Enough to live on for a couple of years if necessary.

He decided to stay overnight at The Old Bell Inn, in Oxted and take a risk by making some enquiries there regarding Floyd. The ride from Thornton Heath to Oxted was a joy to

behold, dropping down off the North Downs with the Vale of Kent stretched out before him, he gave Forest his head and galloped across the undulating open grass and heathland. Forest loved it with the bit between his teeth, sucking in the summer air, with the occasional snort and whinny, Christophe masterly and in full control.

He passed the occasional carriage on the main byways and decided to try out Hind's theory without resorting to robbery. *It's now or never* he said to himself. *I'm not dressed like a Highwayman and need to buy that tricorn hat when I get to Oxted, but at the moment I don't look threatening, with my feathered hat. It's a perfect time to practice judging the character of Parliamentarians versus Royalists.*

He intended to ask the way to Oxted from the first carriage he hailed. Just a stranger, asking the way. No harm in that.

Recognising his Cavalier's hat, he was met with a tirade of abuse; 'Be off with you, you scoundrel, no wonder you lot lost the War, you will get nothing from me,' blurted a rotund soberly dressed old man brandishing a carriage whip with menace.

It did not take much for Christophe to work out where this arrogant man's loyalties lay.

A bit further on he stopped an elegant carriage driven by a footman and carrying a well-dressed, almost flamboyant man with a pretty young maiden young enough to be his daughter. Once again it was obvious to Christophe that they were more likely to have been Royalist supporters.

He decided to take a chance, 'Good afternoon Sir and Madam, I am on my way to Crowborough, and I wondered if you knew of a recent resident to the area. I am trying to trace a man named Floyd who has a daughter not much younger than your companion but no doubt not nearly as pretty'.

He said looking directly at the young lady and giving her a nod and a slight smile. The young girl blushed.

Addressing the man, he continued, 'I believe he may be practising as a lawyer or some legal assistant.'

'I am afraid not' said the man, you might try Old Gwilliam, the local lawyer in Oxted. He might have heard of him. Did you fight in the war?'

'I did sir, as a Cavalier.'

'I thought so, terrible business. Here take this and get a decent meal and lodgings for the night', giving Christophe a King's shilling. 'I can recommend The Old Bell in Oxted.'

'Why thank you kindly sir, and you my lady,' looking at her beguiling figure as he swept his hat off and gave her a secret smile.

With that he continued his journey thinking about his experience. *It can't be that easy*, he thought!

He reached Oxted in mid to late afternoon and after stabling Forest and checking in for the night at The Old Bell Inn under the name of Tristan Cheval.

THE OLD BELL INN, OXTED

He decided to take a stroll around the village which was picturesque and quite beautiful. It was larger than most villages but not quite regarded as a town or coaching stop.

There were numerous shops, a general store, butchers, bakers, an apothecary, and saddlery. He wandered into the general store and purchased a few bits and pieces for his journey around the countryside: A tricorn hat was top of his list, and a bedroll for sleeping out at night and such like. When paying for his goods he casually enquired of the whereabouts of old Gwilliam, the lawyer.

'Old Gwilliam? He doesn't practice much these days since his ticker started to play him up, but he lives in the end cottage along the High Street.'

Christophe paid for his goods, thanked the shopkeeper, and made his way along the road to the end cottage. A small but double fronted building as one might have expected from a retired professional. He knocked on the door to be answered by a frail old man.

'Good afternoon Sir. It's Mr Gwilliam I presume?' enquired Christophe.

'Why, yes indeed, we do not get many strangers in these parts, of whom do I have the pleasure?'

'Tristan Cheval Sir, of the late Dorset Royals,' he replied with a slight bow, suddenly thinking that that was a mistake to reveal his past association with the Royals. No matter, it had been said.

'What can I do for you young man?'

Christophe could not get used to still being called a young man. He was now 28, had fought gallantly in the war, and considered himself well educated and worldly. He could only assume, vainly, that with his bearing, his good looks, even with a scar on his cheek from a war wound, men, and more importantly women, found him to be young and virile in his looks.

'I am just passing through and wondered if you had come across an acquaintance of mine, a lawyer by the name of Floyd travelling with his daughter,' said Tristan.

'No one of that name, but I did engage such a man going by the name of Lord or was it Ford. Yes, Ford, Edmund Ford, that was it. He did some property registry filings for me, but he was only here for a few weeks.'

At last, thought Christophe, *it must be him.* The trail which had gone cold may have come alive again.

What would father do next?

42

Christophe was having what he considered a well-earned tankard of ale in The Old Bell. He had another lead on Floyd, had engaged with two travellers that he deduced one to be a Parliamentarian and the other a Royalist supporter, and had had romantic fantasies at the sight of the pretty young girl accompanying the gentleman. She must have been all of 16.

He ordered supper and sat in the corner taking in the ambience and the clientele. He could have been a Highwayman weighing up those that were spending money freely and those of poorer persuasion. On the far side of the room a well-turned-out couple were arguing, and he strained to listen in to the woman who was accusing the man of making eyes at the serving girl.

A portly old boy sat in the opposite corner, legs wide apart and having finished his meal, his arms were folded over the top of his shelf of a stomach. He caught Christophe's eye as he too looked around the room and nodded to him. Christophe replied with a nod and raised his goblet to him.

He was feeling lonely, lonely for a companion on the road and right then, lonely for female company. The young girl that afternoon reminded him he was attractive to many a maiden, young and old. Whilst eating his meal he came across a particularly tough piece of meat and sitting back in his chair whilst trying to chew it, glanced around the room and spotted the Royalist gentlemen he had met that afternoon with the young girl, presumably his daughter, sitting down at a table on the far side of the room. He had noticed them earlier when to his surprise they had arrived at the Inn.

The girl turned towards him and smiled; Christophe's heart started beating faster with a rush of blood to his loins. The gentleman looked to see who his daughter was looking at, and recognising Christophe from their afternoon encounter, touched his forelock in recognition. He sent word by one of the serving lasses inviting Christophe to join then for coffee and an after-dinner brandy.

Christophe couldn't wait, finishing his meal rather too quickly, he swilled the last of his goblet of wine and then chewed on dried mint leaves he kept in his pocket for such an occasion to freshen up his breath. He eagerly crossed the dining room, clumsily bumping into the chair of a person on the next table. Apologising, he wished he had not had that second goblet of wine.

On reaching the table of his newly found acquaintances he bowed 'Tristan Cheval Sir, at your service.' 'Sir Marmaduke Tillingham-Smythe, but please call me Marmalade, the name used by my Nanny that has stayed with me. May I introduce my daughter Rowena.'

Christophe took the girl's hand and kissed the back of it, 'Delighted to see you again Rowena' he said looking deep into her eyes, 'you are as pretty as the red berries of The Mountain Ash Rowan tree in late summer.' Rowena blushed again, but this time she secretly wished Christophe had kissed her lips, not just her hand. For the first time in her life she found herself sexually aroused. *He is just gorgeous,* she thought.

'She is my pride and joy; we are of Welsh ancestry and both bear the forenames of legendry Welsh icons' said Marmalade. 'Do sit down Tristan and tell us all about yourself.'

Christophe pulled out a chair next to Rowena and opposite her father. He felt at ease in their company and without saying too much about both his father's and his own role in life, proceeded to talk of his Norse and French ancestry, more

to impress young Rowena who was becoming more and more infatuated with him.

They spent the next hour or so idly chatting, with Christophe occasionally brushing his leg again Rowena's under the table and touching hands as he reached across the table for the bottle of brandy that her father had so kindly ordered from the Landlord. Marmalade was beginning to feel his age, and at around ten o'clock said

'I can tell you are a gentleman, a man of breeding and well-educated Tristan, so I shall be off to bed and leave Rowena in your safe care.' He kissed his daughter on the cheek and said, 'don't keep this young man up too late my dear.'

After he had left the room, they both looked at each other and quietly laughed. 'If only father knew', Rowena said, lowering her eyes and smiling so sweetly, so innocently.

'Better that he doesn't,' said Christophe almost in a whisper. After flirting further at the table, teasing each other, Christophe finished his glass of brandy and Rowena her elderflower cordial. He took Rowena by the hand and led her up the staircase to his room, which fortunately was only a few rooms away from hers. As they entered, Rowena was nervous, not knowing how to react, or what was expected of her. *Was he just going to kiss her goodnight and then take her along to her room,* she wondered?

She had never been in a man's room before and knew nothing of love or sex and had never seen a man naked. Christophe sensed this, taking her gently in his arms and just holding her against his chest. After what seemed like ages, she raised her head to look at him, and he was able to gently kiss her lips. Rowena melted in his arms.

They kissed passionately as Christophe kicked the door shut. He could not keep his hands off her any longer. Holding her close, still standing, he started to fondle her breast and said, 'I am so sorry Rowena, you are so beautiful, it has been a long time since for me, way back in the heat of battle in the War.'

She whispered in his ear, 'It is the first time for me, I have led a sheltered upbringing so please be gentle with me.' Christophe gently but passionately kissed her, slowly disrobing her layer by layer, nuzzling her small pert breasts whilst doing so, always aware of her reactions, ready to slow down, stop or even to speed up. At the same time Rowena slowly removed his frilly white shirt, admiring his firm torso and gently stroking the long scar from his left shoulder down his chest that he suffered in the war.

He led her to the wooden framed bed, a luxury in itself, with a soft horse-hair mattress covered in a clean white pressed sheet. *Jenny would be proud* he mused to himself. They lay together and Christophe made love to her, slowly and gently the first time. Rowena was in heaven and responded to his touch more urgently and passionately thereafter. There were no 'I love you' or promises only to be broken, just two young adults engaged in satisfying each other's needs, climbing that mountain and back several times during the long night.

Rowena finally rose at dawn, kissed a sleepy Christophe good morning, and made her way to her, as yet unslept in, room. She threw her clothes off and crept into bed, tired, sated but still in ecstasy, hardly believing what had taken place. She fell quickly into a deep sleep dreaming of 'Tristan'. When she woke late, she lay back smiling, realising she had indeed lost her virginity to a handsome, gallant, Cavalier named Tristan.

Christophe too rose late, washed, and dressed and went down to the dining room for some breakfast. There was Marmalade, who had nearly finished his sumptuous breakfast and Rowena had not long arrived.

'Do join us Tristan, kept you up late, did she? said Marmalade. He glanced at Rowena who was staring intently at her scrambled egg and beaming. 'She does you proud Sir, wonderful company, so well educated with impeccable manners, she will have many a young squire with offers of marriage one day.' After breakfast it was time to say goodbye. They shook hands. 'We live in The Priest House, near East Grinstead, if you are ever passing our way do stop bye.'

'Thank you, Marmalade, it has been a real pleasure to meet you and Rowena. You have a beautiful daughter Sir.'

'I'll leave you young things to say goodbye to each other, we are leaving in about ten minutes Rowena.' 'Yes Papa' she replied.

They stood looking into each other's eyes. Rowena longed for just one more kiss, but they were in a public place, and a distance between them was called for. Christophe picked up her hand and put it to his lips whilst looking into her eyes. 'You truly are gorgeous Rowena. I hope you find that true love who you will love until the day you die, and I hope I shall too, someday.' 'Oh Tristan, if only, another place, another time, I shall never forget you.'

It was time to move on, time to become Tristan Cheval, Highwayman, and pursue Floyd to the end of the earth if need be.

TRISTAN CHEVAL,
ALIAS OF CHRISTOPHE DOUSE

43

It was now the winter of 1651. Christophe had spent nearly
three years searching for Floyd in the Ashdown Forest area
but to no avail. He had enquired in every village and hamlet
he came across; the trail had most definitely gone cold, and
he was becoming disheartened.

The news that Charles 11 had returned to Scotland and
had been crowned King of Scotland at Scone Abbey back in
January, had raised his hopes of England becoming a Kingdom again. News filtered through later in the year that Charles
had raised an army and invaded England.

Christophe's optimism was dashed in September however, when he heard of Charles catastrophic defeat at the
hands of Cromwell in the Battle of Worcester and that he had
fled to France. His only comfort was that Charles was still alive
and had vowed that one day he would regain the throne as
King of England.

He had to keep going, Charles would eventually return
and be crowned, and he, Christophe, had to be ready to present Madrigal to the new King, and to prove how loyal his
father was to King Charles 1. He wanted a pardon for his father's actions in trying to prevent the King's trial and execution.

Over the last three years he had perfected the art of being
a dashing, gallant Highwayman operating across both the
heathland and in the more sheltered forestry areas. He did it,
not so much for personal gain, although his funds were fast

petering out, but with the hope that one or more of the Royalist gentlemen that he held up may have knowledge of Floyd or his whereabouts.

His reputation quickly grew as 'The Blonde Frenchie', spoken in disparaging terms by the Parliamentary fraternity, but revered by Royalists, especially by their wives, lovers, and daughters. He had acquired the nickname on account of his slight French accent and issuing the demand, 'Stand and Deliver, Ton Argent ou ta Vie', which even most of the uneducated Parliamentarians soon got to know as 'Your money or your life'.

Making a good income out of robbing Parliamentarian supporters, he always left them with around ten percent of their purse and was most courteous and flattering to any female companion. He also put aside a further forty percent to go into his fund for destitute ex Royalist and Parliamentarian soldiers from the War. He came across them in his travels, many of whom lived in makeshift shelters in the forest.

His main purpose as a Highwayman however was to hold up and engage in conversation with those travellers he deemed to be Royalist supporters. He asked nothing of them but information, but many offered a sizeable donation to his destitute ex-soldiers fund. Enquiring of Floyd or Ford, as he appeared to call himself, drew several false leads. All had to be followed up which was time consuming, despairing and sometimes expensive, often involving risky overnight stays in various Inns and even bribery.

It was a lonely existence, the early frosts from the long dark nights and the burgeoning red berries on the holly bushes suggested that it was going to be another harsh winter. He longed for his family, particularly his Mama, and for Chaffeymoor, wondering who had taken up residence there. He would go home soon; the thought gave him the strength to carry on with his search.

It was cold, barely rising above freezing point in the low winter's sun. Despite his thick woollen cape that he wore over his tunic, a nightcap under his hat, woollen socks over his leggings and fingerless mittens under his gauntlets, he was still cold when exposed to the wind and snow flurries. It was no life as a romantic Highwayman.

The previous winter he almost gave up, having to spend most nights in make-do shelters that he had made in different parts of the Forest. At first, he avoided lighting a fire at night to keep warm, considering it too risky, but soon found the cold unbearable and in any case, he could see numerous fires alight in the distance at night from the very destitute ex-soldiers that he was trying to help.

If he were challenged, he would just adopt the same persona as them and beg for funds from any intruder.

When the weather became insufferable, he would seek out lodgings in lesser well-known Inns across the Forest. It was a welcome respite, a chance of a decent meal and change of clothes. Sometimes he could even have a hot bath and was able to wash out his soiled underwear, shirt, and leggings in the used bath water. He had the funds to stay longer or to do it more often but that was a risk he was not prepared to take.

On one occasion at The Beechwood Arms in Duddleswell, on leaving in the morning after a good night's sleep and a welcome cooked breakfast, he heard the Landlord, Rogier, who was of French ancestry, quietly say, 'God be with you Blondie.'

Christophe just touched his forehead, smiled, and said' You too Landlord.'

On another occasion he held up a coach-and-four horses with a driver and guard armed with a short flintlock blunderbuss up top, which was capable of firing a number of lead balls of shot in an arc from its flared muzzle.

These coaches usually yielded rich pickings, sometimes they were a mail coach, but they often carried a titled person or at least a wealthy one. They needed to be able afford such luxurious transport and added security. This particular coach was ornate, with thick leather straps and stands suspending the carriage above the wheels, which gently swayed the carriage. The wooden parts were richly carved and gilded, and the doors ordained with the owner's coat of arms.

Pulling out alongside the carriage from behind tall gorse bushes, Christophe gave his customary cry of 'Stand and Deliver, Ton Argent ou ta Vie.'

On this occasion however, the driver flashed his whip at the team of horses and took flight with Christophe instinctively giving chase.

It was a mistake he would rue, and a harsh lesson learned, for as he closed in on the coach the guard fired his blunderbuss which ripped open his thick cape on his upper left arm and shoulder and drew blood.

'Tristan' swerved off the road and sought shelter in a copse. On examining his wound, he discovered that only half of the scatter of balls of shot hit his upper arm and shoulder. The guard had fired too soon, and all but one piece of shot was embedded in his cape. One had penetrated the cape and his upper arm.

Fortunately, it had only torn away some flesh and the bullet had not entered the muscle, but he was bleeding profusely. He stuffed some clean wadding under his clothing to stem the flow of blood and rode in haste to the nearest village seeking out the local blacksmith.

TRISTAN IN FULL FLIGHT

The blacksmith, Little Mick, asked no questions. He had served in the War re-shoeing horses and cauterising wounds, and on examining Christophe, said,

'You are lucky for a Frenchie', acknowledging that he knew who Christophe was. 'If you fought in the war you will know that this will hurt.'

He wasted no time in giving Christophe a swig of brandy, pouring some over the wound and without any hesitation withdrew a hot iron from his Furness and place it on the wound.

Jesus', Christophe cried out as a smell of burned flesh permeated the air.

After downing another swig of brandy, he thanked Little Mick profoundly and gave him a gold one-pound coin. A small price to pay for his swift action in preventing his wound becoming infectious, and for the blacksmith's silence.

'Merci mon Ami,' said Mick, 'I came across many a Frenchie in the war, usually at the end of my pike fighting for those blasted Parliamentarians.'

Christophe just smiled in acknowledgement and agreement.

They may have been on different sides then but were now just victims of an unnecessary war.

44

Christophe took it easy for a several weeks to allow his arm to heal. He took it upon himself to return to the Beechwood Arms in Duddleswell and put his faith in Rogier the Landlord. His trust was not misplaced as it turned out that he was of French Norman descent too and had supported King Charles in the Civil War. He suggested to Christophe that it would be better all-round if he stayed in the converted hayloft away from the clientele of the Inn.

It smelled of the wheat harvest and horse manure. There was a ladder that he could pull up, rudimentary bedding, and pails of clean water. One was for his ablutions which the Rogier's son would empty each night, and Christina, the Landlord's wife would bring meals twice a day. Forest would be stabled below with no-one the wiser.

Christophe welcomed the respite but became increasingly restless as his arm healed. Once on the mend, he rigorously exercised it to strengthen the muscles. Time seemed to drag on endlessly, but he had time to think. He took an unnecessary risk with the four-horse carriage with a guard on top.

If I am to do so in the future, he thought, *I will need a companion. The only person I can think of is my old friend Sam in Oxford.*

He left after six weeks. Words were not enough to thank Rogier for his hospitality, who initially refused any payment. Giving him three gold pounds, more than a month's takings,

Christophe said 'Don't be silly man, think of it as a generous tip made by a Parliamentary squire.'

'In that case I shall reluctantly drink to his health' said Rogier with a smirk on his face. It was early spring in 1652 when an encounter with ex Royalist Officer, Lieutenant Stephen Meursault of the Sheffield Infantry Brigade, gave him his only tangible clue to the whereabouts of Floyd. Christophe had come across him living rough on the outskirts of Coleman's Hatch.

LIEUTENANT STEPHEN MERSAULT
THE ASHDOWN FOREST

It was mid-afternoon with the sun beginning to set on an early March day, with signs of Spring in the air but still chilly at night. Stephen was in the process of re-enforcing his camp with fallen branches from beech trees, bracken, moss, and heather. They lit a fire and shared a mug of herbal tea together, chatting about the War and fallen comrades.

'Before the War, I was a supplier of comestibles to the Godwin's Grocery chain, throughout Yorkshire,' said Stephen. 'He was a beastie when dealing with his staff and suppliers and was always telling me to 'listen and learn Stephen.'

He started to chuckle to himself and continued, 'his advice caused my downfall.'

Christophe told him he was trying to track down a lawyer who was travelling with his daughter, but he wasn't having any luck.

Out of the blue, Stephen said, 'I don't go far and don't meet a lot of folk these days, but back in late last Autumn, I was walking the by-way to Newbridge. I go maybe once a week to scrounge some stale bread from the bakers and mouldy cheese or cast-away vegetables from The Foresters Inn. I know the kitchen hands there who take pity on me. I had spent what few farthings I had begged on some horse oats from the saddlery to make a porridge.'

He got up and threw another branch on the fire, then continued:

'Anyhow, I was met on the road by a gentleman on horse, well clothed but not wealthy, if you know what I mean. A professional man I would say, but he didn't have some of the trappings of a merchant. What struck me most was his companion, a young lass, fine horsewoman, slim, with flaming red hair and good looks to match. He would not slow up to let me pass and almost ran me down, causing me to fall into the ditch at the side of the road, and calling out, 'Out of the way you filthy tramp' and then he just rode on.

'The young lady brought her filly to a stop, swiftly turned round, and dismounted to help me back on my feet. She then said 'You must forgive my Papa, he is ageing, grumpy and feels badly let down by all and sundry, particularly the judiciary. I am so sorry.'

Christophe looked up in amazement.

'It was the red hair, it reminded me of the Regimental colours,' Stephen muttered as he poked at the embers. 'As I say, I don't meet many people, you could say that I avoid them, but she was pretty as a picture and showed me great kindness. I remember it because it was such a strange thing for her to say'.

Christophe was speechless. *It had to be them*, he thought, just had to be.

'She was kind and of good breeding, I would say' he continued, 'a real peach of girl, hard to believe that he was her father. She must have inherited her genes from her mother, whoever she might be' he said with a chuckle. 'After making sure I was all right, she pressed two pennies in my hand, mounted her horse and with a gentle nuzzle in its ear said, 'Forward Scarlet' and they trotted off after her father. I thought about her a lot for some time afterwards.'

'Can you remember where they were going?'

'Well, they were on the Newbridge to Forest Row road, so I assume they either came from Newbridge or were passing through. You may recall the road goes to Forest Row in the direction I came from, that's all I know I am afraid.'

'That's more than enough! I will leave you to settle in for the evening' said Christophe as he rose to leave, bursting with excitement.

'Here are some coins to buy yourself some fresh food to-morrow and a silver sixpence for some lodgings so you can get a decent meal, a bath and a comfortable bed for a night or two.'

'That's far too generous, you look as though you could do with it yourself.'

'Looks are deceptive', said Christophe emphasizing his French accent, and tapping the side of his nose with a grin. 'I shall forever be in your debt with the information you have given me. If anyone asks, just tell them that Tristan Cheval, The French Blondie helped you on your way. In fact,' he said, getting out his leather pouch, 'have a further five gold pound coins Lieutenant, courtesy of a generous Parliamentarian I encountered on the road just yesterday. Get yourself some new clothes and lodgings and go and seek your true destiny. God knows, the world needs a man of your talent in these troubled times. I hear the Americas offer great opportunities. I don't expect to find you still living rough next time I pass this way.'

Stephen looked at the coins that had been placed in his hands and couldn't believe his luck. *America,* he thought, *America.*

'Yes Captain', he replied with a grin, and playful salute, somehow knowing that Christophe was also a commissioned officer in the War. 'The Americas have always been my dream ever since reading about The Pilgrim Fathers.'

Christophe decided time was of the essence once more and set forth to Forest Row to make enquiries of Floyd and his daughter. Sunset had come and gone, it was now dark, and the temperature was falling, but it was only an hour's ride away. He came upon an Inn on the outskirts of town, stopped and left the road to find a suitable place to dismount and change his clothes.

Gone was the tri-corn hat and on went his wide brimmed one, tucking in his tied up golden trestles of hair. It was not as ornate or as fashionable with feathers as befitting a Cavalier, but it looked respectable. Despite the falling temperature, he took off his heavy, well-worn, and soiled great cloak, rolled it up into his sleeping roll and tied it onto the back of Forest.

Riding into the stable yard of the Inn, he handed Forest over to a shivering stable lad, and taking pity on him generously gave him two pence for his troubles and dashed into the bar room. There was a log fire burning in the open grate of an old inglenook with its bressummer beam blackened with years of smoke. Christophe made a bee line for it to warm himself through.

He booked a room in the name of Christophe Harcourt, his Mama's maiden name, for his alias as Tristan Cheval was now well known in the area. He also asked for a meal that night and paid extra for a tin bath and some hot water to be brought up to his room in an hours' time.

The Inn was sparse with a few simple oak tables and chairs on a wooden oak floor sprinkled with sawdust, there was nothing cheery about it apart from the log fire. Ordering a tankard of Sussex's finest ale, it never touched Christophe's sides as he golloped it down in one go. It had been a while since Christophe had enjoyed such nectar. It tasted good, not as good as Anton's at The Winchfield Inn, but good all the same. A second one was on its way.

He felt refreshed, it was surprising how the effect of a tankard or two had on many a young man. He was warming up, and even managed to smile and flirt with the pretty barmaid with large bosoms who served him, and who returned the compliment.

'Your name pretty lady?' he asked. 'Maggie le Blanc' she replied with a sideways smile as she walked away.

You never know your luck Christophe, he mused to himself, *a bit old for me, she must be at least 45, but I could do a lot worse. First, a hot bath and a good meal.*

On retiring to his room, he threw off his riding clothes, poured the ewers of still warm water into the bath and climbed in.

'Oooh such bliss' he murmured as he lay back and soaped himself all over. He changed into dry clean clothes and went down to dinner. The barmaid he had flirted with was nowhere to be seen. *Just as well* he thought, *I might have been dicing with the pox with that one.*

The meal was simple, a rabbit stew, but to Christophe it was sublime compared to the likes of what Stephen would be having that night. He was weary and decided to retire early for the night avoiding too much conversation with other guests. Tomorrow was another day, and as he lay on the bed, he planned what he was going to do. Despite fatigue setting in he felt elated that after many months, in fact nigh on a year, he had now had a reliable sighting of someone who fitted the bill of Floyd and his daughter.

Why Forest Row? he thought. Floyd was taking a risk, as indeed he was. It was a small town, hardly the place to become a recluse and settle down as a local, it was no remote hamlet in the Forest.

I wonder, he thought, *I have looked everywhere in the Ashdown Forest area over the past three years. Were they about to move on?* It suddenly occurred to him that Forest

Row is a staging post for the Canterbury to Salisbury Coaching run. If his instincts were right about Floyd disappearing into either Ashdown or The New Forest, they could have travelled by Stagecoach to Salisbury and started a new life down in the New Forest. He knew the coaching run well, for he had held it up many a time as it crossed the Heath.

He was not a devout religious man, he had witnessed too many atrocities in the War that had challenged his faith, but he prayed that night for guidance. He secretly wished he were right, for he had all but given up. He could not withstand another winter outdoors and needed a safe house, such as James Hind enjoyed at The King's Arms in Malmesbury. He knew just the place, The Winchfield Inn, with Anton and his family. It was ideal, no more than half a day's ride to Ford-ingbridge on the northern edge of The New Forest, which was just eight miles south of Salisbury and two days ride to Bour-ton. From there he could easily get back to see his Mama and everyone from home, and he longed to do that.

First, he had to prove his theory was right, he would en-quire in the morning at the stage post, The Chequers Inn in the main square.

Despite his fatigue he slept fitfully and woke in the morn-ing with signs on his body having been bitten by bed bugs. He could not wait to leave and skipped breakfast, but he had no ill effects from the rabbit stew the night before. He thought he could always grab something to eat at The Chequers. He sad-dled up Forest and they trotted into the village centre. The Chequers was a much larger and welcoming establishment and was the staging post for Stagecoaches going West across the Ashdown Forest from Canterbury and Tunbridge Wells to Winchester and Salisbury.

Christophe dismounted, tied Forest to the hitching post and entered. There was an area in the Reception Room set aside with a clerk's desk where bookings could be made, que-ries raised, and chairs for those awaiting the coach.

Although it was early, only just turned 8 o'clock, the desk was manned, and people were waiting for the next coach which was due in at 8.30am.

Christophe walked confidently up to the clerk and enquired of his friend Ford travelling with his daughter last Autumn.

'I'm busy' said the clerk, 'the next Stage is due in shortly.'

'It won't take a moment' insisted Christophe, 'I'd be most grateful for your help. It is essential that I find them. His daughter has red hair.'

'Ahh, who could forget such a beauty, yes now let me see, I guess I could spare a few minutes. Yes, here we are,' he said as he rummaged through his booking ledger.

'Here it is, Friday 6th of October, single journey to Winchester taking two days with an overnight stop in The Old Drum, Chapel Street, Petersfield. The young lady even paid extra for one of our Mail riders to ride her horse Scarlet to the Salisbury Depot two days later.'

Thank you, God. Christophe thought to himself looking up to heaven. *Off to Winchester we go.*

45

Christophe returned to the Beechwood Arms at Duddleswell to say goodbye to Rogier and Christina and collect some personal belongings he had left in the hayloft. He retrieved, unbeknown to Rogier, a hidden bag of gold coins. This time, instead of hiding in the hayloft, he stayed the night in a comfortable room in the Inn as their guest, under the name of Christophe Harcourt.

The next morning as he bade them both goodbye and Rogier said 'Christophe, we are no fools, but like you were loyal to our departed King. Your air, your breeding, your fluent French tell us that there is more, much more to you than you have chosen to reveal. That we respect, and when you have found what you are looking for and achieved your destiny in life, prey come back and see us'.

'I will Roger and you too Christina. One day the truth will come out and you shall remember me as that "blonde Highwayman" you helped out. You have taken a huge risk in befriending me, and that I shall never forget that'.

With that Christophe mounted Forest and gave them his customary wave of his hat and they trotted off on their way West.

It was another glorious Spring day as they cantered across Selfield Common to the village of Pease Pottage. Fauna and flora were emerging everywhere with new growth of shoots, tendrils and blooms reaching for the light, slowly unfurling. Golden daffodils on the waysides were swaying in the breeze and a maze of wildflowers were everywhere across the Common.

There was not a cloud in the sky with an expanse of blue stretching above distant hill tops. Bird song permeated the air as mating pairs were busily preparing nesting sites to rear their offspring. Blackbirds were calling with their low-pitched fluted-warble, Song Thrushes were singing with their loud clear run of musical tweets often mimicking or mixing other bird sounds, common Sparrows making sharp chirps when excited and a harsh chatter when nest building always on the lookout for swooping birds of prey. Sparrowhawks and Kestrels were common in these parts as well as Red Kites further West.

Christophe felt elated in that, in a sense, he was going home to the South West. Winchester beckoned and beyond that Winchfield, and then The Great West Road to Mere and Bourton for Christmas. First there was a two-day ride to Winchester to visit The Highwayman, the Coaching Station, to find out more about Floyd and his daughter.

Were they staying in Winchester, if not were there any clues as to where they may have travelled on to? He wondered.

This occupied Christophe's mind as he rode through Pease Pottage to towards Horsham Common where he stopped for a late lunch of a tankard of ale, a pork pie, and a rest for Forest at The Beacon Tavern. From there onwards the journey gained momentum as he rode through Loxwood and onto the South Downs towards Hazelmere. The Downs were lush in parts enabling Christophe to give Forest her head as he galloped across the hills and dales.

Other travellers were few and far between. It was the reason why Christophe had deliberately chosen this route as most people either travelled further North or South on the main coaching routes.

He stayed overnight at The Crown Inn, a 15th century Inn by the Green in the centre of Hazelmere on the Chiddingfold to Petworth Road. It was a large establishment, popular with locals as well as travellers. The stable hand was most courteous as he led Forest away to be groomed, fed, and bedded down for the night. The way he handled Forest and the brief discussion with Christophe led him to conclude that he must have been a farrier or groom to the Royalist officers in the Civil War. He generously gave him 3 pence for looking after Forest so well.

The Landlord Ethan was an amiable fellow, spending most of his time serving customers behind the bar and engaging in conversation with them. His Aunt Angelica ran the kitchen and serving wenches, as well as a domestic servant who looked after the resident's rooms.

'Just passing through then are we Mr Harcourt?' the name Christophe had registered under.

'That's right Landlord, I am on my way back to Winchester from Canterbury and thought I would take the scenic route and give the Bay a good gallop over the Downs.'

'And a lovely day it's been for that. What mode of business are you in then?'

'I'm in the fine tooled leather goods business, and both Cathedral Diocese are good customers of mine. They are always looking to replace leather Hassocks, red for Canterbury, blue for Salisbury, emblazoned with the Cathedral's emblem and the Holy Cross.'

'Call me Ethan, everyone round here does, and my Aunt Angelica, runs the Inn with me'.

'You're a lucky one there Ethan, having family to help you.'

'I am, especially as she ran the Inn with my Ma and Pa, Jenny and Alex before they both died of the smallpox, so she knows the business better than me!'

After a while, just as he was enjoying his second tankard of ale, Angelica appeared and asked Christophe what he would like for dinner. 'What do you recommend?' asked Christophe.

'Well, the special tonight is my home-made Cottage Pie, it's Ethan's Grandma's recipe of minced beef, onions and carrots, topped with mashed potatoes from our vegetable garden and covered with grated cheese. I serve it with a thick meaty gravy.'

'Sounds delicious' he said with a smile.

Christophe was famished, he enjoyed the pie washed down with a large glass of Claret so much, that he asked Angelica for a second helping. As much as he was enjoying the meal and convivial chat with Ethan, rather than giving in to temptation and ordering another glass of wine, he decided to retire as he needed to be up early and on the road to Winchester.

The following day he left not long after dawn, continuing his journey across the South Downs through Monkwood on his way to Winchester. All the way he was still unaware that Marchal's son, Alexander, was following him.

He arrived in the evening as the sun was setting and decided to stay overnight at The Highwayman, as he thought he might feel more at home there. It was a Coaching Inn across the green from the Cathedral, and where Floyd and his daughter would have arrived, back in October the previous year.

The Canterbury to Winchester coach had already arrived earlier late that afternoon and the Coach Booking Desk was closed for the night. It would re-open at 6am in the morning to prepare for the onward coach departing for Salisbury at 8am, and the arrival of the Salisbury to Canterbury coach at mid-day.

Christophe washed and changed into a clean white shirt and attended Evensong at the Cathedral. It was a long time since he had attended church way back in Bourton with the Reverend Banks leading the service. That was a homely affair, nothing like the grandeur high service of Winchester Cathedral, which was a blend of Norman and Gothic Architecture with one of the longest Medieval naves in Europe. It was built in the 11th century and was remodelled with soaring Gothic arches in the 14th.

Christophe was in awe of the dulcet tones of the choir reminding him of his time at Christ Church in Oxford. He sat reflecting his past three years and questioned his own motivation. *Had it all become an obsession?* he asked himself. He felt weary. Weary of false leads or a feeling of just missing the boat as Floyd remained one step ahead.

He was close, he felt it in his bones, *more haste less speed,* he told himself, *your destiny awaits, the stars are beginning to line up.* He missed home, he deeply missed his Mama and family and friends in Bourton, he would even entertain the company of young Olivia, but most of all he longed to be back at Chaffeymoor.

Having slept well he was up at dawn, the sun rising at around 6 a.m. The clerk at the Coach Booking Desk had just arrived as Christophe approached the desk.

'You are up early Sir, the Salisbury coach doesn't leave until 8 o'clock', said the clerk to Christophe.

'I wonder if I could just take up just a bit of your valuable time before you get too ensconced in your pressing matters of the day kind Sir?' asked Christophe in a friendly and demeaning way to make the clerk feel important.

'Of course Sir, how can I help you?'

'Some friends of mine, Edmund Floyd and his daughter arrived here on the 6$^{th\,of}$ October last year. You might remember them as the daughter has flaming red hair. I wondered if you knew where there were staying in Winchester?'

'Now let me see', reaching for the ledger from under the desk. 'October the 6th did you say?'

'Yes, here it is. A Mr Edmund Floyd and his daughter Lysette, I do remember them, as they booked for onward passage to Salisbury for the following day, the 7th'. I remember thinking that strange at the time as to why had they not booked straight through as it would have been cheaper. I was off duty the following day but mentioned it in passing to my colleague

over a tankard of ale later that day. He had been on duty and the funny thing was, he said she had blonde hair when she left, and we had a bit of an argument over it and joked about young ladies changing their wigs to reflect the fashions of the day.'

Of course, thought Christophe, *I must be getting weary. How could I have so easily fallen for the red hair disguise. The washerwoman, back in Balham three years hence said she was blonde, I'll wager that is her natural colour. This young maiden becomes more interesting every day,* he mused to himself.

'Thank you kind Sir,' said Christophe, feeling more heartened that he was closing in on Floyd.

A man in the corner of the dining room just smiled as he acknowledged Christophe across the room and continued humming a tune and beating time on table. Little did Christophe know who he was, let alone recognise him.

It was Alexander Marchal.

Having paid his bill for the night, Christophe was off.

Salisbury can wait, time to renew his acquaintance with Anton and his family at The Winchfield Inn.

46

He finally rode into the yard of The Winchfield Inn late afternoon to be greeted with astonishment by Toby.

'Christophe', he exclaimed, 'is that really you?'

'It is Toby, have I really changed that much?'

'No, you are still a handsome devil' he said with a grin, 'but your hair is so much longer and that beard! You look as though you could do with a good bath, feeding up, and some new clothes.'

They both laughed at the thought.

'So, how have things been here, are Anton and Eleanor well?'

'They are fine, but times are hard, I will leave it to Pa to tell you all the news and gossip.'

Anton heard their laughter and came out to see what was going on. Seeing Christophe, he smiled and said,

'Who is this vagabond then, he doesn't look much like a Highwayman to me let alone a dashing Cavalier.'

They all three laughed as Christophe rushed over across the stable yard to give him a hug.

'I am so glad to see you, all three of you. I need respite and a safe house for a few months, maybe longer. I now travel under the name of Christophe Harcourt by the way, it's my Mama's maiden name.'

'You know you are always welcome here, come on in and see Eleanor. We shall put you up in a large room at the top floor of the Inn overlooking the stable yard. The only other person up there is Toby.'

'That sounds ideal, but this time I shall pay you handsomely, courtesy of several wealthy Parliamentary gentry.'

Christophe removed his saddlebags and Toby led Forest away for a well-earned meal and rest in the Inn's stable block.

Anton indicated for Christophe to go in the back entrance of the Inn to be met by Eleanor.

'En, this is Christophe Harcourt,' said Anton with a chuckle, his arm around Christophe's shoulders. 'Do you recognise him? He will be living with us for a few months, maybe longer.'

'Oh Christophe, you are as handsome as ever, but haven't you lost weight! You need fattening up I reckon, come here and give your En a hug.'

Christophe duly did so, he was almost overwhelmed by the kindness shown to him.

That evening after a good soak in a bath including washing his now long locks of blonde hair, he dressed in his last set of clean clothes and joined the others downstairs in their private parlour for a drink before dinner.

En was in the kitchen busy preparing dinner for the few guests that they had for the night, and for the family. The wonderful smell permeating from the kitchen made his stomach start to rumble, he was famished.

Relaxed, in the company of Anton and Toby, drinking a tankard of ale, he briefly told them of his adventures over the last two years, since he last saw them.

'So, are you any closer to catching this traitor Floyd then Christophe?' enquired Anton.

'As close as I have ever been. They boarded the Canterbury to Salisbury stagecoach from Forest Row in Ashdown Forest disembarking at Winchester last October. It was confirmed to me in Winchester that they did indeed continue on to Salisbury. But that was six months ago. Such have been the difficulties I have faced, with false leads here, there, all over

Ashdown Forest, but it is the first real tangible lead I have had from a reliable source. It came from an ex-Lieutenant of the Sheffield Brigade, almost certainly identifying Floyd and his daughter.'

After another tankard and convivial conversation about life at the Inn, it was almost time for dinner.

'How's the fishing been Toby?' asked Christophe looking forward to trying his hand again over this season.

'The trout season has only been going for a couple of months, there are plenty of Blue Olives and Damsels about and a few early Mayflies, so if you fancy a go, how about we go down to the river tomorrow?'

Christophe thought, not too hard, and for not too long about it. Another day or two will hardly make any difference in his quest to find Floyd and he could do with the relaxation, let alone En's cooking.

'Ok you are on, first one to catch buys the first round of drinks!'

En appeared just before 8 o'clock to announce dinner was ready.

'I shall just serve the latecomer in the bar then I will be serving up, so come and sit at the table. It needs new candles Anton, or we won't be able to see what we're eating.'

They ate in their own private quarters so they could continue their conversations without being overheard.

The latecomer who had arrived some-time after Christophe was a muscular fellow in a long dark coat. It was Alexander Marchal. Unknown to Christophe, he had followed him all the way from Forest Row, in Sussex.

Marchal had been tracking him since his altercation with Paul upon the seizure of Chaffeymoor. He too had lost sight of Christophe now and again over the past three years, but it proved a lot easier than Christophe's task; he just had to follow the fortunes, or in the one case misfortunes, of Tristan Cheval, the 'Blonde Frenchie' Highwayman.

He was biding his time to exact revenge for the killing of his father by Robert, Christophe's father. He would not reveal himself however, until the second copy of Madrigal was in Christophe's hand.

En served up one of Christophe's favourites, her renowned Rabbit Pie, with all the trimmings. A cheer went up from them all as she bought the steaming pie to the table for Anton to cut up and serve from his place at the head of the table.

'En, you don't know how much I have missed this, it's delicious,' said Christophe tucking into it as though he hadn't eaten properly for a week.

'I can tell, your clothes are hanging much looser and your breeches almost falling down.'

They all laughed.

'Leave all your dirty clothes outside of your room tonight and I shall wash and press them. I had better put a tuck in your breeches too, we can always let them out again when you have put some weight back on.'

Later that night, after much revelry and a few brandies too many, Christophe decided that he must put himself to bed; an expression he used when he was either extremely weary or extremely drunk!

He lay on his bed thinking of all that had happened since he left home. He had been gone for over three years. *How had they coped without him, had he changed in their eyes?* All these thoughts and many more raced through his head as he fell asleep, but just before he dropped off, he made a vow to himself:

Come what may, I will go home to Bourton for Christmas.

He spent the next two days relaxing, out and about either fly fishing or walking the riverbank and water meadows. On the first morning, Toby took him down to the river to remind him where the best pools and lies were for catching their wily prey. They had both tackled up their willow poles and decided to tie on a piece of duck-down. Toby had dyed it with his own mixture of herbs and urine to get a representative colour match which, together with the hook, gave an imitation of the Blue Winged Olive Flies that were beginning to rise and emerge from the river at around mid-day. It was a warm and overcast day with little breeze, ideal for fly fishing.

It was not long before they heard the quiet splash of a trout, greedily taking the real Olives that had the misfortune to still be in the current of the river before flying off. It was followed by several more, almost starting a frenzy of trout, gorging on their daily feast.

This is going to be easy, thought Christophe, who too eagerly cast his line upstream, but too heavily, causing his line to drag in the river's current. The trout were spooked and were off like a flash to seek shelter in the margins under overhanging branches.

Toby laughed,

'I hope you had a bit more finesse when you were a serving Cavalier, Christophe. The art of fly fishing is stealth and accurate casting, let alone having a tasty morsel on the end of your line. Here, let me show you,' and with that he gracefully and gently flicked a short line up and across the river and let it drift down just off a weed bed, out of which emerged a huge brown trout to grab his fly. He did not snatch the line but counted two seconds and then lifted his pole to let the hook sink in the lips of the trout. With that the trout shot off downstream, jumped out of the water a few times to try to release the hook, but eventually it tired and allowed Toby to bring it in to the bank.

'Marvellous' said Toby 'I reckon he must be all of 3 lb in weight.'

'Well, that showed me,' said Christophe 'the first drink is on me tonight.'

They continued to fish all afternoon, stopping briefly only for lunch of bread and cheese with a bottle of wine between them.

That same heady hour or so they had around noon when they both caught fish and missed many more, was not experienced again. Christophe had landed two, but Toby had three in his bag.

They made their way back along the riverbank spotting a brilliant flash of contrasting colours of orange, cyan and green diving into the shallow margins producing a startling image that could only pertain to one bird. It emerged with a minnow in its beak.

'It's a Kingfisher', cried Toby, 'perhaps it has an early brood to feed back at the nest.'

It's brilliant bright plumage, looking almost exotic, shone in the late afternoon sun.

Further along the riverbank they crossed an old wooden style, crudely made of fallen oak logs, and then across the meadow that ran behind the Inn.

'Mmm' murmured Christophe, *there is nothing on earth that compares to a fine English Spring day. The air is fresh and filled with the scent of new birth of fauna and flora. Is this the year of my destiny* he thought.

After the second day, he felt renewed of energy and fortitude. He was relaxed, had been well fed and enjoyed the comfort and homeliness of his "adopted family". Retiring that night in a contemplative but positive frame of mind, he slept well.

He left the following morning to ride over to The Red Lion, the Coaching Inn in Salisbury, to pursue his enquiries about Floyd and his daughter.

47

The ride over to Salisbury would take Christophe the best part of the day, then would stay at The Red Lion in the name of Christophe Harcourt. He had told Anton and En before departing that he would be away for a few days as he followed the trail of Floyd.

With any luck Floyd may have sought employment in Salisbury as there were a few legal practices in the City, but somehow, I doubt it, he thought to himself.

The journey was in the main pleasant and uneventful, down The Great West Road as far as Andover and then South-West to Salisbury. The only great excitement of the day, and danger, was when a Fallow Deer leapt over a hedge-row in front of them, just before they reached the village of Middle Wallop, almost knocking over Forest who stood firm as he was well used to sudden movement and noise on the battlefields in the Civil War. Having left early, just after dawn, and arrived at The Red Lion late afternoon. Placing Forest in the hands of the stable lad, he immediately made for the Coaching Desk located just inside the front entrance. The desk clerk was only too pleased to help when Christophe en-quired about Floyd and his daughter.

'Yes, here it is', the clerk replied after thumbing back through his heavy leather-bound ledger. 'They arrived here on the Winchester coach around mid-day on the 8th of October last'.

'Have you any idea if they were staying in Salisbury or travelling onwards?' asked Christophe.

'No idea, but they may well have stayed the night here, as many people arriving by stagecoach do. Your best bet is to enquire at the Reception Desk over there,' said the clerk pointing to a much grander desk attended by a smart, well dressed, and attractive mature lady.

Christophe strolled over to the reception desk admiring the architecture of the timber framed building. It was much larger and much grander than any other Coaching Inn he had been in before. The entrance hall was adorned with a large oil painting of the late King Charles and other artefacts indicating that this was still a Royalist supporting household.

THE RED LION, SALISBURY

The original Inn was built in the 13th century to house the stone masons, who were building the nearby Cathedral. A much smaller simpler Cathedral at the top of the hill at Old Sarum had suffered from neglect and storm damage over the years and had started to collapse, so they dismantled it and used much of the stone on the new site to build the lower foundations of the new Cathedral. It was now magnificent, with the tallest spire in the country reaching up to the heavens.

As he approached the reception desk Christophe smiled when he noticed a 'tongue in cheek' verse painted on the wall above it which read:

When the people of Old Sarum
realised there was an excellent Inn
being built in the valley below,
they moved the Cathedral to be nearer to it.

The 'new' Cathedral had suffered severe damage in the Civil War in 1645 when a small contingent of Royalist troops chased Parliamentary forces out of the City. The Parliamentarian forces had barricaded themselves in the Cathedral Bell Tower which was then set alight by the Royalist "to smoke them out". Unfortunately, The Bell Tower and parts of the Cloisters were severely damaged in the fire as the Parliamentary force fled. The City then remained in Royalist hands for the duration of the war.

Christophe was still smiling as he addressed the lady at the reception desk.

'Good afternoon my fair Lady, you are all obviously proud of both your Royal connection and with that of the Cathedral.'

'Why yes kind Sir, it was sacrilege what the Parliamentarians caused by occupying the Cathedral in the war and forcing the Royalist to lay siege. We are all hoping that Charles 11 returns from abroad as King and rebuilds it.'

A further wry smiled came across Christophe as he mused to himself *It was the Royalist troops who set fire to the Belfry! No matter, back to the business of Floyd.*

'I shall be staying the night if you please, maybe longer, do you have a room for me? Christophe Harcourt's the name, and what, prey, is your name?'

'Of course Sir, Daphne Sir. A room with bath, dinner and breakfast will be 2 pence a night. Dinner is served in the dining room between 7 and 9pm, breakfast is 6 to 9am.'

'Thank you kindly Daphne, I feel at home already. If all the ladies on duty are as helpful as you are', he said smiling and looking deep into her eyes, 'I will be in for a very pleasant stay.'

He enjoyed turning on the charm, regardless of the age of the lady, and Daphne started to blush at the very thought of this young man flirting with her.

Christophe turned as he walked away. 'Oh, one more thing. A friend of mine, Edmund Ford, and his daughter, arrived from Winchester last Autumn on the 8$^{th of}$ October. Can you tell me how long they stayed?'

'Just one minute' she replied having overcome the flushing to her cheeks and neck and fumbled below the desk for the Inn's Guest Book.

'Oh yes, I remember them now, the young lady's horse, Scarlet, had been delivered by one of the Mailmen in advance of her arrival. They stayed for two nights, and if I remember correctly, on the second day they were here, Ford attended the local Horse Fair and purchased a fine stallion from an ex Royalist Cavalier who was on hard times.'

How ironic, thought Christophe.

'Any idea where they were going onwards to?' he enquired.

'No, I'm sorry Sir, they kept themselves to themselves and hardly spoke a word. I thought it a bit strange, as if they had something to hide, if you know what I mean. You say they are friends of yours?'

Christophe did indeed know what she meant.

'Yes, from a long time ago, I was hoping to look them up whilst here, that's all. Well thank you anyway. I shall be away to my room and be down in the bar later for dinner. Could you have some hot water for the bath sent up as soon as convenient please. It's a pity you can't bring it up yourself' he teased causing Daphne to blush once more.

'Right away Mr Harcourt', she replied more formally in order to put this young man in his place, and not wishing to say anything she might regret later.

Christophe lay back in his warm bath, having washed in luxuriant soft lavender soap, soaking himself and thinking:

Floyd buying a horse would suggest that they were not staying in Salisbury but were likely to have travelled onwards to somewhere the stagecoaches don't go.

They have come from Winchester and originally Sussex and The Ashdown Forest, so they are not destined either to go back to London or to Kent or the South East. That only really leaves three options:

To travel further into Wiltshire, or South-West to Dorset, Devon, or Cornwall. Or South, he thought, *to my original hunch, Hampshire, and The New Forest!*

He decided that firstly he had to make as sure as he could that they were not still in Salisbury. He would make enquiries in the morning of all the legal firms in the City where Floyd may have sought work. He would also enquire of the landlord letting agencies as they had the funds to rent a respectable town house.

There was nothing more to be done that night, so he got dressed and went down to the bar to sample the best ale Salisbury had to offer. He was not disappointed, despite numerous Taverns in the City brewing their own ale, The Red Lion acquired theirs from the Philip Strong Brewery in Devizes, a town 25 miles away that was rapidly gaining a good reputation in the brewing trade for fine 'strong' malted ale.

Dinner was local haunch of venison, shot and killed in the New Forest under licence from The Crown. The licence had never been challenged by Parliament as many of their officers, when occupying the City during the war, could testify to the succulence of the meat.

The following morning Christophe confirmed that Floyd had not sought legal work in Salisbury and the landlords confirmed that they had not heard of Floyd or Ford. There was of course the possibility that he had rented a property on the 'black market' but Christophe dismissed this idea.

He made his way back to The Red Lion around noon, had a quick lunch of a bowl squirrel stew with chunks of bread, a local delicacy and one which reminded him meals concocted whilst foraging in Ashdown Forest.

For once, he resisted the inclination to immediately set off in haste to The New Forest, which was only 10 miles South.

Funds were running low, as he had given his last 2 pounds to an ex-soldier who had lost a leg and an eye in the war and was begging on the street outside the Cathedral gates on Old Sarum Way.

It was now mid-June 1653. He had four months to seek out Floyd in the New Forest area before the winter started to set in. He needed to prepare to be on the road for a few months and he had left most of his belongings, including his well-worn tricorn hat and pistols, with Anton back at The Winchfield Inn.

Being a Highwayman was a dangerous occupation, as he well knew having been shot at and wounded, but it had allowed him to track down Floyd. He had learnt well from Captain James Hind, the notorious Highwayman whom he had befriended, and from his own exploits. He had also found comradeship with others living rough in the forest, and the likes of Rogier, the landlord and Little Mick the Blacksmith.

The lifestyle was hard but exciting, exhilarating even, and when holding up a stagecoach his heart would pound with the adrenaline coursing through his veins, a feeling he had not felt since the heady days of leading the Dorset Royals on the battlefield.

48

Christophe, having returned to The Winchfield Inn, prepared to go back to his life again as a Highwayman roaming
The New Forest, robbing wealthy Parliamentarians, and seeking help from loyal Royalists as to the whereabouts of Floyd
and his daughter.

He put together his Highwayman ensemble including his
trusty Tricorn hat and packed it in one of the saddlebags. He
had dispensed with the face mask as he was now well known
as 'The Blonde Frenchie', Tristan Cheval.

He also checked over, cleaned, and oiled his Dog Lock
Flintlock Pistol that had served him well from way back in the
Civil War, together with the small pocket pistol that he concealed in either his jerkin or greatcoat depending on the
weather. He made sure his powder supply was dry and that
he had a good supply of pistol shot balls.

Lastly, he honed sharp the blade of his father's stiletto
knife, a weapon of the last resort in hand-to-hand fighting.

As much as he enjoyed the comfort and security of his
'second family,' Anton, En and Toby, it was soon time to go.

Time to finally find and confront Floyd for the betrayal
and murder of his father. He would challenge him to a duel,
no Seconds in attendance and no witnesses.

'You take good care of yourself, Christophe, we will expect to see you at the end of October' said Anton as Tristan mounted Forest for the journey.

En, with tears in her eyes followed with 'Godspeed and protect you Christophe.'

'Have no fear, I shall return, and if God is on my side, I shall find my salvation in exacting revenge on Floyd' replied Christophe.

With that he left with his customary wave of his hat as he rode out of the yard.

Initially he would ride to Lyndhurst, regarded as the capital of The New Forest, dressed as Christophe Harcourt, merchant of fine leather goods. The journey took the best part of the day, and upon arriving late afternoon he sought lodgings for the night in the Crown Manor House, a 15th century Inn located at the top of the High Street.

Lyndhurst, despite being the largest town and the epicentre of the Forest, was also the most readily accessible being on a direct route from Winchfield through Winchester and Romsey and into the Forest itself.

He'd heard there could be rich pickings in the area and that a Highwayman known as Bonny George Prier was notorious for his antics when holding up a coach. It was reported in the Lyndhurst Gazette that on one occasion he had dismounted, dropped his breeches and shown his bare arse to a mature lady he considered to be arrogant and ugly, and who had no money or jewels to offer to save her virtue, but still treated him with contempt. He used to roam the highways and byways in the area, but his luck had run out. He had recently been shot and killed in a dual over the honour of a lady that he had not only robbed of her jewels, but also, with her consent, of her virginity. His demise left the Forest with a false sense of security, which 'Tristan' could take advantage of.

Lyndhurst was not the nearest town to Salisbury, that honour falling to Fordingbridge on the northern edge of the

Forest, but Christophe thought he would check it out while passing through and find out if anyone had seen or employed Floyd locally.

As he half expected, there was no sign of Floyd, or the name of Ford under which he travelled, nor had anyone he enquired of, seen, or heard of him. That evening Christophe decided that, rather than adopting a 'Blunderbuss' approach following many false leads, he would start methodically, learning from some of the mistakes he made when looking for Floyd in the Ashdown Forest. That meant starting in Fordingbridge and working his way south.

He struck up a conversation in the bar with a well-dressed local Wool Trader who led him to believe that he was from a Royalist family who detested the Parliamentarians, none more so than for the implementation of local taxes on trade to fund the army.

Christophe kept to his story of being in the leather trade and enquired of both Floyd or his alias Ford, and the route through the Forest to Fordingbridge.

'Well, the most direct and quickest route would be on the main road up to Cadnam on to Brook, across Nomansland to Godshill and into Fordingbridge, but in your circumstances, you might prefer to go by the bye-ways over Emery Down and on to Stoney Cross and then up to Nomansland and Godshill' he replied.

What a strange reply, thought Christophe, *I wonder what he means "in my circumstances".* Before he could enquire, the Trader suddenly downed the last dregs of his ale, got up and said,

'Well, I must be off' and hurried out of the bar.

Christophe thought no more of it, ate splendidly, and retired for the night. He was still a wanted man and always cautious when staying overnight in an Inn, particularly if he had not stayed there before as was now the case. He slept with his pocket pistol armed but not cocked under his pillow and always checked out the escape route from the premises, should the need arise, before retiring.

That intuition, that sixth sense inherited from his father, proved to be right that night. At dawn he was woken by heavy footsteps on the stairway. He quickly got up, threw on his breeches, stockings and boots and grabbed his remaining clothes and saddle bag. He already had an escape route planned in his mind and was out of the window as quick as forked lightning, crossing the rear roof as a pistol shot cracked, with the bullet shattering one of the roof tiles right next to him.

Dropping down into the stable yard, he remembered his other saddle bag with his Highwayman's attire had been left with Forest's saddle hanging up in the stable.

He found it and saddled Forest in next to no time. In one swoop he attached the saddlebags and in the same motion, tied the leather straps. It was a technique he had mastered in as a Cavalier in the War.

He leapt on Forest and as they galloped across the yard towards the archway entrance, the rear door of the Inn burst open to reveal Parliamentary Soldiers. Christophe let off one volley from his pistol wounding one soldier and momentarily causing the others to retreat behind the door. It was enough time for him to gallop through the arch and down Lyndhurst High Street.

His adrenalin was making him feel euphoric, but he thought that that encounter was too close for comfort. He knew there was something odd in the Trader's reply concerning the route to Fordingbridge. *He must have realised I had a price on my head,* he thought. *He must have been a Parliamentary informer.*

Marchal, who was still following Christophe, thought it all amusing when he heard the commotion during the night. He even admired Christophe's inborne skill when he looked out of his bedroom window and saw him running across the stable yard, clutching his belongings. He was glad he had escaped because he wanted to kill him himself, in his own time. First, he needed Christophe to recover the second copy of Madrigal, because he was sure he knew the whereabouts of it. It was that document that Cromwell had tasked him to find.

Marchal was confident he would soon catch up with this blonde highwayman with a price on his head, as his reputation preceded him wherever he went. He had spies at Bourton where Christophe's mother now resided in the village, their ancestral home having been sequestered and given to a Parliamentarian Lord. Should this ex-Cavalier be so foolish as to go back there, Marchal would soon know of it.

Christophe hastily rode north out of Lyndhurst and sought refuge in the Forest. His destination was Fordingbridge. When he was sure that he was not being pursued by Parliamentary soldiers, and undercover of the thick woodland he changed into his Highwayman clothes. He needed to replenish his funds and would have to take the risk of re-joining the main road from Lyndhurst to Cadnam as there were very few people who took the byways.

It was not long before he came upon a carriage heading towards Lyndhurst. His luck was in. The coach was surprisingly unescorted and contained two Parliamentary Officers carrying gold coinage in bags, to pay the wages of the local Army contingent based in Lyndhurst. They were armed but were reluctant to risk a shoot-out and die for the money that wasn't even theirs, so they offered no resistance, recognising 'The Blonde Frenchie' from wanted posters and knowing of his reputation.

Christophe couldn't believe his eyes, or his luck. He cut open one of the bags and taking a handful of gold and silver coins, scattered them on the ground saying,

'Here, take some of your blood money, England awaits its new King.'

Having relieved them of their pistols and thrown them into the undergrowth, he galloped off on Forest leaving them grovelling in the dirt to pick up the glistening newly minted coins, which he had no doubt they would keep for themselves.

He stopped as soon as it was safe to do so, in a small clearing of heather and gorse with closely cropped grass that had been kept short by the wild ponies, deer and wild boar that roamed freely. A small fast flowing stream that was crystal clear glistened in the sunlight and was inviting for both him and Forest, as he had had no time to fill his leather costrel whilst escaping from The Crown Manor House Inn.

He dismounted and lay down on his stomach at the side of the stream, drinking the cool water from his cupped hands, whilst Forest joined him a little way downstream. Sated, he sat on a grassy mound, and opened one of the nine remaining bags.

Half Pound   Unite (One Pound)   Triple Unite (Three Pounds)

Eureka!

He counted £25 pounds in gold and silver coinage. 'Eureka', he cried and looking up to heaven said to himself *thank you God. I now have enough to survive on now for many a year yet, provide funds for Mama, Sarah, and Paul, as well as help many a destitute veteran.*

I can now put all my efforts into finding Floyd and restoring father's reputation.

Aware of the enormity of the deed he had just performed, he needed to get off of the main road as quickly as he could, so he galloped through the village of Minstead, as this was on a minor track but in the general direction of Fordingbridge. He knew of Minstead from his days at Christ Church for it was here that William Rufus, the third son of William The Conqueror, had been killed in a hunting accident amidst unproven suspicious circumstances.

Once through the village he rode off the main track, deep into the forest, and with the sun as his guide, tried to keep in a North-Westerly direction. He had to go slowly, allowing Forest to pick her way through the undergrowth, and duck in order to miss the low branches of the ancient oaks and sweet chestnut trees.

He quickly changed back into his merchant's clothes for he was sure it would not be long before a Parliamentary Horse Troop would be scouring the Forest looking for 'The Blonde Frenchie'. He thought that at best he may have a two-hour head start on them, but that was time enough to reach Godshill Wood about 8 miles North-West, and a stone's throw from Fordingbridge. Once there he would find a secluded, secure location well within the woods where he would hide and build a temporary shelter whilst he took stock and considered his next move.

Dieu se deplace de manière mysterieuse

49

Floyd and his daughter Lysette had left Salisbury the day after the Horse Fair and travelled south. Fordingbridge and The New Forest beyond beckoned. Floyd was getting older, and tired of constantly moving to keep ahead of an unknown pursuer who he deemed could only be Christophe seeking revenge for his father's death.

They now travelled under the name of Ford, Edmund Ford, and he had decided to stop running and seek gainful employment. It was the least he felt he could do for Lysette who had blossomed into a fine young woman.

They passed through the village of Downton and approached Braemore on the outskirts of Fordingbridge. They both glanced right, and up on the hillside a magnificent Elizabethan Manor glowed in the Autumn sun, with flocks of sheep roaming the acres of meadowland in the foreground.

'Oh father, what a glorious sight, I wonder who could live in such a grand house, it must be wonderful'.

'Hold on to your dreams, Lysette, for one day you shall be carried away by the love of your life to live in the manner that you deserve. You know the old saying *Dare to Dream, for from such precious things come Miracles*? Well, it's true. Unless you dream of it, it will never happen.'

Upon arriving in Fordingbridge they stayed at The George Inn whist Floyd looked for a suitable country cottage or town house to rent temporarily. The George was situated on the banks of the River Avon adjacent to 'The Great Bridge', a magnificent structure of seven medieval arches built in the 14th century and spanning the River. It was the major crossing point for the road from Salisbury to the south coast and the ports of Lymington and Poole.

The road out of town went through the villages of Godshill and Brook and was notorious for Highwaymen. Beyond Godshill was Deadmans Hill and Nomansland. On top of Deadmans Hill a Gibbet had been constructed with oak beams. It was there that many a Highwayman and other criminals had met their maker over the years.

Floyd, having forged legal qualification in his assumed name of Ford, found employment as the Estate Legal Advisor with William Brune, a descendant of the le Brune family, who had held title to the estate and manor of Forde since the 13th century.

Floyd's reward of £1,000 for betraying Sir Robert was more than enough to rent a country house, live comfortably and leave a sizeable dowry for Lysette, but for respectability's sake and to not have to account for his wealth, not even to his daughter, he needed to be seen to be working.

He rented a fine Manor house in Wood Green, a small hamlet between the Breamore Estate and Godshill woods. The house was built in the 16th century of brick from the local Sandleheath brick kilns and stone from Chilmark, near Salisbury. Its high stone mullion windows were adorned with leaden latticed glass windows and the evocative tall brick chimneys mimicked those of Hampton Court.

The three-story house had two large bedrooms and the luxury of two proper bathrooms on the first floor, ideal for Floyd and Lysette, plus two smaller bedrooms. There were staff quarters in the attic space, although they hadn't imagined having live-in staff, and thought a daily housekeeper/cook who lived locally would suffice.

The flagstone entrance hall had an impressive oak staircase to the upper chambers, and to the left was the Drawing room, with a large inglenook fireplace. The other side of the entrance hall led to the dining room with a smaller inglenook and range, and kitchen, complete with wine store. Off the kitchen area, a rear door led to the stable yard and stables for both of their horses and a small rigg.

The large grounds and formal gardens were delightfully secluded with tall oak and beech tress and a myriad of shrubs. They would need a full-time gardener, but again, he could live locally and just come in daily.

It was heaven as far as Lysette was concerned she could just ride out on Scarlet into Godshill woods and the valley beyond, or hopefully with permission granted from the owner of Braemore House, ride over the wooden bridge which spanned the River Avon into the parkland of the house.

Over the course of the next year Floyd went about his business and started to be known and welcomed by the local business, farming community and landed gentry. Floyd and Lysette were invited to local musical soirees where Lysette was often asked to play the harpsichord, when she would play Odes and songs by the composer John Blow. They also attended the occasional dinner party, and she was often introduced to various handsome and eligible bachelors but took no real interest in them.

She loved to ride and the freedom it offered her, spending many a morning out on Scarlet. On one fine Spring day up at the clearing in Godshill wood overlooking the valley below, she came across an elegant mature lady riding a horse as immaculately turned out as his owner. *The lady is obviously important* thought Lysette, *she may even be titled as she had an escort, probably one of her Coachmen.*

'A fine morning young lady, do you often ride over here'? enquired the lady.

'Why yes, replied Lysette politely. My father and I moved into the small manor House in Wood Green last October, he is the legal advisor to the le Brune Estate'.

'Oh, I know the le Brune family well, old William le Brune is getting on a bit but a fair employer I am led to believe'.

'Do you live nearby then my Lady'.

Lady Louise Rees could not help but smile at the innocence of this astonishingly lovely and polite young lady.

'I'm Lady Louise of Breamore House, whom do I have the pleasure of meeting'?

'Lysette, Lysette Ford,' she replied, somewhat taken aback, 'I've always admired your beautiful Elizabethan house from a distance, and longed that one day I would be permitted to ride over the lush parkland.'

'Permission granted young lady, why don't we ride back over there and take some tea on the terrace, come and trot alongside me.'

It was just a short ride over the Miller's bridge, across the Salisbury Road and into the Braemore Estate. A journey Lysette would shortly get to know like the back of her hand.

BRAEMORE HOUSE,
NEAR FORDINGBRIDGE

From that day forth, despite their age difference, they forged a close friendship which resulted in Lady Louise inviting Lysette to become her companion, thus avoiding the necessity of always having to have an escort when either out riding or going into town.

Christophe, venturing out from his secluded camp deep in Godshill wood, spent early Autumn seeking out Floyd in in the Fordingbridge area. Towards the end of September he came across posters nailed to Inns and Taverns that James Hind, the Highwayman he had befriended way back crossing Hounslow Heath, had been hung drawn and quartered at Worcester after being arrested at his 'safe house', The King's Arms, in Malmsbury. He had been tried and found guilty of High Treason.

It was a stark reminder to Christophe of the perilous occupation he had assumed over nigh-on the past four years. *Thank God I no longer have to engage in such activities now I have secured my fortune at the expense of the Parliamentary Army. Justice,* he thought, for the loss of many comrades in the Civil War.

One day, on his way to The Bell Inn at Brook to make further enquiries into Floyd, he was riding out of Godshill wood and up the valley to Deadmans Hill, and he came across Lysette, who loved to ride fast with the wind in her hair, galloping towards him. He had never seen such an accomplished rider, no side saddle for her, she would have shamed many of his Cavalier troops in the war.

Her horse jumped across the small brook at the bottom of the valley, stumbled and Lysette was thrown off. She got up, apparently unhurt showing more concern for her steed than herself. Christophe, the gallant Cavalier that he was, immediately galloped the remaining distance between them and dismounted.

It was love at first sight. He immediately made sure that Lysette and her horse were none the worse for wear, except for a sprained ankle that she had twisted when falling off.

It felt like Zeus had sent a thunder bolt crashing into him leaving him short of breath, like time had stood still, that he had known this beautiful girl all his life. *Where have you been all my life, my dreams have come true,* he mused to himself.

Her blond hair and green eyes reminded him of his Mama, but there the similarity ended. Her beauty was beyond compare to anyone he had ever met before. They had only just met but her beguiling eyes seemed to be looking deeply into his soul, both full of love and for confirmation of his love for her. Her skin shimmered in the autumnal light giving her a serene almost angelic look. He was, quite literally, spell-bound.

Lysette was having similar feelings as she looked up at Christophe, almost in denial that she should be feeling this way towards a member of the opposite sex. *He is the most gorgeous, handsome, blue eyed man I have ever met. His long blonde hair tied back, his bearing, right down to the scar on one cheek, an officer, and a gentlemen no doubt,* she thought.

Christophe helped her to her feet. He had removed his riding gauntlets and despite Lysette's fine cotton gloves a surge of adrenalin flowed between them as they touched. Both hearts were beating fast, and they were lost for words.

Christophe composed himself. 'Tristan Harcourt at your service my lady' he said looking deep into her eyes as he stooped and kissed the back of her hand, now with her gloves removed, it sent a shiver down Lysette's spine.

'Lysette' she replied demurely, 'Lysette Ford'.

From that moment on they were almost inseparable, and over the next few weeks they would meet at their favourite spot beneath a large beech tree in the woods almost every day. Christophe would lay down his thick woollen blanket that had served him so well on his travels and they would lie in each other arms for hours on end. Christophe wo'od her as he knew a gentleman should, with Lysette responding to every embrace, every passionate kiss.

They would lay and talk about anything and everything and laugh at the same silly situations, their hands wandering over each other's bodies, embracing every curve. Sitting hand in hand, gently playing with each other's fingers, every tiny movement sent messages of love. Lysette would lay her head on Christophe's shoulder, and they would watch the sun sink beneath the trees on the opposite side of this most beautiful of valleys in total silence. It was heaven. Parting became so difficult they began to talk of having a future together.

It was a balmy Autumn evening. Lysette had been away with Lady Louise, staying in Bath where Louise was having her winter wardrobe updated to the latest fashion, and four new dresses made for the parties that would be coming. Lysette had been missing Christophe so much, she longed for him to be holding her, to feel his arms around her, and wondered in her innocence whether in the five days that she had been gone, he had found someone else. *Please God let him still love me* she thought as she rode Scarlet to their usual rendezvous.

He was there, waiting, a huge grin on his face on seeing her. She almost fell off Scarlet in her haste to dismount and he caught her, kissing her before she had even touched the ground. Their emotions so raw, so passionate, they immediately consummated their love for each other. Initially it was rushed as they tore away at each other's clothing completely overcome with desire and love for each other. It was the first time for Lysette, Christophe knowing this tried to slow things down and be gentle, but Lysette desperately wanted 'Tristan'. She wanted them to be as one, to belong to him, and for him to belong to her, and she held him tightly inside her. 'Marry me' he whispered. She clung on to him, burying her face in his shoulder, tears of joy streaming down her cheeks.

Lysette confided in Lady Louise of her love for this dashing ex- Cavalier who she had fallen in love with and who had asked her to marry him. Louise, being very fond of Lysette and remembering how the first flush of love felt, so deep, so passionate and all-consuming, that she suggested Lysette move her belongings from her occasional bedroom in the staff quarters in the attic to an unused suite of rooms on the ground floor of Breamore House. It had its own entrance at the rear of the property.

At last Christophe and Lysette could be alone without fear of discovery.

They had never seen each other naked. Making love in the woods, be it against an ancient oak or lying beneath their favourite beech tree, had been exciting and exhilarating, but clothes had to stay basically in place in case someone came by. Here, they could take their time and enjoy each other's body, discovering the sheer joy of flesh against flesh, of legs entwined, caressing, stroking, fondling.

It was intoxicating, culminating in such joy and delight as they had never known as they fulfilled each other's every need, leaving each other breathless. 'I love you like no other,' said Christophe. 'We are one, you are mine, I am yours, forever and a day'.

Lysette, naked and wrapped in his arms, looked into his beautiful eyes, and smiled her agreement. And so it was. She had never been so full of happiness.

50

Ever since Lysette had told Christophe that her name was Lysette Ford and had revealed in conversations between them that her father was working in the Estate Office at Bickton Manor, Christophe was in a dilemma and prayed that her father was not Floyd. He was almost in denial but had to make sure before deciding whether to tell Lysette who he really was, and what her father may have done in betraying his father to Cromwell.

It did not take Christophe long to find Floyd, or Ford as he was now calling himself. He was aware from past events back in Oxted that Floyd often went under the name of Ford when seeking employment, and enquiring amongst local tenanted farmers, he soon established that an Edmund Ford was the Legal Advisor to the le Brune Estate. *The Legal Advisor* he thought, *so he is a Lawyer.*

Most days, unless visiting tenants on the estate, Floyd worked in the Estate office of the ancestral home of the le Brune family. Christophe followed him home one evening to establish where he was living. He was in despair when he watched him turn into the drive of the Manor House, where his daughter, Lysette, was waiting for him.

That night as Christophe lay in his makeshift bed in his secluded camp within Godshill woods, he wrestled with his

conscience as to whether to tell Lysette the full story as to who he was and his quest to find his father's betrayer, which had now led him to her father.

He slept fitfully. Waking up at dawn and he came to the only conclusion he felt was morally right. He loved Lysette from the bottom of his heart and if they were to have a future together, get married and be blessed with children he had to tell her the truth.

That day they met as usual beneath 'their' beech tree. Christophe was dreading the moment and could hardly look Lysette in the eye.

'Whatever is the matter my darling, has something happened?' asked Lysette fearing the answer.

'Let us sit down my sweetheart, I have a story to tell you that you might find hard to believe. I swear to God it is the truth and I am sorry that I have not had the courage to tell you before.'

Christophe proceeded to tell her that his real name was Christophe Douse, the full story of Madrigal, his father's role as Head of King Charles's Secret Service, and his attempt to present it at the King's trial for Treason, only to be betrayed to Cromwell by an unknown lawyer. He finished by telling her that his father was arrested, incarcerated in The Tower of London, and executed without trial.

Lysette was shocked, and almost speechless.

'That is terrible! What a burden you have carried with you all these years.'

'There is more Lysette, I have these past four years been a wanted man, seeking the lawyer who betrayed my father. I found out, with the help of my father's closest associate, the name of the lawyer. It was Edward Floyd.'

Christophe took both her hands in his, and looking into her eyes said,

'I have been living the life as a Highwayman, trying to find you and your father, always one step behind you in your travels across the Ashdown Forest, to Winchester and Salisbury and finally to here in Fordingbridge.'

Lysette immediately knew the consequences of what Christophe was saying. Snatching her hands out of his she cried,

'It can't be true; you must have made a mistake. Tell me that our love affair has not been a ruse for you to get closer to my father.'

'I swear on my mother's life that it didn't even occur to me, not even when you told me what your assumed name was. By that time I was hopelessly in love with you, and just thought Ford was quite a common name. When we lay here talking about our families, you being brought up by your father with no mother known to you, of our adventures, with you living for a while in Balham and not liking the awful washerwoman that lived next door, then moving to the Ashdown Forest for a while. It all started to add up.' Christophe looked forlorn, and continued

'I didn't want it too, and I tried to reason that it was all coincidence. To find that you and your father then came to Salisbury via Winchester was almost confirmation. Did you wear a flaming red wig then?'

Lysette was in floods of tears. *This cannot be true*, she thought, *please God don't let it be true.*

'Just go, I hate you, you're lying, I never want to see you again. My father is the kindest man I know and has always wanted the best for me. You should flee whilst you have the chance.'

Christophe was mortified, but he had no intention of fleeing until he had the opportunity to accuse Floyd face to face of his treachery.

'If you don't believe me, I shall come to your house tonight and give your father the opportunity to deny it to my face.'

'You will be wasting your time, now go, please, just leave me alone', she screamed, with tears pouring down her cheeks.

With that Christophe got up, mounted Forest, and said, 'I'm not lying. I love you more than you will ever know,' and he rode off into the forest.

Lysette was distraught not knowing what to do with her father at work. She got up, still sobbing, mounted Scarlet and rode as fast as the terrain allowed to the only person she could confide in, Lady Louise.

Galloping up Braemore's long drive off the Salisbury to Fordingbridge Road, scattering the sheep lazily grazing in the parkland either side, it seemed an eternity before she reached the house.

Lysette leapt off Scarlet and rattled the large knocker on the Oak Front Door. An immaculately dressed Houseman answered and seeing Lysette, wondered what on earth could have happened to make her so distraught.

'I am afraid Lady Louse is indisposed at the moment Miss Lysette.'

'But I must see her' she cried, tears still flowing freely down her cheeks.

'What's all this commotion, Henry?' asked Lady Louise descending the main staircase. 'Why Lysette whatever is the matter, do pray come in child, let us go into the Morning Room.'

Lady Louise beckoned them both to sit as she handed Lysette her fine lace kerchief, made in Florence, and proceeded to pour two schooners of Amontillado sherry.

After Lysette had sipped half and managed to compose herself, she told Lady Louise the full story.

'What am I to do my Lady?'

'Well first of all you shall stay with me for the rest of the day, and we shall take lunch in the Orangery, as there is still some warmth in there despite the changing seasons. Perhaps we might take a walk in the estate grounds after lunch to clear your mind and think through what you have told me. I am afraid you are going to have speak to your father about this, but you must be prepared for the worst. From what you have told me, Christophe appears to be a fine young man, a war hero and an officer and a gentleman.'

Lysette rode home late that afternoon, calm and fortified by Lady Louise's comforting words and friendship. She still could not believe her father could have been responsible for Sir Robert's death, but deep-down loved Christophe with all her being.

Christophe followed Floyd home from his office at the le Brune Estate to make sure that he was going straight home that evening. He saw Lysette at the front door waiting for her father and seeing her standing their felt torn between the girl of his dreams, the one true love of his life, and the overwhelming compulsion and need to avenge his father's betrayal.

He would return later that evening, giving Lysette plenty of time to tell her father of his allegations. He rode over to The Royal Oak in Gorley to have a tankard of ale whilst passing the time away. His mind was in turmoil. *She must believe me.*

Lysette, gave her father her customary kiss on the cheek welcoming him home as usual.

Once settled in the drawing room she poured him a glass of brandy and a sherry for herself.

'So, what have you been up to today' he enquired, 'have you been over to see Lady Louise?'

Lysette seized the opportunity to tell her father what Christophe had accused him of, not the complete story, that would have taken far too long.

'That is preposterous my love, the man is a liar, how could you doubt your own father?'

'I don't father, it's just I have fallen in love with him and don't know what to believe.'

'He is like all those other popinjay ex- cavaliers, still dreaming of a life under that tyrant of a King, just like his father,' said Floyd.

'He is coming over later this evening to confront you. Please hear him out, he must be confusing you with someone else.'

Lysette turned to leave the room, and as she headed for the kitchen, her father's words struck a horrifying chord. *Why would father mention the King and Christophe's father?*

Floyd knew that the game was up. He would continue to deny it of course but could see no other way out than to eliminate Christophe and move on once again.

Christophe duly arrived an hour later, and without being invited, walked straight in when Lysette opened the front door of the Manor, almost pushing past her to get to the Drawing Room.

Before he could say anything, Floyd took the initiative.

'You sir, are a damned liar, taking advantage of my daughter and spinning her this preposterous yarn about my past.'

Christophe's response was calm, measured, and direct.

'For the sake of your daughter's honour, please don't continue to deny it. I have proof of your involvement in the betrayal of my late father, Sir Robert Douse to The Lord Protector General Oliver Cromwell at the commencement of King Charles's trial for Treason. Your real name, Sir, is Edward Floyd. Furthermore, since my father's arrest and execution without trial, I have followed you for the past four years as you sought anonymity in the Ashdown Forest and since then, your move to Fordingbridge via Winchester and Salisbury.'

Christophe looked across to Lysette who was standing by the door, her hands up to her mouth in disbelief of what she was witnessing.

'This is not the first time you have assumed the name of Edmund Ford to seek gainful employment, probably forging your Legal Accreditation to do so.'

At that point, Lysette knew he was telling the truth.

Floyd by then was puce and in a rage of temper. He slapped Christophe across the cheek with one hand and said,

'You Sir have defamed me in front of my only child with your lies and innuendo. I demand satisfaction. A duel. No Seconds. No witnesses. Your choice of weapons. At dawn, in the top clearing of Godshill Woods, overlooking the valley below.'

He expected Christophe, as an ex-Cavalier, to choose duelling swords of which he, Floyd, was a past university champion. He knew he would not be as fit as his much younger opponent but thought his expertise at fencing would see him through.

He was cocksure of himself and feeling superior, as Christophe would have been used to wielding long, heavy swords in the war, not the light flexible rapiers used in duelling.

'I accept your challenge Sir. May God save your soul. The choice is flintlock pistols, one shot, ten paces.'

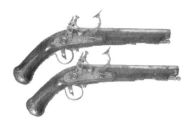

A pair of 17th Century Duelling Pistols

51

'No Christophe, he is my father', cried Lysette.

'I'm sorry Lysette, you now know the truth; it is not me who is the liar. There is no other way to settle this.' and with that Christophe marched out of the room, his head held high, his heart beating fast.

'I shall never forgive you father,' Lysette shouted at her father as she too left.

Christophe had already ridden out of the Manor's grounds and disappeared back up the road to Godshill Wood.

Distraught, trembling, and afraid Lysette knew her only help could come from Lady Louise. She saddled up Scarlett and headed off to Breamore House.

After pouring her heart out to Louise for the second time that day they agreed that there was nothing they could do to stop the duel.

'It is a matter of honour Lysette,' said her Ladyship.

'Christophe had to accept. He could not have endured the shame had he not. We will attend in secret though, in case one or the other is just wounded. I will bring bandages.'

They agreed her Ladyship would ride up to the Manor just before dawn and accompany Lysette to the spot in Godshill Wood as soon as her father had left to do so.

Christophe slept surprisingly well in his make-shift camp considering it may be his last. *This is it,* he thought before

falling asleep, *after four long years I shall finally get to re-venge father, he may be gone but will never be forgotten.*

He woke up with birdsong in the air as many were gathering to fly to warmer climes for the winter. It was still dark with the light just beginning to glint through the boughs of the beech and oak trees, their leaves turning gold in the early morning light and showing off all their autumnal glory.

He felt no nerves just a steely determination to see this through to the bitter end. *This is my fate, my destiny. A son's duty is to avenge the death of his father.*

Having splashed his face with icy cold water, he dressed and put on the finely tooled leather jerkin that was his father's way back in time. The Chaffeymoor shield adorned it with the le Douse crest embroidered on it.

Eating a few oatmeal biscuits and taking a few swigs of brandy, he then checked over his flintlock pistol that he had meticulously cleaned the night before and wrapped in oilskin overnight. Then he checked that his powder was dry. He could do no more, it was but a short walk through the wood to the clearing, so he would leave Forest at the camp. He went over to Forest who whinnied as he approached. Taking her head in his hands, he kissed her nose. 'You have been a faithful friend' he told her. 'This is not the end, but you must wait for me here.'

Floyd slept fitfully, tossing, and turning all night. *I may be older and slower in raising, aiming, and firing my pistol, but I have one last trick up my sleeve*, he thought as he smiled, almost smirked to himself as he lay in bed.

He was up and dressed well before dawn and feeling overconfident. He even managed to make and pour himself several cups of strong coffee causing his adrenaline to rise even further, as if it needed to. He was almost manic in his hatred for Christophe.

Lysette heard him get up and quietly dressed herself in suitable riding clothes, listening for when her father left. As soon as she heard her father close the door to the back yard, she looked out of the landing window to wait to see him ride off.

He wasn't even going to kiss me goodbye, she thought to herself.

Immediately rushing downstairs and out into the stable yard, she saddled up Scarlet and was ready as Lady Louise, who having seen Floyd leave, came cantering up the lane. They rode up the hill to Godshill Wood keeping a safe distance and out of earshot from Floyd.

As soon as they reached the outskirts of the wood, they carefully walked the horses up the long avenue of trees and dismounted at the edge of the clearing. Tethering both horses they proceeded on foot under cover of the trees and gorse. They could make out both Christophe and Lysette's father some 100 yards into the clearing.

Christophe had arrived first and positioned himself on level ground with an unfettered space of over 20 yards. He had paced out 10 paces from a central marker on a line North to South so neither would benefit from the rising sun in the other's eyes. He kicked away the dried wild pony manure on the close-cropped grass making sure there was nothing to distract him on what could be his last walk.

He was ready. He had no intention of asking Floyd to withdraw his challenge, nor did he expect Floyd to offer to do so.

Floyd rode into the clearing shortly thereafter, looking cocky as if it was a no contest. *Such arrogance* thought Christophe, *he is either suicidal or is planning something.*

Lysette and Lady Louise had by now secluded themselves, well-hidden behind gorse bushes, but with a clear view of proceedings.

'Let us not waste any more time Douse, I hope you said your prayers this morning, be prepared to meet your maker and your father.'

'You know the rules Floyd, as a gentleman, we prepare and cock our pistols, then stand back-to-back. On my command we proceed to pace out 10 paces. You will count out those paces and at 10 we turn and fire at will. If we both miss, we repeat the process from the beginning, until one party hits the other. Agreed?'

'Agreed, yes. Yes, just get on with it man.'

Lysette's heart was pounding, she loved Christophe, but Floyd was her father. She prayed for a herd of ponies to gallop through the clearing, or for a thunderbolt, for anything that might make them stop and think again.

Christophe and Floyd adopted the central position and turned back-to-back.

'Ready when you are, you Royalist born loser' said Floyd scornfully.

'Commence' called Christophe.

'One, two, three, four, five, six . . ..

Lysette could stand it no more she buried her head into Lady Louise's shoulder.

'Seven, eight, nine . . .'

Floyd turned and fired. The loud retort from his pistol scattered pigeons lofting in the tall trees.

Floyd's bullet whooshed past Christophe's left ear, nicking, and tearing the collar of his leather jerkin. He hadn't even turned. The count hadn't reached 10. Had Floyd not missed, he would have been shot dead through the back of his head.

On hearing the shot Lysette and Lady Louise broke cover and rushed into the clearing. Christophe turned and held his pistol out, ready to fire. He had all the time in the world to make sure his aim was accurate and lethal. He was seething.

This man has no honour at all, he thought. *He is lower than the vermin who feed on our excrement.*

As Christophe walked slowly forwards, his pistol pointing at Floyd's head who was now on his knees, snivelling, grovelling, and pleading for his life, Lysette reached him and fell to her knees, clutching at his clothing.

'No Christophe. I beg you. No.'

Christophe ignored her. His fury at this grovelling excuse of a man so intense, even she could not get through to him. By now he was standing over him.

'You, Sir, are not only a traitor, but a damned coward, turning and firing on nine. Do you have no honour at all?'

'No Christophe' cried Lysette again. 'If you love me, spare him his life. Please my love, I beg you, don't kill him.'

With that Christophe, looked down at the girl of his dreams who was distraught and sobbing at his feet. Then he looked across to Lady Louise who was standing a few yards away, quietly observing. He looked her in the eye. She returned his look and with a slight sideways movement of her head, and raise of an eyebrow, indicated that he should think about what he was about to do.

Christophe turned back and looked down at Floyd. Raising his pistol, he fired into the ground a few inches from his outstretched hand.

'You, Sir, shall say a final goodbye to your daughter and beg her forgiveness. Then you shall ride like hell to Lymington, set sail for France and never step foot in this country again. Take your blood money, we both want nothing of yours. You have one hour.'

Lysette fell into Christophe's arms where he held her tightly and kissed the top of her head. 'It's over my love' he whispered in her ear.

Floyd composed himself and rode back to the Manor to collect his personal belongings. He was gone by the time Christophe and Lysette returned. He never bade his daughter farewell or asked for her forgiveness.

As they said goodbye to Lady Louise at the end of the drive Christophe turned and said, 'We would love to invite you to the wedding Lady Louise, but I am still a wanted man.'

Looking into Lysette's eyes and putting his arm around her waist he smiled his Christophe smile.

'It will have to be a very quiet affair, but one day I will clear my name, that of my father and regain Chaffeymoor as our rightful ancestral home.'

He looked back at Louise saying, 'when I have regained it for my family, we will invite you as our honoured guest.'

Louise just smiled in acknowledgement.

The news came later that day that Floyd had committed suicide on Deadmans Hill by shooting himself through his right temple. He died instantly.

Despite all they had been through, Christophe and Lysette arranged a Christian burial for 'Edward Floyd, Lawyer, Father of Lysette.' He was buried in the graveyard of the ancient and beautiful St Mary's Church in Fordingbridge, first mentioned in the Doomsday Book of 1086.

As Christophe stood by the grave, holding Lysette's hand in his and looking down on the coffin, he thought *justice father. Justice has been done. Now to clear our names and regain Chaffeymoor.*

52

After the burial, Christophe and Lysette returned to the Manor house in Floyd's Rig, the only item of her father's that Christophe allowed her to keep. The remaining of his possessions they burned. His horse had been sold, and together with the not inconsiderable amount of £800 he had left in gold and silver from the reward for turning in Sir Robert, a princely sum was deposited with a Notary in Fordingbridge. A Trust was to be set up in Lysette's name, the monies to be used for the relief of the poor and destitute living within the boundaries of The New Forest.

They appointed the Notary, Chauncey Gardner as joint trustee of these funds, along with the Vicar of St Marys, The Reverend John Augustus, an ex-Catholic Priest who had decided to be a Protestant to avoid persecution from Parliament.

The Trust was to support the meagre existence of the tenanted Commoners who had grazing rights on the heathland and within the forest. Their cattle were regularly turned out and their pigs let loose in the Autumn to gobble up the acorns as they fell from the oak trees.

Christophe had ridden back up to Godshill Wood the day after the duel to break up his makeshift camp and to recover his own fortune that he had accumulated of ten bags of gold coinage amounting to £240. He had buried it at the foot of the large beech tree within the Forest which held such fond memories of Lysette and himself lying beneath its boughs, making love on many an occasion. Before he left, he carved a heart with the initials CD and LF on its sturdy trunk.

They spent the next few weeks making preparation for their journey to Bourton, where they would get married. They would stay with Marguerite and the family initially. Lysette had given notice on the Manor to the Estate Office from whom her father had rented the property. Christophe ensured that the rig's wheel bearings were well greased and that the harness was in good repair. Scarlet and Forest were reshod by the local blacksmith and meticulously groomed with their manes and tails trimmed.

Lysette had cut Christophe's hair to shoulder length curls and had dyed it brown using a dye made from a combination of Madder, Weld, Cutch and Oak Bark saddened with Copperas, a natural form of Iron Sulphate. He no longer looked like 'the Blonde Frenchie' Highwayman, but like an everyday Leather Merchant.

With a "wife" sitting beside him in a rig, rather than being on horseback, and a trunk on the back seat containing their possessions, he hoped he could go back to Bourton without being recognised, arrested, or shot.

He had few items of clothing. Those that he had, apart from his ex-cavalier hat, his boots, gauntlets, and his father's leather jerkin were, in Lysette's eyes, due for the bonfire. They went shopping together in Salisbury to buy him several sets of new underwear, shirts, stockings and breeches, a doublet, and a new great coat to keep him warm when out riding in winter. Items suitable for a Merchant, not a Cavalier or Highwayman.

With Lysette it was more a case of deciding what not to keep from her vast wardrobe she had acquired since moving into the Manor the year before. Money had been no object and her father had indulged her every whim. However, Christophe insisted when shopping in Salisbury on buying her a complete ensemble to travel in, again, an ensemble suitable for the wife of a Merchant, not a 'Lady'.

'Do I really have to wear these dull clothes, wool and cotton is so not me, and the wool in the skirt will make me itch.' She complained.

'My darling girl, you look stunning in anything, or even nothing.' he said with a grin. 'You don't need silk and satin to look gorgeous, and your cotton petticoats will stop the woollen skirt from annoying you. Anyway, it's cold and getting colder, it will keep you warm.'

'I've got you to keep me warm now' she replied coyly, looking at him from under her eyelashes.

Soon it was time to leave. They would be sorry to say goodbye to Wood Green and Godshill, for it was a beautiful part of the country and aptly named. Despite some painful memories they had fallen in love there, and they vowed to return one day to 'their place' in the woods and find their beloved beech tree again.

They left soon after breakfast on Friday 13th of November 1653. Christophe had harnessed Scarlet to the rig and tethered Forest to trot behind them. Their new life awaited them. Christophe still had much to do, but with Lysette beside him, he felt he could do anything. He felt confident he would succeed. Assured and happy, he smiled to himself as he sat in the rig, waiting for her to join him.

'Hurry up' he shouted. 'It's cold sitting out here.'

'Exactly, that is why I have just rescued an extra blanket from the bundle of things we are leaving for the Reverend to collect and give out. Here, wrap it over your knees, and leave some for me.'

The air was crisp, the sun was rising in a clear blue sky and the frost on the ground and shrubs had begun to melt. They travelled under the assumed names of Robert Asprey, Merchant of Fine Leather Goods, the name his father had used in such circumstances, and his fiancée Miss Lysette Ford.

They took the road from Fordingbridge, up through Cranborne Chase, past William Cecil's other country estate, Cranborne Manor, to Shaftesbury and onwards to Mere, a journey of only some 35 miles. They stopped for lunch at The Red Lion Inn* in the heart of Shaftesbury, an ancient hilltop town.

They ate lunch of freshly baked bread with local cheeses including Goats Cheese and Dorset Vinny, accompanied by a handful of salad herbs and pickles. All washed down with a delightful dry white wine imported from the Loire region of France.

As they ate, they chatted about their future and were excited, visualising the look and reception from Christophe's Mama, and Aunt Sarah and Uncle Paul, for they had no way of letting them know of their pending arrival.

'I am so looking forward to meeting them all' said Lysette 'I do hope they approve of me.'

'Approve? They shall be ecstatic to see us. As for you my darling, you are perfect, and an outrageously beautiful lady. Any man would wish to marry you. God, I fancy making love to you right here, right now.'

'Oh stop it, people might hear you.'

'I don't care, let the world know that I love you so much.'

They perused the shops in Shaftesbury looking for a gift for Christophe's Mama. Lysette spotted the ideal thing, an exquisite short veil in a very pale peach with handmade lace trim.

'I'm sure your Mama would love this to wear to church' said Lysette, 'I know it is a Church of England, but I am sure she would cover her head, as most parishioners do, and this is such a beautiful and unusual colour.'

'Perfect' said Christophe 'and at the same time I will purchase a pink silk ribbon for you to tie in your hair to complete your ensemble and make that rather dull woollen skirt feel more feminine.' They both laughed.

Having re-joined the main road out of Shaftesbury, Scarlet trotted into Mere later that afternoon as the sun was beginning to wane. They would reach Bourton well before sunset.

On arrival they made straight for the Church Cottages.

Marguerite was in the Church, arranging the flowers.

She was using late blooming Chrysanthemums, Witch Hazel and

Achilleas together with White Christmas Roses and their evergreen foliage. She heard the clatter of hooves and cart-wheels on the cobble stones and wondered who on earth that could be at this time of day as there were no further church services.

Out of curiosity she put down the remaining flowers and went out into the churchyard. Out beyond the Lychgate she spotted a young couple in a rig. A decidedly handsome bearded man with shoulder length rich brown hair with his beautiful blonde companion. She was intrigued. *Who could they be outside Sarah's cottage?* She thought.

Christophe, although heading for the cottages on the other side of the road, glanced across at the Church and spotted his Mama. He quickly handed the reigns over to Lysette and leapt out to run to her.

'It's me Mama,' he shouted as he ran towards her.

Marguerite was overwhelmed. She couldn't believe her eyes. Shocked, surprised, she dropped the flowers and looked to the heavens, bursting into tears. 'Pray God is it really you Christophe' she exclaimed.

'It is Mama, I'm home at last' he said with trembling voice as he hugged and kissed his dear Mama.

Lysette had tethered the rig and followed Christophe into the churchyard, her eyes also full of tears on seeing the touching reunion.

'Mama, this is Lysette, we are to be married as soon as practical if the Reverend Banks agrees to officiate.'

Marguerite opened her arms to Lysette, and they all embraced together, laughing, crying, hugging, then hugging again.

'Christophe, what on earth have you done, the beard looks good on you and suits you, but what have you done to those golden locks of yours.'

Christophe and Lysette laughed in unison, 'Lysette cut and dyed it Mama, don't forget I am still a wanted man until I clear father's name. I had to make sure I wouldn't be recognised.'

'And you Lysette, you look pretty as a portrait, how did he persuaded you to marry him?'

'Your son is the most handsome, loving, compassionate and courageous man I have ever known', she replied 'just like his father, from what Christophe tells me.'

With that Marguerite shed another tear. Tears of joy, but sad that her Robert was not going to be there to witness their only son get married to the love of his life.

Christophe walked Scarlet with the rig attached into the rear yard of the cottages. He unharnessed her and led her, together with Forest, into one of the stables, brushed them down and gave them both buckets of water and oats and fresh straw to lie in.

Meanwhile Marguerite had rapped on Sarah and Paul's front door and rushed in with Lysette.

'Christophe's home, this is Lysette, they are to be married' she said proudly, unable to contain her excitement.

Sarah and Paul were sitting at the table having just finished their afternoon tea. They looked up astonished, for a moment lost for words, not realising quite what was going on.

'Well, congratulations Lysette, that Christophe has always been full of surprises. Where is the boy?' Sarah said, aiming her question at her cousin, and at the same time saying to Lysette 'here let me take your cloak and sit yourself down in front of the range my lovely. Have you come far; you must be weary. I'll get you a nice cup of tea.'

'Tea?' said Marguerite. 'What, may I ask is tea?'

'It's a brand-new herbal drink I found out about at the General Store' she said, 'and very nice it is too. It's only just been introduced from China I think he said, or was it India? Do you want a cup too? I had to buy a teapot to make it in.'

Mary moved the already hot kettle onto the hottest plate on the range and it soon boiled.

'The water has to be really boiling, she said, or it'll taste awful. I just have to scold the leaves, leave it a minute or two, then drink it. You can add a drop of milk if you want, and even some sugar.'

She handed a cup of this strange new brew to Lysette:

'Oh, thank you most kindly. We have only travelled from Fordingbridge on the edge of The New Forest today, I have been living there these past two years.'

Christophe burst in through the back door, arms out-stretched, saving Lysette the embarrassment of answering any more awkward questions.

'Hello everyone, what do you think of my new look then?' he said mischievously as only he knew how, bowing and prancing around with a huge grin on his face.

He gave Sarah a big hug, shook hands with Paul and then gave his Mama another caress and kiss before sitting down on the sofa next to Lysette. Marguerite sat in the armchair and Paul fetched two chairs from the dining room. Everyone was smiling.

Holding Lysette's hand he continued

'So, I'm so sorry it has been five long years. I will eventu-ally tell all, but for now suffice to say that I finally traced the traitor who betrayed father, and when confronted he did the honourable thing by ending his own life. God forgive him and rest his soul.'

Lysette squeezed Christophe's hand, she was so in love with him and proud of the way he revealed her father's de-mise.

'This, everyone, is my Lysette', he said with pride and love in his voice. 'We met just a few months ago, and it was love at first sight. Isn't she just adorable, my prayers have been an-swered.'

'You are a lucky man Christophe, and you look as hand-some as ever but are you keeping that ridiculous brown hair'? asked Sarah. 'And you, Lysette, as beautiful as an English Rose in full bloom, you were made for each other.'

'I am afraid I must stay a brunette, as I am still wanted until I can finally clear father's name.'

'What will you do now Christophe, you'll be staying on for Christmas no doubt?' enquired Paul.

'Of course, we shall go and see Reverend Banks tomorrow and see if he will agree to marry us on Saturday the 13th next month. That will allow him to note, privately, in the Parish Records that the required 3 weeks for banns to be read, were met.'

'What's the rush?' asked Marguerite sheepishly, secretly praying to God that Lysette was not with child.

'No rush, we just want to be wed and the 13th has a particular meaning for both of us. We met on a Friday 13th, unlucky for some, but fate had cast its hand for us.'

'Oh Christophe, I am so happy for you', Marguerite said, 'in the meantime Lysette can sleep here in Sarah and Paul's 2nd bedroom, and you shall stay next door with me. Now let us talk of the wedding details.'

Christophe and Lysette glanced at each other and smiled. Lysette had not seen that one coming, even though Christophe had told her that his Mama was actually Catholic.

53

The Gravedigger, Baldy Barnet, finished digging the grave of old Mrs Penelope Stone, a former flower arranger at the church, ready for her funeral the following day, which was his day off.

He smiled too, as Christophe and Lysette arrived. Having witnessed the emotional reunion with Marguerite he knew that he had his man.

He was Marchal's spy, left in Bourton to integrate himself in the local community until Christophe returned one day. That day had come. He needed to get word urgently to Marchal who was now ensconced in Oxford with duties that covered the whole of the South West, so the following morning he set off to ride up to Salisbury where another courier would take his message on to Marchal. He then returned to Bourton awaiting further instructions.

Upon hearing the news Marchal was euphoric. He had lost sight of Christophe in Lyndhurst as he made his escape from The Crown Manor House Inn.

Got you at last, you bastard, he said to himself.

He sent word back to Baldy that he was to maintain observation of the new arrivals, report back with any significant developments and do nothing else until hearing further.

Marchal considered his position. He desperately wanted to revenge his father and kill Christophe but more than that he needed to recover the second copy of Madrigal for Cromwell.

Life in Church Cottages was constrained by living arrangements and reduced income. Elliot had visited every summer with monies from Robert's funds that were deposited at Hoare's Bank and held in trust by old David Paleman, the Lawyer in London, and but they were fast running out. That was no longer an issue with Christophe's good fortune, but Sarah had taken in a lodger, Genevieve Poolman, to help pay the bills. She was the same age as Lysette and helped out at the local school. She agreed to share her double bed with Lysette, and they soon became great friends.

Christophe and Lysette were becoming increasingly frustrated at not having any time to be alone with each other, and Genevieve could see how they adored each other. She conspired with them to be away visiting a sick Aunt from time to time, so that Christophe could sneak in through the adjoining door to the cottages in the middle of the night and creep up to be with Lysette.

They fooled no one except Marguerite.

The Reverend Banks had agreed to officiate at a private wedding and to maintain sacred their true identities. The Reverend's daughter Claire, who had a crush on Christophe for many years when she was younger, was now married to Hugo, and had twin boys. Christophe, and Lysette in particular, agreed to ask both Genevieve and Claire to be bridesmaids. They were thrilled, laughing, and giggling together as to what they should wear.

Christophe had sent word by courier to Elliot inviting him to the wedding of his old friend Robert Asprey and asking him to be his Best Man. Elliot was delighted. He was due to arrive on the day before the wedding and planned to stay at The George in Mere.

The wedding was looming fast, and Marguerite offered Lysette her wedding dress that she had kept these past 30 years. Lysette was beaming at the thought of what would surely be a beautiful dress, and helped Marguerite get the huge box from the attic. They undid the brown string and opened it,

removing the layers of fine paper that had protected it all those years. Marguerite was almost in tears as she gently unfolded the many yards of sumptuous silk skirt to reveal the bodice.

'I haven't seen this since my wedding day' she said. 'My mother packed it away and told me I should leave it packed like this until I had a daughter and that she should wear it for her wedding'.

The dress itself was magnificent as befitted the only daughter of le Duc de Harcourt of Normandy, France. It was pale gold figured silk, which shimmered over an underskirt of cream satin. Handmade Venetian lace and real pearls adorned the top with its low and wide neckline, which made the corset style bodice almost off the shoulder. Voluminous sleeves burst from the bodice and were decorated with the finest lace and embroidery, showing the under garment of satin, and ending in flurries of lace gathered into the elbow length cuffs. Its bodice was heavily embroidered with gold thread, crystals and pearls and it fitted tightly with a deep 'V' front plunging into the full skirt. Lacing down the back drew it in like a corset. It was truly beautiful and a work of art.

'I think it will need a little alteration to fit me' said Lysette, looking at the bodice. We are about the same height, but I think I'm a little thinner than you were.'

'That won't be a problem' replied Marguerite, 'Sarah is a brilliant seamstress and I'm sure she will be able to take it in. I'll ask her to come upstairs and take a look.'

Sarah walked into the room and was speechless at the sight of the beautiful dress spread out across the bed. She had, of course, seen it before when she was bridesmaid to Marguerite, but with a twinkle in her eye, a smile on her face, slipping back into her Scottish lilt she declared,

'Ah lassie, 'tis the bonniest wee dress I have ever seen. I had forgotten just how magnificent it was.'

'But can you alter it to fit Lysette? She's slimmer than I was and has smaller breasts.'

'Of course I can' she replied in her normal English with a slight touch of the French accent she had acquired since she married Paul. 'I will enjoy doing that but leave it up here. Christophe must not see it. Oh, this is so exciting.'

Christophe had decided that they would have to leave Bourton in the New year and settle somewhere else. In the country, but near a large town, until there was news of Charles 11 returning to England, if ever. He thought of heading further West where there were still staunch Royalist areas, perhaps near Exeter, in Devon, but first he needed to retrieve the second copy of Madrigal from its hiding place in Chaffeymoor.

He prayed that it was still there, undiscovered, intact and the mice had not chewed it up to make a nest. He became increasingly anxious to know that it was still where his father had hidden it. Five long years had passed, and it's hiding place had never been spoken of, not even by his father when he told him of it, but he remembered him saying,

'It's in your favourite hiding place when we played hide and seek when you were a boy'.

A week before the wedding, late in the afternoon, Christophe went up the hill through the wooded copse to Chaffeymoor. There was nobody around. *It must be the gardener's day off,* he thought, and prayed that his tree house that he played in for many a year, was still aloft in the great beech tree at the bottom of the garden and the entrance to the copse.

There it was, still intact. *Thank God,* Christophe thought as he climbed the rope ladder and entered. He searched the tree house and thought *where would father have hidden it?*

It suddenly came to him, *where did father hide his parchments in the safe house in Angel Islington, of course, the loft area.*

Searching amongst the eaves, it did not take him long to find a rolled-up oilskin tucked behind one of the rafters and out of site from below. *Well done father,* he said to himself.

One day I shall present this to King Charles 11, just as you attempted to so do with his father Charles 1, and I will seek to clear your name.

On emerging from the copse in the back lane into the village, he clambered down the bank and was spotted by the Gravedigger, Baldy Barnet. He had seen Christophe walking out of the village, rather than riding, which he thought was unusual, so had followed him.

Baldy, a man well trained in the art of espionage, put two and two together and decided that the only reason for Christophe to be in the wood next to Chaffeymoor was to retrieve the second copy of Madrigal. He immediately rode up to Salisbury that same evening and passed a message onwards via courier, to Marchal.

Marchal arrived in Mere on the eve of the wedding.

That same late afternoon Christophe set off for The George in Mere to join Elliot, Paul and Hugo for much merriment and several tankards of ale. He would stay the night at The George, as it was the custom that the groom should not see his bride on the day of the wedding before the ceremony.

Elliot and Paul finally put Christophe to bed at well gone mid-night, exceedingly drunk from consuming far too many tankards of ale, singing at the top of his voice the 17th century love song, Marry, Marry me.

It was the day of the wedding. Christophe finally roused himself, jumping up when Elliot entered his bedroom and threw a jug of cold water over his face.

'Bloody Hell Elliot, I didn't know that was part of the duties of the Best Man. Did I have one too many last night?'

'One? One? That would be an understatement my boy, now get yourself washed and dressed, today's the big day.'

The ceremony was to be at 11.00.a.m. Paul had found his way home the night before and was to walk Lysette over to the church with Genevieve and Claire and, standing in for her father, he was to give her away. Marguerite and Sarah would leave first, ahead of them. Elliot decided that the three mile walk up from Mere to Bourton would help to clear Christophe's head, having already given him a hangover cure of raw eggs and herbs. As they approached the church, looking exceptionally finely dressed in their best clothes, they were laughing and chatting.

Marchal and Baldy could hear them coming up the path and stepped out from behind two tall gravestones, pistols drawn. Elliot threw himself in front of Christophe taking both shots in the chest.

Christophe drew his pocket pistol and shot Baldy dead.

Marchal rushed at Christophe in a wild rage having drawn a knife from his gauntlet, but Christophe side stepped and Marchal lost his footing, tumbling into the ready prepared grave that Baldy had dug the day before, landing face down with his knife piercing his heart. He was dead instantly.

Hugo was in Sarah's cottage and heard the shots, so rushed over to the churchyard, to see what the commotion was. Fortunately, the pistol shots had not brought anyone else running. Christophe ran to Elliot who was slumped face down on the ground and turned him over.

'No' he bellowed 'No Elliot, no' as the lifeless body fell back in his arms.

He looked desperately at Hugo who bent down and checked Elliot's pulse, putting his cheek to Elliot's nose just to make sure, and shook his head at Christophe.

'He's gone, he has died a true hero. From what you have told me about him, he would have wanted it to be him, rather than you, for your father's sake.'

Christophe did not have time to explain, that would come later. His training as a Cavalier kicked in and grabbing hold of Baldy's legs, he said.

'Here Hugo, quickly give me a hand to throw this one into the grave on top of the other body.'

Hugo knew Christophe was a wanted man and assumed these casualties had something to with that, so asked no questions. They picked Baldy up and threw him into the grave on top of Marchal.

'God rest their souls' said Christophe 'grab that spade and cover them with soil.'

He went over to Elliot and knelt beside him.

'You have been such a dear friend to both me and my father' he said, choking back the tears. 'I will make sure that you have a Christian burial, and the very best oak coffin, but I am getting married in 10 minutes time, so forgive me my friend if I move you temporarily to a quieter place, away from the path, but I will be back once I have married Lysette.'

With that he picked Elliot's body up and put it over his shoulder, carrying it to a quiet spot round the side of the church, and behind a large Yew tree. He placed the body down carefully, holding his head so's not to let it land heavily, and straightened his clothing.

For all intents and purposes it looked as though Elliot was asleep.

'I will be back my friend, until then rest in peace, there will only ever be one Elliot Medlar.'

Christophe's new doublet was covered in Elliot's blood and he needed to go back to the cottage to get changed.

'They won't let you in' said Hugo, 'they'll be worried you'll see Lysette and that's really bad luck.'

He offered to go to the cottage and ask Paul to find Christophe something else to wear.

'Fine' said Christophe, still stunned from what had happened and glad that this will give him a few minutes to collect himself.

'Explain to Paul and tell him to delay the others for a few minutes, but don't tell the others. I'll tell them after the ceremony.'

The excitement in the cottages was almost unbearable. Having been up since 6a.m. dressing each other's hair and adding strings of pearls through the curls on top of their heads, Claire, Genevieve and Lysette all looked beautiful.

Marguerite helped Lysette into the magnificent gown that she had married Robert in, 30 years earlier, and that Sarah had altered. It fitted like a glove.

'Pull it tighter' said Lysette to Marguerite as she laced the back of the dress up 'I need a twenty-two-inch waist today.'

They laughed and giggled, Claire saying, 'tonight's the night' and Genevieve and Lysette smiling, knowing that particular night was long passed.

It was 10.55 when they heard Hugo come back in the front door.

'What were the shots?' called Marguerite.

'Nothing, just some lads from the village practising shooting' he replied. 'I sent them packing.'

He took Paul through to the kitchen, told him what had happened and that he needed a fresh doublet for Christophe. Paul climbed the stairs and went through the adjoining door into Marguerite's cottage.

'Christophe's only gone and fallen over and got mud all over his doublet' he said 'can you get me his other one and I'll take it over to the church. He's over there waiting.'

'Honestly, that boy, you'd think he'd be more careful on his wedding day' said Marguerite as she fetched the doublet. 'I trust he's not drunk.'

'No, nothing like that. He's fine apparently, but we could arrive a few minutes late to let him get changed, so there's no rush' he said, trying to get out of the bedroom that was overflowing with ladies dressed in silk and satin as quickly as possible.

They left the cottage at 11.05 a.m. and walked across to the church.

Marguerite looking wonderful in her bottle green silk dress and the little veil Christophe bought her adorning her hair which was piled on top of her head. Sarah walked with her, dressed in a lovely honey coloured satin dress that she had finished making the night before. She preferred the quieter colours and they suited her.

The two bridesmaids were co-ordinated in colour if not style, and both wore pale green. More importantly, they wore huge smiles as they held the train of Lysette's gown as she walked up the long pathway leading to the church on Paul's arm.

She had never been so happy and felt she might burst.

It was a bright sunny morning. The church bell peeled eleven times and Olivia was singing, Greensleeves accompanying herself on the Lute as Lysette entered the church. Olivia's sweet voice resonated throughout.

ST NICHOLAS CHURCH, SILTON, BOURTON, DORSET

Inside the church the Reverend Banks stood in front of the alter, and her groom Christophe awaited her arrival, butterflies galore in his stomach. Hugo stood by his side as his Best Man. He just hoped that in the excitement of the moment, nobody would question the whereabouts of Elliot.

'Do you take this woman to be your lawful wedded wife. . . . . .'

It was over in a matter of minutes.

'You may kiss the bride.'

Christophe took Lysette in his arms, looked deep into her eyes with his beautiful smiling eyes, and she melted as he kissed her.

They were so in love and knew they would live happily ever after.

54

The wedding festivities were in full swing at Marguerite's house. Hugo, crept out to go to see his friend Henry Chippendale the local carpenter who was soon to move from Bourton to Yorkshire, marry a local lass, and produce a dynasty of master craftsmen and furniture designers, including his grandson, Thomas.

Henry agreed to hastily make the finest oak coffin as befitted a man of Elliot's stature, both physically and in respect of him. He had one partly made, but it would take him a few hours to finish and polish it.

'Come back after 10pm and use the back entrance' he said. 'We are close enough to the Church, so you won't need the Bier. Just carry it between you, but it will be heavy, you will need two of you minimum.'

Hugo returned with Paul and collected the coffin under a moonlit sky.

'I know you said it will be heavy' whispered Paul as they struggled up the church path, 'but this weighs a ton.'

'It's empty' whispered Hugo back. 'Wait until we've got Elliot in it before you start complaining.'

They went across to the Yew tree and lifted Elliot into it, placing Christophe's leather jerkin that his father had left at the safe house on top of him. They then nailed the coffin shut.

'It's no good' said Paul 'I can't lift this. I'm not as young as I was. We'll have to get your brother-in-law and Christophe over here.'

Hugo went off to the Forge and Paul returned to the cottage and beckoned Christophe to join him outside.

'We can't lift the coffin with just the two of us. Hugo's gone to get Parker the Blacksmith, but you'll have to come too.'

'OK, but I'll have to tell the others and the Reverend. I can't just disappear for half an hour.'

Christophe took The Reverend Banks to one side, who immediately agreed to conduct a full burial service in the morning.

He then turned to the other guests and called for silence, addressing them, not so much in mourning, Elliot would not have wished for that, but in pride of his late friend.

'Family, friends, I am so sorry to have to inform you that my good friend and intended Best Man, Elliot, died suddenly this morning before the wedding of a suspected heart attack, no doubt brought on by his lifestyle. Elliot, Hugo, Paul, and I had a riotous time last night and he even woke me up by throwing a jug of cold water over me. Something which I'm sure, he thoroughly enjoyed. I got to know Elliot well, and it would have been as he would have wished; to depart this mortal soil, in good company on such a joyous day. So, let us not be sad, but be happy that we knew him, and share one last drink in the name of Elliot Medlar, a finer friend as anyone could ever have.'

The all raised their glasses and proclaimed in unison 'Elliot Medlar.'

'The Reverend Banks has kindly agreed to give Elliot a full private Christian burial in the morning at 11.00 a.m. I'm sure you will all wish to join me there and pay our last respects to a fine man. Meanwhile his coffin needs to be carried into the church for him to lie in peace there for one last night, and I'm going to go over to the church with Paul and help. Please carry on, we won't be long.'

They went over to the graveyard where Hugo and his brother-in-law Parker, were waiting, and together they carried the coffin into the church placing it on trestles in front of the alter.

The festivities continued spilling over into both cottages. Later when retiring, Christophe told Lysette the full story. They just lay in each other's arms that night, it had been an eventful, exhausting day. Their future together would give them infinite time for lovemaking.

The next day, the funeral was a sombre affair, and Christophe was very aware that it should have been him in the coffin as the four men lowered it into the ground.

'Thank you, from the bottom of my heart, thank you. You will never be forgotten', he whispered.

He wrote a moving personal letter to Jenny and John at the safe house in Angel Islington and sent it to them after the funeral by courier. He felt much safer now Alexander Marchal was dead and knew it would take quite a while for Cromwell to realise he was not reporting back. It was certainly enough time for Christophe and Lysette to disappear.

Christmas came and went; the New Year was fast approaching and Christophe and Lysette were busy making plans for their new life in Devon. They had spent a few days in Exeter on their honeymoon, staying at The White Hart, near The Cathedral, and whilst in Exeter they looked around for a suitable country house to purchase and raise a family. Christophe would open a shop and workshop in Exeter selling customised fine leather goods using the contacts passed on by his father and local craftsmen.

They settled on Riverside Court, a fine newly built grand property in the village of Topsham, just 4 miles from the city centre. It had a Dutch gable-end roofline, gated courtyard and the gardens that ran right down to the water's edge of the River Exe estuary. It came with a coach house, ideal for their rig and the horses, Forest, and Scarlet. Lysette fell instantly in love with it.

'Oh it's perfect Christophe, I can just see us living here as a family and God willing raising little Robert and Louise.'

'So, we are having at least two children, are we?' asked Christophe smiling. 'The more the merrier' replied Lysette.

RIVERSIDE COURT,
NEAR TOPSHAM, DEVON

Before leaving Bourton, Christophe made arrangements with a Notary in Salisbury, appointing Paul as his Power of Attorney in relation to the remainder of Robert's funds at Hoar's Bank in London. He himself deposited a further sum of £100 on trust with the Notary to supplement his Mama's income should the need arise.

The New Year was to be another turning point in the family's history and they all decided that they would celebrate it in style. Christophe hired The Church Hall and invited all those that attended the private wedding and many more friends from the village including Hugo's sister and brother-in-law, the blacksmith Parker, and his wife Kim and their daughter Olivia who used to help out at Chaffeymoor. Farmer Peter Quince who continued to rent the lower fields of Chaffeymoor from the new residents also came with his wife Lin and daughters Lottie and Kellie.

The Reverend Banks was in fine form, as he always was whenever there was a party, whirling both Marguerite and Sarah around the dance floor.

'I am going to miss all this darling' said Lysette. 'It's so lovely to be part of a family.'

'We shall return my sweetheart, have no fear of that' replied Christophe, more determined than ever that one day he would regain Chaffeymoor for them all.

They left Bourton on the 4^{th of} January after tearful goodbyes all round. Paul had harnessed Forest to the rig and tethered Scarlet behind. He then helped Christophe load up several cases of all their worldly possessions and wedding presents. Sarah had produced her legendary sumptuous lunch for them in a wicker basket and oats and carrots for the horses.

'I'm not far away Mama, we shall visit, and you must all come down to Topsham in the Summer' said Christophe before departing.

'There is no reason for you not to spend several months with us. We shall be rattling around in the house until a family comes along', said Lysette.

'Oh Lysette, are you with child, that would be wonderful' replied Marguerite.

'Not that I know of, but we do want children as soon as the Lord prevails' she said smiling looking at Christophe.

What the Lord has got to do with it I do not know, thought Christophe, *it's not as if we are not trying hard enough*, he mused to himself.

The journey was easy and comfortable, straight down The Great West Road once more, but this time, all the way to Exeter and then a country road to Topsham. In all it was some 70 miles and would take them the best part of 2 days to get there, so they planned to stop near Ilminster in the village of Broadway overnight to rest the horses. There was a recently built hostelry called The Bell there which had a good reputation.

They arrived in Topsham late afternoon and set to make Riverside Court their home for several years to come.

Christophe being the gentleman and romantic that he was, carried Lysette giggling over the threshold.

Life was kind to them, Christophe established a successful business in Exeter and little Robert came along in the summer of the next year, being born on the 13ᵗʰ August 1655. Fortunately, both Marguerite and Sarah were staying for a summer holiday when Lysette went into labour, so attended the birth with the local Midwife licensed by the Church. All went well, a bonny bouncy baby weighing 8lb. They named him Robert Elliot Douse in memory of Christophe's father and the late Elliot.

A daughter, Marguerite Louis, was born two years later on the 25ᵗʰ May.

The family had an idyllic life spending many hours in the garden overlooking the River Exe estuary. Christophe had returned home one evening with a cocker spaniel puppy named Digby, who was adored by the children, and made their family complete.

The live-in Housekeeper / Nanny would look after the children of an evening, whilst Christophe and Lysette would walk hand in hand through the garden to their small clinker boat, tied to a stake at the river's edge. Christophe would row them up to the Town Quay and join friends for a meal at The Pig and Pallet. The return, in the stillness and blackness of the night with only the moon and stars to guide them, was breath-taking.

It was just over four years later in September 1658 that they heard of the death of Oliver Cromwell. The news sheets being published talked of discontent in the country and political turmoil in Parliament. The Republic that had been led by Cromwell had not produced the promised prosperity for the masses, and the public were angry.

Royalists now had the momentum and after several protests of discontent and debate in the House of Commons Charles 11 was invited to return to England from exile in the Netherlands. On the 29ᵗʰ May1660, his birthday, he was

received in London to public acclaim. He was crowned King on the 23$^{rd\,of}$ April 1661.

Christophe, although a husband, father, and successful merchant was still a wanted man. He had endured over a decade of seeking out his father's betrayer followed by four years of happily married life in "exile". He had one last quest in life; to clear both his father's and his own name and ensure the restoration of Chaffeymoor to its rightful ancestral owners, the Douse family.

There was only one way he could achieve that; by seeking an audience with the new King.

He needed to present to him the complete story of 'The Closely Guarded Secret – Madrigal' and tell him of those that chose to be loyal to his father right to the end. Sir Robert, and others, had sacrificed their own lives whilst trying to bring an end to the Civil War and prevent Charles's trial and execution.

He was a just a merchant living in Devon. The question now was, how?

He remembered the Latin 'Tempus Fugit' from his Alma Mata days at Christ Church.

Time indeed waits for no man, he thought, *I need to strike while the iron is hot. How do I seek an audience with the King, who do I know that might make such an introduction?* he asked himself.

Kathryn Lady d'Aubigny had died in 1650, that left dear old William Cecil, the 2nd Earl of Salisbury, now 70 years of age and a signatory to the Madrigal Agreement. Who better to make the introduction and accompany him in his audience with the King?

55

Christophe could not believe his good fortune. He would go to see Cecil at Hatfield House with due haste taking the second copy of Madrigal with him. He could not wait to discuss his plans with Lysette.

That evening over dinner he shared his ideas with her. For once in his life he was in a bit of a dilemma.

looking concerned he took Lysette's hand and said 'I still worry about you and the children, there could still be someone out there determined that Madrigal never sees the light of day. Would it not be better after all this time to 'let sleeping dogs lie?'

'Of course you must go darling, it's the culmination of your lifetime quest since your father died. You know deep down that you cannot stop now, my love, you are a man of honour. Show everyone that your father and Elliot did not die in vain.'

'Oh, I do so love you, you are right of course. I shall set off for Hatfield in the morning'.

That night they lay cuddled up in each other's arms, once again not knowing what the future might hold. Despite the danger and uncertainty that lay ahead, Lysette felt safe and comforted in the arms of her true love.

Please God send him back to me safe and sound, she thought as she fell into a deep sleep.

Christophe was ready to set off soon after dawn the following morning, kissing Robert and Louise gently so as not to wake them. Upon re-joining Lysette in the master bedroom he whispered to her so's not to awaken the children,

'It will take me 3 days to get to Hatfield my love, I shall go by way of Bristol and Oxford. Whilst in Oxford I shall pay my respects to my late friend Edward's widow and also see Sam, who was at Christ Church with Edward and myself.'

Moving a bit closer and sitting on the side of the bed, holding her hand he said

'Assuming Cecil agrees with my request, I expect that we shall go on by carriage to Cecil's London residence and await an audience with King Charles 11. I shall leave Forest with Cecil's stable hands; she will enjoy the break. Whilst in London I shall also go up to Angel Islington to see Jenny and John.'

'That means you could be away for a month; I just don't know how I shall cope with you not here' replied Lysette with some trepidation.

'Do not fret my love, you have Nanny Trudi the Housekeeper, and I shall send word to Genevieve and Claire to see if they would like to come down for a holiday and to keep you company.'

'That would be wonderful. With all due respect to your Mama, it would be lovely to see them both and have some company of friends my own age.'

Christophe saddled up Forest and left as the early morning mist was dissipating under the late Spring morning sunrise. He journey was uneventful, and he duly arrived in Hatfield three days later in the early evening and sought lodgings for the night at The Wellington Inn.

Just as his father had done way back at the start of The Civil War, he sent a message by a messenger boy at the Inn to William Cecil, 2nd Earl of Salisbury, Hatfield House and prayed that he was in residence.

The message explained that he was Christophe, the son of the late Sir Robert Douse and that he sought an urgent audience to discuss 'Madrigal' in the light of the coronation of King Charles 11.

The reply came by return inviting Christophe over to Hatfield House the following morning at 10 a.m.

He dined and slept well that night confident that Cecil will also see that it was his duty to the late King Charles 1 to see Madrigal through to the very end.

Lying in bed that night Christophe thought, *too many lives had been lost in this quest, none more so than the late King himself and my own father. Cecil too had lost two sons in a war that could have been prevented, surely to God he will concur with my desire to reveal perhaps the most 'Closely Guarded Secret' in history.*

Christophe duly arrive at Hatfield House at the appointed hour having galloped over the Deer Park, just as his father had done many years before. He was met by Cecil's footman and escorted to the Breakfast Room, where the Earl was waiting for him.

'My dear Christophe, you have your father's looks and your reputation from The Civil War goes before you. Welcome to Hatfield House.'

'Thank you, my Lord, it is gracious of you to receive me.'

'Come now Christophe, please call me William, your father and I became great friends as well as co-conspirators in the quest of Madrigal. Now that that braggart Cromwell is dead, and we have a new King in Charles 11, how can I help you?'

'I have spent the last ten years pursuing justice in seeking out the traitor who betrayed my father, Edward Floyd the Lawyer. I finally caught up with him some five years since and the fellow did the honourable thing by taking his own life.'

The butler entered with a tray of coffee and poured them both a cup, giving a slight bow as he retreated backwards before turning and heading for the door.

'This was after I met and fell in love with his daughter Lysette', continued Christoph. 'I was unaware of who her father was when we first met. She knew nothing of her father's betrayal of Sir Robert to Cromwell.'

Christophe smiled at the thought of Lysette.

'We were later wed and have two wonderful children Robert and Louise, so much good has come out of the sordid affair.'

'Congratulations, but I sense that is not the end of the affair as far as you are concerned.'

'Father said you were intuitive William, and you are right. I seek to present Madrigal to King Charles 11 explaining my father's role in his attempt to try to stop the war, but moreover to stop the trial and execution of King Charles 1.'

'Presumably, you are looking to me to arrange an audience with the King?' said William.

'I thought that perhaps you would surely feel the same way as I do, to bring an end to the Madrigal saga?'

'Of course, my dear boy, I have been expecting you since Prince Charles returned to these shores. We shall leave for London tomorrow but tonight over dinner you must tell me all about you family, how is your Mama?'

'She is well, thank you kindly.'

They left the following morning in one of William's horse draw carriages pulled by four magnificent Cleveland Bays, specifically bred as coach horses. They were of strong constitution with brown bodies and black tails.

The carriage itself had all the latest refinements, from its leather slung suspension to an ornate interior mirroring the image of a country house withdrawing room. It was coated in black lacquer with gold gilding and the Earl's Coat of Arms. Up front sat the Coachman accompanied by William's Footman.

It was a pleasant mid-summers day and the journey to William's London residence in Knightsbridge took no more than three hours, arriving in time for afternoon tea.

The following day William went to The House of Lords and met with the King's Equerry, Sir Algenon Fontescue, to seek an audience with the King.

He explained to Fontescue that he wished to introduce Christophe Douse, son of the late Sir Robert Douse, to his Majesty. Fontescue was intrigued and replied that he would send a couriered message to William's London address if the King granted an audience.

It was all that William could do at this stage.

Christophe took the opportunity to go up to the safe house at Angel Islington and see Jenny and John.

John could not believe his eyes when opening the front door, he recognised Christophe instantly and cried out to Jenny.

'Jenny, Jenny come quickly it's Christophe.'

Jenny hugged Christophe with tears in her eyes.

'It's been so long Christophe; we are both dying to hear all your news and that of your family.'

John and Christophe made themselves comfortable in the parlour whilst Jenny went off to the kitchen. She soon returned, poured them all cups of tea, and served a large plateful of her home baked pastries.

'The old house looks the same, have there been any other changes?' enquired Christophe.

'We have kept your room just as it was, and you are welcome to use it anytime you are in London' replied John.

'That's marvellous, thank you. And you two, how have you been keeping?

And what about young Jack? Has he been behaving himself?'

'We are both well thank you. Elliot taught Jack well and he has become a real credit to him. He now reports to the new King's Head of Secret Service, Sir Archibald Windsor.'

Christophe then proceeded to tell them all about the wedding and life down in Devon and went on to talk about Elliot's action in saving his life at the expense of his own.

'He died a hero, and we will never ever forget him. We named our first-born Robert Elliot in his memory.'

'And you have a little girl too, how wonderful', said Jenny.

'Yes, she's a little darling and the spitting image of her mother.'

'What will you do now Christophe?' enquired John.

'William Cecil is, as we speak, seeking an audience for both of us with the King, where I shall seek to clear father's name' replied Christophe.

'I can't believe it after all this time, and everything we have all gone through over the past ten years. It is finally happening. It's a daunting proposition and I'm feeling nervous. I just don't want to let father down.'

'You underestimate yourself Christophe. Like your father, you are a national hero and uphold the name of le Douse with pride. We're both sure that you will rise to the occasion when you meet the King. Do let us know the outcome, won't you?'

'Of course, you know I will. Along with Elliot, father and I have always regarded you both as part of our extended family.'

It was soon time for Christophe to leave and return to Knightsbridge, eager to hear how William's day had gone.

The following day Christophe became anxious, nervous, and tense as the day drew on with no reply for Westminster.

'Stay calm my boy, I have every faith in Fontescue to put our case to his Majesty. That afternoon as they were taking a stroll in the grounds to calm Christophe's nerves came the reply. It came as a personal letter addressed to William with the King's own seal delivered by way of one of the King's own footmen.

The Palace of Whitehall
Westminster
London

11ᵗʰ September 1661

The 2ⁿᵈ Earl of Salisbury

Dear William,

Sir Algernon informs me that you have requested an audience with me to introduce Christophe Douse, son of the late Sir Robert Douse.

I am of course aware of what Sir Robert attempted to do on my father's behalf in attempting to stop his trial for treason. Such heroism is still talked about in Court.

You were one of the few Lords and other members of Court and The Privy Council that my father trusted, and that I believe I can still trust in these troubled times.

I shall be pleased to receive you both at the Palace at 11.30 a.m. on Saturday 13ᵗʰ, after my weekly audience with The Lords Commissioners of The Treasury.

Charles R

On the morning of the 13th, Christophe having slept well, was feeling more relaxed, more confident than he had ever been over the last 10 years in his quest to clear his father's name.

As they were leaving the house and about to step up into the carriage, a familiar face appeared from the opposite side

of the square. It was none other than Sean O'Halloran, the Irish gangster from Kilburn who Christophe had stabbed through the back of his right hand under interrogation after his father's betrayal. He had a flintlock pistol in his left hand, cocked and ready to fire.

Alexander Marchal had paid him handsomely in advance to kill Christophe should he unexpectedly disappear or die at his hands. O'Halloran had heard of Christophe's arrival in London from one of the street urchins he engaged as pickpockets in Knightsbridge and other wealthy areas across the city.

'You bastard, I said you would pay for this', he shouted at Christophe as he started to cross the road, holding up his black gloved right hand that had never healed.

A loud volley rang out as the Coachman let fire with a blunderbuss that he had hidden under the front seat of the carriage. It hit O'Halloran full square in the chest, and his own shot fired into the sky as he felt backwards taking the full blast. He was dead before he hit the ground.

'Well done old boy, well done indeed. Thank you, George. There will be an extra-large bonus for you come Christmastide,' called William dryly. 'Now quickly jump down and run into the house and get Johnson to come and clear up this unfortunate mess.'

Climbing into the carriage and smiling at Christophe he said,

'We have an appointment with The King'.

56

It was but a short ride in the carriage from Knightsbridge to The Palace at Whitehall.

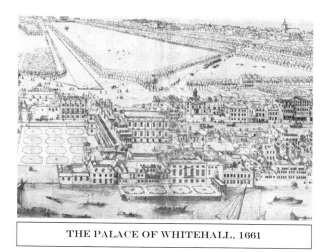

THE PALACE OF WHITEHALL, 1661

The carriage entered through the main gatehouse, The Holbein Gate, and rolled across the cobbled courtyard coming to rest at the main door. Two of the King's household in their fine livery immediately came out and opened each respective door of the carriage, lowered the internal steps, and William and Christophe alighted.

'My Lord, Sir, if you will accompany me to the anti-room of the Receiving Chamber, the King is expecting you,' proclaimed the senior Houseman, Harvard Jones.

After a short wait, Sir Algernon Fortescue, the King's Equerry, came out of the Receiving Chamber and addressed William and Christophe.

'Good morning Your Lordship, and to you, Captain Douse I presume', as he shook hands with both.

'We shall shortly go in. You know the protocol, bow as you enter and let the King speak first. After your audience when leaving the Chamber, you go out of the room backwards, bowing once more as you leave.'

Heading towards the huge heavily carved oak doors, embellished with gold leaf and elaborate handles, he said.

'You are in luck, the King is in fine form having just had The Committee for The Treasury approve the budget to upgrade the indoor real tennis court, built by King Henry V111.'

At last the doors opened, attended by two footmen, and they entered.

The King was standing looking out of the East Window where he was often to be found in the early hours of the day, attending to matters of state whilst watching the sunrise above the city.

As William and Christophe entered, he turned towards them, they bowed as he beckoned them to come forth.

'William, how pleased I am to see you looking so robust, life in Hatfield must be treating you well.'

'You are most kind Sire, one tries ones best, I am afraid real tennis is beyond me now, but I still manage to play the odd game of bowls. May I introduce Captain Christophe Douse, son of the late Sir Robert Douse of Chaffeymoor.'

Christophe lowered his head and said 'Your Highness'.

'Please both be seated', said the King.

'Douse, I understand that you are seeking a pardon for your father's apparent act of Treason under the Cromwell regime. Sir Algernon has already briefed me on the

circumstances of your father's death, and I would have no hesitation in granting such a pardon. He was a hero indeed and is still talked of today in Royal circles.

I will have The Attorney General prepare the document for me to sign and it will be published both in Court and in The House of Commons.'

Christophe was surprised how well the King had been briefed and the speed of his decision.

'Thank you Sire, my mother and I are most sincerely grateful that you are prepared to right this miscarriage of justice. If I may indulge you further, I would like to reveal to you 'Madrigal'. It is a plan that has been 'A Closely Guarded Secret' for the best part of 20 years.'

Christophe took the parchment from beneath his doublet.

'Madrigal, was enabled, negotiated, and signed by the most senior Royalists and Parliamentarians, whose aim was to prevent the Civil War. Once the War had commenced, the aim was to achieve a negotiated settlement between both sides.'

'I have heard such rumours' said the King 'but no evidence has ever been forthcoming.'

'It would not surprise you Sire to hear that William was one of the two Royalist Lords involved, with Philip Herbert, The 4th Earl of Pembroke, sadly no longer with us, the other. However, what may come as a shock to you is that General Sir Thomas Fairfax was one of the two Parliamentarians involved. He, along with Sir William Lenthall, Speaker of The House of Commons, were the other signatories to the agreement.'

The King sat upright in his chair, looking astounded, and Christophe continued:

'It was Fairfax who originally conceived the idea of Madrigal. He and Lord Cecil, here, often met in secret to negotiate terms that they hoped would be acceptable to your father.'

The King was taken aback, looking at Christophe in almost disbelief. 'Fairfax!' he exclaimed.

'Yes Sire, Fairfax was against the war all along and constantly argued with Essex and Cromwell that there should be a negotiated settlement.'

'Do go on Douse,' said the King.

'My father, as your father's Head of Secret Service, first became aware of the Madrigal Agreement in the late summer of 1642, when present at the failed final negotiations on the so called 19 Principles. As you know, it was this failure that led to the Declaration of War by the King.

It became a quest of my father's to find out who was involved in Madrigal and its nature, content, and implications. Several attempts were made on his life as he continued this quest.

Having succeeded however, and in the possession of Lord Cecil's copy of the manuscript, he attempted to present it at the commencement of the King's trial for High Treason.

Cromwell became aware of this and arrested my father as he entered the Court to present the Agreement before the Judges. He was arrested and executed without trial at The Tower that same day.'

'William, is this true, how has this not been revealed before?'

'It is Sire, after the execution of the King, Cromwell asserted power over Parliament, and we have waited for your rightful return to the Throne.'

'My dear Douse, neither I nor any of my Privy Council were aware of the full account of Sir Robert's heroism.'

With that Christophe lowered his head again and gave The King his father's copy of Madrigal.'

The King responded by saying,

'This Agreement shall now remain a secret forever and be locked in a safe place in the Tower along with the Crown Jewels.'

He called for Sir Algernon to join them in the Chamber and to bring the Knighting Sword with him.

Christophe looked shocked; he did not expect what was about to happen for one moment.

'Douse come kneel before me'.

Christophe duly obeyed. The King then dubbed Christophe on his left shoulder then the right, saying,

'Arise Sir Christophe Douse of Chaffeymoor. May you serve God, King, and your country with honour.'

Turning to Sir Algernon as witness to the events, the King said, 'Furthermore, I grant you restitution of Chaffeymoor Grange and its Estate and all chattels upon and therein. Your mother, Lady Marguerite, shall receive a state pension of £1,000 per annum with immediate effect.'

Christophe was overwhelmed and glanced at William in incredulity.

'Well done lad' said William, 'your father would be proud of you.'

'Indeed' said the King. 'The country, and my family and I, owe your father and your good self a great deal of gratitude. Pray let us all drink a toast in your family's honour.' Sir Algernon produced four solid gold goblets of the finest red English wine and proposed the toast.

'Sir Christophe Douse of Chaffeymoor'

*It requires infinitely
a greater genius
to make love
than to make war*

Anne Ninon de Lencos
1620 – 1705
French Author and Courtesan

The Author

Christophe Robert Medler

Christophe, or Chris as he is known by many, was born and raised in Hillingdon, Middlesex. He is a widower and has two children and four grandsons.

He now shares a house in Chippenham and a country cottage in the New Forest with his fiancée and Editor, Lyn, together with their two dogs, Digby and Scarlet.

In his former life he was a graduate of Harvard Business School and a qualified Accountant. He worked as a Corporate Trouble-shooter largely in the Printing and Publishing Industries, travelling all over the world.

It was his fiancée Lyn, a former Events and Marketing Manager for The National Trust and Forestry Commission, who encouraged and inspired him to achieve a lifelong ambition and to write his first Novel. He is now researching his second.

Christophe is a lover of the Arts, History, and the Countryside with a passion for Fly Fishing on the Hampshire and West Country chalk steams.

Bibliography

Cavalier
By Lucy Worsley

Half Hours with The Highwaymen
By Charles G Harper

Killers of The King
By Charles Spencer

Medieval Cookbook
By Maggie Black

Royalists Agents, Conspirators and Spies
By Geoffrey Smith

The Great Philosophers
By Stephen Law

Madrigal:

Real Life Characters:

King Charles 1	*Sovereign, England, Scotland and Ireland 1625-1649*
Earl Edward Sackville	*4th Earl of Dorset, Knole House, Royalist Member of the Privy Council*
General Sir Thomas Fairfax	*3rd Lord Fairfax of Cameron, Commander of Parliamentary Army*
John Hampden	*A Parliamentary Spy and alleged traitor*
Edward Sackville *(son)*	*Viscount, Royalist, Cavalier, Captain of The Kentish Royals*
The 3rd Earl of Essex	*Commander in Chief of The Parliamentary Army*
Lieutenant General Oliver Cromwell	*Parliamentarian Commander of The New Model Army and later Lord Protector*
Prince Rupert	*Duke of Cumberland, Royalist, General of The Horse*
William Cecil	*2nd Earl of Salisbury, Hatfield House, Royalist. Member of the Privy Council*
Philip Herbert	*4th Earl of Pembrokeshire, Wilton House, Lord Chamberlain, Parliamentarian*
Lady Katherine Stuart D'Aubigny	*Cousin by marriage of King Charles, Royalist*
Edmund Waller, Richard Challoner Nathaniel Thompkins, **Henry Heron, Alexander Hampden.** **William Lenthal**	*All members of an unsuccessful conspiracy to to de-throne Charles 1* *Parliamentarian, Speaker of The House of Commons*
Edward Floyd	*Lawyer, Parliamentarian*
Sir Nicholas Crisp	*Royalist, Provocateur*
Samuel Collins	*Provost Marshall Kings College Cambridge*

The Honourable Henry Wray	*Merchant*
and daughter **Bridget**	
Elizabeth Cresswell	*Brothel Owner*
Molly Hardcastle	*Prostitute*
Anthony Steele	*Parliamentarian,*
	Attorney General
John Cook	*Parliamentarian,*
	Solicitor General
Captain James Hind	*Highwayman*
Colonel Robert Hammond	*Parliamentarian,*
	Governor of the Isle of Wight
King Charles 11	*Sovereign 1660-1685*
	(The Restoration period)

Real Life Characters Also Mentioned:

King James 1 / Elizabeth	
King Henry 1V	
King Henry V1	
King Charles V11 of France	
King Henry V111	
Cardinal Wolesey	*Head of the Catholic Church*
William Shakespeare	*Poet*
Christopher Marlowe	*Poet*
John Milton –	*Poet*
Keats	*Poet*
4ᵗʰ Earl of Southampton	*Royalist Statesman*
Sir John Colepepper	*Royalist,*
	Chancellor of the Exchequer
John Tradescant	*Landscape Gardener,*
	Hatfield House
Sir Hugo Boseman	*Head of Chambers, Lincoln's Inn*
2ⁿᵈ Earl of Northampton	*Royalist Officer, Battle of Edge-hill*
Sir James Ramsay	*Parliamentarian Officer, Battle of Edgehill*
Sir William Balfour	*Parliamentarian Officer, Battle of Edgehill*
Sir Henry Wilmot	*Royalist Officer, Battle of Edge-hill*
Lord Fielding	*Parliamentarian Officer, Battle of Edgehill*

Colonel Henry Wentworth	*Royalist Officer,*
	Battle of Newbury
Colonel George Lisle	*Royalist Officer,*
	Battle of Newbury
Sir John Byron	*Royalist Officer,*
	Battle of Newbury
Captain William Willet	*Parliamentarian Officer,*
	Battle of Newbury
Major General Phillip Skippon	*Parliamentarian Officer,*
	Battle of Newbury
The 8th Earl of Rutland	*Neutral, Moderate*
	Member of Parliament
The Earl of Newcastle	*Royalist Officer*
Algernon Percy	*10th Earl of Northumberland,*
	Parliamentarian
Demaris Page	*Brothel Owner*
Dr Michael Hudson	*King Charles 1 Chaplain*
Robert Gatesby	*Parliamentarian, Head of the*
	Gunpowder Plot
Edmond Wingate	*Royalist Mathematician*
Decsartes	*French Philosopher*
Plato	*Greek Philosopher*
Aristotle	*RomanPhilosopher*
Voltaire	*French Philosopher*
Sir Richard Hoar	*Banker, Lord Mayor of London*
William Juxon	*The Bishop of London*
William Rufus	*Son of William the Conqueror*
William Brune	*Landowner*
Henry and Thomas Chippendale	*Carpenters*
Anne Ninon de Lencos	*French Author*
Le Duc de Harcourt	*French Aristocrat and father of the*
	Fictional Marguerite
William Sutton	*Owner of Kelham Hall*

All other characters are entirely fictional and from the Author's imagination.

Madrigal:

Fictitious Characters:

Sir Robert Douse
Christophe's Father, Head of the King's Secret Service
Christophe Douse
Cavalier / Captain of the Dorset Royals
Tristan Cheval
Highwayman
Marguerite Elizabet Douse, nee de Harcourt
Wife of Sir Robert, Mother of Christophe
Lysette Floyd / Ford
Daughter of Edward Floyd, companion to Lady Louise
Elliot Sir Robert's London Agent and Head of Spy Network
Lady Louise Aristocrat and Lysette's employer / confidant
John Marchal Parliamentary Spy
Alexander Marchal Parliamentary Spy
Sarah and Paul Marguerite's cousin & husband. Housekeeper / Manager of the Estate.
Jenny and John Housekeeper / Houseman of Safe House
Jack Daniels Landord of Angel Inn
Geoffrey Chambertin / Dowager Myra Chambertin Fine Wine Importer   / Mother
Denzel Briggs / *Kimberley* Sir Roberts Midland Agent / Mistress
Jack Senior Spy
Matthew Makepiece Senior Spy
Theo Spy
Adam Spy
Sean O'Halloran Irish Gangster
Rogier and Christina Landlord/wife The Beechwood Arms, Ashdown Forest
Little Mick Blacksmith, Ashdown Forest
Sam (Viscount Samuel Fitzherbert) Friend of Edward and Christophe
Anton and Eleanor/En /Toby Landlord / wife / son Winchfield Arms. Winchfield

Baldy Barnet Gravedigger, Bourton

Reverend David Banks, Rosemary Banks, Claire Banks
Vicar, St Nicholas Church, Bourton / wife / daughter

Parker, Kim Parker, Olivia
Blacksmith, Bourton / wife / daughter and housemaid at Chaffeymoor

George and Ida Landlord and wife of The George, Mere

Hugo Birch Parker's brother-in-law

Peter and Lin Quince, Lottie, Kelli Farmer / wife / daughters,
Bourton

Maggie le Blanc Serving Wench, an Inn near Forest Row

David Paleman Sir Robert's Lawyer

Sir Marmaduke Tillingham –Smythe Gentleman

Rowena Tillingham-Smythe Daughter of 'Marmalade'

George Prior Highwayman

Carolann Ward Madame of Seedy Brothel

Scrase Spy, Master Printer

Captain Neil Artfellow Royalist Officer

Ann, Hannah, Janny Welcher Prostitutes

Genevieve Poolman Friend of Lysette

Ethan / Aunt Angelica Innkeeper / Aunt, The Crown, Hazelmere

Primrose Serving Wench

Daphne Receptionist Red Lion, Salisbury

Lieutenant Stephen Meursault Sheffield Infantry Brigade

Penelope Stone Flower arranger

Bob Thatcher Royalist Spy

Harvard Jones Houseman to King Charles 11

Old Gwilliam Lawyer

Nanny Trudi Nanny/Housekeeper, Devon

Austyn Lamborghini Poet

The Reverend David Canten Vicar

Jack Sawyer Gamekeeper

Sister Judy D'Arcy Nurse

Captain Richard D'Arcy Doctor

Captain Henry Wiggins Parliamentary Officer

Lieutenant John Bundy Parliamentary Officer

Madrigal's Very Own

33 Pubs and Inns Pub Crawl

All of the 33 pubs listed below were in business in the 1640's, some as coaching inns, some as ale-houses, and all still exist as pubs, inns or hotels. A few may have changed their names, but a bit of research will soon reveal that.

I have a challenge for you.

Visit every pub – it doesn't matter how long it takes*.

Prove to me you have, by means of a photo of you outside the pub/hotel sign, holding this book. They do not have to be visited in the order listed below.

The first person/couple to do so will receive a two-night stay with dinner at one of the listed pubs/hotels that provide accommodation. Any further persons to achieve this huge, tortuous accomplishment, will receive a bottle of fizz through the post – or lunch for 2 at the establishment nearest to you – booze excluded! Your choice.

Should you achieve this momentous task and have not only enjoyed the book but the journey, my contact details are in the small print!

The Queen's Head	Newark, Nottinghamshire
The Blackmoor's Head	Cambridge
The Swan Inn	Welwyn, Hertfordshire
The Angel	Angel Islington, London
The Boar's Head	Eastcheap, London
The Cloverleaf	Kilburn, London
The Lamb and Flag	Covent Garden, London
The Tabard Inn	Southwark, London
The Old Bell Inn	Oxted, Surrey
The Beechwood Arms	Duddleswell, East Sussex
The Foresters Inn	Newbridge, East Sussex
The Swan Inn	Forest Row, East Sussex
The Beacon Tavern	Horsham, West Sussex

The Crown Inn	Hazelmere, Surrey
The Old Drum	Petersfield, Hampshire
The Highwayman	Winchester, Hampshire
The Crown Manor	Lyndhurst, New Forest
The Bell Inn	Brook, New Forest
The Royal Oak	Gorley, New Forest
The George Inn	Fordingbridge, Hampshire
The Red Lion	Salisbury, Wiltshire
The Three Cups	Stockbridge, Hampshire
The Winchfield Inn	Winchfield, Hampshire
The Swan and Bottle	Denham, Buckinghamshire
The George and Dragon	High Wycombe, Bucks
The Greyhound Inn	Thame, Oxfordshire
The Bear Inn	Oxford
The King's Arms	Malmesbury, Wiltshire
The Marlborough Inn	Marlborough, Wiltshire
The Grosvenor	Shaftsbury, Dorset
The George Inn	Mere, Wiltshire
The Old Bell	Illminster, Somerset
The White Hart	Exeter, Devon

Good Luck! Enjoy!

*These prizes are only offered during my lifetime, so get a move on!!

chris1325@hotmail.co.uk

Madrigal's Very Own Quiz

10 questions, just for fun on your own, or as part of a Book Group discussion.

What is the name of the house where Lady Louise lives?

Who was arrested at The King's Arms, Malmesbury?

Where did Christophe buy a tankard of Mum?

Where is 'The Ring'?

Who bares his arse in front of an arrogant lady?

Who is named after a well-known Burgundy?

What is the occupation of David Paleman?

Who is the father of Rowena?

What was the name of the spaniel puppy?

What was the annual rent and upkeep of the 'Safe House' in Angel Islington?

And if you can also answer these more obscure questions, the first 5 people to email me with the 13 correct answers will receive a bottle of that famous Burgundy wine.

What is the name of Elliot's horse?

Where, specifically, was 'The King Who Does Not Lie' played?

What military action for gallantry was Christophe commended to the King for?

chris1325@hotmail.co.uk

Don't miss the next novel by
Christophe
in the

'Closely Guarded Secret'
Series

Orphan

to be published in 2022
by

Le Douse Publishing

Printed in Great Britain
by Amazon